Exploring Peace Formatic

M000240252

This volume examines the dynamics of socio-political order in post-colonial states across the Pacific Islands region and West Africa in order to elaborate on the processes and practices of peace formation.

Drawing on field research and engaging with post-liberal conceptualisations of peacebuilding, this book investigates the interaction of a variety of actors and institutions involved in the provision of peace, security and justice in post-colonial states. The chapters analyse how different types of actors and institutions involved in peace formation engage in and are interpenetrated by a host of relations in the local arena, making 'the local' contested ground on which different discourses and praxes of peace, security and justice coexist and overlap. In the course of interactions, new and different forms of socio-political order emerge which are far from being captured through the familiar notions of a liberal peace and a Weberian ideal-type state. Rather, this volume investigates how (dis)order emerges as a result of interdependence among agents, thus laying open the fundamentally relational character of peace formation. This innovative relational, liminal and integrative understanding of peace formation has far-reaching consequences for internationally supported peacebuilding.

This book will be of much interest to students of statebuilding, peace studies, security studies, governance, development and IR.

Charles T Hunt is Vice Chancellor's Senior Research Fellow and ARC DECRA Fellow in the School of Global, Urban and Social Studies at RMIT University in Melbourne, Australia. He is editor or author of five books including *UN Peace Operations and International Policing* (Routledge 2015).

M Anne Brown is Principal Research Fellow in the School of Global, Urban and Social Studies at RMIT University, Australia and Co-Director of the Peace and Conflict Studies Institute Australia (PaCSIA).

Kwesi Aning is Director of the Faculty of Academic Affairs and Research at the Kofi Annan International Peacekeeping Training Centre (KAIPTC), Ghana.

Volker Boege is Honorary Senior Research Fellow at the School of Political Science and International Studies, The University of Queensland, Australia, and Co-Director of the Peace and Conflict Studies Institute Australia (PaCSIA).

Series: Studies in Conflict, Development and Peacebuilding
Series Editors:
Keith Krause, Thomas J. Biersteker and Riccardo Bocco
Graduate Institute of International and Development Studies, Geneva

This series publishes innovative research into the connections between insecurity and under-development in fragile states, and into situations of violence and insecurity more generally. It adopts a multidisciplinary approach to the study of a variety of issues, including the changing nature of contemporary armed violence (*conflict*), efforts to foster the conditions that prevent the outbreak or recurrence of such violence (*development*), and strategies to promote peaceful relations on the communal, societal and international level (*peacebuilding*).

Peacebuilding and Ex-Combatants
Political Reintegration in Liberia
Johanna Söderström

Local Ownership in International Peacebuilding
Key Theoretical and Practical Issues
Edited by Sung Yong Lee and Alpaslan Özerdem

Institutional Reforms and Peacebuilding
Change, Path-Dependency and Societal Divisions in Post-War Communities
Edited by Nadine Ansorg and Sabine Kurtenbach

Peacebuilding and Spatial Transformation
Peace, Space and Place
Annika Björkdahl and Stefanie Kappler

Exploring Peace Formation
Security and Justice in Post-colonial States
Edited by Kwesi Aning, Volker Boege, M Anne Brown and Charles T Hunt

For more information about this series, please visit: www.routledge.com/Studies-in-Conflict-Development-and-Peacebuilding/book-series/CONDEVPEACE

Exploring Peace Formation

Security and Justice in Post-colonial States

**Edited by Kwesi Aning, Volker Boege,
M Anne Brown and Charles T Hunt**

Routledge
Taylor & Francis Group

LONDON AND NEW YORK

First published 2018
by Routledge

2 Park Square, Milton Park, Abingdon, Oxfordshire OX14 4RN
52 Vanderbilt Avenue, New York, NY 10017

Routledge is an imprint of the Taylor & Francis Group, an informa business

First issued in paperback 2019

British Library Cataloguing-in-Publication Data
A catalogue record for this book is available from the British Library

Library of Congress Cataloging-in-Publication Data
A catalog record for this book has been requested

ISBN: 978-1-138-99936-7 (hbk)
ISBN: 978-0-367-45772-3 (pbk)

Typeset in Times New Roman
by Wearset Ltd, Boldon, Tyne and Wear

Contents

Figures

Contributors

Kwesi Aning works at the Kofi Annan International Peacekeeping Training Centre (KAIPTC), Accra, Ghana. He was the African Union's first counter-terrorism expert worked as a senior consultant to the UN's Department of Political Affairs in New York. Aning serves on the World Economic Forum's Council on Conflict Prevention and is an Advisory Group member for the Peacebuilding Fund. On two occasions, Aning evaluated the UN's Global Programme on Strengthening the Legal Regime against Terrorism. He serves on several editorial boards, including *Global Responsibility to Protect, Journal of African Security, Afrika Spektrum* and *African Security Review.*

Nancy Annan is a PhD candidate at Coventry University, UK. Previously, Annan worked as a Research Associate with the Peace Support Operations Programme of the Kofi Annan International Peacekeeping Training Centre (KAIPTC) in Accra, Ghana, focusing on conflict resolution, peacebuilding, peace operations and gender issues. Before that, she worked with the Ministry of Foreign Affairs Ghana, Plan International and was a research intern at the UN Headquarters in New York. Nancy holds a Bachelor's degree in Social Work with Psychology, and an MPhil in Social Work from the University of Ghana with a specialisation in Conflict Management and Resolution.

Festus Aubyn is a Research Fellow at the Faculty of Academic Affairs and Research, Kofi Annan International Peacekeeping Training Centre (KAIPTC) in Accra, Ghana. Before joining the KAIPTC, Festus worked with the country office of the United Nations Development Programme (UNDP) in Ghana, and the Institute of Statistical, Social and Economic Research (ISSER), University of Ghana. His research interest is in the area of African Peace and Security, Peace Support Operations and Election Security. He has participated and presented papers at several international conferences and has a number of publications to his credit.

Bruce Baker is Professor of African Security at Coventry University, UK and a Senior Security and Justice Advisor for HMG's Civilian Stabilisation Group. His published articles and books cover African democratisation, governance, policing, security and justice reform and local justice (see www.african

policing.org). His book *Security in Post-Conflict Africa: The Role of Non-State Policing* (CRC Press 2009) won the American Society of Criminology's Prize for Best Book in Comparative and International Criminology 2010. Baker has conducted fieldwork in Zimbabwe, Mozambique, South Africa, Rwanda, Uganda, The Gambia, Sierra Leone, Cape Verde, Seychelles, Liberia, South Sudan, Comoros, Madagascar, Ethiopia and Nigeria.

Volker Boege is a Research Fellow at the School of Political Science and International Studies (POLSIS) at The University of Queensland, Brisbane, Australia. His fields of work include post-conflict peacebuilding and state formation, non-western approaches to conflict transformation, and natural resources, environmental degradation and conflict. His regional areas of expertise are the South Pacific, South-east Asia and West Africa. He has published numerous articles, papers and books on peace research and contemporary history.

M Anne Brown is a Principal Research Fellow at the School of Global, Urban and Social Studies at RMIT University in Melbourne, Australia, and a founding member of PaCSIA, a Peace and Conflict research and practice NGO. Research and practice interests focus on the emergence of political community across division, peacebuilding and state formation, social dialogue processes and the interface of practice and theory. She is the author of articles, chapters and books on peace, conflict and political community.

Lisa Denney is an independent researcher working on issues of security, justice and development in conflict-affected contexts, including Sierra Leone, Sri Lanka and Timor-Leste. She consults for a range of research institutes and development agencies and was previously a Research Fellow at the Overseas Development Institute. Lisa received her PhD in 2011 from Aberystwyth University and is the author of *Justice and Security Reform: donor agencies and informal institutions in Sierra Leone* (Routledge 2014).

Fiifi Edu-Afful is a Research Fellow and the Deputy Programme Head of the Peace Support Operations Programme at the Kofi Annan International Peacekeeping Training Centre (KAIPTC). He previously served with the United Nations Office of Internal Oversight Services on the Prevention of Sexual Exploitation and Abuse in UN peacekeeping. He is currently undertaking research on ECOWAS/UN peacekeeping exit frameworks, international interventions, hybrid security mechanisms and sexual violence against men and boys in conflict. He is an editor for Gov-Enhance Africa, a think-tank for enhancing governance on the continent. He also facilitates training modules on the rule of law, mediation, the protection of civilians and sexual and gender-based violence. He is the author of several academic works on these topics.

Miranda Forsyth is a Fellow in State Society and Governance in Melanesia at the Australian National University in Canberra, Australia. Prior to joining the ANU, Forsyth was a senior lecturer in criminal law at the law school of the

University of the South Pacific based in Port Vila, Vanuatu. The broad focus of her research is the possibilities and challenges presented by the inter-operation of state and non-state justice systems, particularly in the realm of criminal law and intellectual property.

Charles T Hunt is a Vice-Chancellor's Senior Research/ARC DECRA Fellow in the School of Global, Urban and Social Studies at RMIT University in Melbourne, Australia. He previously lectured in International Security in the School of Political Science and International Studies at the University of Queensland. Hunt's research focuses on peace and conflict with an emphasis on security and justice system reform in Africa. He is author of *UN Peace Operations and International Policing: Negotiating Complexity, Assessing Impact and Learning to Learn* (Routledge 2015) and co-author of *Forging New Conventional Wisdom Beyond International Policing* (Brill 2013).

Thomas Jaye is the Deputy Director of Research for the Faculty of Academic Affairs and Research (FAAR) at the Kofi Annan International Peacekeeping Training Centre (KAIPTC), Accra, Ghana. He holds a PhD in International Politics from the University of Aberystwyth. Jaye writes on regional security and has a strong academic interest in post-war recovery and peacebuilding. He is author of *Issues of Sovereignty, Strategy and Security in the ECOWAS Intervention in the Liberian Civil War* (Edwin Mellen Press 2003) and co-editor of *ECOWAS and the Dynamics of Peacebuilding in West Africa* (CODESRIA 2011).

Acknowledgements

A great deal of the work for the chapters in this book was supported by a grant under the *Australian Development Research Awards Scheme* [DFAT agreement 66442] for a project entitled 'Understanding and working with local sources of peace, security and justice in West Africa'. The editors would also like to thank the team of research assistants in Ghana and Liberia, including: Fritz Ba-taa-banah, Sharon Daplah, Rasmus Schleef, Maria Boateng, Nana Bemma Nti, Nana Kofi Abuna IV, Saah N'Tow, Abratha Doe and James Wiles. It is they who conducted and facilitated much of the field work that informs these chapters. Without their efforts and insights this would not have been possible. The editors are also extremely grateful to the Kofi Annan Peacekeeping Training Centre (KAIPTC), in particular its former Commandant Brig. Gen Obed Akwa, who was generous with his time and support for the project. Thanks are due also to Anna Nolan and Mark Love for their dual contributions as project managers and expert advisors, and Glenine Hamlyn AE, Accredited Editor with the Institute of Professional Editors Ltd (IPEd), whose keen editorial eye helped knock this manuscript into shape. The editorial team at Routledge – in particular Andrew Humphreys and Hannah Ferguson – have shown a great deal of patience during the production of this book for which the editors are also very grateful.

Part I

Concepts and thematic treatments

1 Introduction

Seeking peace in West Africa and the Pacific Island region – new directions

M Anne Brown and Kwesi Aning

This book sets out to explore some of the ways peace and security are sought in fragile or fluid circumstances in post-colonial regions of the Global South. The discussion focuses on parts of West Africa and the Pacific Islands, two very different and geographically distant parts of the globe that nevertheless have much to say to each other. By drawing on cases from geographically distinct regions, the discussion enables shared themes to be highlighted, while respecting contextual specificity. Place and context are important here, as all the chapters take peace and social order to be substantially grounded in the circumstances, histories and relational networks of particular places. The fieldwork on which the following chapters draw took place in towns, villages and regions conducted over a number of years in parts of West Africa and Oceania. Nevertheless, many of the insights and approaches raised have broader applicability. Some chapters address countries or regions that have undergone protracted violent conflict in the relatively recent past (Liberia, Sierra Leone, Bougainville, Solomon Islands), while others draw on experiences where conflict manifests in more structural ways. The following discussion is less focused on conditions of hot conflict, however, and more on the demands of everyday peace and security. Nevertheless, in both regions, countries face intense socio-political pressures that could spiral into significant violent conflict. The 'everyday' management of these pressures can play a critical role in whether serious conflict erupts or is contained, and whether the sources and legacies of violence are transformed or kept alive.

While this book emphasises the contextual nature of efforts to work against violence, it is also conceptual in orientation. In considering the ways people seek to build relative peace and social order under challenging conditions, discussion engages current debates about peacebuilding and statebuilding, the formation of political community and the state and the foundations of security and social order in conflict-affected or fragile environments.

This opening chapter gives an overview of some of the interweaving themes, framing debates and key terms upon which the following chapters draw; the chapters, however, engage with these terms, themes and debates from varying perspectives and with varying emphases. This chapter also considers the significance of bringing in cases from the diverse regions of West Africa and the Pacific Islands, and introduces the book's structure and individual contributions.

Themes throughout the discussion include interrelated questions about key sources of peace and security, the place of the state in the provision of peace and security, and different ways of understanding, but also of crafting, the political order and political community of the state. These are questions without easy or ready-made answers; answers take shape through conceptual exchange but also from practical actions, realities and experimentation on the ground.

Providing security, externally and internally, has long been seen as the fundamental business and *raison d'etre* of the state (Baker, see Chapter 4 in this volume). Seeking to respond to violent conflict, or support stability and economic growth, the international donor community has thus put significant effort into strengthening the state, through support for key state institutions and processes and governance reform programmes (Paris 2004; Ghani and Lockhart 2008). As discussed below, 'building the state' has been understood as a key path to peace, security and justice. Quite particular, if also generic, templates of the state have guided these efforts. At the same time, in many parts of the world, other significant forms and sources of socio-political order and authority are enmeshed with state institutions. These forms of order are often embedded in longstanding community practices and values and can be expressed in a range of associations and institutions, from very localised to widespread. Customary forms of social order, however, in all their diversity and complexity, are often the most extensive and important of these. For many communities in the regions discussed here, it is these that are a primary source of everyday security and justice (Boege, see Chapter 10 in this volume; Mac Ginty 2011). As an OECD policy review has noted, 'in sub-Saharan Africa at least 80% of justice services are delivered by non-state providers' (OECD 2008, p. 17). Customary sources of order include not just the more visible chieftancy institutions or other leadership arrangements, but kinship networks and associated patterns of authority and obligation.

The socio-political dynamics of many post-colonial regions are significantly shaped by long historical interaction and multilayered, shifting relationships between the demands, principles and practices of state-making and customary life (Boege, see Chapter 12 in this volume; Albrecht and Moe 2014). These entangled relations, and particularly the role of customary and broader community practices within them, have often been seen by national elites or external commentators as a cause of political fragility, weak states and violence (Fukuyama 2011). There is increasing argument, however, evident in the following discussion and elsewhere, that these relations could also be seen as contributors to peace and resilience (Aning and Aubyn, see Chapter 2 in this volume). Moreover, as discussed in the final chapter, if national, international and community actors were able to work with the grain of these dynamics, they could potentially play more constructive roles in peace and community well-being (Dinnen and Peake 2013; Mac Ginty and Richmond 2016; McWilliam 2008; Lederach 2005).

This debate raises questions about the make-up, operation and governance of states, and how 'being a state' is understood. As Bruce Baker notes, '[a] government cannot run a state with multiple authorities as if there were one single central authority' (see Chapter 4 in this volume, p. 74). The relations between state institutions and customary or traditional systems of authority, and what this means for statehood, form a prominent theme throughout the following chapters. More broadly, a number of chapters point to the need for state institutions and practices that are more fully and accountably engaged with the realities of their own context, as African states or Pacific Island states (see, e.g. Aning, Annan and Edu-Afful, Chapter 7; Baker, Chapter 4 and Boege, Chapter 12, all in this volume).

Peace formation and the 'local'

The idea of 'peace formation', a term associated with the work of Oliver Richmond, is also a way of underscoring the fundamental significance of local efforts to work against and undo the effects of violence, and the importance of those efforts being effectively part of subsequent peace settlements (Richmond 2013, 2014). 'Peace formation' as a term highlights the reality that in the midst of violent conflict or widespread insecurity there are people working against violence, to create spaces of peace, collectively or individually (Nordstrom 2004; Sawyer 2005; Lederach 2005). This focus marks a shift from dominant conceptual and policy approaches that have come to be associated with peacebuilding and, even more so, statebuilding (Richmond 2013). For many, peacebuilding has become almost synonymous with international action and international agencies. International interventions into or following violent conflict are often essential, life-saving and intensely sought. The intention here is not to reject the involvement or importance of international actors in potentially securing stability or helping to overcome the legacy of violent conflict. The international drive to restore political order after conflict, however, while often vital, can easily overlook the work of local actors against violence and abuse, and the approaches they have forged (Sawyer 2005).

Echoing 'state formation', 'peace formation' as an idea draws attention to the role of those people who every day work to survive and overcome violence in achieving workable peace. Moreover, it underscores the need for international and national elite actors to acknowledge and work with this reality. Ending protracted conflict and crafting peaceful relations are not primarily international endeavours, nor solely the products of elite action or bargaining between warlords, faction leaders or international interests, despite the undoubted importance of these elements. The Women of Liberia Mass Action for Peace is just one high-profile example of local action, in this case explicitly linked to international engagement, but there are persistent, everyday examples from across Liberia and elsewhere, taking place on streets, in villages, across towns and regions (Sawyer 2005; Nordstrom 1997; Boege and Forsyth, see Chapter 11 in this volume; UNDP and The Ministry of State, Timor Leste 2003). The renewal or re-creation of political community following violent conflict needs to be substantially grounded in the lives of local communities and populations (Brown and Gusmao 2009). Recognising communities and regions as not only 'war zones' but also sites of fundamental ethical values, resistance to violence and capacity for innovation and creativity is an important step towards this (Lederach 2005). This emphasis is relevant not only to crafting peace in the face of or following hot conflict, but also to working against violence in the context of everyday collective insecurity.

Peace formation draws attention to local efforts to work against violence, alongside the efforts of international actors and national elites. To be called 'local' often means being relegated to the bottom of a vertical hierarchy, below national, international and global. In this positioning, local forms of knowledge are seen to carry less weight than the more elevated perspectives (Escobar 2011). That is not the sense in which 'local' is used here. 'Local' can be a way of referring to 'bottom up', rather than 'top down' endeavours, or of working with practical, concrete and lived experience, but it can refer to more than that. The 'local' can be saturated with the national and the global, and vice versa; issues emerging or playing out within towns and neighbourhoods can have real national and global ramifications. The local is also a way of addressing place (Escobar 2008). Place holds a fundamental meaning for many peoples; across much of the Pacific Islands and West Africa, for example, kin networks, which are the basis of social order and belonging, are part of an ancestral domain, an ecology and a landscape. Place can thus bear on who has authority to speak, when, and in what way.

Addressing local sources of social order highlights both social context and people's agency. Cities, villages and regions are places where people shape collective meaning and live out 'values, ideas, narratives, feelings, political and moral projects, and visions of what social life should be' (Stasch 2010, p. 43).

> The local can be small-scale, geographically contained and parochial; it can also be where far-reaching networks of communication, trade, criminality, security and migration intersect and are grappled with, where people struggle with dilemmas of war and peace, terrorism, climate change, or epidemic disease and where creative responses to existential challenges can emerge.
>
> (Brown 2017)

While general answers to problems of violent conflict can offer valuable insights, working with violence and its legacy needs to be grounded in the concrete realities, histories, needs and relationships of particular places and contexts (Lederach 2005). 'The local' is thus a decisive arena for the formation of peace and political community.

Statebuilding as the path to security

For some decades, the United Nations, major multilateral organisations and international donor states have shared a broad, overarching consensus concerning the fundamental underpinnings of peace and social and political order (Doyle and Sambanis 2006; Paris 2004). While changing emphasis in various ways over time, this broad consensus continues to form the framework for much international effort on security, peace and development (Ramsbotham, Woodhouse and Miall 2011). In this account, peace, justice and social order rest primarily upon the foundations of an effective state. In the words of former UN Secretary General Kofi Annan (2005),

> [i]f states are fragile, the peoples of the world will not enjoy the security, development, and justice that are their right. Therefore, one of the great challenges of the new millennium is to ensure that all states are strong enough to meet the many challenges we face.

This statement underscores the fundamental significance attached to states in contemporary political life, and the responsibilities seen to belong to them. The questions then are: what is meant by the state, how are strong states (understood as states able to ensure security, development and justice) achieved, and how can the international donor community support this? The predominant international response to these questions has been statebuilding.

International statebuilding efforts have purveyed a powerful discourse and idea of the state (Paris 2004; Eriksen 2016). This discourse of the state purports to provide a thumbnail sketch of the essential elements of actual states that have successfully provided security, development and justice to their populations (Fukuyama 2011; Ghani and Lockhart 2008). In post-conflict contexts, this template can play a leading role in the orientation and scope of international assistance. In development scenarios, it may define the efforts to strengthen governance and justify institutional transfer, interacting with state institutional practices already in play (Larmour 2005). More generally, and perhaps more importantly, this discourse promotes certain ways of thinking about the state, about peaceful political community, and about what does not fit the template.

Underpinning a complex variety of institution-building efforts, the statebuilding template offers a technocratic, standardised and simplified version of the Weberian nation-state. Because it is widely taken to be rational, it is often considered as able to be replicated anywhere (Larmour 2005). This is a discourse of centralised, hierarchical power, exercising a monopoly over the legitimate use of violence and thus over fundamental security provision (Weber 1994). The state is understood as comprising a unitary system of political and legal institutions, operating through bureaucratic decision-making processes, according to frameworks set by law and regulation. The centralised, unitary institutions are generally themselves identified as the state and are the focus of statebuilding efforts (Eriksen 2016). The state is categorised as distinct from society, which it governs (Miller and Rose 2008). Citizens in turn exercise control over the state through a range of accountability mechanisms and democratic representation managed through elections. Security, justice, order and ultimately peace are vested in the state; in practical terms, this means in state institutions. Citizens, as one half of the social contract, appear (in theory at least) as recipients of services, a source of taxes, a voting public, and as 'civil society'. Many dimensions of society, however, for example, customary networks, would not be classified as 'civil society'. In this idea of the state, society appears as that which is governed. Society, in its diversity, agency and unruliness, its forms of order and governance, its collective meaning and value, scarcely appears at all.

There are other elements to the statebuilding template, including principles of accountability, participation and human rights. Accountability and participation are critical to the operation of the liberal democratic state and its ability to support justice and peace. The way of thinking about the state enabled by this template, however, arguably weakens the conceptual and practical capacity to support realisation of these values (Eriksen 2016; Brown 2009). Well-operating institutions are a vital part of the life of a state. Nevertheless, in its focus on state institutions, this model overlooks the critical significance of the relations between those institutions and the broader field of often diverse values, social institutions and ways of life within which state institutions operate and with whom they must meaningfully communicate and interact. Yet it is the relations between government and people, in their various forms of social, political and economic organisation, that make up the life of a state, and certainly of a democratic state (Bevir 2013). The political, economic and legal institutions of government are effective and accountable largely because they are part of networks of exchange with social norms and practices (Krygier 2006; Krygier and Mason 2008). Effective processes and habits of accountability, participation and legitimacy speak directly to the range and quality of relations between state institutions, including political leadership, and society in its many aspects.

International statebuilding programmes generally work with state institutions that are already in place, and which already refer in principle to broadly liberal, Weberian models, even if such models do not describe the actual workings of those institutions. Rather than strengthening states' capacities to provide security, development and justice, however, statebuilding models may be weakening them by promoting this powerful but eviscerated idea of the state (Eriksen 2016). The Weberian model of the state is not oriented towards the challenges of building viable relations with significantly different socio-cultural approaches to governance or across a disaggregated sovereignty (Brown and Grenfell 2017). Yet in much of the post-colonial world, this is exactly the situation that exists. Multiple linkages have developed historically and in practice between the operations of government agencies and diverse customary or community forms of governance. On the ground, different forms of authority are interwoven, both competing and cooperating, with police calling on customary and community bodies and vice versa in order to operate, for example (Baker and Scheye 2007). Social welfare often depends significantly, even primarily, on community networks, rather than provision through government. In effect, 'the state' and its operations are enabled and underpinned, as well as sometimes challenged and threatened, by these complex, shifting alliances (Hunt, see Chapter 5 in this volume). The dominant idea and discourse of the state, however, offers no way to conceptualise the need to work constructively with different logics of governance and multiple sources of authority as part of the challenge of accountability and legitimacy in political order (Tully 1995). Because government appears as a technical project that can be replicated anywhere, there is little incentive to see the significance, or work with the grain, of local realities. Because the state is identified simply with the formal institutional framework rather than with the broader political community, of which state institutions are part, the fundamental significance of the body of relations between state institutions and diverse societal networks and institutions is obscured.

In post-conflict situations, the drive of state-builders to see society as an empty, chaotic space awaiting the ordering of state institutions is even stronger (Autesserre 2010). According to Roland Paris, for example, '[f]or countries just emerging from civil wars, the relevant starting point is something closer to the "state of nature" of early liberal theory, in which government is largely, or entirely, absent' (Paris 2004, p. 50). The state of nature, in Hobbes' famous phrase, is a state of 'the war of all against all' or 'conditions of virtual anarchy' (ibid., p. 47). The region in question is seen only as a site of conflict; the life of resistance and survival, and the forms of mutual support and order communities have constructed, are obscured (UNDP and The Ministry of State, Timor Leste 2003). This perspective does not equip state-builders to 'see', let alone engage with, the efforts to move beyond violence that community and societal networks are already undertaking (Sawyer 2005; Nordstrom 2004). As Hunt notes (see Chapter 5 in this volume, pp. 79–80), 'the dominant imaginaries of the state as a set of institutions and mechanisms of state power act as an impediment to "seeing politics as it is"' (Frödin 2012).

The statebuilding discourse appeals to the idea that it captures the essential operation of successful liberal democratic, western states. This presumption is misleading. There is much that is valuable and relevant to others in the experience of liberal democratic states. International agencies have experience and approaches to share. The idea of the state put forward, however, does not describe fundamental dimensions of the actual operation of governance in liberal states, which are more heterogeneous and socially and culturally embedded than the template suggests (Rhodes 2007; Miller and Rose 2008). More importantly, it does not describe the relationship between state institutions and social institutions and networks in democratic states. These relationships are the result of long and ongoing processes of state formation. While the distinction of state institutions from society is part of the operation of modern, liberal government and has been carefully cultivated and policed, state and social institutions and networks have taken shape over time as part of, and in dialogue and struggle with, each other (Krygier 2006). As a result, they share significant socio-cultural vocabularies. These socio-cultural vocabularies are far from being technical or culturally neutral, however (Tully 1995). In liberal democratic states, governance and accountability rest significantly on the quality, character and system of relations and communication joining government and society.

The hybrid turn

There has been widespread critique of the standardising, homogenising approach to the state embedded in statebuilding and much peacebuilding. One of the more prominent critiques centres around notions of 'hybridity'. Hybridity, or the hybrid turn, is used in different ways, even within the context of peacebuilding and critiques of statebuilding, and so can be associated with different conceptual and policy approaches and practical engagements (e.g. see Mac Ginty and Richmond 2016). As many of the following chapters draw on these ideas, discussion of some key analytical moves enabled by 'the hybrid turn' is useful here. The uses of hybridity discussed here are those which address peace formation, political community or the state.

The hybrid turn begins by recognising the reality of different logics of political order making up the life of the state in post-colonial contexts. These other logics of governance often have their roots in 'local', perhaps even face-to-face, social relations and forms of authority, as discussed earlier. The recognition of difference is significant in view of the standardising, centralising drive of statebuilding efforts and the discounting of social sources of order by dominant versions of the Weberian model of the state. For many post-colonial states, recognising heterogeneity involves taking customary and locally embedded forms of governance seriously as part of the collective political and social order underpinning the state. This does not mean accepting all aspects of customary or community governance, but recognising them, rather than overlooking, marginalising or co-opting them, and where relevant engaging seriously with them (Aning and Aubyn, see Chapter 2 in this volume). Engagement in genuine exchange is likely to involve changes for all parties. Liberal democratic models of the state accommodate a spectrum of different political perspectives and demand different political parties; societies are understood as characterised by cultural, linguistic, religious or ethnic differences which the state must manage. Despite this, the dominant idea of the state does not offer ways of recognising or working across significantly different logics of governance and collective identity (Tully 1995). By contrast, the hybrid turn affirms the validity of such difference. The entanglement of diverse logics of governance is not taken as a sign of 'failure' to be a 'proper' state. Customary life does not represent the corruption of supposedly pure forms of state institutions, or vice versa, although the friction and competition between different actors, modes of understanding and values can be corrosive of both. Rather, these dynamics are part of difficult, slow and ongoing processes of state formation. Moreover, they are likely to mark the emergence of a different form of state – potentially one that can work constructively across different ways of being in the world (Tully 1995; Baker, see Chapter 4 in this volume). States in which government institutions have strong, visible and accessible relations across the diverse social networks and institutions in play throughout the population are more likely to be accountable and participatory and in a better position to 'meet the many challenges we face' (UN 2005).

As Charles Hunt's chapter notes, recognising different logics of governance does not mean that state institutions and customary, religious or community bodies are settled and distinct entities that have only recently been interacting (Hunt, see Chapter 5 in this volume). Historically and in practice, they are entangled, competing for authority, but also interdependent and at times cooperating (Bagayoko, Hutchful and Luckham 2016, Boege and Forsyth, see Chapter 11 in this volume). Practices are dynamic and shifting, actors are challenging and changing each other, and sometimes innovating together (Albrecht and Moe 2014; Baker, see Chapter 4 in this volume). Hybridity describes the 'messy mix' of different forms of socio-political order in practice or investigates the interaction of 'local and liberal' governance processes and values (Boege, see Chapter 12 in this volume; Mac Ginty and Richmond 2013). This orientation enables better analysis of actual circumstances in many states. Shared recognition of heterogeneity in turn provides a better basis upon which institutions and communities can craft ways of grappling with inevitable conflicts of values, processes and meaning-making. Positive coexistence across a heterogeneous state needs a range of ways of working with, bridging, adjusting and simply listening to difference. The hybrid turn does not set out a new model of the state, but it does carry implications for thinking about and making the state. State formation, understood as the processes by which political communities and the institutions that structure them take shape over time, comes to the fore, rather than statebuilding. International agencies can play roles in supporting state formation but cannot expect to drive it. Notions of hybridity also call for approaches to international peacebuilding built on working with local efforts to undo violence (Mac Ginty and Richmond 2013). Working seriously with the implications of these directions could enable emancipatory approaches to political order more broadly (Mac Ginty and Richmond 2016). As discussed in some of the following chapters, the hybrid turn opens ways of thinking about the state to greater diversity, not as merely a 'good enough' state or, worse, a failing state, but potentially as a political community with institutional structures and processes that are grounded in the histories and social and cultural values of their countries and communities.

Two world regions

Addressing cases from the Pacific Islands (the Melanesian sub-region in particular) and from West Africa in the same volume might seem unusual but opens fertile spaces for conversation. This volume is not a work of comparative politics, and its chapters do not undertake systematic regional or national comparisons. Being informed by cases from geographically distinct regions, however, offers particular insights. It is an effort to respect the specificity of place, while engaging with what is often the persistence of themes in regions struggling with the legacies of colonialism, the pressures of economic globalisation and the demands of state formation in societies not historically oriented towards Weberian style states. It points out that stepping aside from universalist claims about the necessary structure of the state does not entail uncontained relativism, but rather paying attention to what is there. Drawing on case studies from the Pacific

Islands and West Africa also steps aside from the notion that the African continent is peculiarly generative of disorder, a notion that says more about western
imaginings of, and preoccupation with, Africa than about the continent itself
(Chabal and Daloz 1999). There is a history of pejorative comparison of Melanesia and Africa (Denoon 1999). Melanesia is not especially chaotic, but rather,
in Anthony Regan's phrase, a place with 'clever people working on difficult
problems' (Brown 2007, p. 300). This resonance of the regions in western imagination is itself a significant, if murky, link, which will be touched on briefly
below.

West Africa and the Pacific Islands are different in fundamental respects,
including the simplest statistics of geography, demography and history. In contrast
to the massive continental presence of Africa, of which West Africa is part, the
Pacific Island region is made up of clusters of literally thousands of mostly relatively small islands. These island clusters are scattered over approximately 30
million square kilometres, of which 98 per cent is ocean. The human geography of
both regions is extraordinarily diverse. West Africa is patterned by successive
waves of migration and conquest; it was and is traversed by major global trading
routes and has been shaped by the rise and fall of empires and pre-modern states,
as well as networks of smaller political units. This has formed the substrata of a
dense and dynamic layering of cultures, languages, religions and forms of socio-
political organisation. Altogether, the 16 countries of West Africa have a population of approximately 370 million people. For the Pacific Islands, ocean distances
and the volcanic mountain terrain of many islands meant that communities often
developed at a distance from each other and valued their independence. Communities were generally relatively small but highly complex and interlinked, connected through multiple networks of exchange. Reflecting this, the Pacific Islands
are home to over a quarter of the world's total number of languages and a great
variety of socio-political organisation, despite there being only approximately 14
million people across 28 states and territories.

Historically, the regions are linked by elements of colonial experience, and by
the desires, ambitions, obsessions and fears of colonial Europe, along with their
lingering imprint (Denoon 1999; Chabal 2009). Curiously, the island of New
Guinea in the South Pacific, the largest land mass in Oceania, was named by
passing Spanish explorers in the sixteenth century after a supposed resemblance
of the people there to inhabitants of the Gulf of Guinea (West Africa) and similar
dreams of gold (Quanchi 2005). Nevertheless, significant European interaction
began later in the Pacific Islands than in West Africa; when it did begin, the
'British empire did not dominate the Pacific as it did Africa', despite being the
major imperial presence across the broader region (Denoon 1999, p. 289). Nor
did the Pacific 'engage the British imagination as Africa did' (ibid.). Similar
statements could be made regarding French and German imperial rule (although
French Polynesia and New Caledonia continue to be French territories in the
Pacific, in an arrangement regarded as 'shared sovereignty').

In British colonies in West Africa, diverse kinds of traditional leadership were
simplified into the English word 'chief', though some leaders may rule a

kingdom (great or small) or a territory within the larger ambit of a kingdom; some may be elders, while others may be priests tending the earth (Odetei and Awedoba 2006; Aning and Aubyn, see Chapter 2 in this volume). Nevertheless, as Odetei and Awedoba point out regarding Ghana, chieftancy institutions were, and remain, a vital part of life, embedded 'in complex belief systems' and interwoven with other institutions and ways of life (2006, p. 16). At the same time, dominant European conceptions of 'chiefs' were shaped less by observation of African socio-political, philosophical and spiritual life and more by their interpretation at the time of their own history and their confidence in their own progress and superiority (Rathbone 2006, p. 45). This interpretation,

> inherently accepted that ... what had happened in the west would, in the fullness of time, happen elsewhere [and that African experiences] were an echo ... of the European past. Just as the primitive ancestors of European states had been designated chieftancies ... the entirety of that condescending taxonomy was imposed upon Africans.

Customary institutions were altered by relations with, and rule by, European colonising powers. As Kwesi Aning and Festus Aubyn's discussion makes clear, the nature of British colonial rule meant that local leaders 'were transformed into local potentates' while communities with more collective forms of leadership frequently had 'warrant chiefs' imposed (Aning and Aubyn, see Chapter 2 in this volume, p. 29). Indigenous systems distributing authority and enabling accountability to communities were thus reshaped, reducing accountability to communities but demanding local leaders be answerable to the colonial power, to raise taxes and control the population where necessary. Traditional authorities' relations with colonial power were complex and changing; there were forms of resistance, but also co-option and efforts at management through compromise (Odetei and Awedoba 2006). Nevertheless, across much of West Africa chiefs became associated with the colonisers and so in tension with those leading self-determination struggles (Aning *et al.* see Chapter 7 in this volume). The leaders of these nationalist struggles were part of modernising elites. They saw value in significant aspects of what European interaction and approaches made possible, and drew on some of those approaches, particularly ideas of a modern, self-determining state, as tools to fight against imperialism itself. For these elites, customary authorities and practices seemed simultaneously signs of a glorious past, but also 'primitive, unaccountable ... and doomed to extinction' (Rathbone 2006, p. 48).

British imperial experience in Africa influenced their approach to rule in the Pacific Islands. The generalised and simplified representations of African societies and chiefs informed how Pacific Island socio-political culture was understood, not only in Britain, but more broadly. Addressing the history of policy orientations in near neighbour Australia, for example, Denoon notes that often, 'Melanesian affairs were seen through an African lens' (Denoon 1999, p. 285). Melanesia has a long, dynamic history of customary leadership; nevertheless,

figures acting as the highly autonomous leaders of the 'chiefs' of western imagination seemed rare. In Vanuatu, for example, '"chief" is not an indigenous category' (Bolton 1998, p. 180). It is a colonial category, introduced by the British
and French to help control the local population. As in West Africa, the idea of
'chiefs' is a simplification of different, extensive networks of authority, some
relatively stable in form, with authority passing through lineage, and some
highly fluid, with authority subject to regular forms of community assessment.
Melanesia did not lend itself to kingdoms. Indeed, the relatively negotiable
nature of authority in much of Melanesia was taken by the colonial British to be
a sign of lack of civilisation in contrast to the more centralised political arrangements of the Polynesian sub-region (Jolly 1996). 'Chiefs' were in important
ways a colonial translation of, and imposition upon, a range of complex systems
– a translation which cloaked but also altered the actual workings of power and
authority across Melanesia (Bolton 2003, pp. 10–11; Boege and Forsyth, see
Chapter 11 in this volume).

Colonial administrations endeavoured to instrumentalise and in the process
reshape customary or traditional authority in both regions, with mixed success.
Despite this, across much of the Pacific Islands, custom became a basis for
claims for independence and national identity. In contrast to the independence
politics in much of West Africa, the assertion of self-determination in the Pacific
Islands drew in large part upon ancestral sources of identity, grounded in place
and the particularity of ancestral domains, even as it reshaped those ancestral
claims (White 1993; Bolton 2003). Vanuatu, for example, now has a National
Council of Chiefs, referred to in Volker Boege and Miranda Forsyth's chapter
(Chapter 11). In varying ways across both regions, this contrasting history has
influenced how customary social order and authority, and the independent state,
are seen and operate in relation to each other.

In both regions, however, custom, culture and tradition enjoy significant legitimacy, and forms of customary authority remain alive and important to the well-
being of many. As such, claims to customary authority can act also as something
to be competed for, used and misused in electoral and other forms of competition for power (Lentz 1998). Both regions are patterned by complex interplays
of diverse, competing, but also interdependent and interwoven networks of
authority and centres of power (Jaye, see Chapter 8; Hunt, see Chapter 5; Baker,
see Chapter 4; Denney, see Chapter 9, all in this volume). These can include
religious, commercial, community and other sources of power (Lentz 1998).
Traditional or customary forms of authority have proved extremely resilient as a
significant source of social order, collective meaning and value, however. This is
not to idealise such forms of order – they can be oppressive and violent (as can
the modern state).

For many, however, customary life is rooted in kinship structures and family
relations, including ancestors. In that sense it cannot be reduced to 'chiefs' and
their actions, although the varying authority structures could be understood as
expressive of this fabric of collective ties. Closely associated with this, custom is
expressive of culture and identity, values and the world of the unseen and the

spirit, alongside widely embraced forms of Islam and Christianity (Rathbone 2006; Ellis and ter Haar 2004). Nor should customary forms of social order be seen as fixed in the past. 'Tradition' persists because of a capacity for adaption, refashioning and renewal (Keesing 1996). Depending on their context and outlook, chiefs might 'travel abroad to seek economic aid and investment for their communities' (Odetei and Awedoba 2006, p. 19), coordinate overseas worker programmes for community members, promote education for girls in their communities, set up support programmes for youth in town, collaborate to manage crime in urban areas, initiate far-reaching conflict resolution and reconciliation processes, as well as enact local 'traditional' duties (ACPACS 2012; Boege and Forsyth, see Chapter 11 in this volume, field research 2014). As the first Prime Minister of Vanuatu, Fr. Walter Lini, noted, '[c]ustom is part of life, but as our way of life changes, so must custom. Its strength in the future must lie in its flexibility' (Government of Vanuatu 1990, in Jolly 1994, p. 256). While customary patterns of life are intrinsically conservative in many respects, rooted in collective and kinship patterns of life, they are often also dynamic and adaptive.

As suggested by Richard Rathbone's comments above on earlier European interpretations of 'chiefs', the legacy of colonialism has also affected ways of knowing and what counts as valid knowledge (Chilisa 2012; Smith 1999). Historically, both regions were seen by the colonising capitals as undeveloped, uncivilised (particularly Melanesia), and expressions of moral darkness (Nakata 2007). The violence of tribal battles in Melanesia, for example, was put forward as a reason justifying colonial control, while the violence of colonial conquest was portrayed as the civilising spread of progress (Jolly 1996). Echoes of these judgements about the nature of social, cultural and political organisation in both regions persist. In popular but also some scholarly and policy discussion, Melanesia and Africa more generally can still be sweepingly portrayed as zones of threat, inherent violence and Hobbesian chaos (Autesserre 2010; Richards 2005; Dinnen 2000). Africa, as an almost generic category, is burdened by representations of 'new wars' occurring in the 'interzones – the places where weak states had withdrawn or collapsed' (Richards 2005, p. 2). Melanesia has been identified as 'an arc of instability', a zone of economic 'basket cases' and 'failing states', open to penetration by terrorism and organised crime. Loose comparisons and 'untested African analogies [shape] perceptions and policies, and [become] a source of confusion' (Denoon 1999, p. 289).[1]

Both regions face profound challenges. Significant parts of West Africa are struggling with multifaceted, entrenched patterns of violent conflict. Nevertheless, sweeping generalisations and their implications of inherent violence are profoundly misleading. They sidestep the causes, contexts and histories of violent conflict – histories and contexts in which the 'developed world' often plays a role – and instead label whole areas as inherently given to violent conflict and so beyond the need of serious understanding or the possibility of serious engagement. Such perceptions support top-down interventions but do not support the kinds of engagement that listen to communities or pay attention to less obvious causes of conflict; nor are they alert to local efforts to undo violence. Such generalisations overlook the dynamics of order, resilience and creativity that are the basis of peace formation. These representations themselves become obstacles to working together against violence.

The book

This book proceeds in two parts. The first part explores the conceptual and thematic questions already raised here. These discussions draw on empirical cases, however, and are linked to the case studies in the second part of the volume. The authors write from different experiences, some as active citizens of states discussed and some not, some as direct participants in the struggles of post-colonial political community and some not, but all are engaged with questions of peace formation and the changing nature of the state as political community. The second part of the book provides case studies from Ghana, Liberia, Sierra Leone, Solomon Islands, Papua New Guinea (Bougainville) and Vanuatu, which in turn link back to the concepts and thematic treatments of the first part. These contexts differ significantly. Liberia and Sierra Leone have experienced deep-reaching international intervention, carried out by the United Nations, with significant involvement by the security arm of ECOWAS (the Economic Community of West African States) and, in the case of Sierra Leone, Britain. Solomon Islands provides an example of a comparatively small regional intervention, carried out by neighbouring countries in the context of a regional organisation, the Pacific Islands Forum. Bougainville is not a state, but an autonomous region within Papua New Guinea. It was the site of the region's most severe conflict since World War II; Bougainville leaders themselves invited in a relatively contained UN peacebuilding force and unarmed regional forces. Vanuatu is a small Pacific Island country and a latecomer as a nation-state. Ghana is by comparison substantial, with a relatively long history as a post-colonial state. Both are relatively stable, though they display some of the qualities and characteristics witnessed in the other cases. The final chapter draws together some of the conceptual, practical and policy implications of the earlier discussions.

Kwesi Aning and Festus Aubyn's chapter argues that the 'Weberian paradigm of the state is fundamentally irreconcilable with the underlying realities of the African context' (p. 24). Indeed, as Aning and Aubyn point out, 'the character of the state inherited after colonialism strengthened the position of those in power at the expense of the population' (p. 30) and created a context where 'the post-colonial political order resorted to protecting itself against the population' (p. 29). The reality on the ground in Ghana and Liberia, particularly, but not only, in rural areas, is that traditional authorities continue to provide much of the security, justice and general welfare that is available. These authorities, however, are enmeshed in multiple relations with state institutional authorities. The chapter argues that these complex interdependent relations underpin community resilience and peace. The discussion proposes that routes to functioning statehood can emerge and are emerging from these realities of West African life.

Volker Boege's later discussion of Bougainville picks up this point in a Pacific Island context.

The question of the appropriate form of the state is continued in Bruce Baker's reflection on the dilemma facing African states. Governments want to demonstrate that they can assert a monopoly over the legitimate use of violence, 'a service that almost defines what a state is according to the West', as well as to secure their own position and authority (p. 74). Despite being 'the most powerful player' overall, however, governments have had to accept that they must work with a heterogeneous range of bodies, norms and practices underpinning security and justice. Establishing what counts as justice and order are social processes, and these norms and practices are expressions of often widely held views concerning the nature of these goods. This chapter provides a valuable overview of some of the different arrangements that have arisen as governments and other authorities navigate their relations through particular histories and circumstances. Like Aning and Aubyn, Baker argues that the dilemma facing African states will not be resolved within the context of current models of the state. Rather, the relationship between state and society needs to be reworked, enabling 'new security and justice networks appropriate to local conditions' to emerge and African forms of state to take shape (p. 74). Baker touches on the question of what frameworks and processes might guide this state-making. He points to the importance of accountability to local communities as well as to state law, the need for non-state actors to be open to change, and the need for all parties to engage in deeper forms of consultation with a willingness to see through long, uncertain processes of collaboration and change.

Accounts of the interaction of different actors and different logics of governance can easily become fixed in binary oppositions: state and non-state, modern and traditional (or customary), liberal and illiberal, western and non-western. While it can be important to note these distinctions, it is equally important to grasp the interdependence and overlapping identities of the actors involved. Charles Hunt's chapter on relational dimensions of peace formation emphasises two related moves – a shift of focus from entities (state institutions, chiefs, etc.) to the network, or eco-system, of relations, and a more nuanced exploration of the different kinds of relations in play. The chapter argues that a focus on entities has produced static analyses, often preoccupied with identifying an entity as good or bad, state or customary, liberal or illiberal. By contrast, a relational, systemic view, informed here by complexity theory, enables clearer, more nuanced analysis of the ways people seek security, justice and social order in conflict-affected or socio-politically heterogeneous environments. This chapter proposes a framework of analysis based on three guiding categories of symbiotic relations: predatory, parasitic and mutual.

Lisa Denney's discussion of justice and security provision in Sierra Leone (in Part II) also emphasises the value of understanding different actors as part of a broader symbiotic, interactive system, rather than simply as competitors for the same 'space'. Taking the perspective of the 'end-user', this chapter highlights the multiple roles that security and justice actors play in heterogeneous states or plural justice systems, as well as people's agency navigating 'between different providers in order to find the most suitable outcomes' (p. 159). Denney argues that the view that security and justice provision in heterogeneous states is made up of discrete, competing bodies has dominated many international academic and policy approaches and, in the case of Sierra Leone, has led to a misunderstanding and neglect of the roles of chiefs, despite their leading role in security and justice.

Many political communities and bodies have struggled, and continue to struggle, to embed principles of human rights, including those addressing gender relations, into the framework and practices of states. Progress in these fundamental dimensions of working against violence and marginalisation is hard won and uncertain (Brown 2009). Formal commitments to human rights can be incorporated into state legislation, as a potent tool and with potential for impact on practice. Whether in West Africa or the Pacific Islands, however, there can be considerable tensions between customary orientations and practices and ideas of human rights and gender equality. It is not surprising, therefore, that some of the strongest objections to more fully recognising the role of customary actors in the political community of the state are grounded in concerns about upholding human rights and undoing oppression rooted in gender roles. Nancy Annan broaches the question of gender in hybrid political contexts, noting the relative lack of writing on this key issue. Focusing on West Africa, this chapter sets out some of the leadership roles played by women, including in customary contexts, and draws attention to their roles in community justice and security. It argues that sustainable security requires recognition of the contributions of all actors, including women. Turning to the Pacific Islands, Anne Brown discusses approaches to working with questions of human rights in heterogeneous or hybrid political contexts. Drawing primarily on a case study from Vanuatu, the chapter suggests the value of a dialogic approach to promoting human rights across differences of culture and historical division.

Chapters by Volker Boege, and Volker Boege and Miranda Forsyth, draw on cases or examples from Vanuatu, Solomon Islands, Bougainville, Ghana and Liberia. Although these countries are situated in geographically distant regions, and although they are highly diverse with regard to their current state of peace and order, in all five countries or territories 'illiberal' local actors, such as chiefs, elders and religious leaders, play important roles in conflict resolution and peace formation. Their interactions with state institutions lead to the emergence of context-specific, hybrid forms of peace, order and socio-political authority. Moreover, customary dispute resolution is not only of relevance for the everyday life of people in peripheral rural areas and for locally confined conflicts (as conventional wisdom has it), but is also utilised in urban environments and in the context of the state and national politics (as the Vanuatu case illustrates).

These cases demonstrate that the distinction between state and non-state actors is helpful in grasping the realities of the provision of peace, security and justice; nevertheless, they also indicate that while some entities can at first sight be seen as 'state' (the police, the army, the courts) or as 'non-state' (elders, vigilantes, land-guards, chiefs), a closer look reveals intersections and entanglement, for example, with customary authorities playing formal roles in state institutions, or community police referencing state authority in some contexts and non-state authority in others. As Selwyn Garu, formerly of the National Council of Chiefs of Vanuatu (itself a hybrid body) noted, chiefs are 'turtles' living in the water and on land (Boege, Chapter 12, pp. 212–213). In underlining the enmeshment of different logics of social order, these case studies demonstrate the hybridisation of order and security governance, introduce the non-state dimension to analysis, policy and practice, and step aside from liberal peace-building's overwhelming focus on state institutions.

In Bougainville a home-grown variety of political order is emerging, imbued with the features of hybrid governance and security arrangements. This form of polity is not necessarily 'second best' in comparison to the ideal type Weberian state, but can potentially serve people's needs and interests in effective and legitimate ways, including in the domain of peace and security. In Vanuatu it was the complementarity and cooperation of state agencies and chiefs and the combined utilisation of state-based and customary instruments of conflict resolution (such as court cases and customary reconciliation) in the case discussed that restrained violence, averted disaster and laid a basis for ongoing relations. While illustrating complementarity, however, the cases discussed in these chapters also disclose frictions, competition and incompatibilities, demonstrating that relations remain deeply challenging. It may be the relations – the interstices, liminality and performativity out of which hybridity emerges and evolves – that matter most to the formation of a political community grounded in, and responsive to, communities' needs and values.

In their discussion of justice and security provision in Ghana, Kwesi Aning, Nancy Annan and Fiifi Edu-Afful address common representations of the relationship between the 'modern' and 'traditional' modes of governance within Ghana, examining historical and current relations between state and chieftancy institutions. The chapter argues that the processes of colonisation and the nature of the independence struggle have led to the polarisation of 'modern' and 'traditional' modes of governance. Despite frequent cooperation in practice, this polarisation has contributed to lack of trust between chiefs and state bodies and has been an impediment to understanding the 'contemporary realities of power, legitimacy, justice, and security provision' in the country (p. 122). The chapter argues against efforts by state authorities to co-opt or 'manage' customary actors. Formal structures for the 'harmonisation' of these modes of governance may also prove an obstacle to genuinely effective, open cooperation. Rather, processes of cooperation need to place 'the interactions and relationships between the traditional authorities and other non-state and state institutions' at the centre of the discussions (p. 123).

Both this chapter and Thomas Jaye's discussion of Liberia counter common assumptions of historical, traditional socio-political life as merely reactionary, violent, or in a state of Hobbesian anarchy. They note that forms of social contract and accountability mechanisms existed (and continue to exist), and that social order, peace and justice did not wait for the arrival of a Westphalian state. Liberia's case is unusual and instructive, as Jaye's discussion sets out. Formally independent since 1847, but ruled by freed settler slaves and their descendants, unrelated to the indigenous population, the relations between state institutions and the indigenous population and their forms of governance has been highly divisive and exclusionary. At the same time, forms of co-option, but also of cooperation and complementarity, have developed. As the site of protracted violent conflict flowing in part from this history, Liberia has also experienced a major international peacebuilding and statebuilding effort. Jaye underscores the critical significance of paying attention to community sources of governance in the ongoing efforts to build peaceful political community.

Jaye's chapter, and in different ways all the following chapters, highlights the need to engage with the heterogeneity of political life. In part this can be justified on pragmatic grounds. Enquiring into, and taking seriously, the character of everyday politics and what people value is more likely to generate insight than judging communities according to an 'imaginary' of the state or how well they uphold institutions they have only partially embraced. Working with the grain of what people value is more likely to be effective than approaching communities as empty vessels to be filled by others. There are also serious ethical reasons for recognising and working with what is important to communities, however. These concern respect for others as interlocutors in ongoing questions of how to live. Many of the following chapters, however, also indicate some of the difficulty of these efforts, while the final chapter will consider some possible ways forward.

Note

1 In a notable example from a major Australian newspaper, the columnist expostulated that 'Melanesian culture is tribal and warlike.... Melanesia is often tellingly compared with Africa.... There are no solutions. Nothing works' (Sheridan 2006).

Bibliography

ACPACS (Australian Centre of Peace and Conflict Studies) 2012, *Kastom governance is for everyone: activities and impacts of the Vanuatu Kastom Governance Partnership 2005–2012*, The University of Queensland, Brisbane.

Albrecht, P and Moe, LW 2014, 'The simultaneity of authority in hybrid orders', *Peacebuilding* vol. 3, no. 1, pp. 1–16.

Autesserre, S 2010, *The trouble with the Congo*, Cambridge University Press, Cambridge.

Bagayoko, N, Hutchful, E and Luckham, R 2016, 'Hybrid security governance in Africa: rethinking the foundations of security, justice and legitimate public authority', *Conflict, Security* and *Development*, vol. 16, no. 1, pp. 1–32.

Baker, B and Scheye, E 2007, 'Multi-layered justice and security delivery in post-conflict and fragile states', *Conflict, Security and Development*, vol. 7, no. 4, pp. 503–28.

Bevir, M 2013, *Governance: a very short introduction*, Oxford University Press, Oxford.

Bolton, L 1998, 'Chief Willie Bongmatur Maldo and the role of chiefs in Vanuatu', *Journal of Pacific History*, vol. 33, no. 2, pp. 179–95.

Bolton, L 2003, *Unfolding the moon: enacting women's kastom in Vanuatu*, University of Hawai'i Press, Honolulu.

Brown, MA 2007, 'Conclusion', in *Security and development in the Pacific Islands: social resilience in emerging states*, Lynne Rienner, Boulder.

Brown, MA 2009, *Human rights and the borders of suffering: the promotion of human rights in international politics*, Manchester University Press, Manchester.

Brown, MA 2017, 'Global and national governance', in Farazmand, A (ed.) *Global encyclopedia of public administration, public policy and governance*, Cham, Springer Link.

Brown, MA and Grenfell, D 2017, 'An ecology of governance: rethinking the state and political community in Timor-Leste', in Viegas and Feijo (eds), *Transformations in independent Timor-Leste: dynamics of cohabitation*, Routledge, Abingdon.

Brown, MA and Gusmao, AF 2009, 'Peacebuilding and political hybridity in East Timor', *Peace Review*, vol. 21, no. 1, pp. 61–9.

Chabal, P 2009, *Africa, the politics of suffering and smiling*, Zed Books, London.

Chabal, P and Daloz, J-P 1999, *Africa works: disorder as political instrument*, Indiana University Press, Indiana.

Chilisa, B 2012, *Situating knowledge systems in indigenous research methodologies*, Sage, Los Angeles.

Denoon, D 1999, 'Black Mischief: the trouble with African analogies', *Journal of Pacific History*, vol. 34, no. 3, pp. 281–9.

Dinnen, S 2000, 'Violence and governance in Melanesia: an introduction', in Dinnen and Ley (eds), *Reflections on violence in Melanesia*, Hawkins Press/Asia Pacific Press, NSW/Canberra.

Dinnen, S and Peake, G 2013, 'More than just policing: police reform in post-conflict Bougainville', *International Peacekeeping*, vol. 20, no. 5, pp. 570–84.

Doyle, MW and Sambanis, N 2006, *Making war and building peace: United Nations peace operations*, Princeton University Press, Princeton.

Ellis, S and ter Haar, G 2004, *Worlds of power: religious thought and political practice in Africa*, Hurst and Co., London.

Eriksen, SS 2016, 'State effects and the effects of state building: institution building and the formation of state-centred societies', *Third World Quarterly*, vol. 10, pp. 1–16.

Escobar, A 2011, *Encountering development: the making and unmaking of the Third World*, Princeton University Press, Princeton.

Escobar, A 2008, *Territories of difference: place, movements, life, redes*, Duke University Press, Durham and London.

Fukuyama, F 2011, *The origins of political order: from prehuman times to the French Revolution*, Farrar, Straus and Giroux, New York.

Ghani, A and Lockhart, C 2008, *Fixing failed states: a framework for rebuilding a fractured world*, Oxford University Press, Oxford.

Jolly, M 1994, *Women of the place: kastom, colonialism and gender in Vanuatu*, Harwood Academic Publishers, Melbourne.

Jolly, M 1996, 'Women ikat raet long human raet o no?' Women's rights and domestic violence in Vanuatu', *Feminist Review*, vol. 52, pp. 169–90.

Keesing, R 1996, 'Class, culture, custom', in Friedman, J and Carrier, JG (eds), *Melanesian modernities*, Lund University Press, Lund.

Krygier, M and Mason, W 2008, 'Interpersonal violence, the rule of law and its enforcement', paper delivered at the Global Development Network Conference, Brisbane, 29 January–5 February.

Krygier, M 2006, 'Introduction' in Sadurski, W, Czarnota, A and Krygier, M (eds), *Spreading democracy and the rule of law? The impact of EU enlargement on the rule of law, democracy and constitutionalism in post-Communist legal orders*, Springer, Dordrecht.

Larmour, P 2005, *Foreign flowers: institutional transfer and good governance in the Pacific Islands*, University of Hawai'i Press, London.

Lederach, JP 2005, *The moral imagination: the art and soul of building peace*, Oxford University Press, Oxford.

Lentz, C 1998, 'The chief, the mine captain and the politician: legitimating power in Northern Ghana', *Africa*, vol. 68, no. 1, pp. 46–67.

Mac Ginty, R 2011, *International peacebuilding and local resistance: hybrid forms of peace*, Palgrave Macmillan, New York.

Mac Ginty, R and Richmond, O 2013, 'The local turn in peacebuilding: a critical agenda for peace', *Third World Quarterly*, vol. 34, no. 5, pp. 763–83.

Mac Ginty, R and Richmond, O 2016, 'The fallacy of constructing hybrid political orders: a reappraisal of the hybrid turn in peacebuilding', *International Peacekeeping*, vol. 23, no. 2, pp. 219–39.

McWilliam, A 2008, 'Customary governance in Timor-Leste', in Mearns, D (ed.), *Democratic governance in Timor-Leste: reconciling the local and the national*, Charles Darwin University Press, Darwin.

Miller, P and Rose, N 2008, *Governing the present: administering economic, social and personal life*, Polity, Cambridge.

Nakata, M 2007, *Disciplining the savages, savaging the disciplines*, Aboriginal Studies Press, Canberra.

Nordstrom, C 1997, *A different kind of war story*, University of Pennsylvania Press, Philadelphia.

Nordstrom, C 2004, *The shadows of war*, University of California Press, Berkeley.

Odetei, IK and Awedoba, AK 2006, 'Introduction', in Odetei, IK and Awedoba, AK (eds), *Chieftancy in Ghana: culture, governance and development*, Sub-Saharan Publishers, Accra.

OECD 2008, *The OECD DAC handbook on security system reform: supporting security and justice*, OECD Publishing, Paris.

Paris, R 2004, *At war's end: building peace after civil conflict*, Cambridge University Press, Cambridge.

Quanchi, M 2005, *Historical dictionary of the discovery and exploration of the Pacific Islands*, The Scarecrow Press, Lanham.

Ramsbotham, O, Woodhouse, T and Miall, H 2011, *Contemporary conflict resolution; the prevention, management and transformation of deadly conflicts*, Polity Press, Cambridge and Malden.

Rathbone, R 2006, 'From kingdom to nation: changing African constructions of identity', in Odetei, AK and Awedoba, K (eds), *Chieftancy in Ghana: culture, governance and development*, Sub-Saharan Publishers, Accra.

Rhodes, RAW 2007, 'Understanding governance: ten years on', *Organization Studies*, vol. 28, no. 8, pp. 1243–64.

Richards, P 2005, 'New war, an ethnographic approach', in Richards, P and Helander, B (eds), *No peace, no war: an anthology of contemporary armed conflicts*, Ohio University Press, Ohio.

Richmond, OP 2013, 'Failed statebuilding versus peace formation', *Cooperation and Conflict* vol. 48, no. 3, pp. 378–400.

Richmond, OP 2014, *Failed statebuilding: intervention, the state and the dynamics of peace formation*, Yale University Press, New Haven.

Sawyer, A 2005, 'Social capital, survival strategies, and their potential for post-conflict governance in Liberia', *Expert Group on Development Issues*, UNU-WIDER, Research Paper, 5.

Sheridan, G 2006, 'Melanesia is a huge disaster', *The Australian*, 20 April, p. 12.

Smith, L 1999, *Decolonizing methodologies: research and indigenous people*, Zed Books, New York.

Stasch, R 2010, 'The category "village" in Melanesian social worlds: some theoretical and methodological possibilities' *Paideuma*, vol. 56, pp. 41–62.

Tully, J 1995, *Strange multiplicity: constitutionalism in an age of diversity*, Cambridge University Press, Cambridge.

UN, United Nations 2005, *In larger freedom: towards development, security and human rights for all*, Report of the Secretary General, UN.

UNDP and The Ministry of State, Timor Leste 2003, *Local government options study: final report*, prepared by Tanja Hohe, UNDP, Ministry of State (AGLD), Dili.

Weber, M 1994, *Political writings*, Cambridge University Press, Cambridge.

White, GM 1993, 'Three discourses of custom', *Anthropological Forum*, vol. 6, no. 4, pp. 475–94.

2 Challenging conventional understandings of statehood

West African realities

Kwesi Aning and Festus Aubyn

Introduction

The issue of what constitutes a modern state has been discussed extensively by scholars, but most often in absolute terms confined to a list of criteria that must be met before an entity may be deemed as a state. In Africa especially, most of the arguments about statehood have drawn from the Weberian model of what constitutes a state (Wulf 2007). In Max Weber's political thought, the state lays claim to the monopoly of legitimate use of physical violence over a given territory and population (Weber 1964; Wulf 2007, p. 3). The state is also seen as the provider of general welfare or public goods including peace, justice, security and development. Analytically, the rigidity of this very notion implies that the term 'state' has a fixed meaning that provides an unambiguous yardstick for measuring what an effective state should look like and what it should be able to deliver. Thus, the state must have a definite territory over which effective legitimate control is exercised and the capacity to provide for, as well as maintain, the welfare of its population (Jackson and Rosberg 1984, p. 2S; Jackson 1987; Jeng 2012). Based on this conception, many states in Africa are said to be seriously deficient in the essentials of statehood and exist primarily by means of international legitimacy. The African state is, furthermore, conceived as fragile, failing and in extreme cases collapsed due to an inability to 'capture' and control all its constituent parts (Zartman 1995; Rotberg 2004). The typical cases often referred to are Somalia and, more recently, Libya, Guinea-Bissau and the Central African Republic (CAR), to mention only a few.

The Weberian paradigm of the state is fundamentally irreconcilable with the underlying realities of the African context, where state authority and the provision of welfare services are not only contested but also exercised by a vast array of different, recognisable non-state actors (Jackson and Rosberg 1984, p. 3). As argued by Clapham (1996), it would be more 'appropriate to place all states on a continuum, focusing not only on the level of effective government power over the states' territory, but also the extent to which the "idea" of each state is both shared and implemented' (Clapham 1996, p. 8).

Cognizant of and underscoring the realities in West Africa, we argue in this chapter that states can, and often do, develop in functional forms that do not necessarily follow a Weberian model. Thus, the chapter argues that in several West African societies, focusing especially on Ghana and Liberia, it is the complex and interdependent relationships between what are often characterised as the modern and the traditional system of governance that explain the resilience of the state. A mix of conflict and cooperation characterises these linkages. The authority to exercise legitimate force and the provision of welfare services do not rest exclusively with the institutions of central government, which in most instances have not penetrated local societies and are often perceived as an imposition. Due to this factor, as well as modern governments' institutional frailties in delivering key services, traditional authorities have continued to play key roles in the provision of welfare services, including peace, justice, and security. This is especially so in fragile situations where states are sometimes incapable of providing, and in worst cases unwilling to provide, basic security and welfare services, or in rural and semi-urban areas where local customary practices and relationships shape everyday social reality and provide support for basic livelihoods. Essentially, the West African state and its institutions overlap, interrelate, interpenetrate and operate alongside a diverse array of non-state governance systems and localised security providers, some violently challenging its authority, others working alongside or cooperating with it (OECD 2010; Africa Security Sector Network [ASSN] 2014).

The chapter is divided into three sections. The first section examines the conventional notion of statehood and is followed by a discussion of the nature of the African state in the second section.[1] The subsequent section explores the interface between the modern state and traditional governance systems by looking at the notion of hybridity, juxtaposing the conventional notion of statehood and the West African traditional systems of governance. While there can be a range of bodies providing various forms of security, and their exercise of force is seen (locally at least) to have varying degrees of legitimacy, traditional systems are the most widespread, far-reaching and persistently important sources of social order beyond state institutions. This chapter, therefore, focuses largely on these traditional systems and authorities.

The conventional notion of statehood

States are the principal actors in international politics and have been the dominant form of political organisation since the nineteenth century. Under international law, the attributes of statehood have traditionally been considered as: territory; population; and recognition by other states. The legal document often quoted is the 1933 Montevideo Convention on the Rights and Duties of States, which defines the state as a person of international law that should possess the following qualifications: (a) a permanent population; (b) a defined territory; (c) government; and (d) capacity to enter into relations with the other states.[2] It is commonly assumed that these four criteria must be met before an entity can be said to be a 'state'.

In the post-colonial era, dominant arguments about the legitimate forms of statehood have derived primarily from the Weberian model of what constitutes a state. According to Weber, the state is 'a corporate group that has compulsory jurisdiction, exercises continuous organisation, and claims a monopoly of force over a territory and its population, including all action taking place in the area of its jurisdiction' (Weber, quoted in Jackson and Rosberg 1982, p. 2). Thus, Weber describes the state as a human community that successfully claims for itself the monopoly of the legitimate use of physical force within a given territory with determined boundaries. By this definition, it can be assumed that the basic essential feature of the existence of a state according to Weber is whether it can lay claim to a monopoly of force in the territory under its jurisdiction. He claimed that the capability of the modern state in administering this assignment is in three classical areas of normative order: norm setting by means of legislation, sanctioning in cases of deviation from the norm and the execution of sanctions (Simone 1989; Akude 2007). Weber further makes the point that the feature distinguishing the modern state from its predecessor is its impersonality: the detachment of the office from the occupant and a rational-legal basis of exercising authority. Without social institutions acting together as government claiming a monopoly of the legitimate use of force within a given territory, Weber argues, a condition of anarchy would quickly ensue and it would be doubtful whether a state existed or not (Weber 1964; Wulf 2007).

Other writers have similarly theorised the state. While Young and Turner give six factors of the concept of the state as territoriality, sovereignty, nation, institutions of rule, a legal system, and an idea, Zartman points out that the basic characteristics of a state are a population, territory, a governmental apparatus, and authority (Young and Turner 1985; Zartman 1995). Migdal (1988), on the other hand, defines the state as:

> an organization, composed of numerous agencies led and coordinated by the state's leadership (executive authority) that has the ability or authority to make and implement the binding rules for all the people as well as the parameters of rule making for other social organizations in a given territory, using force if necessary to have its way.
>
> (Migdal 1988, p. 19)

As argued in the subsequent sections of this chapter, most states in Africa do not fit such Weberian-inspired conceptions of the state. States' claim to force is rarely effective and much less monopolistic; their frequent predatory nature fails the test of legitimacy; and their territoriality is generally at best hesitant and contested (Jackson and Rosberg 1982, p. 4; Englebert 1997).

The nature of the African state

Attempts at a more detailed and clear definition of the 'African' state have proved abortive. States in Africa are arguably the most demonised social institution on the continent – allegedly dysfunctional and unable to manage larger social, economic, security and political challenges. States across the continent have been variously described as 'rentier', 'parasitical', 'predatory', 'failed', 'collapsed', 'patrimonial', 'prebendal', 'crony', 'kleptocratic', just to mention a few descriptors (Jackson and Rosberg 1982; Jackson 1990). To better understand the nature and character of Africa's post-colonial states, it is important to examine the historical and social state formation processes through which they have evolved. In that regard, we analyse and categorise the historical trajectories of the African state into three different phases. The nature of political order in African societies can be understood with reference to these three particular historic types or modes of governing: 'pre-colonial', 'colonial', and 'post-colonial' (Hagmann and Péclard 2010).

Pre-colonial political order

Prior to colonisation, many African societies were organised according to distinctive ethnic identities with differences in terms of language, religion and geographical locations. Two main political systems of governance existed during the pre-colonial period to help generate stable communities and foster prosperity. Ayittey (2006) classifies these political formations into centralised and non-centralised societies. Kisangani similarly describes the two types of systems as hierarchical political systems and horizontal or acephalous societies (Kisangani 2005). Political systems of governance through which communities were governed differed from highly centralised political systems to highly decentralised political structures. The centralised political systems comprised large empires or kingdoms governed by emperors, kings or chiefs, who carried out executive, legislative, and judicial functions with the help of councillors and advisors (ibid.). The chief was the head assisted by an inner council whose membership he selected. Chiefs, according to Agbese (2004), were in theory and in practice de facto and *de jure* governors of their communities. The chiefs were not dependent on any higher authority to exercise their power, though their authority and behaviour were limited by conventions and customs. They personified the political community and served as the guardians and custodians of the people's common heritage. The role of the inner council was to provide advice to the chief, prevent him from abusing his powers and participate in the decision-making process. The chief was seen as both the religious leader of the tribe and the living representative of the ancestral spirits, as well as the governance leader, responsible for maintaining order and acting as the decisive authority (Beattie 1967; Busia 1968; Jones 1983; Coplan and Quinlan 1997). The authority of the chief was based on his religious roles and ability to collect revenue and tribute, usually through the control of trade, and defend his sovereignty from external aggression. The empires of ancient Egypt in North Africa; Nubia and Axum in North East Africa; Ghana, Mali and Songhai in West Africa; and Zimbabwe in Southern Africa; Buganda and the Busoga in Uganda; and the Tswana of Botswana, were examples of such centralised political systems (Ayittey 2006). It is significant to note that the power of the centralised authority in the centralised societies was counterbalanced by the devolution of power to regional, zonal and district chiefs. Among the Ashanti of Ghana, the Tswana of Botswana, and the Busoga of Uganda, for instance, there were systems of checks and balances defined in customary laws authorising a council of elders, religious leaders, and administrative staff of the chiefs to check the power of the leaders and keep them accountable (Busia 1968; Jones 1983).

The acephalous systems did not have a well-defined and centralised system of government. They were decentralised with law-making, social control, and allocation of resources carried out by local entities, such as lineage groupings, villages and communities (Crowder and Ikime 1970; Ayittey 2006). Some of these decentralised societies included the Igbo of Nigeria, the Kung of Liberia, the Talensi of Ghana, the Somalis, Jie of Uganda and Mbeere of Kenya (Crowder and Ikime 1970; Ayittey 2006). Most of these decentralised societies did not have a system of chiefs and were mainly ruled by a 'headman' or council of elders, generally comprising the elderly male people in the community. They lived in small-scale, egalitarian societies in which government was more a matter of consensus among the entire adult population than rule by an elite few. This system ensured 'checks and balances' and accountability, as no group exercised too much power.

Generally, the pre-colonial political systems, whether centralised or decentralised, had some important attributes that are worth noting. First, the welfare of members of the community was the primary concern and almost everyone took part, either directly or indirectly, in the daily affairs of the society. Thus, the pre-colonial systems embedded practices of participation and accountability and were concerned for welfare and stability. Second, the traditional political and social structures were organised on the basis of lineage. The lineage connected the family to the overarching political order (Ayittey 1991). To put it briefly, pre-colonial Africa was arguably characterised by autonomous, relatively stable political systems with relatively significant degrees of participation and accountability.

Political order under colonialism

During the colonial period, between 1800 and the 1960s, the pre-colonial political systems were incorporated into colonial forms of rule, reduced in terms of their formal powers or in some instances summarily abolished (Olowu 1994, p. 6). The colonial powers superimposed on these pre-colonial institutions new systems borrowed from western historical experiences, which were comparatively alien to most African cultures. Colonial rule involved centralising local or lower-level government units and installing a chief to rule over particular areas. These units were sometimes artificially delineated for purposes of control and in the interests of the colonial powers, rather than to the benefit of local communities. To maintain direct control, effective occupation and administration of their African territories, the colonisers employed methods and strategies such as conquest, forced labour, taxation, and payment of low wages to compel Africans to submit to the colonial administration (Busia 1968; Ayittey 1991; Olowu

1994). The colonial administration exercised control based on the monopoly of power and ability to use force. To be able to rule effectively and maintain law and order, the colonial administration, especially the British, adopted a system of 'indirect rule' by which the colonial powers ruled through local chiefs and existing local power structures (Busia 1968; Ayittey 1991; Olowu 1994). The system of indirect rule was designed to provide the colonial authorities with a viable low-cost administrative structure to maintain order, mobilise labour, enforce the production of cash crops, and collect taxes. Under this system, the local chiefs were transformed into local potentates with absolutist powers similar to those of the colonial governors. In areas where there were no chiefs like the acephalous societies, 'warrant chiefs', who were not always supported by the local population, were selected. This was particularly the case among groups such as the Ibo of Eastern Nigeria, the Tonga in Zambia and the Masai in Kenya (Tosh 1977; Gartrell 1983; Uwazie 1994). As noted by Busia (1968), African leaders who resisted colonisation or rebelled after colonisation were either demoted or eliminated.

The chiefs were placed under the authority of district officers/commissioners who served as advisors and ensured that the chiefs effectively performed their duties, including the administration of law, the collection of taxes, and other administrative tasks. This practice modified the traditional system of governance and altered the basic functions of the chiefs in the societies by giving them more power than they had before. As intermediaries between the colonial administration and local peoples, chiefs were expected to maintain peace and order within their communities. However, although the Chiefs were supposedly ruling, the colonial administration actually made the decisions. The colonial administration ruled by suppressing the population and regarded them as subjects rather than citizens. This led to the resistance of some colonial policies and practices by some local people. The 1929 Aba Women's Revolt or Igbo Women's War in south-eastern Nigeria was an example. The Aba Women's Revolt was an effort on the part of Igbo women to protect their economic and political interests by resisting the imposition of taxes by the local colonial administration (Dike 1995). In some countries, such as Guinea, Ghana, South Africa, Zimbabwe and Kenya, civil protest brought colonial rule to a close.

Post-colonial political order

In their struggle to assert themselves and be recognised as independent states, post-colonial states took on many of the elements of the colonial state in terms of philosophy, structure and organisation. The post-colonial political orders emulated western institutions of governance. It was, in fact, during the period of colonialism that modern Africa took on many of its most familiar characteristics (Englebert 1997; Hagmann and Péclard 2010). Instead of enhancing its capacity to provide the essential public goods and welfare services to all segments of the society, the post-colonial political orders resorted to protecting itself against the population (Hagmann and Péclard 2010). The rhetoric of unity, and the ideologies imposed by the new political elites on African countries, contributed to alienating the state from society (Economic Commission for Africa [ECA] 2004, 2005a, 2005b). Thus, the character of the state inherited after colonialism strengthened the position of those in power at the expense of the population. Hence, instead of building on the pre-colonial institutions and systems of governance, it suppressed them or perpetuated the colonial era bastardisation of them.

Chiefs were regarded as anachronistic and functionaries of the colonial arrangements. They were denied the powers and authority they had during the indirect rule system of the colonial period, and some countries even went as far as abolishing chieftaincy (ECA 2004, 2005a, 2005b). Nigeria is an example where the current 1999 constitution of the Federal Republic failed to make any provision for the role of traditional rulers in the democratic governance of the country (Peter 2014). As noted by Peter (2014), the 1999 Nigerian constitution was the most radical among all the previous constitutions in Nigeria after independence in quashing, abrogating and preventing the traditional chiefs from exercising any political power in the country. Hence, in most cases, government policies to 'Africanise' the bureaucracy failed to indigenise the institutions of governance. Underlying this purposeful neglect of the traditional system was the fact that the new political elite, which grew increasingly self-serving and autocratic, could not tolerate the existence of contending points of power. Nevertheless, chiefs were often co-opted to facilitate 'the extension of despotic control over the population and, more crucially, to enhance the legitimacy of the state and their own legitimacy within communities' (ECA 2004, p. 8).

In spite of the suppression of the traditional systems in the post-colonial political system, they have continued to operate, particularly in the rural areas but also in some urban areas of Africa. However, unlike the urban centres, where the impact of constitutionalism and western-oriented laws is evident, in the rural areas, where the majority of citizens live, people look to their chiefs and elders for development, security, the settlement of disputes and other welfare services (Boateng and Schleef 2014; Aubyn and Edu-Afful 2015). That is to say, the traditional system has endured in spite of the efforts to distort, supplant and suppress it during the colonial and post-colonial periods, though there have been some changes and adaptations over time. In some rural areas in West Africa, such as Mali, Niger, Burkina Faso, Ghana, Liberia, and Nigeria, the traditional systems of governance are virtually the only institutions of governance in some rural areas, as there is a total absence of the central government institutions and services in these places. The traditional rulers act as agents of cohesion, peace, dispute management, reconciliation, and land administration in many of the communities (Annan 2013). Public law and order, as well as welfare services, are also provided through various traditional political structures. Therefore, contrary to the view by some state elites and international actors that traditional authorities are no longer relevant, they continue to exercise significant power and influence over the lives and well-being of the population in most West African states. Agbese (2004), for instance, argues that the virtual collapse of the institutions of the modern Nigerian state since the imposition of military rule, corruption and privatisation have accentuated the importance of traditional systems of governance in many rural communities in the country. He further maintains that these traditional systems of governance elicit greater confidence and legitimacy in the eyes of many Nigerians than the institutions of the modern Nigerian state. This situation challenges the primacy of the central government's legitimacy – the basic essential feature of statehood as posited by Weber.

More significantly, in places where both state and traditional societal structures have proven incapable of delivering peace and security, people have turned to other social entities, such as warlords and their militias, and ethnic-based protection groups, who are in some cases linked to the traditional system for support. For example, in Somalia warlord systems are embedded in the local societal structure of clans and tribes (Boege, Brown and Clements 2009). These new formations, which sometimes control whole regions of a state's territory, have shown the capacity to exert and control violence within their respective areas. Their presence and competition has substituted the state's monopoly over the legitimate use of violence. Religious institutions and actors also figure prominently in some communities. There are Christian and Muslim religious leaders, as well as witch doctors, secret societies (the male *Poro* and female *Sande* in Liberia) and other representations of indigenous authority (for example, the *asafo* companies[3] in Ghana) and spirituality to whom people tend to turn for peace, security and justice provision (Ellis 2007). The point being made here is that there is a plurality of service providers that communities rely on for the provision of security, peace and justice in places such as Ghana and Liberia in West Africa, and this is in contrast with the Weberian model of the modern state.

Notions of hybridity: negotiating the Weberian conception of statehood and traditional governance systems in West Africa

In their article 'Hybrid political orders, not fragile states', Boege, Brown and Clements (2009) posit that many states outside the OECD countries are political entities that do not closely resemble the western-style Weberian state. This assertion is true with reference to many West African states, which practically exist as hybrid political orders in which governance is carried out by the central government and a range of non-state actors. Although the modern African state operates according to formal rules that appeal to the model of the rational-legal political order, they coexist with other forms of socio-political orders that have their roots in traditional political orders (Wulf 2007, p. 7). The central government is only one actor among many others, and the 'state order' is only one of a number of orders claiming to provide public goods and services to the population (Boege, Brown, Clements and Nolan 2008, p. 6). The traditional governance structures in many places also function to deliver public goods and services in a constantly negotiated relationship with the formal institutions of governance to fill critical gaps in state capacity.[4]

Recognising the resilience and significance of traditional governance systems, most countries in West Africa have incorporated them into their national constitutions or enacted legislative instrument with designated roles. For example, in Ghana, the place of traditional authorities has been guaranteed in each of the five constitutions since independence, namely, the 1957, 1960, 1969, 1979 and the current 1992 constitutions. The 1992 Ghana Constitution and the 2008 Chieftaincy Act (Act 759) establishes at the state level a triple-layered chiefly system, comprising: (1) the National House of Chiefs; (2) the Regional House of Chiefs; and (3) Traditional Councils. The National House of Chiefs and its affiliates at the regional and district levels have responsibility for all matters relating to, or affecting, chieftaincy in Ghana, such as the interpretation and codification of customary law, and eliminating outmoded and socially harmful custom. However, this incorporation has not been undertaken in a way that enables deeper acknowledgement of the work of traditional governance in the political community of the state or more conscious, reflective exchange across government institutional and traditional governance practices. The interaction remains fragmentary and is frequently characterised by distrust and suspicion.[5] Similarly, in Liberia, the National Council of Chiefs and Elders, which was formerly the National Traditional Council of Liberia, was established in 2012 with an autonomous legal status to help implement the National Policy on Decentralization and Local Governance. The Council focuses mainly on peacebuilding, advocacy, dialogue, reconciliation and the protection of the cultural heritage of the Republic of Liberia (Johnny 2012). Like Ghana, the Liberian state has not been able to effectively involve the traditional authorities in the governance of the country. The provision of peace, security and justice by the central government is mainly centralised in the capital Monrovia and at the county levels, with limited involvement of the traditional authorities from the rural areas.

Nevertheless, it is instructive to note that in many places in West Africa, state bodies operate alongside traditional authorities and in most cases actively seek the cooperation of traditional authorities to enhance the performance of state institutions (Aubyn and Edu-Afful 2015; Boateng and Schleef 2014). In some areas, traditional authorities play representational roles by serving as a link between government and the people especially in the rural areas. In Burkina Faso, for instance, the most powerful chief, the Moro-Naba, who is emperor of the Mossi people, has so much influence that the government often consults him before making any major decisions that have an impact on the lives of the people. Some traditional rulers also inspire respect for the law and urge their people to participate in the electoral and governance processes of their countries. During elections in Ghana state institutions such as the police and judiciary, also work together with the traditional authorities in several ways to provide peace, security and justice in the communities, although more efforts are needed to enhance the relationship (Hunt, see Chapter 5 in this volume). The 'Kumasi Declaration or Kumasi Peace Pact' championed by the National Peace Council (NPC) of Ghana and the Manhyia Palace before the 2012 general election, is worth noting here (Kotia and Aubyn 2013, p. 26). Thus, to ensure a peaceful and transparent election in 2012, the NPC, the Manhyia Palace and the Institute for Democratic Governance (IDEG) jointly convened a meeting of all the 2012 presidential candidates to publicly denounce electoral violence, impunity, and injustice, and to make a declaration that they would accept the electoral results. This event was historic because it was the first time in the history of Ghana that political parties had committed themselves to such a peace accord. The signing of the peace pact by the presidential candidates was witnessed by His Royal Majesty Otumfuo Osei Tutu II (king of Asante), former president Jerry John Rawlings and John Agyekum Kufuor, the Chief Justice (Her Lordship Georgina Theodora Wood) and the Inspector General of the Ghana Police Service. Although the impact of the meeting was difficult to measure, it calmed the heightened political tensions in the period and helped to avert potential violence that could have plunged Ghana into conflict (Kotia and Aubyn 2013, p. 27).

In some communities, the traditional authorities first of all attempt to resolve community problems, apart from criminal issues such as rape and murder, using indigenous methods of dispute resolution.[6] The issues are only escalated to state actors such as the courts or police when the community is unable to solve them in this way. The police and the courts, on the other hand, work with the community leaders and members in the resolution of criminal matters and other societal problems which require their participation.[7] The traditional authorities and the state institutions also work together through dialogues, community meetings, sharing of information and collective actions to solve problems.[8] This was particularly demonstrated during the Ebola virus disease outbreak in Liberia. The community, the security agencies and health workers collaborated as first responders to limit the spread of the disease in the communities by sharing information, raising awareness and undertaking collective actions (Aubyn and Edu-Afful 2015; Obinna and Aning 2017). This collaboration helped minimise the spread of the disease among the population.

In places where the capacities of state institutions like the courts and police are generally weak, their effectiveness and legitimacy very much depends on their working relationship with traditional authorities on the ground. Thus, in most rural and remote peripheral areas in West Africa, where state institutions are virtually non-existent, traditional societal structures (extended families, clans, tribes, religious brotherhoods, village communities etc.) and traditional authorities (such as village elders, headmen, clan chiefs, women leaders and religious leaders) play an important role in the everyday life of the people (Boateng and Schleef 2014; Aubyn and Edu-Afful 2015). These traditional structures and authorities often determine the everyday social reality of the majority of the population. In fact, there are areas where no courts, police and other law enforcement agencies, government ministries and public services exist. In areas where they do exist, the police, for instance, are either seen as lacking capacity in terms of logistics and personnel, or even as being corrupt and inefficient (Aubyn and Edu-Afful 2015). The same can be said of the courts, which are often seen as inaccessible, slow in pronouncing judgement and too expensive for ordinary people to patronise (Aubyn and Edu-Afful 2015). Citizens are alienated from the state, and the social contract between the state and citizens is weak. In many areas, such as the Sahel region of West Africa, the state has virtually failed in its responsibility to deliver basic law, order and security, which would ensure the loyalty and participation of citizens. Hence, the people define themselves as members of a particular sub-national group (kinship group, tribe, village), rather than perceiving themselves as citizens of a particular state (Boege, Brown and Clements 2009).

Due to the weakness and often relative lack of legitimacy of state institutions, the people have turned to their own communities, with which they identify, for security, justice and order (see also Baker, Chapter 4 in this volume). The traditional authorities, led by the chiefs and community elders, have sometimes filled the security vacuum by maintaining peace, security and justice based on local culture and customary laws (Boateng and Schleef 2014). They do this by handling a number of issues that have the potential to impact on the security and development of their localities through the application of customary laws. The issues dealt with are multifaceted, usually consisting of marital problems, divorce cases, adultery or infidelity, intra- and inter-ethnic conflicts, and interpersonal conflicts (Boafo-Arthur 2003; Aryee 2007). Others comprise land and property disputes, witch-craft, and youth 'indiscipline', including refusal to perform community work such as the cleaning of roads to the streams where they fetch water. In the provision of security, dispute resolution and law enforcement, for example, chiefs in Ghana, Liberia, Nigeria and other places in West Africa have provided these functions over time. Boafo-Arthur (2003) confirms this when he posits that in Ghana 'there are many instances, at the rural and some urban areas, where societal conflicts are referred, first and foremost, to the traditional ruler for arbitration' (p. 135).

The traditional system of dispute resolution among the Ashanti kingdom in Ghana, led by the Asantehene, His Royal Majesty Otumfuo Osei Tutu II, is worth noting in this regard. Applying the norms of customary law, the king, in council with his chiefs, sub-chiefs and elders, has been able to settle disputes or dispense justice to the satisfaction of parties who appear before the traditional court. Some of the matters dealt with include land issues, chieftaincy succession, and criminal and civil cases. These are issues which can sometimes drag on in the law courts for longer periods, but through the intervention of the chiefs, peace has returned to communities. In the community of Yendi, for example, in the northern region of Ghana, development had halted because of conflicts, and now families have been reunited.[9]

It is important to stress that people generally prefer the traditional arbitration system to settle their issues due to its accessibility, cost-effectiveness, and because they have more confidence in the chiefs to give a fair judgement than the court system due to its deficiencies.[10] The relationship between traditional governance systems and the state institutions has, however, been fairly problematic due to competition for space, resources and expressions of authority and power. For instance, on the issue of land administration, the distribution of land and the signing of contracts for the development of such resources have generated, or been a potential source of, conflict between traditional authorities and the central government in Ghana.[11]

The discussion above shows that in many West African societies, the provision of welfare services does not rest exclusively with the central government. The traditional systems that existed before colonialism continue to play key roles in the provision of welfare services. This is because people prefer traditional authorities and see them as more legitimate. Thus, most people prefer the traditional systems due to the weakness or sometimes the unwillingness of modern states' institutions to deliver key services including peace, justice and security. The inability of the state to penetrate local societies has also contributed to the preference for the traditional system. Therefore, far from possessing an effective monopoly of force, states and their security institutions share their authority, legitimacy and responsibilities by operating alongside, and in collaboration with, traditional structures.

Conclusion

In this chapter, we have argued that the Weberian ideal-type/model of a state does not sufficiently explain or capture the empirical nature of political community/order in West Africa.

Rather, it is the interdependent relationships and the nature of those relations, characterised by a mix of conflict and cooperation between modern state institutions and the traditional system of governance, that explain the resilience of the state. That is, the levels of resilience of West African states reflect both the reality that the authority to exercise legitimate force and the provision of welfare services do not rest exclusively with the institutions of central government and the nature of the interaction between modern and traditional governing institutions. Citing the experiences of Ghana and Liberia, the chapter has shown the crucial roles traditional authorities play in the provision of welfare services, including providing peace, justice and security to their people. This is particularly noticeable in fragile situations or in rural and semi-urban areas where states are sometimes incapable of providing, and in worst cases unwilling to provide, basic security and welfare services. Traditional authorities continue to serve the needs of the majority of the people, especially in the rural areas, indicating the plurality of actors that communities rely on for the provision of security, peace and justice. Therefore, promoting the Weberian idea of a modern state as the ultimate model of statehood is to ignore the contemporary realities and historical context of the emergence of the modern states in Africa. It is obvious from the above discussion that many (West) African states do not fit the description or criteria of the Weberian model of statehood.

The modern state, therefore, has no monopolistic position as the only agency providing peace, security, justice and other welfare services; it has to share authority, legitimacy and capacity with other non-state institutions. There is, therefore, the need for the recognition of a multiplicity of actors in order to effectively combine the elements of the Weberian model of governance and elements stemming from traditional systems of governance. The question, therefore, is how the different systems, which are already overlapping and entangled, can work together more effectively and accountably to better serve citizens in terms of service delivery, provision of peace, security and access to justice.

Notes

1 Most African states share similar characteristics in terms of their historical development from the pre-colonial period and the governance structures inherited after colonialism. Therefore, to make our analysis simple and manageable, we used 'African state' as a generic term to refer to the general characteristics of states in Africa.
2 See 'Montevideo Convention on the Rights and Duties of States', signed at the International Conference of American States in Montevideo, Uruguay on 26 December 1933. It entered into force on 26 December 1934.
3 These are traditional warrior groupings of the Akan people of Ghana, especially the *Fantes* that were established many years ago to defend their towns in times of war. (See Ghana Web 2004.)
4 Interviews with traditional rulers in the Western region of Ghana, August 2013.
5 Interviews with traditional rulers in Ghana and Liberia, 2013 and 2014. (See also Brown, Boege and Hunt 2016.)
6 Interviews with chiefs and community elders in Sekondi-Takoradi, Busua, and Kalsegra in Ghana, August and November 2013.
7 Interview with representatives at the regional police headquarters, Wa, Upper West Region of Ghana, 12 January 2015; interview with representatives of the Ghana Judicial Service, Western Regional Office, Sekondi of Ghana, 15 August 2013.
8 Interview with traditional rulers in Liberia, Monrovia, 2015.
9 See His Royal Majesty Otumfuo Osei Tutu II, Asantehene 2004.
10 Interviews with chiefs and community leaders in Busua, Sekondi-Tarkoradi, Kumasi and Kalsegra, August and November 2013.
11 Ibid.

Bibliography

Agbese, OP 2004, 'Chiefs, constitutions, and policies in Nigeria', *West Africa Review*, Issue 6.

Africa Security Sector Network 2014, *Hybrid Security Orders in Africa: Concept paper*, http://africansecuritynetwork.org/assn/idrc-project-2/ (accessed 6 July 2017).

Akude, JE 2007, *The failure and collapse of the African state: on the example of Nigeria*, FRIDGE, Abuja.

Annan, N 2013, 'Providing peace, security and justice in Ghana: the role of non-state actors', *KAIPTC Policy Brief* 7/2013.

Aryee, JRA 2007, 'Traditional leadership and local governance in Africa: the Ghanaian experience', paper presented at 4th Annual Local Governance Conference on the theme, 'Traditional leadership and local governance in a democratic South Africa: Quo Vadis' 30–31 July, Durban.

Aubyn, FK and Edu-Afful, F 2015, 'Report of national stakeholders workshop on understanding and working with local sources of peace, security and justice in West Africa', Golden Gate Hotel, Monrovia, Liberia, 29–30 June.

Ayittey, G 1991, *Indigenous African institutions*, Transnational Publishers, New York.

Ayittey, G 2006, *Indigenous African institutions*, Transnational Publishers, New York.

Beattie, J 1967, 'Checks on the abuse of political power in some African states: a prelimi-nary framework for analysis', in R Cohen and J Middleton (eds), *Comparative political systems: studies in politics of pre-industrial societies*, University of Texas Press, Austin.

Boafo-Arthur, K 2003, 'Chieftaincy in Ghana: challenges and prospects in the 21st Century', *African and Asian Studies*, vol. 2, no. 2, pp. 125–53.

Boateng, M and Schleef, R 2014, 'Report of national stakeholders workshop on under-standing and working with local sources of peace, security and justice in West Africa', Golden Tulip Hotel, Kumasi, Ghana, 24–27 August 2014.

Boege, V, Brown, A, Clements, K and Nolan, A 2008, 'On hybrid political orders and emerging states: state formation in the context of fragility', *Berghof Handbook for Conflict Transformation*, Dialogue no. 8.

Boege, V, Brown, A and Clements, K 2009, 'Hybrid political orders, not fragile states', *Peace Review*, vol. 21, no. 1, pp. 13–21.

Brown, A, Boege, V and Hunt, CT 2016, 'Understanding and working with local sources of peace, security and justice in West Africa – Ghana and Liberia', *Policy Brief pre-pared for DFAT*, Brisbane, University of Queensland.

Busia, KA 1968, *The position of the chief in the modern political system of Ashanti: a study of the influence of contemporary social changes on Ashanti political institutions*, Frank Cass and Co. Ltd, London.

Clapham, C 1996, *Africa and the international system*, Cambridge University Press, London.

Coplan, DB and Quinlan, T 1997, 'A chief by the people: nation versus state in Lesotho', *Journal of the International African Institute*, vol. 67, no. 1, pp. 27–60.

Crowder, M and Ikime, O (eds) 1970, *West African chiefs: the changing status under colonial rule and independence*, Africana Publishing Company, New York.

Dike, CP 1995, *The women's revolt of 1929. Proceedings of a national symposium to mark the 60th anniversary of the women's uprising in South-Eastern Nigeria*, Nelag and Co. Ltd, Lagos.

Economic Commission for Africa (ECA) 2004, *Relevance of African traditional institu-tions of governance*, ECA, Addis Ababa.

Economic Commission for Africa (ECA) 2005a, *ADF IV: Governance for a progressing Africa*, ECA, Addis Ababa.

Economic Commission for Africa (ECA) 2005b, *Striving for good governance in Africa. Synopsis of the 2005 African Governance Report*, ECA, Addis Ababa.

Ellis, S 2007, *The mask of anarchy. The destruction of Liberia and the religious dimen-sion of an African civil war*, New York University Press, New York.

Englebert, P 1997, 'The contemporary African state: neither African nor state' *Third World Quarterly*, vol. 18, no. 4, pp. 767–75.

Gartrell, B 1983, 'British administrators, colonial chiefs, and the comfort of tradition: an example from Uganda', *African Studies Review*, vol. 26, no. 1, pp. 1–24.

Ghana Web 2004, *Asafo companies have crucial role in community dev't – chief*, 18 March, www.ghanaweb.com/GhanaHomePage/NewsArchive/artikel.php?ID=54123 (accessed 27 December 2015).

Hagmann, T and Péclard, D 2010, 'Negotiating statehood: dynamics of power and domi-nation in Africa' *Development and Change*, vol. 41, no. 4.

His Royal Majesty Otumfuo Osei Tutu II, Asantehene 2004 'Traditional systems of govern-ance and the modern state', Keynote address, Fourth African Development Forum, Addis Ababa, 12 October 2004, http://dspace.africaportal.org/jspui/bitstream/123456789/10101/1/

Traditional%20Systems%20of%20Governance%20and%20the%20Modern%20State.
pdf?1.

Jackson, R 1990, *Quasi-states: sovereignty, international relations and the Third World*, Cambridge University Press, Cambridge.

Jackson, RH 1987, 'Quasi-states, dual regimes, and neoclassical theory: international jurisprudence and the Third World', *International Organization*, vol. 41, no. 4, pp. 519–49.

Jackson, RH and Rosberg, CG 1982, 'Why Africa's weak states persist: the empirical and juridical in statehood', *World Politics*, vol. 35, no. 1, pp. 1–24.

Jackson, RH and Rosberg, CG 1984, Popular legitimacy in African multi-ethnic states. *Journal of Modern African Studies*, vol. 22, no. 2. pp. 177–98.

Jeng, NH 2012, 'Why has the Westphalia state failed to function effectively in Africa?' Paper presented at Cultural Diplomacy in Africa – A Forum for young leaders, Institute for Cultural Diplomacy (ICD), Berlin, 23–28 July.

Jones, DS 1983, 'Traditional authority and state administration in Botswana', *Journal of Modern African Studies*, vol. 21, no. 1, pp. 133–9.

Johnny, TM 2012, 'Liberia: Traditional Council Granted Autonomy Status', http://all africa.com/stories/201211281261.html.

Kisangani, EF 2005, 'Development of African administration: pre-colonial times and since', *Public Administration and Public Policy*, vol. I.

Kotia, EW and Aubyn, FK 2013, 'Building national infrastructures for peace in Africa: understanding the role of the National Peace Council in Ghana', http://works.bepress. com/emmanuel_kotia/10/.

Migdal, J 1988, *Strong societies and weak states: state-society relations and state capabilities in the Third World*, Princeton University Press, Princeton.

Obinna, IF and Aning, K 2017, 'West Africa's Ebola pandemic: towards effective multilateral responses to health crises', *Global Governance*, vol. 23, no. 2, April–June.

OECD 2010, 'The state's legitimacy in fragile situations – unpacking complexity, conflict and fragility', www.oecd-ilibrary.org/development/the-state-s-legitimacy-in-fragile-situations_9789264083882-en.

Olowu, D 1994, 'The nature and character of the African state', paper presented for AAPAM 15th Roundtable at Banjul, Gambia, 24–29 January.

Peter, I 2014, 'Reconsidering place of traditional institutions under the Nigerian constitution: a comparative analysis', *Journal of Law, Policy and Globalization*, vol. 31, pp. 135–48.

Rotberg, RI (ed.) 2004, *When states fail: causes and consequences*, Princeton University Press, Princeton.

Simone, D 1989, *Max Weber: the profession of politics*, Plutarch Press, Washington DC.

Tosh, J 1977, 'Colonial chiefs in a stateless society: A case study from Northern Uganda', *Journal of African History*, vol. 14, no. 3, pp. 473–90.

Uwazie, EE 1994, 'Modes of indigenous disputing and legal interactions among the Ibos of Eastern Nigeria', *Journal of Legal Pluralism*, no. 34, pp. 87–103.

Weber, M 1964, *The theory of social and economic organisation*, Free Press, New York.

Wulf, H 2007, 'Challenging the Weberian concept of the state: the future of the monopoly of violence', *Occasional Papers Series*, no. 9, Australian Centre for Peace and Conflict Studies, Brisbane.

Young, C and Turner, T 1985, *The rise and decline of the Zairian state*, The University of Wisconsin Press, Madison.

Zartman, WI (ed.) 1995, *Collapsed states: the disintegration and restoration of legitimate authority*, Lynne Rienner, Boulder.

3 Working with 'illiberal' sources of peace and order

Talking about human rights

M Anne Brown

Introduction

Social order everywhere relies substantially on the dense, dynamic patterns of social relations that shape everyday lives, and the behavioural norms and expectations that these relations generate and by which they are ordered. As other chapters in this work have pointed out, however, in much of the world, societal systems and networks not only support a general context of social order (or disorder) and local norms of behaviour, they are the primary providers of security and justice, or at least play a very extensive role in their provision (Aning *et al.,* see Chapter 7; Baker, see Chapter 4; Boege and Forsyth, see Chapter 11; Brown and Aning, see Chapter 13, all in this volume; UNDP, UNICEF and UN Women 2013). Providing security and justice is often asserted as 'a', if not 'the', fundamental task and *sine qua non* of the state and statutory institutions (Gerth and Mills 1946). In many countries, however, the state does not work in this way, and statutory institutions such as police, courts and associated bodies do not play this role, even though they may be significant, and at times vital, actors in these arenas. Similarly, in many post-colonial states, societal networks underpin available social welfare and food security to a significant extent, with kinship structures often playing a key role (Brown 2012, 2017).

The networks underpinning security, justice and peace can include varying combinations and forms of societal and statutory leadership and activity (Hunt, see Chapter 5 in this volume; Baker and Scheye 2007). Individuals can themselves be dynamic amalgams, performing and reshaping different roles in different contexts. Nevertheless, in this shifting interplay, customary patterns of social order and customary authorities of many kinds continue to play significant and socially wide-ranging roles in providing security and justice, even in many urban areas, across much of West Africa and the Pacific Islands (Moore 2007; White 1993; Sawyer 2005; UNDP *et al.* 2013). These roles are not necessarily 'traditional' and are certainly not unchanging. On the contrary, they may be innovative responses to shifting circumstances and demands (Vanuatu *Kastom* Governance Partnership 2012). To take two examples from Vanuatu, town councils of chiefs or festivals such as the Namakura festival are contemporary responses to urban life that are nevertheless rooted in culture and kin patterns of social interaction and order. In the Pacific Islands, it may be that 'the role of chiefs in large part [is …] to mediate modernisation' (Fraser 2003, p. 2011).

International policy circles, scholars and commentators have recognised the significance of societal and customary forms of order for some time. Often, such forms of ordering have been viewed as fundamentally negative, backward or 'tribal', however, with their significance read as a threat to the progressive potential of the state and an obstacle to the work of statutory authorities (Fukuyama 2011). Indeed, as noted later, custom can be implicitly equated with violence, abuse and dark irrationality as a point of contrast to 'progress', 'modernity' and the liberal norms associated in principle with international interventions. Even as customary networks have come to be viewed more positively in some quarters, there has nevertheless been significant reticence among many multilateral, government and non-government agencies regarding working with them in pursuit of peace or justice, or recognising their importance in a practical way. This reticence reflects a range of factors, including what can be restrictions on governments working with societal bodies in other states, or the serious complexity of dealing with multiple, localised, overlapping and often cross-border networks. The bureaucratic structure of donor agencies also imposes particular limitations, as Lisa Denney has pointed out (2013). In any individual case there may also be good reasons not to work with particular groups. More generally, however, questions about levels of accountability, human rights standards and practices, and levels of direct and structural gender violence in particular are seen by international agencies as significant challenges to closer engagement with customary bodies. This is a question not only for these agencies directly, but also in terms of how they communicate their work to the domestic or donor audiences to which they must appeal (Denney 2013). This can mean that programmes, such as the UK Department for International Development's (DiFID) security sector reform programme in Sierra Leone, might work almost exclusively with the statutory bodies (the formal police, courts and army, etc.) in the security sector, despite recognising that 'informal actors … provide approximately 80% of policing and justice services in rural Sierra Leone' (Denney 2013, p. 5).

This chapter addresses key elements of this dilemma, drawing particularly on examples from Vanuatu regarding questions of violence against women and gender rights. This discussion complements Nancy Annan's contribution, which focuses on highlighting the contribution of women, particularly women in leadership roles, to customary governance. The chapter argues for a subtle but significant shift in emphasis regarding how human rights are often understood, promoted and approached in practice, particularly when working across cultures (Brown 2009; Merry 2009). This is a shift to a relational, dialogic approach to working against violence and abuse, where rights are understood more as 'the product of negotiation and discussion rather than imposition' (Merry 2009, p. 180; Brown 2009). Working dialogically against violence is consistent with an emphasis on peace formation in that it seeks to recognise and work with local efforts to undo patterns of abuse. Continuing these themes, the discussion briefly considers the debate about culture and human rights. It then looks at aspects of custom and women's rights in Vanuatu, and the tendency to automatically or categorically link abuse with custom or culture. The chapter concludes with an account of some community discussions of gender violence. Human rights, including gender rights, raise pressing questions to be pursued – not only as lists of harm, victims and perpetrators, but as investigations of larger contexts of social relations and dynamics of power, and the efforts to undo the patterns of suffering that we collectively impose and experience. Local struggles for freedom from abuse and prevailing forms of justice and solidarity are critical elements of this broader context. These contextualising frameworks can provide both insight into patterns of violence, and valuable perspectives in working to undo it.

Questions of framing: human rights

Notions and mechanisms of human rights offer a powerful way of identifying and working against systemic marginalisation, exploitation, humiliation and violence. While there are significant continuities across time and place regarding what is recognised as imposed suffering or abuse, there are also differences regarding what forms of violence are seen as legitimate, or as a matter of human responsibility, or are even recognised as violence (Merry 2009). This is not an argument for leaving difference as it is. It is rather to point to the contentious and dynamic nature (if often only very slow to change) of how we collectively demarcate what is acceptable and what is not, what is our concern and what is not, and of how we come to see pain and our part in it, or render it invisible. The slow process in many countries of coming to see domestic violence as criminal violence, or of becoming aware of the sexual abuse of children, are simply two examples of this process of change in what we collectively 'see'. The thresholds of what is recognised as abuse changes, individually and collectively, often as a result of exchange, interaction and expanded experience, including coming to recognise oneself in the pain of others (Merry 2006; Mohamad 1994; Brown 2009; Scarry 1985).

This is to point to the relational, dialogic dimension of human rights (Reilly 2012). While ideas of human rights are often put forward as universal, there is less emphasis on exchanges about what people in different places and different roles experience as suffering or harm, or on conversation and shared experience regarding what different means of working against systemic violence or marginalisation might be. Yet such exchanges, across class, genders, roles, cultures and other forms of division and differentiation, are fundamental to rendering silenced forms of suffering and harm visible and to recognising the dynamics of power by which systemic violence is produced and experienced. If access to fundamental values is treated as primarily international, generated only by a liberal elite, or accessible only to those shorn of 'culture', it offers no foundation for dialogue or simply for listening to the experiences of others. Under such conditions, claims of universality pre-empt exchange and exploration and dim realisation of the need for it. The claim of universality has the critically important function of including those who are excluded (in effect or categorically) from the circle of human being, mutuality and exchange. The emphasis on mutuality could come more sharply to the fore, however, enabling the universality of rights to be understood as a practice and a process of becoming aware of each other, collectively, systemically and individually, and of the patterns of suffering we inflict and experience (Brown 2009).

Exploring how 'transnational ideas such as human rights approaches to violence against women become meaningful in local social settings' is thus an important and practical dimension of the relational character of human rights (Merry 2006, p. 38). The articulation and operation of human rights in practice could be understood as fundamentally dialogic, however, in that they require recognition of others as being part of a circle of exchange, and as 'human' (Brown 2009). Violence can be both one way of expelling individuals and groups from the category of 'human' and the outcome of such rejection or 'othering', as Elaine Scarry's account of torture details (Scarry 1985). To bring the relational dimension of human rights to the fore thus entails a shift from treating the promotion of rights as the delivery of a message from those who have the answers to those with the problems, to working against abuse as part of a long, often difficult conversation in which all parties have things to learn. It also implies investigating what are often the more far-reaching patterns which set the conditions for violence. The potential of such long conversations, conducted through actions and well as words, is that we learn more from each other about the experience of being human, and undo patterns of entrenched violence.

A relational approach to human rights thus involves seeking 'to locate interpersonal violence within wider patterns of power and inequality' (Merry 2009, p. 59; UNDP *et al.* 2013). If we do not seek to understand the context of abuse, enquiry stops at the event (or the practice), encouraging narratives of 'inherent violence' or of the 'violence-prone areas' (Das and Kleinman 2000) repeatedly associated with non-state forms of social order and 'the state of nature' (Autesserre 2010). Sub-Saharan Africa and Melanesia, among other regions, have both suffered from such representations and their consequences (Brown and Aning, see Chapter 1 in this volume). Patterns of violence or abuse are often shaped by dense histories of exchange, however, which confound closed categories of self and other, indigenous and exogenous, and interweave the most local and personal details with national and global interactions, shifts and pressures. Exploring questions of violence against women in Vanuatu in this broader context brings somewhat different perspectives to the fore.

'Culture' and 'rights'

When applied to statutory institutions (such as the police or the armed forces) human rights concerns often lead to programmes of engagement, such as the DiFID security sector reform programme in Sierra Leone noted earlier. When applied to customary networks or authorities, human rights concerns can have the opposite effect. There is a pervasive unease regarding customary or 'traditional' networks and a strong tendency to see 'cultures' in post-colonial states (but not only post-colonial states) as a fundamental source of violence. Ideas of 'custom' or 'tradition' often operate as part of a highly polarised (if sometimes implicit) set of dichotomies. They stand as 'tradition' in contrast to 'progress'. Within the terms of this dichotomy, the modern liberal state lays claim to being the reasoned form of political order – it is the 'rational-legal state' liberated from the parochial blinkers of localised tradition (Brown 2006). When 'modernity [operates] as the normative referent', other forms of life are repeatedly discounted (Mohanty 2003, p. 22; Grenfell 2018). Rather than appearing as a diverse and often pragmatic mix of ways of shaping collective life, customary and other community forms of life implicitly function as a point of comparison (or of 'Third World difference') against which the progress of the 'west' can be measured (Mohanty 2003, p. 19; Tully 1995; Brown 2008).

Not paying attention to community and customary ways of life, or not taking communities seriously as interlocutors who also have things to say about undoing patterns of suffering, encourages approaching communities on questions of human rights solely through the delivery of instruction or training. When it operates as a model for engagement, instruction is 'based on the assumption that there [are] no strong concepts or ideas existing at the local level' or that what ideas there are need to be replaced as quickly as possible (Hohe 2002, p. 570; Grenfell 2018). There is a place for instruction and training when they are part of a more expansive, inclusive and 'two-way' engagement. This is different, however, from monologue operating as a dominant mode of approach, rather than conversation with what people already know, value and hope for (Friere 1996). There are certainly exceptions to an 'instructional' or 'banking' approach (to use Frierian terminology) among groups working against violence. These exceptions often emerge from the work of local community organisations or from bodies (sometimes including international bodies and government agencies) grounded in community life; nevertheless, they remain exceptions. Meanwhile 'culture', or people's various ways of life and the complex, often contradictory things people value, tends to be either substantially ignored, or seen as an obstacle to appropriate behavior: 'invoked in explanations of forms of violence against Third-World women' in ways that culture is rarely invoked in explanations of violence against 'mainstream Western women' (Narayan 2006, p. 62; Grenfell 2018).

Ideas of culture and of human rights are often framed as explicitly or implicitly in contradiction to each other. On one hand, claims of upholding culture can be used as a weapon against people's efforts to be free of the systemic infliction of suffering (Merry 2009). On the other hand, culture (as collective worlds of meaning) and with it those people who identify with the ways of life in question, can be belittled, as irrational, inferior and to be swept aside when deemed necessary (Mohanty 2003). In both cases, culture and human rights are treated as fixed, abstract, reified categories instead of complex but also concrete engagements, concerning practices, material life and embodied experiences that are always part of context, dynamic human interaction and change (Brown 2009).

Even efforts to engage positively across this dichotomy are often cast in terms 'of "balancing" ... rights with culture and custom rather than taking a more dynamic and process-oriented view of culture' (UNDP *et al.* 2013, p. 12).

In Vanuatu, ideas of human rights are perhaps most prominently associated with women's rights (as well as children's rights) as this has been the main locus of international rights campaigns as well as a lively site of local activism (Taylor 2008). Assertions of culture or custom are often pitted against the promotion of human rights and women's rights in particular, as over a decade of public debates around the introduction of the Family Protection Bill in 2009 (which criminalises gender-based violence) made clear (Kenneth 2012; see also numerous letters to the editor of the *Vanuatu Daily Post* as well as vigorous debate on social media).

If upholding custom and culture can be used as a weapon against the assertion of rights, however, it also works as a vibrant expression of the desire for self-determination and the maintenance of longstanding community values – something to which women and men are widely committed (Jolly 1994, 2000; Tor and Toka 2004). Semi-structured interviews as well as informal conversations over a number of years with ni-Vanuatu women involved in a range of forms of gender activism made clear widespread commitment to customary values and practices.[1] In contrast to some regions of West Africa, the assertion of custom formed a significant basis of the independence movement in Vanuatu. This was articulated through the strength of collective claims to land, as the foundation for community, but also national self-determination, articulated through the diverse, lived community practices which came to be identified as 'custom' (Bolton 2003). For most ni-Vanuatu, land is held through custom and is a touchstone for everyday food security, welfare and some level of community self-determination. In Vanuatu as elsewhere, culture and custom are also tied to questions of economic survival. As touched on later, however, the idea of 'custom' that emerged from the struggles of decolonisation – and that continues to take shape in the often tense exchange with the dynamics of globalisation and 'Westernisation' – produced a new, generalised, indeterminate, but *gendered* discourse of custom as 'the way we do things round here' (Bolton 2003). These tensions render questions of human rights and gender particularly fraught insofar as they are articulated as a battle between competing, and seemingly incompatible, goods. How human rights and gender issues are framed bears directly on people's capacities to find ways through these dilemmas.

Questions of framing: violence against women

As noted above, among international agencies and more urban circles in Vanuatu, questions of gender discrimination and violence are routinely expressed so that violence towards women is identified with custom and culture, while nonviolent, positive gender relations are identified with liberal modernity. This is not surprising. Struggles against violence and marginalisation are often given voice in the language of human rights, as this language has become internationally the leading mechanism for protesting suffering and abuse. The language of human rights, including women's rights, is broadly part of liberal international-ism and liberal political ideals more generally. Relevant official statements, such as the Government of Vanuatu's National Gender Equality Policy (2015–19) (Government of Vanuatu, Department of Women's Affairs 2015) situate them-selves within a spectrum of international events, meetings, goals and instru-ments. Despite the extensive community work of groups such as the Vanuatu Women's Centre and Wan Smol Bag, the language of rights evokes the imagery of large cities, elites in business clothes and the commodity economy. This is a complex imagery for many ni-Vanuatu; while it can have multiple attractions it is also deeply threatening (including in its potential implications for the privati-sation and alienation of land). 'Rights talk' has become part of 'the drive to define "modern" human subjects' (Taylor 2008, p. 166; Brown 2009). At the same time, when responding to questions on domestic violence, international agencies and many ni-Vanuatu themselves will refer to custom as an explana-tion, with bride-price, for example, being a common point of reference (Govern-ment of Vanuatu 2002; CEDAW 2007). A report by the UN Committee on the Elimination of Discrimination Against Women (CEDAW), for example, noted 'the persistence of adverse cultural norms, practices and traditions, as well as patriarchal attitudes and deep-rooted stereotypes regarding the roles, responsibil-ities and identities of men and women in all spheres of life' in Vanuatu (CEDAW 2007, p. 4; see also Government of Vanuatu 2011).

This framing, it is suggested, is both deeply misleading and a serious obstacle to working against violence. It infers an inherent link between ni-Vanuatu custom and violence against women. It is not only that certain practices or con-texts are put forward as a reason for why men hit women; the identification of custom with violence becomes embedded in the trajectory of the argument. The CEDAW report mentioned above, for example, goes on to identify specific prac-tices with damaging effects on women. The statement that systemic patterns of behaviour and belief are significant factors in what drives gender violence is beyond question. The problem occurs when 'adverse cultural practices' are seen to characterise ni-Vanuatu, or more generally customary or 'traditional' ways of living. At the same time, a link between liberal modernity and nonviolent gender relations is powerfully inferred. Nonviolent gender relations can then seem to be tied to embracing liberal conceptions of political community and the human, and moving away from locally prevailing (but widespread) understandings of human interconnection. Yet, gender relations in 'modern' states are themselves marked by significant levels of violence, marginalisation and exploitation, with decades of political, economic and social structures and policies failing to eradicate this form of violence. As Sally Engel Merry points out, patterns of structural and direct abuse are not less prevalent in 'modern' than 'traditional' societies.

> Traditional or rural societies are not systematically more violent than modern or urban ones. In fact, the transition to a modern, capitalist society can exacerbate gender violence.... Violence does not diminish with the shift

to more modern or urban forms of social life, but it may change its form and meaning.

(Merry 2009, p. 21)

Not only is it mistaken to infer that adopting modern, capitalist, liberal ways of life will in themselves lead to nonviolent gender relations. This inference also undermines the potential of working together to find ways of undoing violence in particular contexts. Discussing gender violence campaigns in Timor-Leste, Damian Grenfell notes that identifying particular cultures as patriarchal, as if this were a point of distinction, rather than a point of commonality to be explored, 'is a kind of 'rendering' that labels a population negatively and ... in need of treatment' (Grenfell 2018). It also asserts a difficult division between (in this case) Timorese and 'international intervenors'.

> [A]ssertions of Timor-Leste as patriarchal per se ... as an all-encompassing categorisation risk missing the agency of those who struggle against it, and ... the identification of subsequent counter spaces. Such an approach also closes rather than opens pathways to build spaces for solidarities and mutual learning across societies. The latter may, for example, promote esteem and disable shame or self-blame if survivors of violence come to understand that they are not an exception, either individually or as a defined populace.
>
> (Grenfell 2018)

Orientations guiding policy and engagement which implicitly or explicitly identify gender violence with 'custom' or certain cultures, rather than with particular discursive practices, create obstacles on many levels to the kinds of conversation, exchange and change that may be fundamental parts of undoing violence. Approaches which implicitly turn upon a distinction between intervenors or outsiders (who are supposedly rights-respecting, hostile to gendered violence and thus superior) and recipients or insiders (who are supposedly perpetrators or victims of violence, inhabiting sites ripe for intervention) can generate anger, resistance or alienation, or shame and a sense of inferiority, so reinforcing negative patterns of exchange already established through neo-colonial histories of interaction. Such orientations do not themselves enact the kind of mutual respect and acknowledgement that is argued here to be at the core of a working human rights practice.

Custom and gender

This brief discussion does not set out to summarise the complex and shifting interplay of contemporary custom and gender in Vanuatu. (For relevant discussions of gender in Melanesia or Vanuatu, see for example, Strathern 1988; Jolly 1989, 1994, 2000; Bolton 2003; Taylor 2008). Nevertheless, some indicative, contextualising points can be made. There is a substantial history of western commentary not only positing sharp distinctions between Melanesian and western ways of life, but taking (genuine and often profound) difference and polarising it. The idea of the tribe and tribal life, for example, has come to be an almost wholly pejorative description, whether discussing Melanesia or Africa. It is challenging for contemporary western approaches to matters, such as gender, which are intimate to the collective experience of life in Melanesia (and other regions) not to reproduce these embedded assumptions and postures. Yet the historical record of the Pacific Islands, while contentious and ambiguous, is clearly enough an account of enmeshment, of the explosive and continuing impact of capitalist economic dynamics on subsistence and exchange economies, and of the unexpected outcomes of various efforts on the part of western interventions to enlighten the locals (e.g. see Jolly 1994; Keesing 1996).

Custom (or '*kastom*' in Bislama, the ni-Vanuatu pidgin) is a multi-layered term, open to different purposes and meanings (White 1993). Custom often simply refers to indigenously grounded ways of life and forms of meaning. The archipelago did not and does not have one culture or custom, but different languages, different clan groups, and different but overlapping and enmeshed ways of life. Kinship patterns, land tenures and usage, systems of exchange and sharing, marriage arrangements, patterns of settlement, making of textiles, story-making and narratives of place and origin are some of the interweaving dimensions shaping the indigenous roots of people's ways of life. The processes of colonisation and missionisation, the formation of Vanuatu into a single state, and its incorporation as a vulnerable player in the global political economy, have reshaped political, economic and social life profoundly. Embedded in kinship networks, however, significant elements and currents of customary practice, value and meaning-making continue to form life, particularly in rural, subsistence-based regions. Customary values and practices, however, also shape urban contexts (Boege and Forsyth, see Chapter 11 in this volume). The point here, however, is not to draw a sharp boundary between customary or indigenous and exogenous ways of life, but simply to emphasise the contemporary reality and power of indigenous sources of meaning-making and patterns of life.

From commentary by nineteenth century missionaries in Vanuatu onwards, traditional values and practices have repeatedly been seen by expatriate observers as oppressive towards women and marked by male violence. The rhetoric of earlier (and still some contemporary) Christian missionaries characterised conversion as the 'transformation from the time of darkness ... typified by ancestral violence, killing and cannibalism, to the time of light characterised by Christian peace, love and togetherness' (Jolly 2000, p. 129). In some areas missionaries strategically reoriented local land tenure systems away from matrilineal (female) descent (which was seen as 'ungodly') towards a system based on male descent (Naupa and Simo 2008). Missionaries also endeavoured to remodel the family as a basis for Christian life. This entailed the movement of men and women into smaller family units and women away from heavier agricultural activities outside, to newly created 'private' domestic spaces inside the new, individual family homes (Tor and Toka 2004). 'The women no longer took part, for example, in building a house; the men started moving away from food preparation and cooking, caring for the children and other shared duties' (Tor and Toka 2004, p. 20). The impact of western divisions of public and private space has been particularly significant for gender constructions. Jolly notes that:

> although gender difference was encoded spatially in the traditional settlement, the forms and meanings of these separate spheres and sacred spaces is very different to those prevalent in the West.... Indeed the very basis of the division [of public and private] is missing since the most central and public institutions revolved around the sacralisation of domestic life. Growing crops, herding pigs, nurturing children and perpetuating the cycles of kinship linking ancestors and descendants was the stuff of public as well as private life.
>
> (Jolly 1989, p. 222, in Malloch and Kaloran 2006, p. 9)

Colonial and later, western accounts significantly overlooked the contributions of women's activities to the political life or governance of indigenous communities, and have rendered invisible forms of activity in which women's work was and continues to be highly valued. Lissant Bolton points to a 'study of banana-leaf bundles and skirts [which] provided a new assessment of women's role in exchange, highlighting women's power and importance, but ... also [drawing] attention to the importance of these object types, which Western eyes easily overlook' (Bolton 2003, p. 127). This overlooking is in part grounded in the observers' placement of women in the private sphere – that is, in a realm other than the political life of the community and thus outside processes of community decision-making. Rendering women invisible applied also to the critical issue of land.

> Men practice their relationship to land by having enduring rights to it; women practice their relationship to land by bearing children to it. Both men and women practice their relationship to land by using it for gardens and by living on it. The colonial interpretation of such systems accounted men as landowners and discounted women's relationship to land, and this perspective has been upheld by ni-Vanuatu since independence.
>
> (Bolton 2003, p. 188)

As well as rendering women less visible in the operation of political community, private domestic spaces created areas hidden from direct physical scrutiny. Various studies have drawn attention to the 'strong ... ideals of the inviolability of the person and the sanctity of the body' and the extensive system of customary controls and supports which ensured that family life was open to the wider community and created obstacles to domestic violence (Jolly 2000, p. 130; Bolton 2003). By contrast, one of the factors seen to increase the vulnerability of women in Vanuatu to domestic and other violence is the 'spread of the cash economy and the weakening of traditional forms of social cohesion' (Government of Vanuatu 2006, p. 35). The spread of the cash economy is, inevitably, a key point of reference and foundation of the development framework of nearly all international development activities, including those aimed at gender (e.g. see Commonwealth of Australia, Department of Foreign Affairs and Trade 2016).

Bride-price, which is widespread in Vanuatu, is often identified as a traditional practice that leads to domestic violence, on the basis that the man has 'paid' for his wife, and can therefore do what he likes. Roselyn Tor and Anthea Toka's study considers the contemporary practice of bride-price in five geographical areas. The authors, drawing on extensive interviews, argue that rather than being 'traditional', contemporary bride-price has been increasingly assimilated into the cash economy and to a significant extent now represents a break from the functions and significance of gift-giving to the young woman's kin. Far from enabling 'ownership', such gifts were part of a broader, cross-generational pattern of two-way exchange which bound the extended families in mutual obligation. Bride-price practices continue to help establish the access to land and thus security of any children of the union, and remain important. It is worth remembering, however, that the term 'bride-price', and its associated imagery, is not an indigenous term, just as 'chief' is not indigenous (Bolton 1998). Changing economic systems have fundamentally altered the context in which this exchange finds meaning. In the exchange or gift economy, the concept of payment is significantly different than in a commodity, market economy (Tor and Toka 2004; Mauss 2001). 'In the cultural soup of today's society, the contemporary "*kastoms*" and beliefs that have evolved are discriminatory to women and some quite contrary to past practice' (Tor and Toka 2004, p. 63).

The question here is not whether bride-price practices are customary or modern. They are part of the ongoing interaction between local practices and meanings and a jumble of global forces and influences; part of the complex and changing picture of Melanesian communities' struggles to make their way through the relentless pressures and pace of change driven by global economic dynamics. Contemporary bride-price practices, however, which are held up as symbols of custom, are not inherently or essentially ni-Vanuatu or Melanesian. Rather, they have been shaped by 'development' processes and international commerce as much as by local cultures. Rather than being dismissed as demonstrations of culturally embedded structural violence, bride-price practices are an example of those issues that could benefit from processes of community and national exchange, reflection and debate.

Custom and the state

'Custom' as a singular English or Bislama term is a relatively new idea; it has only been around since approximately the 1950s or 1960s. Custom refers not only to those life practices that are grounded in indigenous forms of meaning, but also to the self-conscious assertion of identity or the 'externalisation of culture as a symbol' (Keesing 1982, p. 300, in White 1993, p. 476). In this sense, custom is also a response to the far-reaching, wrenching impact of foreign, western forms of political, economic and social relations; it articulates an 'awareness of a collective selfhood' contrasting 'with a collective other' (White 1993, p. 476). It is not only western discourse that polarises categories of indigenous and exogenous life in Melanesia. There are elements of rejection – of modernity, of otherness, of the very real threats of loss – but oppositional dynamics are not the only transaction at work. Custom is a mixed response – one not simply of assertion, but also of exploration and engagement.

Nevertheless, these oppositional dynamics have gendered effects. The reification of custom can create conditions for heightened forms of and calls for control of women (Jolly 1994). 'The self-conscious need to "hold women tight" becomes not just an internal imperative but part of the resistant relation to external pressures ... [an] anti-colonial defence of tradition' that Jolly points out is commonplace in nationalist movements (Jolly 1994, p. 257). A powerful division of roles can take shape, as men patrol the symbolic barricades to keep away the forces of disintegration from their identities and their kin.

Talk of custom emerged as part of the language of independence (Bolton 2003). It provided a vocabulary in which the independence movement could assert indigenous rights to land in the face of colonial dispossession – a central driver of independence. At the same time, as the independence movement joined the political and cultural debate with colonial interests and powers, they faced no option but to argue upon the political ground of the state. 'Independence' is a function of statehood, and the independence movement thereby took on the space of the state, with no alternative but to be the inheritors of that mantle. This itself entailed a profound reworking of key dimensions of ancestral values and practices, which is still very much working its way through Vanuatu's political and cultural life. The historical and contemporary 'state' was, and is, a gendered space, as Wendy Brown has argued (Brown 2006). Ancestral life was deeply emplaced. There was, and continues to be, however, a process of remaking custom at the new level of the state, where it had not been. This 'national custom' was marked by the conceptual life of 1960s and 1970s colonial state practices and norms. The notions of custom that came to the fore were those that seemed best suited to doing battle with the colonial powers of Britain and France. Perhaps as a result, those notions centred around land ownership and amalgamated versions of men's custom. As a newly formed national category custom thus came, through the dynamics of independence, to be identified with a shorthand of men's custom and with public spaces (Bolton 2003). As a result, the National Council of Chiefs, created just preceding independence in 1980, is entirely male, despite important forms of female leadership (pre-independence), notably in the largely matrilineal north of the country (Tor and Toka 2004). Grace Molisa, a leading figure in the independence movement, noted the absence of women from the construction of independence. 'When men talk about *kastom* at [the national] level, they omit women; they pretend that women don't have *kastom*.... If we make women's work of no importance, much will be lost' (Bolton 2003, p. 183).

Social change

Rapid economic and social change have deeply affected gender roles and expectations in Vanuatu – what it is to be a 'good' woman and a 'good' man – but also what it is possible, or necessary, for men and women to do to survive, to look after families or to prosper. These are changes of the most basic kind, in the ways that people eat and obtain food, earn their livelihood, become educated, arrange their housing, meet and partner, create entertainment. An increasing number of young people are growing up in urban environments, seeking jobs in a capitalist labour market and are influenced by the changing expectations created by globalisation. The market economy is also reshaping rural women's and men's activities. Women's roles, for example, have been closely connected with the provision of food within their extended families and communities, but also more broadly with providing nurture, and maintaining community networks which nourish well-being. For many people, however, the provision of food and the structures and needs of families and communities have changed profoundly with the advent of the cash economy, among other things. Extended families are increasingly becoming nuclear, often intensifying parents' burdens (Kalontano, Vatu and White 2003, p. 84).

Social and economic changes have led to new opportunities but also to new burdens and pressures. In both urban and rural areas, people increasingly need access to cash 'to meet their family and community obligations and expectations', adding to family workloads and generating insecurity and complexity (Kalontano *et al.* 2003, p. 46). The market economy may have led to women carrying a particularly heavy burden, and drawn them away from traditional routes to community respect. Many women are increasingly making items to sell, for example, but this can also take them away from making items for customary exchange or from caring roles in the family – both traditionally sources of community standing and well-being (Tor and Toka 2004; Cox *et al.* 2007).

The sources of men's self-esteem are also under serious pressure. Whereas men previously played fundamental community roles, including through fishing, hunting and growing food, many must now also provide, or are dependent upon, commodities or services requiring cash. The formal cash economy remains small, however, with only 37 per cent of men and 23 per cent of women having any regular paid employment (Vanuatu National Statistics Office 2009). Nevertheless, the drive for access to the cash economy has contributed to rapid urbanisation, with urban populations growing much faster than rural populations and approximately 40 per cent of the urban population living in squatter settlements (UNICEF and Government of Vanuatu 2005, p. 3; see also Keen and Barbara 2016). Moving to town, however, takes men away from the land and kin network, which is a significant source of community standing, support and livelihood (Taylor 2008). The squatter settlements can be characterised by poverty, unemployment and reduced access to the support systems, social control and sources of community standing offered by more traditional rural zones. 'It is these populations that fall more quickly and severely through the traditional safety net provided by access to custom land' (Naupa 2014).

These conflicting factors create conditions for insecurity and alienation. '[M]any young men no longer enjoy the satisfaction of a real contribution to their community ... [leading to] increasing rates of substance abuse, particularly kava and alcohol', which in turn leads to violence and sexual violence (Vanuatu Association of Women Graduates 2001, p. 3). At the same time, access to land is becoming less reliable. 'Growing land alienation from weakly regulated speculative land transactions [and flowing from incorporation into the global market] has resulted in increasing tensions amongst communities and a dilution of social cohesion' (Naupa 2014). Many men are left 'struggling to cope with a profound sense of disempowerment and both personal and cultural loss stemming from what they see as large-scale socio-economic, political and ideological changes attached to neo-colonialism' (Taylor 2008, p. 172). Through the same dynamics, '[u]rban women are particularly vulnerable to poverty and hardship due to diluted clan identities, and therefore weaker land claims' (Naupa 2014 p. 41). For many ni-Vanuatu, however, both women and men, the language of rights can simply situate women on the side of liberal modernity, symbolised at worst, but potently, by the *nouveau riche* and the land speculators (Taylor 2008).

While there is no suggestion here that traditional life was free of violence (structural or direct) towards women, the violent dimensions of contemporary Vanuatu life seem likely to be less manifestations of traditional culture, than processes of cultural, social, economic and physical displacement, with people taking out their stress on the more vulnerable. New areas of poverty, including the emergence of what is effectively landless poor, a sense of humiliation and loss, the gradual construction of a national public political space from which women are marginalised, the weakening of traditional forms of social order and support, the notable presence of Christian fundamentalist views of gender roles, the increasing use of alcohol and kava – all these factors have driven the emergence of a kind of machismo. How often is it this machismo that is called 'custom' by husbands, boyfriends or angry and alienated young men? While changes in gender roles have enabled men and women greater access to equal opportunities in certain contexts, 'negative consequences of these changes include a decline in respect between men and women' (Kalontano *et al.* 2003, p. 46).

Conversations

For most ni-Vanuatu, 'custom', however understood, is entwined with the sense of family relationship and kin network, access to livelihood or food security through land, emplacement, identity and collective self-determination. It is a sense of interconnection with, and emplacement within, relations and networks of fundamental value. Conversations about difficult subjects which are framed by the assumption of the inferiority of customary values and practices can be expected to be both deeply familiar and alienating for many ni-Vanuatu. There are other ways of engaging with questions of violence against women (e.g. see the work of the Vanuatu Women's Centre).

One small example of engagement could be drawn from a project, the Vanuatu *Kastom* Governance Partnership (VKGP), that I was part of. VKGP was a collaboration between the Malvatumauri Council of Chiefs in Vanuatu, the then Australian national development agency, AusAID and an Australian university. The collaboration revolved around a series of workshops bringing together community leaders and members at sites around the country over a number of years (Westoby and Brown 2007; Westoby 2010; Walker and Garu 2009). These workshops did not follow the model of the transmission of expert knowledge, but were dialogic in approach and essentially facilitated conversations. The workshops were largely concerned with how urban and rural communities might respond to a range of contemporary pressures and problems. They addressed a range of themes concerning working with conflict and governance and provided a platform for community and cross-community discussion and reflection on issues important to the participants. Ni-Vanuatu facilitators came together from around the islands, and included chiefs, women, a young man and a Church elder.

> [T]here was often a clear and active willingness, on the part of ni-Vanuatu facilitators [and ...] the workshop participants, to engage in exactly this kind of conversation, in which *kastom* was taken seriously as a potentially dynamic source of social ethics, that could have something to say to new, contemporary social problems.
>
> (Love and Brown 2014)

Within this context, partners from the Council of Chiefs and ni-Vanuatu facilitators devised a module addressing vernacular languages and kin terms (which was called the 'Language and Relationship module'). This element of the workshops became so popular that it was also offered as a stand-alone short workshop, travelling to additional groups and communities that asked for it. On their own initiative, participants also ran their own versions of the module in their local communities. A variation of the module has continued to be offered. The basic idea of the module was simple. There are over 80 languages still spoken in Vanuatu, but many are weakening. The facilitators would ask the group (nearly always a mixed language group) for their language names for different family relationships, and then for the roles and significance that went with these positions. The kin network is exhaustively identified and the roles, entitlements, responsibilities and prohibitions associated with different family relations extensively set out. Kin networks are the basis of social order but also of a broader sense of social relationship, mutual obligation and cooperation. Language is understood as playing an active role in maintaining 'respect, unity and peace' in communities, and the revitalisation of even simply kin terminology is seen to play a role in community life more broadly (Love and Brown 2014).

The workshop, run by ni-Vanuatu for ni-Vanuatu about something they consider precious, became a context for searching conversation over many issues. Violence within the family, and how to stop it, figured prominently. While a difficult conversation, it was discussed without the division of seeming to be rejecting your own communities, cultures and place and without being wholly trapped in the polarisation of men and women, custom and rights. Rather than appearing as an opposition between culture and rights, domestic violence was discussed as a difficult problem for which people wanted solutions. The well-being of the family appeared as central to the well-being of communities, and domestic violence was widely seen as undermining the well-being of the family. The ni-Vanuatu facilitators included men and women, chiefs and women who had worked with the Vanuatu Women's Centre and the Department of Women's Affairs. They guided discussion without dominating it. This helped support the expression of sufficient diversity of views and experience to avoid the simple assertion of male dominance as the solution to conflict being left as the only, or principal voice, while also giving space to such views and to the concerns that they can articulate.

It is difficult to assess whether these workshop modules have changed behaviours over time. Nevertheless, they have continued to be popular, some years after the modules were initiated and the original partnership has come to an end. At a concrete level, one outcome was the production of a picture book (produced by Daniel Lukai) for children and adults in a vernacular which is strongly represented in the capital, Port Vila. The book addresses the importance of the safety and welfare of children and of respect for children; in effect, it covers the issues raised by the Convention of the Rights of the Child, but through the language of custom and customary ideals. More broadly, the workshops enabled a space for broader conversations between and among women and men about the changing nature of respect and of their relationships. They became the site of relatively non-polarised conversations about difficult issues that participants – both women and men – wanted to discuss. These smaller workshops continued beyond the life of the formal collaboration, simply because the conversations they opened up have been welcomed by people. This is an approach to working against violence, and to supporting peace formation, through 'incremental work across many fields that can shift abuse by reconstituting fundamental social relationships' (Brown 2009, p. 23).

Conclusion

Structural and direct violence against women is not something that movement along an ideological trajectory from customary practice to liberalism can be expected to fix (Merry 2009). While 'rights talk' is a liberal language, it is certainly not only liberal actors who are concerned with, or open to, working against violence. In the case of the Pacific Islands, as the New Zealand Law Commission report *Converging Currents: Custom and Human Rights in the Pacific*, points out, human dignity, respect and standing are central principles of Pacific cultures (New Zealand Law Commission 2006). Similar observations can be made around the world. To work with ni-Vanuatu or other peoples on questions of gender violence or human rights requires being attentive to different understandings of gender and human community, to different apprehensions of the sacred or understandings of the human person (Brown 2009). It also asks for exploration of the context of the violence in question. Even when a particular customary practice is associated with violence (such as bride-price in Melanesia) or is directly violent towards women (such as female genital mutilation in West Africa) a wider understanding of the practice and of the functions and meanings it holds, as well as relations with communities and community authorities that are based on trust and cooperation, are more likely to enable ways of reshaping or replacing such practices to emerge.

The acknowledgement of socio-cultural difference is a critical step in working with and across difference on issues of violence (Tully 1995). Recognising difference, however, is distinct from polarisation, which acts to fix and contain, and which, along with idealisations of male and female, is a powerful strategy in battles for discursive power (Taylor 2008). The polarisation of liberal and traditional or customary ways of life is not only misleading, it does not serve well the goal of undoing abuse. It does not enable building mutual recognition and respect, or an exchange in which all those participating can be seen and listened to as interlocutors (Tully 1995; Brown 2009).

When we look more carefully into the context of abuse, we might, to greater or lesser degrees, find our collective selves in these broader contexts and their knots of suffering, whether this is through the contemporary global dynamics of intensifying enrichment and immiseration and the international politics of poverty, the afterwash of colonialism, or more immediate dynamics. There is already a dense history of exchange and, except in quite rare circumstances, we are already part of each other in ways we are not likely to fully grasp. Moreover, this history is likely to be contentious, often violent and oppressive. This is not an effort to apportion blame or to shift a key moment of responsibility from people engaged in harm, but to recognise the bigger, more complex picture, including often enough the unintended consequences of liberal economic, political or social interventions. It is often not only the actions of individuals, but elements within this bigger picture that need to be managed or to shift, even slightly, if ways of entering into and undoing these knots are to become available.

Engagements within states and societies and among them are marked by both difference and entanglement, as many chapters in this volume have discussed (e.g. Hunt, see Chapter 5 in this volume). Cultures are part of each other and changing in response to each other, but are far from being clear to each other. To be conscious of these entanglements, and of patterns of marginalisation, systemic violence and abuse generated by and within the Global North as well as the South, encourages a relational awareness that helps to reframe the ways we approach questions of human rights and 'culture'. This is an approach to working against abuse that sees it as an exchange in which all parties have things to learn from each other about forms of suffering, humiliation and systemic abuse, and the contexts which give rise to such abuse and suffering. To approach the pursuit of human rights as the transmission of a fixed truth of which only one party is in possession may be to undermine the conditions within which undoing patterns of abuse becomes possible. We are, rather, part of an ongoing and difficult conversation about how we live together without systemically harming each other. This is far from meaning agreement, or lack of confrontation or struggle.

This approach does not offer a high road to human rights observance across cultures. Rather, it is a way of working with and across the entrenched oppositions that have emerged around 'local culture' and of opening conversations about patterns of harm. To conclude with a comment from Sally Engle Merry:

> Violence in intimate relationships is inseparable from societal conflict, violence, and injustice ... [I]nterpersonal gendered violence and structural violence – the violence of poverty, hunger, social exclusion, and humiliation – are deeply connected. It is impossible to diminish violence against women without reducing these other forms of violence and injustice. The conditions which breed gender violence include racism and inequality, conquest, occupation, colonialism, warfare and civil conflict, economic disruptions and poverty.
>
> (Merry 2009, p. 18)

Such conversations are ongoing. They need to engage with communities and community leaders, including customary actors. This is not only for the pragmatic reasons, that this is where the locus of much everyday social order rests, although such reasons are powerful. It is also a recognition that other societies and other ways of life, including customary ways of life, also bring values, practices and insights that contribute positively to social well-being. Such engagement also speaks to the core of how human rights might be understood; that is, it speaks to the relationship between undoing violence and the recognition of each other in continuing exchange about what it is to be human.

Note

1 Semi-structured interviews with a number of women active in working against domestic violence and violence against women in a range of capacities (working with the Vanuatu Women's Centre, central and regional offices, Vanuatu National Council of Women, local women's support organisations, and the Mothers Union) were conducted by the author, by herself or with Roselyn Tor, in Laneki, Tanna in August, 2007; Port Vila, January, 2008; Luganville, Santo, January, 2008; Port Vila September, 2012. Informal conversations are ongoing.

Bibliography

Autesserre, S 2010, *The trouble with the Congo*, Cambridge University Press, Cambridge.

Baker, B and Scheye, E 2007, 'Multi-layered justice and security delivery in post-conflict and fragile states', *Conflict, Security and Development*, vol. 7, no. 4, pp. 503–28.

Bolton, L 1998, 'Chief Willie Bongmatur Maldo and the role of chiefs in Vanuatu', *Journal of Pacific History*, vol. 33, no. 2, pp. 179–95.

Bolton, L 2003, *Unfolding the moon: enacting women's kastom in Vanuatu*, University of Hawaii Press, Hawaii.

Brown, MA 2008, 'Custom and identity: reflections on and representations of violence in Melanesia', in Slocum-Bradley, N (ed.) *Promoting conflict or peace through identity*, Ashgate, Farnham.

Brown, MA 2009, *Human rights and the borders of suffering: the promotion of human rights in international politics*, Manchester University Press, Manchester.

Brown, MA 2012, 'Entangled worlds: villages and political community in Timor Leste', *Local-Global: Identity, Security, Community*, vol. 11, pp. 54–71.

Brown, MA 2017, 'Hybridity and dialogue – approaches to the hybrid turn', *Third World Thematics*, doi.org/10.1080/23802014.2017.1353893.

Brown, W 2006, 'Finding the man in the state', in Sharma, A and Gupta, A, *The anthropology of the state*, Blackwell Publishing, Oxford.

Committee on the Elimination of Discrimination Against Women (CEDAW) 2007, 'Concluding comments of the Committee on the Elimination of Discrimination Against Women: Vanuatu, CEDAW/C/VUT/CO/3, United Nations, New York.

Commonwealth of Australia, Department of Foreign Affairs and Trade 2016, *Gender equality and women's empowerment strategy*, Department of Foreign Affairs and Trade, Canberra.

Cox, M, Alatoa, H, Kenni, A, Naupa, A, Rawlings, G, Soni, N and Vatu, C 2007, *The unfinished state: drivers of change in Vanuatu*, AusAID, Canberra.

Das, V and Kleinman, A 2000, 'Introduction', in Das, V, Kleinman, A, Ramphele, M and Reynolds, P (eds), *Violence and subjectivity*, University of California Press, Berkeley.

Denney, L 2013, 'Liberal chiefs or illiberal development? The challenge of engaging chiefs in DFID's Security Sector Reform Programme in Sierra Leone', *Development Policy Review*, vol. 3, no. 1, pp. 5–25.

Fraser, I 2003, 'Human rights vs custom in the Pacific: struggle, adaption or game?', in Anita Jowitt and Tess Newton Cain (eds), *Passage of change: law, society and governance in the Pacific*, Pandanus Books, Canberra.

Friere, P 1996, *Pedagogy of the oppressed*, Penguin, London.

Fukuyama, F 2011, *The origins of political order: from prehuman times to the French revolution*, Farrar, Straus and Giroux, New York.

Gerth, HH and Mills, CW (eds) 1946, From *Max Weber: essays in sociology*, Oxford University Press, New York.

Government of Vanuatu 2006, *Priorities and action agenda 2006–2015*, Government of Vanuatu, Port Vila.

Government of Vanuatu, Department of Women's Affairs 2002, *Violence against women in Vanuatu*, Policy paper, 2002–2006, Port Vila.

Government of Vanuatu, Department of Women's Affairs 2011, *Review of Vanuatu's national machinery for women*, Naupa, A and Olul, R, Ministry of Justice and Community Services, UN Women and AusAID, Port Vila.

Government of Vanuatu, Department of Women's Affairs 2015, *National Gender Equality Policy 2015–2019*, Government of Vanuatu, Port Vila.

Grenfell, D 2018, 'Hybridity on the ground in peacebuilding and development', in Wallis, J, Kent, L, Forsyth, M, Dinnen, S and Bose, S (eds), *Hybridity in peacebuilding and development; critical conversations'*, ANU Press, Canberra.

Hohe, T 2002, The clash of paradigms: international administration and local political legitimacy in East Timor', *Contemporary Southeast Asia*, vol. 4, no. 3, pp. 569–89.

Jolly, M 1989, 'Sacred spaces: churches, men's houses and households in South Pente-cost, Vanuatu', in Jolly, M. and MacIntyre, M. (eds), *Family and gender in the Pacific*, Cambridge University Press, Cambridge, Melbourne.

Jolly, M 1994, *Women of the place: kastom, colonialism and gender in Vanuatu*, Harwood Academic Publishers, Melbourne.

Jolly, M 2000, 'Woman ikat raet long human raet o no?: Womens' rights, human rights and domestic violence in Vanuatu', in Hildson, A, MacIntyre, M, Mackie, V and Stevens, M (eds), *Human rights and gender politics*, Asia-Pacific Perspectives, Routledge, London.

Kalontano, A, Vatu, C and White, J 2003, *Assessing community perspectives on governance in Vanuatu*, FSPI (Foundation of the Peoples of the South Pacific), Vanuatu, Port Vila.

Keen, B and Barbara, J 2016, 'Pacific urbanisation: changing times', Devpolicy Blog, 25 February, 2016, http://devpolicy.org/pacific-urbanisation-changing-times-20160225/ ANU, Canberra.

Keesing, R 1982, 'Kastom in Melanesia: an overview'. *Reinventing traditional culture: the politics of kastom in island Melanesia. Mankind*, vol. 13, no. 4, pp. 297–301 (Special Issue).

Keesing, R 1996, 'Class, culture, custom', in Friedman, J and Carrier, JG (eds), *Melanesian Modernities*, Lund University Press, Lund.

Kenneth, D 2012, Statement by Ms Dorosday Dhressen Kenneth, Director, Department of Women's Affairs, Government of Vanuatu, to the 56th Session on the 'Commission on the Status of Women', The Commission on the Status of Women, New York.

Love, M and Brown, MA 2014, 'Language and social capital: localising social develop-ment in Vanuatu', unpublished paper. The University of Queensland.

Malloch, M and Kaloran, M 2006, 'A report on equity and women in Vanuatu', Report presented at the 'After 26 Years: Collaborative research in Vanuatu since Independ-ence, Vanuatu Research Conference', Port Vila.

Mauss, M 2001, *The Gift: the form and reason for exchange in archaic societies*, Routledge Classics, London.

Merry, SE 2006, 'Transnational human rights and local activism: mapping the middle', *American Anthropologist*, vol. 8 no. 1, pp. 38–51.

Merry, SE 2009, *Gender violence: a cultural perspective*, Blackwell, Chichester.

Mohamad, G 1994, *Sidelines: writings from Tempo, Indonesia's banned magazine*, Hyland House in association with Monash University, South Melbourne.

Mohanty, C 2003, *Feminism without borders: decolonising theory, practising solidarity*, Duke University Press, Durham and London.

Moore, C 2007, 'External intervention: The Solomon Islands beyond RAMSI', in Brown, MA (ed.), *Security and development in the Pacific Islands: social resilience in emerg-ing states*, Lynne Rienner, Colorado.

Narayan, U 2006, 'Cross-cultural connections, border-crossings, and "death by culture"', in Hackett, E and Haslanger, S (eds), *Theorizing Feminisms*, Oxford University Press, Oxford.

Naupa, A 2014, 'Vanuatu case study', in *Falling through the net? Gender and social pro-tection in the Pacific*, UN Women Discussion Paper, UN Women, New York.

Naupa, A and Simo, J 2008, 'Matrilineal land tenure in Vanuatu: *"Hu i kaekae long basket?"*, case studies of Rgaa and Mele', in Huffer, E (ed.), *Land and women: the matrilineal factor*, Pacific Islands Forum Secretariat, Suva.

New Zealand Law Commission 2006, *Converging currents: custom and human rights in the Pacific*, Law Commission, Wellington.

Reilly, N 2012, 'Doing transnational feminism, transforming human rights: the emancipatory possibilities revisited', *Irish Journal of Sociology*, vol. 19, no. 2, pp. 60–76.

Sawyer, A 2005, 'Social capital, survival strategies, and their potential for post-conflict governance in Liberia', *Expert Group on Development Issues*, UNU-WIDER, Research Paper, 5.

Scarry, E 1985, *The body in pain: the making and unmaking of the world*, Oxford University Press, New York.

Strathern, M 1988, *The gender of the gift: problems with women and problems with society in Melanesia*, University of California Press, Berkeley.

Taylor, JP 2008, 'The social life of rights: 'gender antagonism', modernity and *raet* in Vanuatu', *Australian Journal of Anthropology*, vol. 19, no. 2, pp. 165–78.

Tor, R and Toka, A 2004, 'Gender, kastom and domestic violence: a research on the historical trend, extent and impact of domestic violence in Vanuatu', a paper prepared for the Government of Vanuatu and the Canadian University Service Overseas (CUSO), Port Vila.

Tully, J 1995, *Strange multiplicity: constitutionalism in an age of diversity*, Cambridge University Press, Cambridge.

UNDP, UNICEF and UN Women 2013, *Informal justice systems: charting a course for human rights-based engagement*, Danish Institute for Human Rights (eds), UN Women, New York.

UNICEF and Government of Vanuatu 2005, *Vanuatu, A situation analysis of children, women and youth*, UNICEF Pacific Office, Suva.

Vanuatu Association of Women Graduates, 2001, 'The girl child'; contribution to the Pacific workshop on the girl child, International Federation of University Women Conference, Ottawa, Canada.

Vanuatu *Kastom* Governance Partnership 2012, *Kastom Governance is for everyone: activities and impacts of the Vanuatu Kastom Governance Partnership 2005–2012*, The University of Queensland, Brisbane.

Vanuatu National Statistics Office, 2009, *Special Report: 2009 National Population and Housing Census*, https://vnso.gov.vu/index.php/census-and-surveys/censuses (accessed 17 May 2017).

Walker, P and Garu, S 2009, ' "A few more arrows" ': strengthening mediative capacity in Vanuatu', in Bagshaw, D and Porter, E (eds), *Mediation in the Asia-Pacific region: transforming conflict and building peace*, Routledge, London.

Westoby, P 2010, 'Dialogue and disentanglement: navigating tensions for sustainable community economic development within Vanuatu', *Journal of Environmental, Cultural, Economic and Social Sustainability*, vol. 6, no. 1, pp. 81–92.

Westoby, P and Brown, MA 2007, 'Peaceful community development in Vanuatu: a reflection on the Vanuatu *Kastom* Governance Partnership', *Journal of Peacebuilding and Development*, vol. 3, no. 3, pp. 77–81.

White, G 1993, 'Three discourses of custom', *Anthropological Forum*, vol. 6, no. 4, pp. 475–94.

4   What to do with informal security and justice

The dilemma for African states

Bruce Baker

Introduction

Can those who govern states live with those who enforce alternative laws? This question has been asked for at least 2500 years. The ancient Greek plays *Electra* and *Antigone* reminded their audiences that family revenge following customary law challenged the new city rulers and the city laws that demanded submission by all (including kings and royal families). The pros and cons of both types of law, and the difficulty of the relationship between them presented in those dramas, are still with us today. In Africa, as in every other continent, numerous normative modes of policing and ordering are found. Each arises from different views of security: what should an ordered and just society look like? Who should have order and justice (who are insiders and outsiders)? How should order and justice be provided? How should disorder and injustice be punished?

In part, the answering of these questions is a social process. A 'security issue' is not inherent – it emerges, since it is socially constructed. Everyday conversation, social media, journalism and political speeches drive some 'fears' to the top of the agenda, requiring urgent attention. Economics, too, will play a part in determining answers to the key questions. What can be afforded is questioned by state providers of public goods and the consumers of private goods. The latter 'shop around' for security in a fragmented, 'multi-choice' and increasingly privatised market (Baker 2007b). Security, then, is economically constructed. But security is also politically constructed. Security is about politics and power. It matters keenly who defines security, how they deliver it and on behalf of whom (Luckham and Kirk 2012). And that is determined by power. Power determines who gets (and is denied) security. Traditionally in the west, it has been thought that this power is, and should be, the state's prerogative; elsewhere it may be assumed that the immediate neighbourhood or wider social, cultural and religious community is the final arbiter.

The complexity of the social, economic and political patterning of African societies has been overlooked by the west, as it has sought to penetrate Africa and transform it into its own image. The western colonial programme of change imposed a legal positivism which shifted the source of law away from local social norms to legislation. It transplanted its own legal cultures, which were alien to many local customs and legal systems. Subsequently, newly independent political leaders (educated in the west) adopted international (that is, western) standards. However, despite the self-evident 'solution' for Africa's security needs, many localities retained their own definition of acceptable order and prioritised communal views of identity and responsibility, as opposed to an individual-rights approach. Inevitably they frequently disengaged from, distorted or resisted state law. That is not to say that they rejected the rule of law. As Woodman observes:

> The rule of law cannot be limited to the rule of state law. If the law of a state is largely disregarded because subjects consider it to be an alien element which enjoins them to flout their own sense of right, but general rules expressed in a customary law are largely observed, the conditions for the rule of law would appear to be present.
>
> (Woodman 1996, pp. 4, 6)

It is of course state law that the police and judiciary enforce with their coercive powers. Nevertheless, the security and justice system that is supposed to be the evidence of the state's supreme authority, has never held a monopoly of legitimate violence in Africa. Instead, governments are faced with a multitude not just of justice and ordering norms, but of institutions and organisations that implement them (Baker 2009; Albrecht and Kyed 2015). Instead of homogeneity under central control, they are challenged by a complex network of security and justice actors, where agencies overlap in territory and in service provision. It is a security and justice sector of duplication, competition or cooperation. In such a complex social system the government and its agencies can never be certain of the outcome of their interventions. Programme inputs will bring change to the lives of all citizens, but not necessarily the intended changes. Even not to act and be indifferent to the other actors will still have consequences for this security and justice system. The state, then, cannot avoid the dilemma: what should it do with informal security and justice actors?

In constructing an answer, the state, and in particular its government, has to begin first by having a clear view of itself, its role in society, what it thinks it ought to do regarding citizens' security and justice, and how it sees its relationship with society. Only then can it consider strategies to respond to the informal security and justice actors.

How African states view themselves in terms of security and justice

When it comes to security and justice, states make grand and exclusive claims. The Nigerian constitution asserts: 'There shall be a police force for Nigeria, which shall be known as the Nigeria Police Force, and ... no other police force shall be established for the Federation or any part thereof' (Constitution of the Federal Republic of Nigeria 1999, Chapter 6, Part 111, B: 214). South Africa's constitution says that:

the security services ... consist of a single defence force, a single police service ... The objects of the police service are to prevent, combat and investigate crime, to maintain public order, to protect and secure the inhabitants of the Republic and their property, and to uphold and enforce the law.

(South African Government 1996: *Constitution of the Republic of South Africa*, Chapter 11)

They have, in other words, adopted Weber's description of western states in the early twentieth century as a prescription for African states in the twenty-first.[1] As true states, they shall have the monopoly of the legitimate use of violence. Weber's qualification that legitimate violence may also be delegated by the state to others has passed them by.[2]

In addition to monopolistic claims, states also make optimistic claims about the nationwide capacity of their security and justice services. Sierra Leone's 1991 constitution stipulates that:

the security, peace and welfare of the people of Sierra Leone shall be the primary purpose and responsibility of Government, and to this end it shall be the duty of the Armed Forces, the Police, Public Officers and all security agents to protect and safeguard the people of Sierra Leone.

(State House, Republic of Sierra Leone 1991: *Constitution of Sierra Leone*, Chapter 1: 4)

In the DRC,

[t]he National Police is charged with public security, the security of persons and goods, the maintenance and restoration of public order.... The National Police operates on the entire national territory in respect of this Constitution and the laws of the republic.

(Government of the Democratic Republic of the Congo 2005, Section 7, Articles 182–3)

Despite the clear absence of the police over most of the territory of DRC, other actors are excluded by virtue of Article 17: 'No one may be prosecuted, arrested detained or sentenced except by virtue of a law and in the manner in which the latter prescribes'. In their attempt to demonstrate to the world that they are proper states and equal to any others, African states in their constitutions, and their governments in their rhetoric, lay claim to service provision that they know they cannot deliver. Their claim to guarantee the security of their citizens is aspirational rather than a guaranteed right.

That local people provide most of the justice and security in their countries may be an empirical fact (Baker 2009), but for governments, it is often an uncomfortable fact. It is not only an embarrassment that they do not have the resources to replace them with state services for all, but also a challenge to their authority. A polity of parallel authorities is not the system they aspire to. It means uncertain control. It means sharing the power: power over determining and enforcing social order; of deciding right and wrong, guilty and not guilty; of taking life or granting pardon. For rulers it means the state that they control is not the single pinnacle of a hierarchy, the unchallenged most powerful authority. There are others, that might not be *the* state, but that nevertheless act in a *state-like* fashion, defining collectively binding decisions in the name of the common interest (Lund 2006). There are other sovereigns in their territory, or at least 'partial sovereigns', seeking exclusive control over the lives and deaths of others (Comaroff and Comaroff 2006). It means a cohabitation. The colonial authorities, focused on economic extraction, could choose to be indifferent to alternative security and justice systems, as long as expatriates could enjoy Western law. How the 'natives' behaved could be left to chiefs and missionaries. For the independence leaders, however, there was a political necessity to demonstrate that they, not customary rulers, determined the social conduct of all. To legitimate this claim of supreme authority they turned to state law: this would authorise their monopoly. And the instruments of enforcement would be the security forces and judicial system. Thus, in the initial years of independence, Cameroon's President Ahidjo staged 'elaborate ceremonies of executions of death sentences through firing squads, [and] populations were often enjoined to come out massively to be entertained by the spectacle of death by the military firing squads' (Orock 2014, p. 422).

It is not hard, therefore, to understand the motivation for the legislation that was passed in many African countries immediately after independence designed to weaken or eliminate the customary chiefs' judicial function. The young states wanted to centralise political power, to establish a national identity as opposed to a tribal one, and to introduce 'modern' state laws as the 'supreme' law concerning land, inheritance, marriage and serious crime. They wanted to control conduct. With the exception of Malawi, Ethiopia, South Africa, Nigeria and Sierra Leone, customary chiefs either lost their judicial powers or had them severely restricted. What was vital was the symbolism, since for both pragmatic and political reasons, customary law was usually recognised in some form in the new justice structures established by the state at the local level. And although the judgements of customary leaders did not have the force in law, they continued to preside over as many disputes as before. What had changed, however, was that they had been shown their place as subordinate to the constitution and law of the state. Hence some were put in the pay of, and under the control of, the government and were obliged to do its bidding (Malawi, Cameroon, Botswana, South Africa, South Sudan). The new constitutions told them that their practices were to be consistent with it and with international human rights (South Africa, Angola, DRC, Ethiopia, Ghana, Kenya, Liberia); they were to apply statutory law only or alongside customary law (Zimbabwe, Liberia); they were to do nothing 'contrary to public order' (DRC); they were confined to civil cases (DRC, Liberia, Zimbabwe, Chad, Nigeria); and they were subject to the state either repealing their customary law (Namibia) or harmonising customary law with the constitution (Côte d'Ivoire, Niger, Togo) (Cuskelly 2011, pp. 8–11;

Miles 2006). No state was going to give customary authorities and their courts free rein. And the increasing demand of the late twentieth century that states integrate their legal systems with their trading partners only confirmed them in their approach (Aning and Aubyn, see Chapter 2 in this volume, p. 28).

Attempts by local people to protect themselves from rebels and criminals in the light of perceived indifference or unavailability on the part of the state consistently meets with official hostility. The Nigerian Minister for Economic Matters, announcing a decision by The Federal Executive Council 1999, called on the Nigeria Police to immediately stop the activities of the vigilante group, the Bakassi Boys since they had 'taken laws into their hands and were killing innocent people' (Smith 2006, p. 137). In November 2014, DRC Defence Minister, Alexandre Luba Ntambo, told civilians in the east that despite a string of massacres at the hands of the Allied Democratic Forces and National Army for the Liberation of Uganda (ADF-NALU), they were not to form militias to protect themselves (News24 2014). Also in November 2014, the Acting Provincial Commissioner of the South African Police Service in Mpumalanga issued a warning against vigilantism in certain communities:

> Under no circumstances is anyone allowed to carry out any judgement against anyone who is suspected of having committed a crime. In terms of the law, if you are found having acted in an unpalatable manner wherein your actions are labelled as unlawful, police will act against you in accordance with the prescripts of the law.
>
> (Arrive Alive 2014)

Similarly, in Cameroon in 2006, the Divisional Officer for central Douala asserted publicly that only state law enforcement officers were permitted to arrest and discipline offenders through the courts. He warned that anyone caught taking the law into their own hands in the punishment of suspects would be arrested and in the case of deaths, charged for murder (Pefok 2006).

The state antagonism against citizen violence is welcome, but in light of the evidence that police in Nigeria, DRC, South Africa and Cameroon frequently use violence against criminal suspects, that Nigeria has been very inconsistent in its enforcement of bans on violent vigilante groups, that the DRC security forces have set up their own militias, and that the police in South Africa have informal relationships with vigilantes, this suggests the additional agenda is one of wanting to perpetuate the belief that, as truly sovereign states, these countries can ensure security unaided by citizens' self-help groups.

Ministers and police chiefs across the continent repeatedly condemn people who 'take the law into their own hands'. Though this rarely occurs without people lacking confidence in the criminal justice system to tackle crime, the authorities base their prohibition of the private use of violence on the premise that the state security forces can guarantee the necessary protection. To admit state inability would be to undermine the very *raison d'être* of the state. Security and justice is seen as a core function. The challenge is clear. 'Having taken over social control functions and responsibilities which once belonged to the institutions of the community, the state is now faced with its own inability to deliver the expected levels of control of criminal conduct' (Garland 1996, p. 449). The state and its government, therefore, are caught between image and reality. With its image of itself as monopoly provider of security and justice, the government has to officially outlaw all providers outside its authority. And yet it knows it is unable to accomplish its task single-handed. Attempts to square this circle constitute much of the rest of this chapter.

Four broad state policy options towards non-state security and justice provision have emerged in Africa: exclusion, delegation, partnership and imitation.

Strategies of exclusion

It might appear that the exclusion of informal security and justice providers offers a straightforward approach for governments. Governments can simply exclude all alternative providers or clearly define the required standards of conduct and procedure and registration so as to exclude those who do not meet those requirements. On the basis of this criminalisation, existing providers can be closed down or prosecuted and new initiatives can be stalled. Yet it is one thing to legislate and another to enforce the law. Civilian policing groups, believing that they are preventing crime in the absence of the police, may resist foreclosure and in doing so be able to call upon popular support. In this context, does a government persist with an unpopular action, especially when it knows that it cannot replace the proscribed group with an effective (or even popular) police?

When the Liberian government closed down the local policing groups in Monrovia under pressure from the police and international community, violent crime rose again, prompting public outcries against the government policy and, with an upcoming election, a rapid about-turn by the government. Political considerations at a more local level have been prominent in Kenya. Despite legislation prohibiting vigilante groups, they have often been tolerated, at least by local politicians, in the fight against cattle rustling in rural areas. In Kuria district, for instance, the local communities sought protection from the District Commissioner before beginning their assault on the criminals. Without his tacit approval of their activities, they knew they were vulnerable to arrest by the police (with whom they had a very bad relationship) and to prosecution by the courts for their use of violence against suspects and for holding their own courts. Why did successive DCs and the local MP protect them? Certainly because they were effective in a way the police were not. But ultimately, because they were so popular that to counter them would be political suicide (Heald 2007).

In Nigeria, local political interests in security and justice are more explicit. States, local government and politicians have all been implemented over time with high-jacking vigilante groups for political purposes, turning some of them into what appear as little more than personal militias. This has made prosecuting them and closing them down problematic for the federal government. Take, for example, the vigilante group in Anambra State known as the Bakassi Boys.

Though they were outlawed by the federal government in 1999 for their violence, a little later, the Anambra State Governor simply established a new vigilante group known as the Onitsha Main Market Vigilante Services, claiming (as he had done for the Bakassi Boys) that it would be run in collaboration with the Nigeria Police. It was still operating throughout the state in 2013 (*Orient* newspaper 2013). Similarly, when the Nigerian federal government in 1999 announced a ban on the Yoruba cultural, political and security group the OPC (The O'odua People's Congress), scores of OPC members may have been killed or arrested by the police, but the OPC still continues to function, if less openly. As Human Rights Watch observes, far from being eliminated,

> [t]hese groups have benefited from the financial and political support of influential political figures, including state government officials. Several government officials maintain close links with the OPC leadership, and OPC members have provided security arrangements at official and public functions, in the presence of government officials…. In some of the states where it operates in the southwest, it enjoys close relations with state government authorities and even the explicit support of governors – a support which, to some extent, may have provided it with a level of protection.
>
> (Human Rights Watch 2003, p. 1)

Many explain the ambiguity of the federal government, which on the one hand bans the OPC and yet on the other has a private cordial relationship with them, as due to the government's need of the political support that the OPC can garner or withdraw (the OPC is said to have something between one and three million members) (Human Rights Watch 2003).

Even the police have at times reason to be wary of prosecuting illegal vigilante activities. They have often been recorded watching passively as local groups violently punish alleged criminals in Nigeria. And in Uganda, South Africa and elsewhere there are reports that police at times 'farm out' to less accountable local policing groups the 'dirty work' of extracting criminal intelligence or of teaching well-known thieves a lesson, which they as the police were not entitled to do (Titeca 2009; Buur 2006). In another reported incident in South Africa, police were faced with a tribal policing group that was violent. The local commander of a small station with 35 police officers covering an extensive area was only too glad to have their help. How did she justify the violence?

> Sometimes you have to turn the blind eye for the sake of crime. If you for instance have someone coming in accused of raping a three year old and he has been beaten up, then you do turn the blind eye. You know that it is like victim support.
>
> (Jensen 2007, p. 111)

When faced with low rates of conviction due to lack of strong evidence, it is not surprising that the regional police in Ethiopia have been willing, informally, to refer a case to the elders to use the customary oath process to get at the truth. It may not be legal, but getting the families of the accused to swear on pain of divine anger that the accused did not commit the crime is effective, as far as the police are concerned.

Faced with a public, politicians and police who may have their reasons for not confronting illegal policing, governments may well ask themselves what store to put on legislation and whether the criminalisation of those tackling it in their own way is a workable or even wise policy. Or put another way, can legislation that has limited support achieve much?

Strategies of partnership

This approach starts with the recognition that the state is not in a position to replace non-state security and justice actors, at least in the short to medium term and therefore consideration should be given to partnering with actors that may well be the principal providers and often enjoy widespread local support.

From the state's perspective, of course, the questions surrounding partnership are multiple. There are political considerations. Will this approach undermine the government's legitimacy in being seen as a failure to provide a basic service; or is this going to garner more political support, as the state is seen to support popular local provision? Will partnership be resisted by the police with their concerns about work encroachment and of working with 'untrained amateurs'? Will this policy aggravate the donors over issues of human rights abuses by some potential partners?

There are also very practical issues. Are all the active providers known and mapped in terms of the services they offer, the quality of those services and the local support they enjoy from all sectors of the community? Which groups currently meet the basic requirements of legality, effectiveness and non-violence (or at least are willing to consider reform in areas where they are weak)? Would it be better for the state to initiate a local group itself as a partner for the police to work with, along the lines favoured by 'community policing'?

Partnership policies not only have to tackle the issue of 'who' but of 'how'. If it is apparent that there is considerable diversity among local policing groups, can a single partnership approach be designed? And what should be the level of partnership – that is, what will be the roles given to the partners? Is it one of equality, or is it assumed that the police will be the dominant and lead partner that accepts assistance from others? Four variations on this theme have emerged, although there are overlaps.

There is *open cooperation*, even though there is no formal agreement. This is the recognition between two parties that they share common goals and thus can support one another. Commercial security is often prepared to share intelligence with the state police and vice versa. In South Africa, commercial security firms frequently make citizens' arrests and take the suspects to the police station. It has been known, too, for a customary dispute resolution by a chief or an NGO to find enforcement of fines and community service difficult to ensure, in which cases they have turned to the state's enforcement machinery for assistance, as is reported in South Africa (Population Council and Ubuntu Institute 2010, p. 18). In Ethiopia, police and courts diverted cases to local elders or Sharia courts and vice versa long before there was any government policy to support this. More informally, South Sudan police have been seen to maintain order in chiefs' courts and to undertake the proscribed beating of someone found guilty (Baker and Scheye 2009).

In Somaliland, the very weakness or absence of a formal security and justice sector has meant that the 'central government' has relied on clan leaders using customary law *(Xeer)* as the main providers of security and justice. When a government has few pretensions about its power, it more willingly recognises that there must be a shared authority, in this case between 'the state' and the clan leaders. Thus, police endorse and facilitate clan leaders when they assert jurisdiction over a matter or call for an arrest. Similarly, state courts ratify *Xeer* rulings that are registered with them. 'As such, traditional authorities and state authorities are mutually dependent on each other's articulations of authority' (Moe 2014, p. 71).

In Malawi and Sierra Leone, governments have supported donor programmes that engage paralegals without formal legal qualifications to promote awareness and understanding of basic legal rights. Since paralegals help to reduce backlogs in the system, their contribution is valued by the police and judges. Development NGOs that aim to enhance the prospects of improved safety and security of person and property, as well as significantly increasing access to justice, are also often welcomed. Zambia is a good example of such NGOs. The Legal Resources Foundation mediates more than 1000 cases a year; Women for Change empowers village women to understand their rights and to find the appropriate forum for their problem; the Legal Resources Foundation and National Women's Legal Aid Clinic assist women to navigate the complex court structures; and Zambia Civic Education Association provides legal advice, civic education, legal representation and advocacy.

The loosest form of partnership is *coordination* with what remain autonomous non-state actors, with or without a formal agreement. In this relationship, the services of non-state providers are coordinated with, but not subordinated to, those provided by state police. Take, for example, Sierra Leone, where the state has its own armed police wing, the OSD, co-guarding with unarmed bank guards and co-manning vehicles with unarmed diplomatic missions. And at the country's largest diamond mine, Koidu Holdings has a partnership between the mine guards and the OSD that is overseen by the security firm. In the case of Sierra Rutile's mine, the mine has been allowed to have private security that is itself armed (Abrahamsen and Williams 2005). As far back as 2002 in Mozambique, private security companies were explicitly asked to cooperate with the police, requesting security guards to act as police officers in the fight against crime and to share their vehicles in emergencies.

Similar close coordination was found between the Ugandan state and the Ugandan taxi drivers association, UTODA, when in 1993 the latter was given authority to run bus parks in Kampala. This included dealing with crime and disputes in the parks, and policing drivers' vehicles and driving. In addition UTODA undertook traffic duties with the police during rush hour, helped drivers acquire permits and played a mediation role between drivers and the police (Atwine 2009). In 2012, Kampala Capital City Authority had a change of heart and refused to renew the contract for the management of the taxi parks. Kampala taxi drivers apparently backed the City takeover, amidst stories of harassment of drivers by UTODA. However, it was also clear that the opposition-led City Council wanted control of this sector and of the revenues paid by the drivers daily.[3]

South Africa's Improvement Districts grant authority to city neighbourhoods, if they have electoral consent, to form associations that among other things seek to improve security. They may do this by hiring commercial security to 'supplement' the work of the police, primarily in patrols and intelligence gathering. Where implemented, the two work in close cooperation, with allegedly good results in reducing (or at least displacing) crime (Berg and Shearing 2015).

Similarly, the UN-Habitat's 'Safer Cities Programme' has seen local authorities over the last 20 years attempt to tackle crime by coordinating the work of NGOs, Community Based Organisations and the police within large African cities. This programme has been implemented in Abidjan, Antananarivo, Dakar, Dar-es-Salaam, Durban, Johannesburg, Nairobi and Yaoundé. In addition to sensitising communities and building local capacity in urban safety, it also seeks to promote job creation as a means of tackling the root causes of crime. Little research has been conducted on them, but early reports suggested that the initiatives 'are most often hampered by lack of effective support from the local government' (Kisia 2004, p. 14).

A much tighter partnership is *incorporation*, where elements of the informal are brought into the formal. An example would be the community/lay assessor system of having two community members as lay assessors, as occurs in Zimbabwean and South African magistrates' courts (South African Law Reform Commission 2008). Zimbabwe has no jury system, and cases are routinely tried by a judge sitting with two lay assessors. Matters of law are decided by the judge alone. Questions of fact must be resolved by a majority of the panel of three. They can familiarise the magistrates of the circumstances prevailing in, and peculiar to, that community, and matters of customary justice, and they can overrule them on the facts, although the magistrate remains the authority on the law. They were more popular in South Africa immediately after the end of apartheid, when most judges were white and there was concern lest justice be seen to be 'white man's justice'. The District Appeal Court in Sierra Leone has two customary law officers to advise the Chairman on matters relating to local practice.

Another form of partnership is *co-optation* by the state, by which the entirety of an informal provider is taken over by the state. This is favoured when a non-state group is seen as popular and thus as undermining the state's forms of security and justice. The strategy has the advantage of bringing the informal provider operationally under the umbrella of the state police so that their popularity can be harnessed for the state, excesses can be more readily controlled and, officially, such activities can then receive central or local government funding.

Initially the Tanzanian state, for instance, was intensely wary of the highly successful and popular anti-rustling vigilantes (*sungusungu*) (Fleisher 2000). Its official line was to praise them for their initiative, while insisting that they hand over suspects to the police and leave the determination of guilt and punishment to the courts. In time, however, the Tanzanian state saw the benefits of co-optation to neutralise their threat, and they were formalised in 1990. A similar story has occurred in Liberia with the government's co-optation of Monrovian vigilantes.

The most common form of partnership in recent years has been government initiated *co-production*, that is, the setting up of local groups according to government-approved rules with whom the government and its agencies, such as the police, can partner. The obvious example is 'community policing' groups. These are formed by the state after 'consultation' with citizens and offer partnership with the police to reduce crime (Denney and Jenkins 2013). There is usually talk of listening to the people's concerns and of 'working together', and even of opportunities to hold the local police to account, but in practice the police retain their dominance as the 'professionals', and the citizen group become their sources of intelligence. From the government's perspective the advantages are clear. This will enrol the public as the unpaid informers and surveillance personnel for the police. It is also hoped that it will improve public trust in the police and remove the legacy of suspicion and hostility. Finally, should it be desired, it offers a way of engaging communities in the monitoring of police effectiveness and efficiency and in evaluating its service provision. Whatever the government goals, the likelihood is that in the hands of the police, who oversee the local groups of volunteers, this partnership will be run so as to enhance their achievements and will be nothing other than 'police property' (Reiner 2000). Thus, in Ethiopia, community police officers see their role as being, unequivocally, leaders in local security and justice (despite their lack of local knowledge and police training). As such they take on the responsibility of organising and leading the community meetings, gathering statistics, undertaking patrols, giving advice, fundraising, running youth clubs and controlling militias (Denney and Kassaye 2015; Kassaye 2013).

Whatever the form of partnership, the aims of the governments are clear – they are seeking to harness the energies, knowledge and local legitimacy of other security and justice players. They recognise their capital and want to share in it. To enrol them in the services of the state and its government is seen as a benefit, although maintaining a relationship where the state actor(s) is dominant is not necessarily easy. At times it is not clear who is enrolling whom, and the dividing line between 'state' and 'non-state' becomes blurred. The end-products of these interactions are complex, dynamic security networks, where the providers, both formal and informal, while acknowledging their need of others nevertheless constantly seek to concentrate power (see Hunt, Chapter 5 in this volume). Under the friendly terminology of 'partnership', the individual partners are often seeking to enforce, within the space they claim, their authority, their definition of right and wrong and guilty and innocent and their right over life and death.

Strategies of delegation

Lack of trust leads to strategies of exclusion and partnership. Both assume that the non-state actors are suspect in some way and therefore should be either banned or linked with responsible state agents to ensure their good conduct. Yet both enforcement and supervision require resources that may be thin on the ground. In this situation, it may be attractive for the government to consider delegation, that is, handing over to others certain (limited) security and justice responsibilities. This can be done through constitutional provision and/or legislation and has been applied most often with regard to customary and commercial security and justice services.

For governments, customary provision comes with baggage: rival political authorities competing for local loyalties; presumably conservative practices such as gender discrimination and corporal punishment being incompatible with the international standards and donor requirements; a large diversity of practices that are probably not codified; accountability issues, at least to the laws and institutions of the state, if not to the community; and, probably, donor anxiety. Little wonder that many governments, on acquiring independence, decided to rid themselves of these perceived troublesome anachronisms. Yet not all have followed this path. Some have seen the potential for security and justice to be delegated away from over-pressed state services. These have also seen the potential for customary provision to make access to justice much more of a reality for rural areas and reduce criticism of the government for failing to provide formal services. Furthermore, in countries with major ethnic fault lines the recognition of cultural difference might weaken secessionist tendencies. Those who have made this calculation have therefore been happy to make constitutional provision for customary justice, usually within certain limitations to eliminate what is deemed unacceptable.

In practice, many perceived deficiencies in customary provision have continued. Governments have been reluctant to enforce statutory limitations on customary courts' powers, such as the nature of cases that can be handled, and reluctant to introduce reforms concerning female participation, recording of cases, and the right of legal representation. The strategy adopted has been one of 'letting sleeping dogs lie' and retaining the political support of influential local leaders, as long as they are deemed by the local population to be 'working' and 'popular'. Minimal activity, therefore, has been seen as the best way of handling the tension between establishing a unitary legal system that offers uniform legal rules, and the political wisdom of recognising diversity and flexibility within a large multinational state. And delay seems the best policy of reconciling the dominant customary justice that often closely reflects local popular demands, with the protection of human rights as expressed in international conventions that the government has agreed to abide by. The mixture of principle and politics is seen clearly in both Malawi and Ethiopia.

The Malawi Constitution of 1994 recognised customary law as an integral part of the legal system and provided for 'traditional courts' with limited jurisdiction over civil and minor criminal cases. The legislation to set up such courts, however, was not introduced until 2011. Local traditional courts can now handle most civil cases and some minor criminal cases. Interestingly, from 1970 there had been regional traditional courts with jurisdiction over virtually all criminal trials involving Africans of Malawian descent. Their allegedly authoritarian and punitive justice was said to accord with the views of President Banda. They also had a reputation for being used to prosecute government political opponents and being corrupt. Hence, with Banda's fall they were suspended.

Mozambique has changed its mind as regards the role of chiefs in providing security and justice. Independence brought an official government ban on traditional leaders, but this was reconsidered following the end of the civil war in 1992, when in view of limited government resources the importance of traditional leaders was recognised. Traditional authority was also seen as having potential in national reconciliation. In addition, the FRELIMO government was well aware of how its civil war rival, RENAMO, had called upon chiefs for governance in the rural areas and the popularity there of its use of traditionalist rhetoric. If nothing else, a pro-traditional chief strategy would undermine its political rival's chief 'selling point'. Hence from 2002, chiefs were recognised by the government as community authorities and as assistants of the local tiers of the state in a range of state administrative matters. This brought the return of state recognition of chiefs' roles in policing and justice. They are now required to collaborate with the local state police in identifying troublemakers and to undertake resolution of civil conflicts in liaison with the local community courts. The legislation is, nonetheless, full of ambiguities. Strangely, chiefs' courts and system of policing are not recognised by law, and there is no official incorporation of chiefs within the justice and security sectors (Kyed 2009).

As part of its decentralised policy of government, Ethiopia's 1994 constitution provides legal recognition to pre-existing religious and customary courts, and allows federal and regional legislatures to recognise the decisions of such courts. Yet though customary courts are widely used, the Ethiopian government appears to be keeping its options open by delaying the issuing of a law for their official recognition, as envisaged under the constitution. This, perhaps, is reluctant delegation. It is never easy for a government to hand over core state functions to others, the more so if the government sees itself as progressive and developmentalist, and those delegated powers are seen as reactionary.

Strategies of imitation

It might not be admitted publicly, but the very popularity and success of informal security and justice groups evokes from governments something close to jealousy. For all the social capital governments have (long-standing official recognition), as well as economic capital (state and donor finances) and cultural capital (its corporate knowledge and skills acquired by training and experience), they often lack the symbolic capital (prestige and attention) that many informal providers possess. This can of course be secured through linkages with resource-strong partners. Alternatively, the basis of that capital can be imitated.

One obvious example of this strategy has been the adoption by courts of restorative justice principles taken from customary practices in their country. Both Rwanda and Uganda allowed their lowest level of administration to undertake security and justice functions and to do so using the customary processes of dispute resolution that local people were familiar with and preferred (Baker 2005, 2007a). Another example concerns community policing, which despite its western origins has been widely introduced into African settings by external consultants through donor police reform programmes. Less well known is how African police have admired and copied aspects of local community groups' efforts to provide policing and justice in their neighbourhoods. Police have even adopted these self-help groups' effective style as a 'community policing' programme – or at least, that is how some interpret what happened in Swaziland (Kyed 2015, p. 59).

In recent years there has been a recognition by the state in Ethiopia that the formal justice system needs to be supported by the informal system for capacity reasons. In addition, the government has realised that for greater popularity and legitimacy it could usefully adopt informal justice approaches such as mediation, inclusion, reparation, reconciliation, compensation and reintegration. Thus, alternative remedial measures have been incorporated into the criminal procedure code and stages and instances in the criminal justice process identified where diversion to non-state actors is allowed. Disputing parties are given a choice by the police of handling the conflict through mediation (whether offered by customary leaders or a mediation service provided by the police themselves) or of pursuing the case through the formal processes. If the mediation is concluded, the victim submits a written request for case withdrawal. This is sent to the prosecution office, which has the legal mandate to dismiss such cases. Similarly, some district (*woreda*) courts have established an ADR system and have selected elders for this process. Some *woreda* courts have established committees of two elders and one woman to intervene in family and other cases to avoid such cases coming to court. They advise the community to use these structures and only afterwards to refer to the *woreda* courts. Homicide, as a criminal offence, is dealt with exclusively by the formal courts, and yet even in these cases a place had been found for a parallel informality: the police use customary mediation to bring reconciliation between the victim/family and the accused. The object is to avoid the risk of revenge killings. Part of the mediation includes compensation.

Conclusion

The challenge of informal security and justice to African states and their governments is not simply a policy challenge. It certainly has very significant policy dimensions, but beyond that it fundamentally challenges how states as political communities are 'supposed' to be construed. The self-image of having a mono-poly of legitimate coercion through the police and courts has proved for the most part to be undeliverable. In other words, governments may not be able to fully offer a core service, a service that almost defines what a state is, according to the west. The informal providers demonstrate not just the weakness of African gov-ernments and their failure to create a state that follows the Weberian norm. The political reality demands that governments think again – and think differently – about their view of themselves. They may not like it, but they are faced with legal and policing pluralism and, more fundamentally, with a hybrid polity. A government cannot run a state with multiple authorities as if there were one single central authority. Moreover, the government may not be in a position to either totally ignore or criminalise such important players in the security and justice sector as informal providers.

What has been shown in this chapter is that governments are being forced into some sort of negotiation, accommodation and 'living arrangements' with informal providers of security and justice. They cannot simply take their security and justice policies off a western peg – that policy approach is for another world that is not their own. The African state and its government may still be the most powerful players, but they are not the only players in the room, and they have to come to terms with that. This entails more complex governance. It requires com-promise rather than signing treaties whose terms they can never fully meet. It necessitates heterogeneous or hybrid institutions. It demands a review of the police, perhaps along the minimalist lines of specialist organisation for serious and complex cases only (Marks, Shearing and Wood 2009); or what Brogden and Shearing call 'dual policing' (Brogden and Shearing 1993), where the state police would bear primary responsibility for enforcement, while problem-orientated (community) policing would be provided by state police in conjunc-tion with commercial, municipal and voluntary organisations. It requires a degree of confidence in communities' abilities to police and resolve disputes based on their social skills and in the absence of 'professional' skills. It requires new levels of consultation beyond the 'usual suspects' of 'key stakeholders'. It means an emphasis as much on the importance of accountability to the local community as accountability to state law. It means accepting a willingness to reform as the entry point of partnership with non-state actors, in the place of making the highest international standards the starting point. It means a commit-ment to what must inevitably be a slow and sometimes haphazard progress of developing new security and justice networks appropriate to local conditions. It means, more fundamentally, defining what the state and its government is in African terms.

In the final analysis, then, we are not talking about the question of how states deal with informal security and justice – we are talking about how societies deal with states. *That* is the dilemma.

Notes

1 'A state is a human community that (successfully) claims *monopoly of the legitimate use of physical force* within a given territory' (Weber 1948, p. 78), emphasis in the original.
2 'The right to use physical force is ascribed to other institutions or individuals only to the extent to which the state permits it' (ibid.).
3 Police officers stationed at the parks' exits now ask the 20,000 drivers for the Shs4500 that is required of drivers daily and the monthly Shs25,000 sticker fee.

Bibliography

Abrahamsen, R and Williams, M 2005, *Globalisation of African Security: Sierra Leone*, http://users.aber.ac.uk/rbh/privatesecurity/country%20report-sierra%20leone.pdf (accessed 7 January 2015).

Albrecht, P and Kyed, HM (eds) 2015, *Policing and the politics of order making*, Routledge, Abingdon.

Arrive Alive 2014, 'Police urge communities towards caring for our children and warn against vigilantism', 18 November 2014, www.arrivealive.co.za/news.aspx?s=1&i=13859&page=Police-urge-communities-towards-caring-for-our-children-and-warn-against-vigilantism (accessed 7 January 2015).

Atwine, A 2009, 'Management agencies and public road transport services in Uganda: A case study of Uganda Taxi Operators and Drivers' Association (UTODA)', http://hdl.handle.net/10570/3121 (accessed 7 January 2015).

Baker, B 2005, 'Multi-choice policing in Uganda', *Policing and Society*, vol. 15, no. 1, pp. 19–41.

Baker, B 2007a, 'Reconstructing a policing system out of the ashes: Rwanda's solution', *Policing and Society*, vol. 17, no. 4, pp. 1–23.

Baker, B 2007b, *Multi-choice policing in Africa*, Nordiska Afrikainstitutet, Uppsala.

Baker, B 2009, *Security in post-conflict Africa: the role of non-state policing*, CRC Press, Boca Raton.

Baker, B and Scheye, E 2009, 'Access to justice in a post-conflict state: donor-supported multidimensional peacekeeping in Southern Sudan', *International Peacekeeping*, vol. 16, no. 2, pp. 171–85.

Berg, J and Shearing, C 2015, 'New authorities: relating state and non-state security auspices in South African Improvement Districts', in Albrecht, P and Kyed, HM (eds), *Policing and the politics of order making*, Routledge, Abingdon.

Brogden, M and Shearing, C 1993, *Policing for a new South Africa*, Routledge, Abingdon.

Buur, L 2006, 'Reordering society: vigilantism and sovereign expressions in Port Elizabeth's townships', *Development and Change*, vol. 37, no. 4, pp. 735–57.

Comaroff, JL and Comaroff, J (eds) 2006, *Law and disorder in the postcolony*, University of Chicago Press, Chicago.

Cuskelly, K 2011, *Customs and constitutions: state recognition of customary law around the world*, IUCN, Bangkok, https://portals.iucn.org/library/efiles/documents/2011-101.pdf (accessed 3 January 2015).

Denney, L and Jenkins, S 2013, *Securing communities: the what and the how of community policing*, ODI, London, www.odi.org.uk/publications/7633-community-policing (accessed 12 January 2015).

Denney, L and Kassaye, D 2015, *Securing communities for development: community policing in Ethiopia's Amhara region*, ODI, London.

Federal Republic of Nigeria 1999, *Constitution of the Federal Republic of Nigeria*, www.nigeria-law.org/ConstitutionOfTheFederalRepublicOfNigeria.htm (accessed 6 July 2017).

Fleisher, ML 2000, 'Sungusungu: state-sponsored village vigilante groups among the Kuria of Tanzania', *Africa*, vol. 70, no. 2, pp. 209–28.

Garland, D 1996, 'The limits of the sovereign state: strategies of crime control in contemporary society', *British Journal of Criminology*, vol. 36, no. 4, pp. 445–71.

Heald, S 2007, 'Making law in rural East Africa: Sungusungu in Kenya', *Crisis States Working Paper*, no. 12 www.lse.ac.uk/internationalDevelopment/research/crisisStates/download/wp/wpSeries2/wp122.pdf (accessed 3 January 2015).

Government of the Democratic Republic of the Congo 2005, www.parliament.am/library/sahmanadrutyunner/kongo.pdf (accessed 6 July 2017).

Human Rights Watch 2003, *The O'odua People's Congress: fighting violence with violence*, www.hrw.org/reports/2003/02/27/oodua-peoples-congress-opc (accessed 7 January 2015).

Jensen, S 2007, 'Security and violence on the frontier of the state: vigilant citizens in Nkomazi, South Africa', in Ahuluwalia, P, Bethlehem, L and Ginio, R (eds), *Violence and non-violence in Africa*, Ashgate, Aldershot.

Kassaye, D 2013, 'Transformative policing in Ethiopia: community policing as a new paradigm of policing in Ethiopia', PhD thesis, School of Social Work, Addis Ababa University, Addis Ababa.

Kisia, P 2004, 'Promoting peace, safety and security: the role of communities and local governments', paper prepared for Africa Local Government Action Forum.

Kyed, HM 2009, 'Mutual transformations of state and traditional authority the renewed role of chiefs in policing and justice enforcement in Mozambique', *Cadernos de Estudos Africanos*, 16/17, http://cea.revues.org/192 (accessed 30 December 2014).

Kyed, HM 2015, 'Rival forms of policing and politics in urban Swaziland', in Albrecht, P and Kyed, HM (eds), *Policing and the politics of order making*, Routledge, Abingdon.

Luckham, R and Kirk, T 2012, *Security in hybrid political contexts: an end-user approach*. Justice and Security Research Programme, paper 2, http://eprints.lse.ac.uk/56358/1/JSRP_Paper2_Security_in_hybrid_political_contexts_Luckham_Kirk_2012.pdf (accessed 7 January 2015).

Lund, C 2006, 'Twilight institutions: public authority and local politics in Africa', *Development and Change*, vol. 37, no. 4, pp. 685–706.

Marks, M, Shearing, C and Wood, J 2009, 'Who should the police be? Finding a new narrative for community policing in South Africa', *Police Practice and Research*, vol. 10, no. 2, pp. 145–55.

Miles, J 2006, *Customary and Islamic law and its development in Africa*, African Development Bank, https://papers.ssrn.com/sol3/papers.cfm?abstract_id=1015783 (accessed 6 July 2017).

Moe, L 2014, 'The "turn to the local": hybridity, local ordering and the new governing rationalities of peace and security interventions in Somalia', PhD thesis, University of Queensland, Brisbane.

News24 2014, 'Vigilante warning after massacres', 5 November, www.news24.com/Africa/News/DRC-vigilante-warning-after-massacres-20141105 (accessed 16 May 2017).

Orient newspaper 2013, 'Vigilante services in Anambra mark 10 years', 25 March, Nigeria.

Orock, R 2014, 'Crime, in/security and mob justice: the micropolitics of sovereignty in Cameroon', *Social Dynamics*, vol. 40, no. 2, pp. 408–42.

Pefok, JD 2006, 'Wouri SDO says mob justice tarnishes Cameroon's image', *The Post*, 17 November, www.postnewsline.com/2006/11/wouri_sdo_says_.html (accessed 15 January 2015).

Population Council and Ubuntu Institute 2010, *The role of traditional leaders in preventing and addressing sexual and gender-based violence: findings from Kwa-Zulu Natal, North West and Limpopo Provinces, South Africa*, www.k4health.org/toolkits/hiv-and-traditional-leadership/role-traditional-leaders-preventing-and-addressing-sexual (accessed 8 January 2015).

Reiner, R 2000, *The politics of the police*, Oxford University Press, Oxford.

South African Government 1996, *Constitution of the Republic of South Africa*, www.gov.za/DOCUMENTS/CONSTITUTION/constitution-republic-south-africa-1996-1 (accessed 6 July 2017).

South African Law Reform Commission 2008, *Review of the Law of Evidence*, Issue Paper 26, Project 126, January.

Smith, D 2006, 'Violent vigilantism and the state in Nigeria', in Bay, E and Donham, D (eds), *States of violence: politics, youth, and memory in contemporary Africa*, Charlottesville, VA: University of Virginia Press, pp. 127–47.

State House, Republic of Sierra Leone 1991, *Constitution of Sierra Leone*, www.sierra-leone.org/Laws/constitution1991.pdf (accessed 6 July 2017).

Titeca, K 2009, 'The "Masai" and Miraa: public authority, vigilance and criminality in a Ugandan border town', *Journal of Modern African Studies*, vol. 47, no. 2, pp. 219–317.

Weber, M 1948, *From Max Weber: essays in Sociology* (ed. and trans. H Geth and C Wright Mills), RKP, London.

Woodman, G 1996, 'Legal pluralism and the search for justice', *Journal of African Law*, vol. 40, no. 2, pp. 152–67.

5   Relational perspectives on peace formation

Symbiosis and the provision of security and justice*

Charles T Hunt

Introduction

In post-colonial states, the production of socio-political order is contingent on the interaction of myriad sources of social governance (Boege, Brown, Clements and Nolan 2009). While the machinery of central government plays a vital role, it is far from the only or main provider. The governance of everyday life for the majority is overseen and underwritten by a plethora of other community-based and private actors.[1] This includes traditional chieftaincies, village and tribal elders and religious figures who preside over customary dispute resolution. A range of civil society organisations, youth and women's groups, guilds or associations, private security companies and vigilante/community watch groups are also important – as are 'secret societies' and those who act as a bridge to the spiritual realm. Their appeal is multifaceted (Baker and Scheye 2007, p. 512)[2] and their importance is evidenced by the large numbers of people dependent on them for as much as 80 per cent of their security and justice needs (OECD 2007, p. 6; UNDP 2009, p. 9; Chirayath, Sage and Woolcock 2005, p. 5; Albrecht and Kyed 2010). Social order is argued to be the result of *polycentric governance* epitomised by multiple sources and sites of political legitimacy, authority and agency (Ostrom 1999; Sawyer 2005). What could be broadly termed a *Weberian* notion of the state – i.e. a 'statist imaginary' contingent on a state monopoly on legitimate violence (Gerth and Mills 1946) – simply does not correlate well with the enactment of the social order this multilayered system brings about in the post-colonial context.[3]

Despite some acknowledgement of the importance of actors beyond government institutions (World Bank 2011; DfID 2010, pp. 28–31), this 'statist' imaginary endures in the scripts and standard operating procedures of international peacebuilders. The majority of security and justice reform programming continues to prioritise and flow through the central government and its institutional architecture (Gordon 2014; Hughes *et al.* 2015, p. 823). The post-conflict transition frameworks co-conceived in national capitals, and the international organisations that shape engagement, have tended to reject many of the locally emplaced entities that contribute to social order as unacceptable partners, deemed unfit for peace-building – often treating them as anachronistic, illiberal and undemocratic (e.g. UN 2014, p. 10). In effect, the empirical reality presented above is subverted. However, the outcomes have been at best mixed, producing policing and justice systems that vary in quality and sustainability (Richmond 2014).

In response, a growing body of conceptual and empirical work has high-lighted the hybrid nature of socio-political order in conflict-affected settings (Boege *et al.* 2009; Scheye 2010), culminating in a so-called 'local turn' in peacebuilding discourse (Mac Ginty and Richmond 2013). This has contributed to the increasing acceptance that local sources of peace and order play important roles in the emergence of social order, and as such they are beginning to feature more prominently in the discussions around (and, to a lesser extent, approaches to) peace formation (Richmond and Mitchell 2012).[4] However, these developments have met with their own critiques (Chandler 2011).

First, this counter-critique contends that concepts such as hybridity and the focus on 'the local' run the risk of uncritically romanticising traditional and customary bodies (Meagher 2012, pp. 1080–1; Paffenholz 2015, pp. 857–74). In doing so, it is alleged that these approaches have unhelpfully pitted one source of authority against a counterpart and display a tendency to reify Cartesian categorical thinking and draw binary distinctions between, for instance, liberal and local or west and non-west (Heathershaw 2013, p. 277; Laffey and Nadarajah 2012, p. 417; Sabaratnam 2013; Randazzo 2016). The language used in debates about legitimate actors in providing social peace has been subject to some scrutiny in the peacebuilding literature, and authors synonymous with the liberal peace critique have raised concerns about the 'lazy dichotomies' found in main-stream scholarship and practice (Mac Ginty 2010, 2011; Richmond 2009). However, these and other efforts to unpack the semantics involved (Lemay-Hébert, Onuf, Rakić and Bojanić 2013), have not sufficiently addressed questions that remain about the epistemological, political and practical consequences of using such analytics and labels.

Second, and related, the relationships between all of the actors involved are underappreciated and poorly understood. This has resulted in them being onto-logically demoted in favour of assessments of the types and qualities of the entities involved.[5] While there is an extensive body of literature on the relationships between formal and informal institutions in Africa and beyond (e.g. Baker 2010; Lund 2006; Reno 1998), the majority treats these actors as discrete systems that relate to each other in various fixed ways, as opposed to a complex eco-system of entities that all relate to each other in a multitude of dynamic ways. Further-more, much of this literature is predicated on the understanding that the Weberian ideal-type state is the only viable foundation for, and standard for judgement of, social order and political community. 'Non-state' institutions are consistently characterised as obstacles to proper state functioning. While such analyses can bring valuable material to light, they have a tendency to investigate informal institutions and the societies that depend upon them from a perspective of deficit, instead of looking at the empirical reality and the work that such actors actually do and how they do it. Consequently, the dominant imaginaries of the state as a set of institutions and mechanisms of state power act as an impediment to 'seeing politics as it is' (Frödin 2012, p. 271.) This has ramifications for understanding how these 'other' entities enact change. Additionally, the dominant descriptions of state functions can play a distorted and distorting role within the dynamics of power and accountability in play, obscuring more than they reveal.

There is consequently a need to problematise the reductive binaries that enable this and develop a more comprehensive understanding of the unique networked relationality that exists between these players, as well as the ways in which that leads to emergent (dis)order. The remainder of this chapter addresses these issues and proceeds in four main parts.

The first section interrogates the veracity, and examines the consequences, of the prevalence of analytical binaries and dichotomies in peacebuilding discourse and practice. The second section emphasises the centrality of the linkages between providers and makes the case for an ontology of relationships when articulating formations of peace. Drawing on this depiction of relational social order, the third section introduces the concept of symbiosis into the discourse on peace formation and develops an innovative analytical framework designed to unpack the relations between sources of social peace. The fourth section identifies the possible implications of this development for research and policy.

The chapter argues that a framework that sheds light on the nature and significance of the multiplicity of relationships between a range of providers of security and justice has the potential to provide analytical leverage when understanding socio-political order in conflict-affected and fragile settings. It argues that it is the nature of the *relationships between entities* rather than the *characteristics of entities* that matters most for understanding how hybridisation occurs and how hybrid (dis)orders emerge. Furthermore, it posits that despite significant inertia, such understanding and analyses may be able to better inform the shape and substance of international assistance to peace formation processes in future.

Problematic binaries: inaccurate labels, composite identities and consequences

The polycentric and pluralistic nature of governance in post-colonial states presents a taxonomic problem. What language and labels are appropriate when distinguishing between the nimiety of actors described above? Efforts to differentiate between sundry providers of security and justice services – particularly those that fall within and beyond the state's accountability frameworks – are an imprecise art and fraught with dangers. Despite efforts to finesse their usage, the tendency to talk and think in terms of dichotomies endures (Paffenholz 2015). Cartesian thinking often underpins the articulation of numerous binaries – *inter alia*, state/non-state, formal/informal, traditional/modern, autochthonous-indigenous/exogenous, licit/illicit, public/private and liberal/local.

The most prominent binary delineation is between *state* and *non-state* domains (Albrecht, Kyed, Isser and Harper 2011). Divisions such as this imply arenas that are distinct and separate, when more often than not some collaboration between the two is occurring, making neither of them purely one or the other. For example, customary authorities are often recognised and formalised in constitutions of state, albeit with significant limitations and caveats. Chiefs, for example, often have an advisory and sometimes judicial role – providing public goods in the form of decisions and actions on behalf of the community. Actors such as these – commonly referred to as 'non-state' – are often essential to service provision, making them very 'state-like' in their conduct, and by some definitions more state-like than the state itself. While roles and responsibilities might be clear *de jure*, the way things play out de facto is often quite different and does not abide by delineations of state and non-state law or rules in practice.

Certain entities providing everyday dispute resolution at the local level are frequently labelled as *informal* despite often being extremely well-organised and predictable with known procedures, avenues of appeal and accountability mechanisms.[6] In many ways, these can be much more *formal* than institutions of government commonly assumed to inhabit the formal sphere but which have little capacity or even presence in many parts of their official jurisdiction.

Similarly, the notion that there is a clear distinction between entities that are *traditional* and those that are *modern* is hard to defend.[7] A Chief in a Ghanaian village may still be referred to as a 'traditional authority'; however, the tradition enshrined in his/her role is not fixed in space or time (Odotei and Awedoba 2006b, pp. 16–17). Individual chiefs and their coterie of advisors can accumulate western education, property on different continents and international business ventures. It is also increasingly common for chiefs to seek economic assistance and direct investment into their community from overseas. Therefore, they embody tradition but also reflect modernity and are affected by changing societal norms and influences including the economic and cultural forces of globalisation. Similarly, the institutions they lead are altered in the collision between indigenous and exogenous (Odotei and Awedoba 2006a). For instance, the incorporation of customary law and roles for chiefs within post-independence constitutions fundamentally altered the power and privilege of chiefs, as did attempts to enact indirect rule through their offices by colonial powers.[8] Therefore, the interpenetration of traditional and modern, customary and formal-legal mean that the entities these labels are attached to are actually much more adaptive and liminal in nature (Denney 2014a, pp. 8–10).

There are also instances where an actor may not be acting under a single identity at all times or in a particular instance. Many individuals (though possibly groups of individuals) who play important roles in community order embody multiple sources of authority. This set of actors possesses numerous social, political, legal, ritual and spiritual roles and responsibilities and derive legitimacy from different realms. Gluckman, Mitchell and Barnes recognised this as an important political reality in parts of Africa, referring to the 'dilemma of the village headman' who had to navigate competing demands on him as a simultaneous agent of both the state and societal kinship-based bodies (Gluckman, Mitchell and Barnes 1949, pp. 93–4). This duality or 'double-embeddedness' importantly works in both directions. That is, as well as competing claims on them as authority figures, powerful figures may have the option of drawing on different strands of their identity when exercising control. For example, in northern Ghana it is often the case that sources of authority derive power from multiple roles as a traditional chief, successful businessperson and elected representative on a local council or decentralised provincial government (Lentz 1998, p. 59). Similarly, in Liberia, a *Zoe* (ritual officer in the Poro secret society)[9] could also be a religious official, while at the same time having heritage that ordains him as a traditional chief, meaning that through state-sponsored customary law he could also play a role in the formal dual legal system (Herman and Martin-Ortega 2011, p. 146; Ellis 2007, p. 225).

In these cases, different forms of authority coexist and intersect as entities draw on different fields of action. These actors are accordingly able to access different registers of power (e.g. formal-political, traditional-customary, spiritual, etc.). The need to be able to convert economic and social into political capital (and vice versa) means that actors are often traversing spaces/domains.[10] However, it may not be immediately, always, or sometimes at all, possible to determine which authority a particular entity is acting under. For instance, when acting in his capacity as a representative of the state (e.g. local politician or district assembly representative), he who is also a religious leader does not entirely relinquish his claim to authority/legitimacy through either channel – whichever capacity he may seem to be acting in. While it might appear obvious which 'hat' is being worn (particularly when it is evidently a chiefly hat, robes and the hearing is occurring in the Chief's palace), if it is known to claimants that the same individual is also a high priest within a secret society or is believed to be a conduit/bridge to the spiritual realm, the construction of the authority that allows them to act and pass judgement on the post-colonial subject is less clear and more multifaceted (Fanthorpe 2007). These actors do not necessarily identify which 'string to their bow' allows them to lead and exercise authority in any particular instance. Moreover, even if they were to explicitly declare the authority they were acting under, who is to say that everyone responds to that particular office if/when they adhere to the decisions and resolutions meted out?

Key providers of order can therefore possess *composite identities* and hence potentially compound legitimacies. Actors can be at once state and non-state, formal and informal, traditional and modern. They are better understood as powerful and integral to what emerges in terms of social order (Lubkemann, Isser and Chapman 2011, p. 81). There are boundaries, and indeed a continuous process of boundary-making (Kyed 2015); however, the boundaries are blurred. As Lentz has argued, 'it seems more adequate to speak of the "combination" and "complementarity" of different registers of power than of "straddling" of different spheres' (Lentz 1998, p. 61).

In summary, *entities* are rarely as discrete or quarantined as the reductive binaries imply. The boundaries between these dichotomous categories are simply not as prevalent as is habitually made out. To the extent they do exist, they are certainly more porous and penetrable than is often portrayed (particularly in the formal scripts of government and international peacebuilders). The interpenetration of traditional and modern, customary and formal-legal means that a range of government institutions and societal bodies are often given *inaccurate labels*. These entities are actually much more fluid and transgressive in nature. In other words, while certain actors may be autochthonous, they are not impervious to influence and adaptation. The distinctions between different actors and the binaries deployed exist more for political purposes than any empirical assessment of service provision in many parts of post-colonial states and societies.

It seems clear then that the binaries commonly in play do not stand up to scrutiny. While nuanced analyses seek to do justice to the empirical complexities (e.g. Mac Ginty 2010), their use remains strong in both the scholarship and praxis of peacebuilding (Lubkemann *et al.* 2011). To be sure, they can be useful in allowing categorisation for some sorts of typological analysis. Indeed it is difficult to avoid them and it is almost impossible to abandon them altogether. Much of the work generated in the 'critical turn' in peacebuilding literature is careful to avoid the accusation of uncritically using these dichotomies – laden with caveats acknowledging the vagaries of using one terminology or another (e.g. Denney 2014a). However, this is not simply a semantic issue. As well as being misleading, the categories and labels applied to various entities involved in formations of peace can present very real epistemological, political and practical problems (de Guevara 2010; Peterson 2012).

Epistemologically, the use of limiting dichotomies places stringent constraints on how stakeholders are understood as individual agents. They can also be to the detriment of attempts to understand if, and if so how, a plurality of providers is enmeshed in the formation of peace. *Politically*, the simplistic depiction of these entities can conceal or discount power relations between the various actors as well as between external peacebuilding organisations and the systems they intervene in. This can result in certain actors seen as 'simply local' or merely cultural, in contrast to the 'State', seen as not local but universal and not cultural but rational. Furthermore, these 'other' actors can be eagerly dismissed as discriminatory and arbitrary, illiberal and anachronistic. In this sense, the binaries are not just overly simplistic analytical frames but can obscure the politics that frame orthodox peacebuilding. They can be instrumentalised by those with power to reinforce their privilege and control while undermining the standing and potentiality of other vital contributors to social order. This is what Leonardsson and Rudd (2015) refer to as 'efficiency-oriented' uses of the local and can have deleterious consequences for the people who rely on the whole gamut of providers to meet their everyday needs and claims. *Practically*, this can result in the derivative conceptual and analytical tools at our disposal for understanding and working with the hybrid orders described above being rendered inadequate and misleading. Furthermore, the epistemological and political considerations can have flow-through implications for whether or not, as well as how, entities are factored into visions for the future. As a corollary, those deemed ineligible can end up falling through the cracks between categories and end up outside of analysis and engagement (Albrecht 2010, pp. 6–7).

The case for relationality: relationships over entities in complex social systems

The reductive binaries problematised above are implicit in an *ontology of entities* that dominates discourse and practice in peacebuilding. That is to say, the focus of conventional approaches is on questions of what set of actors exists and is deemed to be important in the provision of security and justice. It is certainly important to grapple with ontological questions about the types of 'entities' in order to establish who the important stakeholders are and enhance our analytical leverage over their social governance roles, resources and power. However, it is important to go further and examine the relationships between them that are constitutive of emergent order.

The peacebuilding literature has begun to respond to some of these challenges (e.g. Denney 2014b; Luckham and Kirk 2012; Albrecht and Moe 2014, p. 16). Specifically in response to the prevalence of the ontology of entities described above, others have argued for a more 'relational sensibility' and approach to peacebuilding and understanding peace formation (Gadinger, Chadwick and Debiel 2013). For instance, building on similar developments in other areas of the social sciences, Brigg has argued: '[T]he language of relationality is a useful vehicle for navigating the complexities of contemporary peacebuilding' (Brigg 2016, p. 57). Similarly, Thelen and colleagues have proposed a relational approach – which they call 'stategraphy' – in their attempts to theorise the state (Thelen, Vetters and von Benda-Beckmann 2014).

These approaches embrace depictions of societies affected by conflict as complex social systems. To represent political order as such is not simply to say it is difficult to understand and work in. Instead, drawing on concepts from complexity theory, it is to emphasise the centrality of linkages between systemic actors and emergent order. Complexity thinking implores us to recognise that complex social systems are characterised by the existence of *intricate interdependence* between system elements constituted by *feedback processes* that lead to *emergence* and *non-linear change* that ultimately produces *self-organisation* and *co-evolution* (Mitchell 2011; Heylighen 2001). Therefore, it is the nature of the *relationships between entities* rather than the *characteristics of the entities* in a complex social system that matter most for understanding how hybridisation occurs and how hybrid (dis)order emerges.

Consequently, the relationships between sources of security and justice are not just important for formal legalistic reasons of jurisdiction and apportion of responsibility. These relationships shape, empower and at times constrain the extent to which social systems are resilient or otherwise. These bonds between social governance providers lead to emergent outcomes such as peace, security and justice. It is therefore important to focus as much on how the various actors are networked and how these inter-linkages lead to emergent order as it is to identify their individual character. The ways in which these different actors relate to one another, interpenetrate and co-evolve, is what matters fundamentally and may tell us more about the hybrid forms of peace that exist, as well as emancipatory forms that might be possible. However, these relationships are seldom well-understood, and the ramifications for peacebuilding remain underexplored.

State institutions, societal actors and international agencies engage in, and are shaped by, a host of relationships in the local arena. This makes 'the local' contested ground on which different discourses and praxes of peace, security and justice coexist, intertwine and overlap. Several logics of governance – sometimes profoundly different – are entangled with each other through a range of relations that are dynamic, variegated and constitute a diffuse form of political community. The relationships between a diverse array of sources of order are invariably more nuanced, mutable and context-specific than simplistic binary accounts suggest (Baker 2009, pp. 32–5). There is, in effect, much more overlap, cooperation and complementarity between entities than simple contestation or competition. Nevertheless, as Albrecht and Kyed put it, 'There may be full recognition and close collaboration, limited partnership, unofficial acceptance, competition and even open hostility' (2010, p. 2). Entities outside of the machinery of government will have a range of relationships amongst themselves that fundamentally impact on daily politics. For instance, there might be a clear hierarchal order between chiefs of different jurisdictions and perhaps a council of elders, but the relationships between private security companies securing a local gold mine and community watch groups comprised of ex-combatants retaining war-time command and control structures is likely to be less clear but no less important to the everyday day experiences of security and justice for people in those communities (Themnér 2013).

In the course of interactions, forms of peace and socio-political order can emerge that are far from being captured, described or governed through the familiar notions of a liberal peace grounded in a Weberian ideal-type statist imaginary. The exchanges that occur between providers of public goods, and between them and 'end-users', are actually critical to what constitutes political community as well as its substance and dynamics.

While this focus on relationships may appear obvious or simply common sense, it is not manifest in the practice and discourse around peacebuilding. This relational account of order-making demands that peacebuilding scholars and practitioners turn away from the preoccupation with the individual attributes of entities and move towards their linkages and embeddedness as the locus of analysis. Primacy should be given to relationships and better understanding the networked relationality at play. It is therefore necessary to shift from an ontology of *entities* to embrace an ontology of *relationships*. The ontology of relationships advocated here – a reflection of a self-organising and co-evolutionary complex social system – resonates with what Brigg refers to as a 'thick' understanding of relationality in his schematic (Brigg 2016, pp. 58–62). The following section builds on this ontological shift to develop an analytical framework designed to unpack the symbiotic relations between providers of security and justice.

A framework for analysis: unpacking symbiotic relations

When unpacking the linkages between entities, a range of possibilities exist. Realities on the ground in conflict-affected and fragile situations are characterised by a varied and fluid mixture of friction, competition, complementarity and collaboration between agents providing (and indeed threatening) various forms of security and justice.

As explained above, the whole gamut of entities usually coexist, sometimes with a de facto division of labour, but can also substitute for each other. In other words, it may be that societal actors are doing the work the formal institutions of state *cannot* or *will not* do, but with tacit approval and even some material assistance. This 'outsourcing', and the nature of the 'sub-contract' varies, can be dynamic and often ambiguous or obscured in the formal procedural accounts of governments or their international sponsors (Lund 2006, p. 688).

The ecology of these arrangements is neatly captured by the concept of *symbiosis*. Originating in the biological sciences but increasingly applied to the study of human society, *sym-bio-sis* refers to the state of entities 'living together'. For the purposes of this framework, symbiosis is understood as: the association between two or more dissimilar entities coexisting and displaying interdependence, each member receiving succour that may – but not necessarily – constitute a net benefit for them. The analytical framework that follows includes three sub-categories of symbiotic relations: (1) predatory amensalism; (2) parasitic commensalism; and (3) mutualism.[11]

Predatory amensalism

The first category relates to instances where there is a confrontational relationship between providers. A predatory/amensal approach suggests that one actor can only fulfil its objectives if it is able to undermine or degrade the capabilities and/or reputation of the competition. This may be an attack on a rival in terms of material resources but could also refer to a battle for socio-political capital. Such a relationship implies a significant level of incompatibility and to some extent an attempt at substitution. An example of this is an armed insurgency set on overthrowing an incumbent government and obtaining sovereign power. While such groups can provide protection and settle disputes for populations in the territory they control, the need for such services may have arisen due to its own act of dislodging or degrading the capacity of competitors to do so. That is to say, it provides services and engages with communities to the detriment of another, be that the central state or other non-state actor (Utas and Bøås 2013, p. 9; Bøås and Torheim 2013).

This form of relation can also exist where the central government becomes a predator, preying on societal bodies and (society itself) as politics becomes little more than patrimony towards a predatory elite exploiting masses for the enrichment in perpetuity of the rent-seekers (Mbeki 2014, p. 13). Similarly, entities beyond the purview of the government are often in competition over scarce resources – often social, political and economic capital – such that an amensalism typifies strategies employed by a range of community-based actors in pursuit of influence. Sometimes a strategy may be to emulate or mimic the approach of a competitor in order to draw on their strengths and sources of legitimacy.[12] The contest for authority is intricately linked with the tussle for legitimacy and a predator that can outmanoeuvre its enemy may gain both. In sum, the point with predatory relations is that these antagonistic relations do not necessarily take the form of an existential battle to the death. Coexistence is still possible, and actors will learn and adapt their strategies in the face of predatory behaviour by others.

Parasitic commensalism

The second category comprises relationships between providers characterised by sustainable asymmetry. In other words, the relationship is parasitic/commensal if one provider preys on and feeds off the strengths, and particularly the weaknesses, of another in the competition to be the most legitimate – but also just a viable – provider of security and justice. Importantly, the ecology of this relationship is maintainable. That is to say that the leaching of resource or structural support is either negligble or can be tolerated and endogenised by the 'host', which is substantively unaffected in a process of iterative co-evolution (McGlade and Garnsey 2006, pp. 3–4). Examples of this category often display substitution effects. For instance, one provider may have contributed to (even created) well-functioning and socially just communities, only to have their role appropriated by a competitor. This could be agents of central government harnessing the effective work of local actors and extending its territorial authority, vice versa, or indeed one societal actor (e.g. paramount chief) out-ranking and over-ruling another (e.g. village chief).

The parasitic category also captures those situations in which one entity cannot survive alone in its environment without the support and sometimes sustenance of another. For instance, while chiefs in rural Ghana derive authority and legitimacy locally due to pre-colonial governance structures, they are still dependent on the state (often via District Assembly men) for resources to improve basic services like health, sanitation, and education. Consequently, the chief may be fulfilling integral security and justice roles in the community, but the chieftaincy institution itself has been rendered reliant on the state for its continued existence. Similarly, in Liberia, successive governments sought to control customary authorities through integrating 'town chiefs' into more formalised local government, regulating their conduct through oversight by district commissioners and county superintendents appointed by the state (Government of Liberia 2000). However, co-option between central government and traditional authorities has worked both ways, with chiefs attempting to extract patronage from central government in return for their continued support and compliance (Sawyer 2005).

In cases of extreme criminality (e.g. murder) it is not uncommon for emplaced entities such as a Chief's court or elders of the secret society to be first responders.

Particularly, in more rural areas, these actors may be integral to investigating, gathering evidence and hearing elements of a case before it is transferred to relevant state authorities. For example, in Liberia the integrity of the civil-criminal threshold for customary courts often goes unheeded, and ambiguity reigns (Sandefur and Siddiqi 2011, p. 112). Thus, even in cases where the customary system is formally disqualified, it still plays vital facilitating roles in relation to the statutory criminal justice system (Kofi Annan International Peacekeeping Training Centre [KAIPTC] 2015, p. 6). Similarly, while high levels of vigilante mob justice are often assumed to indicate failing state law enforcement capacity and overall state fragility (Whitehouse 2013, p. 48) community watch groups working with national police forces to tackle armed robbery in the suburbs of the Liberian capital, Monrovia, represents a certain degree of acquiescence or even outsourcing of the monopoly on enforcing law and order.

This category therefore applies to relations where one entity may feed off another – even thrive as a result – often as a consequence of cycles of interaction, incorporation and co-option. This reflects the long history and perpetual process of hybridisation that occurs between the various actors involved in providing social order (Boege 2011).[13]

Mutualism

The third category concerns relationships characterised by complementarity. In these relations, various sources cooperate in ways that lead to mutually beneficial outcomes. Indeed, mutualism often refers to *obligative* relationships, in which entities are existentially bound to each other. In other words, providers coexist and operate together to the benefit of all and perpetuation of the status quo. Where mutualism pertains, the emergent security and justice landscape people experience on the ground will be characterised by certain synergies between various sources coexisting. Outcomes are co-produced through a process that draws on the web of inter-linked providers and 'marriages of convenience' where articulations of authority by one will reinforce that of another in tandem.

For example, the ability of chiefs in rural Ghana and Liberia to exercise authority can often depend on collaboration with a range of other actors. On occasion, a spell or curse on a litigant in a dispute may need to be removed before adjudication can take place in a chief's court. This would likely require the services of the local *witch-doctor* or *ju-ju* man. Similarly, if and when it is established that the dispute under consideration involves matters of a serious criminal nature (e.g. the spilling of blood) it may be that the interface between the community and the state – perhaps a district assembly man or magistrate – may be involved in escalating the case to the formal state criminal justice system (PBO 2014). On the flip side, disputes that are deemed fit for resolution within the community are also often transferred from police to local chiefs and elders to resolve.[14] Constitutional provisions often place the responsibility for the protection and support of traditional authorities on national government.

Even the secret societies in Liberia are linked to the formal bureaucracy of central government in a mutually beneficial way, with the Poro having status as a 'cultural society' to be 'protected' by the government of Liberia (Olukoju 2006). These sorts of provisions and arrangements make the relationships between key stakeholders in this domain obligative and are indicative of mutualistic relations.

Another example relates to the privatisation of public security. In many natural resource extraction sites it is private security companies that protect the mines and plantations. However, this outsourcing of public security to the private sector takes many forms. Sometimes the statutory authorities will acquiesce to the substitution effect or officially sanction it. However, these commercial guards often work closely with – and are sometimes even embedded within – national security agencies such as police or border control (e.g. Niger delta, see Abrahamsen and Williams 2010). Similar scenarios play out in the Liberian rubber plantations and Ghanaian gold mines (Kofi Annan International Peacekeeping Training Centre 2015). In these cases, notwithstanding their fluid and changeable nature, accommodative relationships are grounded in mutually beneficial payoffs.

These and many more potential partnerships for reaching security and justice outcomes – capturing varying degrees and forms of cooperation, coordination and co-production – speak to the significance of mutualistic relations in the recognition of comparative advantage as well as the perpetual (re-)construction of authority and jurisdiction. Many of the providers involved in the provision of security and justice-type services will exist in a mutualistic relationship with the institutions of the central state as well as each other.

The framework depicted in Figure 5.1 below – elaborating symbiotic relations and a range of strategies that can be adopted by symbiotes – sheds light on the nature and significance of the multiplicity of relationships between the range of providers of security and justice. Whether *predatory-amensal*, *parasitic-commensal* or *mutualistic*, the relations captured in the framework are the product of interactions that lead to intricate interdependence. This complex system of order is characterised by on-going processes of accommodation,

Type	Definition	Examples
Predatory amensalism	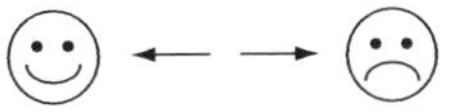 🙂 ← → 🙁	e.g. Armed insurgency
Parasitic commensalism	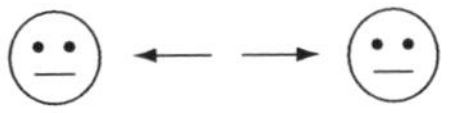 🙂 ← → 🙂	e.g. Community Policing Programme in Liberia
Mutualism	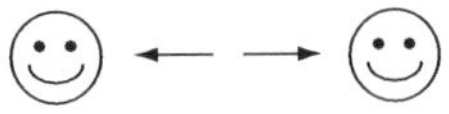 🙂 ← → 🙂	e.g. Chiefs vis-à-vis *ju-ju* man, assembly man and state law and justice system

Figure 5.1 Framework for symbiotic relations.

negotiation and exchange between and across different elements of the system. The feedback intrinsic to these symbiotic relations renders all actors altered by the interactions and their influence on each other. Through bouts of contestation or cooperation, entities exercise their agency, adopt strategies towards those they work with/around and re-define their own identities, as well as their perceived mandates and responsibilities in relation to each other. As a result, relationships between actors are in a constant state of flux – shifting and continuously renegotiated. Fluidity and malleability in response to interests, power and context dictates that the bonds flex and shift over time. This, in part, explains why these networks (hybrid orders) are not institutionalised. Moreover, it is these continual processes – in complexity terms, self-organisation and co-evolution as pursuits of long-term power and authority as well as the resolution of everyday challenges to societal stability – that lead to subtle new systemic patterning and substantively different forms of emergent order (Lentz 2006).

In sum, the various providers of security and justice and the realms they inhabit do not simply exist conterminously alongside each other. Nor do they resign themselves to 'endure' what is at times unavoidable but inconvenient overlap. In effect, they have genuinely symbiotic relationships that are generative of emergent and hybrid forms of peace and political order. This is not always transparent – indeed, often it is not. While certain entities may be formally delegitimised – and in extreme cases criminalised – by the state, the reality may be very different, with acquiescence or even active support and partnership the norm. Often the government and its institutional architecture is involved as much as an orchestrator, and possibly coordinator, of many contributors rather than a monopoly-wielding authority. While governments can be detached from their publics and even be seen as working against their interests, the linkages via other sources of authority – often more locally legitimate forms – can allow central state authority to hold the reins on an outsourced yet loosely centralised political authority over the territory.

Implications for research, policy and praxis

Relational perspectives and the framework presented here offer a number of benefits to researchers and practitioners. *For scholars* they provide analytical leverage and argument to push beyond the narratives that have tended to dominate discourse on peacebuilding and post-conflict statebuilding to date. On the one hand, it offers support to those who would challenge change theories predicated on unproven visions of a 'liberal' peace. On the other hand, it allows analysts to problematise reductive and simplistic critiques of the liberal peace approach that might have us romanticise the 'traditional-local' and see a clearer division between that and the 'liberal-international' than the empirical reality attests. The framework also has the potential to enable better understandings hybrid and emergent formations of peace in conflict-affected and fragile settings – that is to say, a systemic context in which all sources of security and justice are operating in some loosely, self-organised order, where legitimacy and authority are contested and granted from multiple sites, not simply captured in the idea of a state-society social contract, nor existential threats to it.

The framework and relational understanding of peace formation, therefore, promises to contribute to embracing the empirical reality. In other words, it offers a way of grasping the production of order and authority in post-colonial societies based on what exists and pertains to everyday politics. Such an approach allows for highlighting existing strengths and sources of resilience rather than applying a failure lens and simply identifying the deficits perceptible when compared with unrealistic (and often unrealised) visions for ideal liberal-democratic polities. This would require a move away from the hubris associated with reflections of western modernity towards a more accommodated, open and interpretive imaginary for political community and order. This opens up the space for, and could facilitate a reinvigorated debate about, possible formation(s) of peace that are more grounded in what exists on the ground as well as sophisticated thinking. Moreover, this space affords scholars the room to countenance a truly different imaginary for what constitutes political community and what forms of state and statehood could be possible. This is vital in an era where the 'extension of state authority' is increasingly part of the prescriptive lexicon of big international stabilisation and peacebuilding interventions (UN 2014).

These shifts may also be useful *for practitioners* who are in the business of struggling with these 'wicked problems', pragmatically implementing difficult programmes in resource-scarce settings while navigating rigid bureaucracies. Even modest amounts of fieldwork with practitioners make it clear that many of the experts engaged in security and justice reform on behalf of development agencies are very aware of the empirical realities (i.e. plurality of networked providers in hybrid social order). However, they lack sufficient *agency* to overcome the bureaucratic inertia and dislodge deep epistemological footholds to alter the way their organisations engage with those empirical realities – or do not, as the case may be (Autesserre 2014). Enhancing the awareness of all stakeholders about the presence, relevance and intricate interdependence of a myriad of providers of security and justice may be one way of supporting a sea change and surmounting structural impediments. The framework promises to facilitate this in two key ways.

First, it can enable mapping of the nuanced and dynamical symbiotic relationships between entities and draw attention to the way in which social order emerges from the local context in such settings. This may offer some ammunition for these experts who can, albeit only incrementally, inform and influence future policy prescriptions, project design and implementation on the ground (ODI 2012, p. 4). In practical terms, this means international agents undertaking engagement with a wide range of entities – engagement that is not wholly governed by understanding of these actors as 'spoilers' but rather as potential partners for peace. For instance, programmes aimed at 'formalising the informal', 'incorporating the non-state into the state sphere' and 'codifying the customary' (but also 'decentralising central government') can be aided by the framework's capacity to identify how entities are already related in ways that blur boundaries.

Doing so can reveal existent pathways that may make such 'harmonisation' efforts possible, while highlighting when this might be more difficult and implausible due to the long history of accommodation and contestation (i.e. hybridisation). Second, a clearer understanding of the relationships between the constellation of providers might allow for internationals – where appropriate – to support key local actors in shaping and transforming their relationships in ways that appear to lead to stability, resilience and enhanced security (Brown, Boege and Hunt 2016, p. 4). This is what Baker (2010) refers to as 'link-building not state-building', de Coning (2016) describes as facilitating self-organisation, and Oliver Richmond has labelled 'peace enablement' (Richmond 2014). Linkages that lead to greater mutual understanding and reflective exchange will nevertheless remain contingent on the will and perseverance of the local stakeholders.

Such breakthroughs may be slow to emerge or not be forthcoming at all. On the part of internationals, this will necessarily require more humility, patience and realistic expectations around what can be achieved. It will also demand more genuine valuation of, and engagement with, local actors and emplaced sources of knowledge in the iterative analysis and understanding of the context where peace formation is occurring.[15] This, in turn, may support a shift towards genuinely 'evidence-based policy-making' and away from the extant obsession with 'policy-based evidence-making' (de Waal 2016).

Conclusion

Some have argued for a post-biological phase in peacebuilding scholarship (Richmond and Mac Ginty 2015). However, it has been argued here that – whether stringently applied or loosely used as a metaphor – the ideas, concepts and language of relationality, complexity and symbiosis are useful in better understanding the nature of polycentric political and social order. This chapter has also argued that a relational approach to understanding the nature of governance in the post-colonial state will generate better analytical leverage and potentially practical approaches for those interested in appreciating and supporting processes of peace formation. It elaborated the need to move beyond the deployment of limited and limiting dichotomies that do not stand up to scrutiny and underplay the variation of the relations between entities in complex social systems. It has argued that it is the nature of the relationships between entities rather than a frequently fixed conception of the characteristics of those entities that matters most for understanding how (dis)order emerges. It therefore emphasised the need to shift away from the reductive binaries that are implicit in an ontology of entities to emphasise an ontology of relationships. It introduced the concept of symbiosis in its different forms (amensalism, commensalism and mutualism) into the peacebuilding and peace formation discourse as an innovative analytical framework for understanding how peace, security and justice emerge in these settings.

Shifting towards a relational ontology presents both promise and problems. In particular, such a move could have ethical implications and challenge established human rights standards while raising concerns around the plight of vulnerable and disempowered constituencies including gendered concerns. However, this is not an argument for disavowal or non-involvement of internationals in supporting conflict-affected populations. The promotion of relational peace formation must not be seen as an attempt absolve western donors of their responsibilities to support the realisation of peaceful societies in the post-colonial world. On the contrary, if relationality dictates that we are 'co-implicated' in the construction of one another's lives, then it might follow that we are similarly responsible for the well-being of those with whom we are interdependent. This is not, however, a call for a normative project. It does not promote any particular type or form of hybrid, emancipatory or post-liberal peace according to a new set of blue-prints. The normative commitment of such an approach calls for paying more attention and attributing greater importance to what exists locally and in the everyday experiences of the post-colonial subject. What it then advocates is a way of better analysing and understanding the complex relational orders that emerge so as to inform more effectively approaches to peace formation that include or value these empirical realities more highly.

The state will remain a critical piece of the puzzle and perhaps an indispensable part of the solution to security and development in post-colonial states, as in the rest of the world, for that matter. Therefore, it is important to grapple with its empirical realities and work towards enhancing its responsiveness and resilience. This work needs to be undertaken in the context of broader discourse and a body of research that seeks to re-envision the nature and role of the state (in Africa), including questions of reach, sovereignty and legitimacy (Miti *et al.* 2012). A relational approach to peace formation is not offered as a panacea to the problems facing the peacebuilding industry or the post-colonial subjects who continue to suffer from its failings. It is, however, proposed as an important corrective to existing analytical frames emerging from the critical turn in order to better understand and work with conflict-affected societies and post-colonial states. Making relationships the focus of analyses can present new insights about the nature and formation of political community. Doing so presents the possibility of countenancing substantively different forms of peace that focus on polycentricism and a more heterogeneous state as a source of resilience and strength, rather than applying a deficit-model concerned with identifying ways in which the state is absent, ineffective or illegitimate.

Enhanced analytical leverage through the framework put forward here offers possibilities for moving beyond well-made critiques of the failed state paradigm and liberal peacebuilding, highlighting ways in which theory and practice can better understand and engage with the empirical reality of emergent order after violent conflict and processes of peace formation. This shift, in turn, has the potential to inform incremental change in policy and praxis that may improve the outcomes of policies designed to restore peace and justice after destructive conflict. However, if new developments in international approaches to peace formation are to connote anything other than 'lipstick on the gorilla', peacebuilding discourse and praxis should be less about deconstructing and abolishing the linkages that clearly exist and underpin everyday order, and more about better understanding and facilitating these relationships. Such an understanding might allow for collective efforts to manoeuvre relationships towards more productive and less violent forms that generate more legitimate, equitable, efficient and resilient processes of peace formation. In turn, these processes would enable a more constructive engagement of discourses and praxes, and actors of peace, security and justice in the local context.

Such efforts at order-making in so-called fragile societies can be made under the auspices of a stabilisation and statebuilding paradigm, strategy and budget line – as long as 'the state' is more broadly conceived, beyond the confines of the conventional institutional architecture and Weberian notions of state monopolies over anything much at all. This might facilitate approaches that reflect the *Afropolitanism* emerging in some contemporary African societies (Mbembe 2007, pp. 26–30) – a worldview from the continent that is not stuck in the sterile dualisms that the policies designed to fix it seem to be.[16]

Notes

* The work for this chapter was supported by a grant under the Australian Development Research Awards Scheme (DFAT agreement 66442).

1 Regarding Ghana, see Aning and Aubyn, Chapter 2 in this volume. For Liberia, see Jaye, Chapter 8 in this volume. See also: ICG 2006, pp. 6–9; Robinson, Valters, Strauss and Weah 2015.

2 Many boast comparative advantage when it comes to accessibility, cultural appropriateness, affordability and timeliness.

3 The (post-)colonial state was never actually substantively anything like a Weberian ideal type but rather a shell and avatar of one, with a bifurcated arrangement between statutory and customary authority for elites and non-elites (Mamdani 1996, pp. 109–10).

4 For an elaboration of the concept of 'peace formation', see Brown, Chapter 1 (Introduction) in this volume.

5 While this is the usual business of ontological enquiry, this chapter understands an entity to be: 'something that exists as itself, as a subject or as an object, actually or potentially, concretely or abstractly, physically or not. It need not be of material existence'.

6 For example, procedures of traditional authorities. Indeed, these processes are often better understood and formally acknowledged than a so-called formal statutory system.

7 Sometimes articulated as the *local-customary/liberal-state* or *autochthonous/exogenous* dichotomy.

8 The appointment of high-profile chiefs to statutory entities such as the government's Council of State, and the provision of government stipends to recognised chiefs, speak to this hybridisation.

9 The Poro are known as a tribal 'secret society' that draws its authority from its respect for, and obedience to, the traditions of the ancestors. The Poro also upsets simple spatialities, transcending national territorial borders and having a Pan-Poro solidarity and community across the Mano River basin, which includes Liberia, Sierra Leone and Guinea. It functions as a system of social control, administering customary law and providing conflict resolution. (For further details, see Gibbs 1962; Fahey 1971.)

10 It is important to acknowledge that this possibility/access to discretion in decision-making can lead to abuse. This is an example of how emergent order is not objectively or exclusively a 'good' thing.

11 This approach draws on the work of: (1) James Cockayne and Adam Lupel (2009, pp. 4–19), writing in relation to organised crime entities in conflict-affected environments and (2) Johnston (2008) relating to the sub- and supra-national privatisation of security.

12 For further elaboration of some of these strategies, see Baker, Chapter 2 in this volume.

13 See Boege, Chapter 12 in this volume.

14 See Denney, Chapter 9 in this volume.

15 One particularly helpful example is the work of the Carter Center in Liberia. For details, see Flomoku and Reeves (2012, pp. 44–7).

16 Although the empirics provided in this chapter are from fieldwork in West Africa, the development of the analytical framework is informed by similar work conducted in the Oceania region. Therefore, while evaluations of its utility should be subject to further research and application to different contexts, it is not meant to be useful only for understanding post-colonial societies in West Africa, or even more broadly, in Africa, but in a more general sense.

Bibliography

Abrahamsen, R and Williams, MC 2010, *Security beyond the state: private security in international politics*, Cambridge University Press, Cambridge.

Albrecht, P 2010, 'Betwixt and between – chiefs and reform of Sierra Leone's justice sector', *DIIS Working Paper 2010:33*. Danish Institute for International Studies, Copenhagen.

Albrecht, P and Kyed, HM 2010, 'Justice and security: when the state isn't the main provider', *DIIS Policy Brief*, Danish Institute for International Studies (DIIS), Copenhagen.

Albrecht, P, Kyed, HM, Isser, D and Harper, E (eds) 2011, *Perspectives on involving non-state and customary actors in justice and security reform*, International Development Law Organization, Rome.

Albrecht, P and Moe, LW 2014, 'The simultaneity of authority in hybrid orders', *Peacebuilding*, vol. 3, no. 1, pp. 1–16.

Autesserre, S 2014, *Peaceland: conflict resolution and the everyday politics of international intervention*, Cambridge University Press, Cambridge.

Baker, B 2009, *Security in post-conflict Africa: the role of nonstate policing*, CRC Press, Boca Raton.

Baker, B 2010, 'Linking state and non-state security and justice', *Development Policy Review*, vol. 28, no. 5, pp. 597–616.

Baker, B and Scheye, E 2007, 'Multi-layered justice and security delivery in post-conflict and fragile states', *Conflict, Security and Development*, vol. 7, no. 4, pp. 503–28.

Bøås, M and Torheim, LE 2013, 'The trouble in Mali – corruption, collusion, resistance', *Third World Quarterly*, vol. 34, no. 7, pp. 1279–92.

Boege, V 2011, 'Hybrid forms of peace and order on a South Sea island: experiences from Bougainville (Papua New Guinea)', in Richmond, OP and Mitchell, A (eds), *Hybrid forms of peace: from everyday agency to post-liberalism*, Palgrave Macmillan, Basingstoke, pp. 88–106.

Boege, V, Brown, A, Clements, K and Nolan, A 2009, 'Building peace and political community in hybrid political orders', *International Peacekeeping*, vol. 16, no. 5, pp. 599–615.

Brigg, M 2016, 'Relational peacebuilding: promise beyond crisis', in Debiel, T, Held, T and Schneckener, U (eds), *Peacebuilding in crisis? Rethinking paradigms and practices of transnational cooperation*, Routledge, Abingdon, pp. 56–69.

Brown, A, Boege, V and Hunt, CT 2016, 'Understanding and working with local sources of peace, security and justice in West Africa – Ghana and Liberia', *Policy Brief* prepared for DFAT, University of Queensland, Brisbane.

Chandler, D 2011, 'The uncritical critique of "Liberal Peace"', in Campbell, S, Chandler, D and Sabaratnam, M (eds), *A liberal peace? The problems and practices of peacebuilding*, Zed Books, London, pp. 174–89.

Chirayath, L, Sage, C and Woolcock, M 2005, *Customary law and policy reform: engaging with the plurality of justice systems*, 2, http://siteresources.worldbank.org/INTWDR2006/Resources/477383-1118673432908/Customary_Law_and_Policy_Reform.pdf.

Cockayne, J and Lupel, A 2009, 'Introduction: rethinking the relationship between peace operations and organized crime', *International Peacekeeping*, vol. 16, no. 1, pp. 4–19.

Denney, L 2014a, 'Justice and security reform: development agencies and informal institutions in Sierra Leone', *Law, development and globalization*, Routledge, Abingdon.

Denney, L 2014b, 'Overcoming the state/non-state divide: an end user approach to security and justice reform', *International Peacekeeping*, vol. 21, no. 2, pp. 251–68.

de Coning, C 2016, 'Implications of complexity for peacebuilding policies and practices', in Brusset, E, de Coning, C and Hughes, B (eds), *Complexity thinking for peacebuilding practice and evaluation*, Palgrave-Macmillan, Basingstoke, pp. 19–48.

de Guevara, B 2010, 'Introduction: the limits of statebuilding and the analysis of state-formation', *Journal of Intervention and Statebuilding*, vol. 4, no. 2, pp. 111–28.

de Waal, A 2016, 'African academics face a huge divide between their real and scholarly selves', 10 March, *The Conversation*.

Department for International Development (DfID), 2010, 'Building peaceful states and societies', *A DFID Practice Paper*, www.gov.uk/government/uploads/system/uploads/attachment_data/file/67694/Building-peaceful-states-and-societies.pdf (accessed 6 July 2017).

Ellis, S 2007, *The mask of anarchy: The destruction of Liberia and the religious dimension of an African civil war*, 2nd edn., Hurst, London.

Fahey, RP 1971, 'The Poro as a system of judicial administration in Northwestern Liberia', *Journal of Legal Pluralism and Unofficial Law*, vol. 3, no. 4, pp. 1–25.

Fanthorpe, R 2007, 'Sierra Leone: The influence of the secret societies, with special reference to female genital mutilation', *A Writenet Report* commissioned by United Nations High Commissioner for Refugees, Status Determination and Protection Information Section (DIPS).

Flomoku, P and Reeves, L 2012, 'Formal and informal justice in Liberia', *ACCORD*, vol. 23, pp. 44–7, www.cartercenter.org/resources/pdfs/news/peace_publications/conflict_resolution/formal-informal-justice-liberia-accord-issue23.pdf (accessed 6 July 2017).

Frödin, OJ 2012, 'Dissecting the state: towards a relational conceptualization of states and state failure', *Journal of International Development*, vol. 24, no. 3, pp. 271–86.

Gadinger, F, Chadwick, W and Debiel, T (eds) 2013, 'Relational sensibility and the "turn to the local": prospects for the future of peacebuilding', *Global Dialogues 2*, Käte Hamburger Kolleg/Centre for Global Cooperation Research, Duisburg.

Gerth, HH and Mills, CW (eds) 1946, *From Max Weber: essays in sociology*, Oxford University Press, New York.

Gibbs, JL 1962, 'Poro values and courtroom procedures in a Kpelle chiefdom', *Southwestern Journal of Anthropology*, vol. 17, pp. 341–50.

Gluckman, M, Mitchell, JC and Barnes, JA 1949, 'The village headman in British Central Africa', *Africa: Journal of the International African Institute*, vol. 19, no. 2, pp. 89–106.

Gordon, E 2014, 'Security sector reform, statebuilding and local ownership: securing the state or its people?', *Journal of Intervention and Statebuilding*, vol. 8, no. 2–3, pp. 126–48.

Government of Liberia 2000, *The rules and regulations governing local government officials of the political sub-divisions of Liberia*, Revised edn., Ministry of the Interior, Republic of Liberia, Monrovia.

Heathershaw, J 2013, 'Towards better theories of peacebuilding: beyond the liberal peace debate', *Peacebuilding*, vol. 1, no. 2, pp. 275–82.

Herman, J and Martin-Ortega, O 2011, 'Narrowing gaps in justice: rule of law programming in Liberia', in Sriram, CL, Martin-Ortega, O and Herman, J (eds), *Peacebuilding and rule of law in Africa: just peace?*, Routledge, Abingdon, pp. 142–60.

Heylighen, F 2001, *The science of self-organization and adaptivity*, Center Leo Apostel, Free University of Brussels, Brussels.

Hughes, C, Öjendal, J and Schierenbeck, I 2015, 'The struggle versus the song – the local turn in peacebuilding: an introduction', *Third World Quarterly*, vol. 36, no. 5, pp. 817–24.

ICG 2006, *Liberia: resurrecting the justice system*, International Crisis Group, Dakar/ Brussels.

Johnston, L 2008, 'Glocal heroes: transnational commercial security companies in the 21st century', paper presented at a workshop on 'New Economies of Security', Merton College, Oxford, 3–4 July.

Kofi Annan International Peacekeeping Training Centre (KAIPTC) 2015, 'Ghanaian and Liberian Fieldwork Notes', Australian Development Research Awards Scheme Project, University of Queensland, Brisbane.

Kyed, HM 2015, 'Hybridity and political dynamics: the case of Mozambique', Paper presented at a workshop on 'Hybridity: History, Power and Scale', Australian National University, Canberra, 2–4 December.

Laffey, M and Nadarajah, S 2012, 'The hybridity of liberal peace: states, diasporas and insecurity', *Security Dialogue*, vol. 43, no. 5, pp. 403–20.

Lemay-Hébert, N, Onuf, N, Rakić, V and Bojanić, P 2013, *Semantics of statebuilding: language, meanings and sovereignty*, Routledge, Abingdon.

Lentz, C 1998, 'The chief, the mine captain and the politician: legitimating power in Northern Ghana', *Africa: Journal of International African Institute*, vol. 68, no. 1, pp. 46–67.

Lentz, C 2006, *Ethnicity and the making of history in Northern Ghana*, Edinburgh University Press, Edinburgh.

Leonardsson, H and Rudd, G 2015, 'The "local turn" in peacebuilding: a literature review of effective and emancipatory local peacebuilding', *Third World Quarterly*, vol. 36, no. 5, pp. 825–39.

Lubkemann, S, Isser, D and Chapman, P 2011, 'Neither state nor custom – just naked power: the consequences of ideals-oriented rule of law policy-making in Liberia', *Journal of Legal Pluralism and Unofficial Law*, vol. 43, no. 63, pp. 73–109.

Luckham, R and Kirk, T 2012, *Security in hybrid political contexts: an end-user approach*, London School of Economics and Political Science (LSE), London.

Lund, C 2006, 'Twilight institutions: public authority and local politics in Africa', *Development and Change*, vol. 37, no. 4, pp. 685–705.

Mac Ginty, R 2010, 'Hybrid peace: the interaction between top-down and bottom-up peace', *Security Dialogue*, vol. 41, no. 4, pp. 391–412.

Mac Ginty, R 2011, 'Hybrid peace: how does hybrid peace come about?', in Campbell, S, Chandler, D and Sarabatnam, M (eds), *A liberal peace: the problems and practices of peacebuilding*, Zed Books, London, pp. 763–83.

Mac Ginty, R and Richmond, O 2013, 'The local turn in peace building: a critical agenda for peace', *Third World Quarterly*, vol. 34, no. 5, pp. 763–83.

Mamdani, M 1996, *Citizen and subject: contemporary Africa and the legacy of late colonialism*, Princeton University Press, Princeton.

Mbeki, T 2014, 'Tasks of the African progressive movement', *The Thinker*, vol. 59, pp. 12–18.

Mbembe, A 2007, 'Afropolitanism', in Simon, N and Durán, L (eds), *Africa remix: contemporary art of a continent*, Jacana Media, Johannesburg, pp. 26–30.

McGlade, J and Garnsey, E 2006, 'The nature of complexity', in Garnsey, E and McGlade, J (eds), *Complexity and co-evolution: continuity and change in socio-economic systems*, Edward Elgar, Cheltenham, pp. 1–21.

Meagher, K 2012, 'The strength of weak states? Non-state security forces and hybrid governance in Africa', *Development and Change*, vol. 43, no. 5, pp. 1073–101.

Mitchell, M 2011, *Complexity: a guided tour*, Oxford University Press, Oxford.

Miti, K, Juma, M and Adar, K 2012, 'Confronting Africa's development challenges', in *The State of Africa, 2010/2011*, Pretoria: Africa Institute of South Africa, pp. 245–52.

ODI 2012, 'Non-state security and justice in fragile states: lessons from Sierra Leone', *Briefing Paper 73*, Overseas Development Institute, London.

Odotei, IK and Awedoba, AK (eds) 2006a, *Chieftaincy in Ghana: culture, governance and development*, Sub-Saharan Publishers, Accra.

Odotei, IK and Awedoba, AK 2006b, 'Introduction', in Odotei, IK and Awedob, AK (eds), *Chieftaincy in Ghana: culture, governance and development*, Sub-Saharan Publishers, Accra, pp. 15–24.

Olukoju, A 2006, *Culture and customs of Liberia*, Greenwood Press, Westport.

OECD 2007, *Enhancing security and justice service delivery*, Organisation for Economic Co-operation and Development.

Ostrom, V 1999, 'Polycentricity (Parts 1&2)', in McGinnis, MD (ed.), *Polycentricity and local public economies: readings from the workshop in political theory and policy analysis*, University of Michigan Press, Ann Arbor, MI, pp. 75–103.

Paffenholz, T 2015, 'Unpacking the local turn in peacebuilding: a critical assessment towards an agenda for future research', *Third World Quarterly*, vol. 36, no. 5, pp. 857–74.

PBO 2014, *Public perception survey on justice and security in Bong, Lofa and Nimba Counties, Liberia*, Peacebuilding Office, Ministry of Internal Affairs, Monrovia, Liberia.

Robinson, KB and Valters, C, with Strauss, T and Weah, A 2015, 'Progress in small steps: security against the odds in Liberia', *ODI Development Progress, Case Study Report: Security*, Overseas Development Institute, Londonwww.odi.org/publications/9191-progress-small-steps-security-against-odds-liberia (accessed 6 July 2017).

Peterson, JH 2012, 'A conceptual unpacking of hybridity: accounting for notions of power, politics and progress in analyses of aid-driven interfaces', *Journal of Peacebuilding and Development*, vol. 7, no. 2, pp. 9–22.

Randazzo, E 2016, 'The paradoxes of the "everyday": scrutinising the local turn in peace building', *Third World Quarterly*, vol. 37, no. 8, pp. 1351–70.

Reno, W 1998, *Warlord politics and African states*, Lynne Reinner, Boulder.

Richmond, OP 2009, 'A post-liberal peace: Eirenism and the everyday', *Review of International Studies*, vol. 35, no. 3, pp. 557–80.

Richmond, OP 2014, *Failed statebuilding: intervention, the state, and the dynamics of peace formation*, Yale University Press, New Haven.

Richmond, OP and Mac Ginty, R 2015, 'Where now for the critique of the liberal peace?', *Cooperation and Conflict*, vol. 50, no. 2, pp. 171–89.

Richmond, OP and Mitchell, A 2011, 'Introduction – towards a post-liberal Peace: exploring hybridity via everyday forms of resistance, agency and autonomy', in Richmond, OP and Mitchell, A (eds), *Hybrid forms of peace: from everyday agency to post-liberalism*, Palgrave Macmillan, Basingstoke, pp. 1–38.

Sabaratnam, M 2013, 'Avatars of eurocentrism in the critique of the liberal peace', *Security Dialogue*, vol. 44, no. 3, pp. 259–78.

Sandefur, J and Siddiqi, B 2011, 'Rights or remedies? Shopping for justice in Liberia's dualistic legal system', in Harper, E (ed.), *Working with customary justice systems: post-conflict and fragile states*, International Development Law Organization, Rome, pp. 109–26.

Sawyer, A 2005, 'Social capital, survival strategies, and their potential for post-conflict governance in Liberia', *WIDER Research Paper no. 2005/15*, World Institute for Development Economics Research, Helsinki.

Scheye, E 2010, 'Redeeming statebuilding's misconceptions: power, politics and social efficacy and capital in fragile and conflict-affected states', in Hughes, BW, Hunt, CT and Kondoch, B (eds), *Making sense of peace and capacity-building operations: rethinking policing and beyond*, Martinus Nijhoff, Leiden, pp. 33–60.

Thelen, T, Vetters, L and von Benda-Beckmann, K 2014, 'Introduction to Stategraphy: toward a relational anthropology of the State', *Social Analysis* vol. 58, no. 3, pp. 1–19.

Themnér, A 2013, 'A leap of faith: when and how ex-combatants resort to violence', *Security Studies*, vol. 22, no. 2, pp. 295–329.

UN 2014, 'Peacebuilding in the aftermath of conflict', *Report of the Secretary-General*, 23 September 2014, A/69/399–S/2014/694, www.un.org/ga/search/view_doc.asp?symbol=S/2014/694 (accessed 6 July 2017).

UNDP 2009, *Community security and social cohesion: towards a UNDP approach*, United Nations Development Programme, New York.

Utas, M and Bøås, M 2013, Thematic focus on Francophone Central and West Africa, *Strategic Review for Southern Africa*, vol. 35, no. 2.

Whitehouse, B 2013, '"A festival of brigands": in search of democracy and political legitimacy in Mali', *Strategic Review for Southern Africa*, vol. 35, no. 2, pp. 35–52.

World Bank 2011, *World Development Report 2011: Conflict, security and development*, World Bank, Washington DC.

6   Gender and hybridity

Exploring the contributions of women in hybrid political orders in West Africa

Nancy Annan

Introduction

In the context of this discussion, hybridity is a concept that highlights not only the contributions of different actors toward peace and their relationships, but also the interaction of different ideals of socio-political ordering. A conceptualisation of hybridity in gender terms, however, is lacking in the scholarly literature (McLeod 2015), which has focused primarily on the operationalisation of, and the contestations around, the hybridity concept, without looking at its gendered dimensions.

The concept of hybridity acknowledges the multiplicity of actors and roles in peace formation and shifts focus from the state as the sole entity in governance. Providing peaceful, stable and constructive governance under conditions of hybridity requires the collective efforts of multiple actors playing diverse roles. It is important that these roles be understood and analysed through a gender lens. For African societies the question of gender in hybrid political orders is critical. When looking at the web of interactions between various institutions and actors, such as police, traditional authorities, community groups and the judiciary, which all contribute to generating (sometimes competing) forms of social order, one question is seldom raised, namely: What limits and what enables women's contribution and authority? Interrogating the gender dimension of hybrid political orders will not only highlight the patriarchal socio-cultural and traditional norms, practices and beliefs that influence the roles of men and women in the governance systems in Africa, and their challenges, but also pave the way for appropriate strategies to be developed and implemented to make these systems more gender-sensitive. As Laura McLeod has pointed out, analysing hybridity from a gender-based or feminist standpoint 'is not merely a matter of "adding women" or looking at gender-related initiatives. Rather, a feminist lens means rethinking the way in which power functions to shape the world around us' (McLeod 2015, p. 49). This chapter does not seek to romanticise the importance of women in hybrid contexts but seeks to add to the limited knowledge and understanding of the contribution of women in such contexts. It posits that the sustainable provision of security and justice hinges on inclusive governance, in which the contributions of various actors, including women, are recognised and promoted.

Women are indeed important contributors to peace, security and justice in times of both peace and violent conflict. However, these contributions are hardly recognised and documented. This can be attributed to the fact that women's roles and contributions hinge on social and cultural factors that often create the notion that women do not have the strength, are unfit, or lack the capacity to lead (National Commission for Civic Education [NCCE] 2011). While this disparity is evident in most societies, it is highly pronounced in West Africa, where many societies are patriarchal. As a result, the lived experiences of queen mothers, female chiefs, female *Tindana* (earth priestess), community women's groups, girls' youth groups, and other actors within traditional governance structures and at the local level in West Africa are often overshadowed by the roles of male chiefs and community elders (NCCE 2011). For instance, the military bravery and leadership of women like Queen Adisa of Nanumba, Dokua of Akyem and Yaa Asantewaa of Asante of Ghana during the struggles for independence are hardly noted, nor are the important roles of the *Sande* (Women's secret society) of Liberia and the *Umuada* ('native daughters') of Nigeria (NCCE 2011; Asogwa 2015, p. 136).

Traditional systems of governance were in existence in West African societies, including societies which later became the independent states of Ghana and Liberia, long before the advent of colonial rule. Traditional governance structures were critical in maintaining the peaceful (co-)existence of communities. However, colonial and post-independence regimes introducing the western-style or 'modern' systems of governance tried to circumscribe, overthrow or co-opt traditional authorities and institutions, in some cases turning them into agents and puppets of the state (Nyei 2014). This substantially undermined the relevance of traditional institutions (Kessey n.d.). Of the Liberian context, Nyei (2014, p. 2) writes:

> The co-optation of the chiefs further strengthened the predatory and patrimonial nature of the central government and facilitated the erosion of any form of perceived parallel authority in the hinterlands thus strengthening presidential autocracy or the imperial presidency in Liberia.

Despite these attempts to limit and control their relevance and roles, traditional authorities and institutions are still respected and preferred as guardians of social order and providers of public goods such as security and justice. Moreover, the failure of modern state institutions to address contemporary peace, security and governance challenges has sparked a growing interest among scholars and practitioners in the role of traditional institutions in peace formation in West Africa and the continent as a whole. Precisely because of this wave of interest in the traditional and local structures, highlighting gender issues is critical for creating the space for a more nuanced understanding of women's contributions in hybrid political orders.

Using Ghana and Liberia as empirical cases, this chapter explores the contribution of women in hybrid political contexts, with a particular focus on their roles in the context of traditional governance and leadership. This analysis is based on findings from field research conducted in the two countries.[1] The chapter proceeds in four main sections. Section one provides a background of the traditional institutions and how they have evolved over time, as well as their functionality in relation to the institutions of the modern state. In Section two, the concepts of gender and hybridity are discussed in more general terms. Section three highlights the contributions of women in traditional governance and at the local level. Section four addresses some of the limitations that women face, especially within the context of traditional governance structures. The chapter concludes with some recommendations for gender mainstreaming.

Contextualising 'the traditional' in a modern state

Before colonialism, traditional chiefdoms co-inhabited the territory which later was to become Ghana; they operated largely according to agreed rules and modes of conduct. Traditional governance in Ghana can be traced back centuries before the arrival of Europeans in 1471 (Adjei 2015). Communities had their system of governance, in which chiefs, queen mothers, community elders and other kinship authorities worked together to ensure cohesion, peace, safety and order. They resolved family disputes, land disputes, connected the people with the ancestors (as a fundamental element in the generation of social order and collective meaning), and provided security and justice (Busia 1951). The arrival of colonial rule and the later introduction of the 'modern state' led to competition for power in which the traditional governance authorities were often seen as a threat to the colonial and, later, the state authorities (de Zwaan and Frerks 2011). For example, the British intended to suppress the leadership of the chiefs of the Gold Coast and expand British territory; they wanted to capture the Ashanti Golden Stool, which was, and still is, perceived to be the 'supreme symbol of Asante kingship and unity' (Adjei and Adebayo 2015, p. 105). As Adjei and Adebayo (2015) explain: '[T]he very existence of the Ashanti nation is rooted in the presence, sanctity, cultural, spiritual contagion, and power of the Golden Stool' (p. 105). Hence, capturing the stool would constitute a threat to the power, security and defence of the Ashanti people. In a speech to the Ashantis after the exiling of King Prempeh I in 1896, British governor Lord Frederick Hodgson reportedly said:

> Your King Prempeh I is in exile and will not return to Ashanti. His power and authority will be taken over by the Representative of the Queen of Britain.... Then there is the matter of the Golden Stool of Ashanti. The Queen is entitled to the stool; she must receive it. Where is the Golden Stool? I am the representative of the Paramount Power. Why have you relegated me to this ordinary chair? Why did you not take the opportunity of my coming to Kumasi to bring the Golden Stool for me to sit upon?
>
> (cited in Adjei and Adebayo 2015, p. 107)

These pronouncements infuriated Nana Yaa Asantewaa, the queen mother of Ejisu at the time, who was noted to have enquired how the Asante authorities could heed to such 'nonsense' (ibid.). Yaa Asantewaa's display of courage and defiance led the Asante leaders, mostly men, to select her to lead the seven-months 'War of the Golden Stool', also known as the 'Yaa Asantewaa War' from 28 March to late September 1900 (Adjei and Adebayo 2015, p. 108). Although the Ashantis were defeated and eventually became a British protec-torate in 1902, the role of Yaa Asantewaa, queen mother of Ejisu, empowered both men and women in her kingdom to fight against oppressive rule. This show of bravery indicates the significant role that women in positions of rel-ative power could play in the highly patriarchal power structure of Ashanti leadership.

After conquering many of the territories in the Gold Coast and finally adding the area to its colonies, the British 'established strategic, political, legal and military structures that weakened the powers of Chiefs and their elders' (Adjei 2015, pp. 85–101). With their supremacy established, the British intensified their control with the introduction of 'Indirect Rule' by Sir Gordon Guggisberg in 1927 (Boulton 2004). Even though the indirect rule, in principle, conserved the traditional system, it weakened the authority of, and respect given to, the traditional leaders, as well as giving the British power to remove chiefs who did not obey their directives (Owusu 2006). This was done in utter disregard to chieftaincy succession regulations (ibid.). Thus, the indirect rule policy, though it gave the chiefs some freedom to oversee traditional and cultural practices under the strict supervision of the colonialists, turned the former into 'stooges' of the latter. This consequently created tensions between the chiefs and their people, including, importantly, the educated elites who were fighting for inde-pendence against British rule (Boulton 2004; Adjei 2015). Consequently, when post-independence regimes were established by these educated elites, they also saw the traditional authorities as a threat; this further fuelled tensions and misunderstandings.

An expression of this conflictual relationship was the Chieftaincy Act adopted by the Nkrumah government in 1961. This Act reduced the roles of chiefs as rulers of their communities to merely custodians of traditional cultural practices (Kessey n.d.). Consequently, as the role of chiefs diminished in the new modern state, so did the position and influence of queen mothers, whose role comple-mented the leadership of the former. As noted by Beverly Stoeltje, before colo-nial and post-colonial rule, queen mothers 'exercised considerably more power' (Stoeltje 2003, p. 6). The tension has continued to date: the traditional institu-tions still feel that the state undermines their authority, power and influence. One respondent from the Ghana Police Service indicated: 'sometimes the Chiefs feel that we are here to take their job'.[2]

It is, however, noteworthy that the relationship and interaction between the traditional and the modern institutions has seen some progress over the years. Currently, traditional institutions are recognised and legitimised in Ghana's 1992 Constitution. As indicated in Chapter 22, Articles 270 (1) and 270 (2):

The institution of chieftaincy, together with its traditional councils as established by customary law and usage, is hereby guaranteed. Parliament shall have no power to enact any law which – (a) confers on any person or authority the right to accord or withdraw recognition to or from a chief for any purpose whatsoever; or (b) in any way detracts or derogates from the honour and dignity of the institution of chieftaincy.

(Republic of Ghana 1992)

The inclusion of this clause in the Constitution demonstrates the enduring prominence of the traditional institutions in the affairs of the modern state. This contrasts with the impediments placed on traditional institutions during the Nkrumah regime, as described by Kwesi Aning and Festus Aubyn (see Chapter 2 in this volume).

Similarly, before colonial rule, Liberia, then known as the Malaquette Coast, had traditional systems governing its 16 ethnic groups (Jaye, see Chapter 8 in this volume). Traditional rulers, elders and communities lived together, mutually bonded by systems of norms and practices. The *Poro* (male) and *Sande* (female) secret societies wielded power and authority across much of the country (Nmoma 1997).[3] However, the arrival of the freed slaves in 1821, also known as the settlers (and, later, Americo-Liberians) marked the beginning of changes in the country's social make-up. The newcomers introduced American practices and systems of governance that incorporated deeply exclusionary and hierarchical governance approaches. These quickly alienated and undermined the indigenous Liberians and the traditional systems of governance. As indicated by Ballah and Clemente (2003, p. 56):

Upon their arrival, the Americo-Liberians segregated themselves from the indigenous Liberians and colonized them. They believed that they were more civilized than the indigenous Liberians, since they had experienced western civilization and acquired western cultural values, skills and attitudes … the freed slaves that settled in the colony saw themselves as a distinctly enlightened group in comparison with the Africans they met on the land, whom they often referred to as 'heathens and savages'.

The indigenes were forced by law to 'convert to Christianity' and had to denounce their traditional religious beliefs and practices for three years' before they were given full citizenship (Ballah and Clemente 2003, p. 58). With the foundation for segregation and exclusion set, successive governments continued their bid to turn Liberia into a supposedly 'modern state' by further limiting the influence and power of the traditional authorities. By the 1920s, 'the local traditional units of clans and chiefdoms previously self-administered through traditions and with customary laws, gradually merged into the state' (Nyei 2014, p. 2). The chiefs were used by the state to enforce government policies, including taxation and recruitment of personnel for large foreign companies (Nyei 2014). Subsequently, the introduction of British systems of Indirect Rule further reduced the authority of the traditional rulers, whom the Americo-Liberians perceived as a threat to their political and economic agenda. As Amos Sawyer noted in an interview with Louise Andersen:

> Throughout its development, the Liberian state structure has manipulated indigenous political and social systems. It did so by appointing – and therefore deciding – who the local chiefs were; and by giving these chiefs the same kind of state functions as in the British system. The chiefs were in a sense turned into state officials.
>
> (Andersen 2007, p. 10)

This contrasts with the situation in Ghana. Whereas in Ghana chiefs maintained the right to elect and remove their leaders as per their traditions and customs without state interference, in the Liberian case the 1847 and 1986 constitutions notably bestowed the president with 'the power to remove locally elected paramount chiefs' (Nyei 2014, p. 3). This affected the legitimacy of the chiefs, as they were no longer seen as respected traditional leaders but merely a branch of the government (Gerdes 2013). This, by extension, had implications for the legitimacy of the state, as its control even through the chiefs remained questionable.

The continuous marginalisation of the indigenes and their traditional authorities resulted in increased tensions and bitterness against the Americo-Liberian elite, leading to civil demonstrations both by Liberians within the country and in the diaspora (Ballah and Clemente 2003). An example was the resistance led by the Kru, Gola and the Grebo to stop the territorial enlargement of the Americo-Liberian autocratic rule (Ballah and Clemente 2003). The two subsequent *coup d'états*, led by Master Sargent Samuel Doe and Charles Taylor in 1980 and 1989, respectively, which sparked over a decade of civil war that claimed many lives, were linked to this history of discrimination and civic exclusion. The often difficult and highly instrumentalised relationships between traditional governance and Liberian communities on the one hand, and the modus operandi of state institutions on the other, has thus been a fundamental factor in the protracted violent conflict in Liberia. According to Amos Sawyer, if the country intends to address its bitter past, it has to 'figure out how the system of "customary law", as we call it, can be sufficiently integrated into the formal rule of law' (Andersen 2007, p. 11).

Notwithstanding the introduction of a western system of governance, traditional governance continues to exist, helping vast numbers of people, the majority of whom the state institutions are often unable to reach, to address societal challenges. Whether they contribute positively or negatively to peace and security, the traditional political institutions remain an important agency for peace formation and peacebuilding. Many local populations feel at ease reporting cases to their chiefs rather than the police.[4] This is perhaps evidence of the respect and authority that chiefs have in their communities.

The main dilemma this poses, however, 'is to understand how traditional and formal systems interact in any particular context and to look for ways of constructively combining them' (Luckham and Kirk 2013, p. 9). Indeed, despite their differences, the traditional authorities and state institutions have been making efforts to collaborate in the provision of peace, security and justice. In Ghana, for instance, they collaborate in organising outreach campaigns and workshops, training, neighbourhood security watch, and alternative dispute resolution mechanisms.[5] The same can be said for Liberia, where chiefs worked with national and international actors to provide support for victims after the conflict (Sawyer 2005).

Gender and the discourses on hybrid governance

The concept of hybridity is fairly new in peace and security discourses. As discussed in Chapter 1, this concept is a way of acknowledging and exploring the combinations of actors and groups, including government and traditional authorities, which interact, engage and collaborate (or clash) in the pursuit of peace, security and development in post-colonial states in particular. Addressing 'hybrid peace', for example, Roger Mac Ginty (2010) describes hybridity as a situation 'whereby different actors coalesce and conflict to different extents on different issues to produce a fusion peace' (p. 397). Although it is a concept that highlights difference, complexity, interaction and enmeshment, its proponents seldom raise the issue of gender in hybrid political contexts. As Laura McLeod (2015) argues, 'hybridity is rarely conceptualized in a feminist way (by placing gender at the centre of analysis), and yet the concept echoes many elements of feminist scholarship relating to post-conflict contexts' (p. 49).

Indeed, including gender in the discourse on hybridity is crucial, as gender is of fundamental importance for the formation of any kind of political community or society as a whole. For instance, the moment a child is born, society through its norms and practices determines the function or role that the child should play in order to be accepted as a member of that society. In the same way, peace formation is inextricably linked to the roles assigned to men, women, boys and girls. Described as the socially constructed positions, roles and opportunities attributed to male and female, gender has been society's way of dividing and sharing responsibilities between men, women, boys and girls. It is often used to define the value and expectations placed on a man or a woman (UN Office for the Coordination of Humanitarian Affairs [OCHA] 2012). In hybrid contexts, these disparities along gender lines are more complex, and tensions more pronounced, as women and men have to negotiate the dynamics ensuing from the interaction and entanglement of the modern state and traditional institutions and their associated gender expectations.

The formal and informal rules, practices and norms have often been skewed towards creating dominant roles and opportunities for men, while placing women in subordinate positions. Not only does the modern state compete with traditional institutions to affirm its power (and vice versa), but within it, men and women also compete to establish their influence in governance, as well as in peace and security delivery. As Felix Asogwa (2015) explains, '[E]very social group in the community, including women, strive to give their existence some degree of relevance and to identify and defend their role in the process of social engineering' (p. 139).

The power dynamics often do not favour women, and social norms limit their roles and influence in governance. In most societies, including those in Africa, 'the male is the provider and holds the power while the women are more submissive nurturers' (Mahama 2014, p. 25). This places a limit on what a woman can do, the position she can occupy, and the career she can choose, while placing the man in a more powerful position with more opportunities. According to Girard (2015), in a patriarchal society the way '[w]omen are perceived within the context of tradition and culture might create substantial pressure on *how* women ought to behave, but it might also lead to expectations on what women *ought* to be interested in' (Girard 2015, p. 532).

This explains why most leadership roles or positions in both the modern state and the traditional realm are occupied by men. Chiefs, community elders and leaders in the traditional context in West Africa are overwhelmingly male, and executive bodies, legislatures and the judiciary of state are also dominated by men. With fewer women occupying leadership roles, the needs of women and vulnerable groups often tend to be neglected and enjoy lower priority, a position which Cynthia Enloe (2004) describes as the 'patriarchal time zone' (p. 215). Following on from Enloe's observation, many scholars have linked the continuous existence of gender roles and disparities to patriarchy and hegemonic masculinity. Sylvia Walby (1990), for instance, describes patriarchy as social arrangements which give men the opportunity or right to 'dominate, oppress and exploit women' (p. 20). Others such as Adrienne Rich (1986) see patriarchy as the 'power of the fathers' used to 'determine what part women shall or shall not play, and in which the female is everywhere subsumed under the male' (cited in Puechguirbal 2010, p. 172). To Connell and Messerschmidt (2005) and Elias and Beasley (2009), while patriarchy entrenches gender roles and relations, hegemonic masculinity legitimises the dominance of men in society (particular ways of being a man) and is often promoted through rigid cultural and institutional norms (Connell and Messerschmidt 2005; Elias and Beasley 2009). Arguably, these notions mirror the characteristics of most societies, including those in Africa, where sociocultural and institutional norms and practices create imbalances in gender relations and roles.

At the same time, the dynamics and scope of roles and positions of women varies in different contexts. In some Ghanaian and Liberian communities, women are respected and occupy some decision-making roles. For instance, among the Akans of Ghana, who follow the matrilineal lineage system, women are sometimes given a strategic position, such as being part of the college of kingmakers. By contrast, most tribes in northern Ghana follow the patrilineal system.[6] Like the Akans of Ghana, the Glebos of south-eastern Liberia entrust women with some leadership functions in their community (Moran 1990).

The above-mentioned gender issues reflect the realities of African societies and many other societies worldwide, albeit to varying degrees and with differing dynamics. Thus, it is important to study, understand and highlight these gender dynamics and how they shape and mould the roles, positions and perceptions of men and women, in order to create the space for developing new strategies towards bridging gender disparities.

Women's contributions in hybrid political orders

Women contribute in several ways to social cohesion and order in West African communities. Their role in the provision of peace, security, justice and governance, though limited due to societal norms, cannot be overlooked. In the traditional context, as well as at macropolitical levels, women have made efforts to consolidate peace and stability. In the state context, women have risen to become presidents, ministers and cabinet advisers. In 2005, Liberia elected its, and Africa's, first female president, Her Excellency Ellen Johnson-Sirleaf, who in the shadow of a volatile past has contributed to rebuilding, restoring and consolidating the country's democratic governance (Forbes 2013). Liberia is notably enjoying relative stability and rule of law after 14 years of civil war (Kamara and Kanubah 2013). Furthermore, President Johnson-Sirleaf led the passing of several policies, including the rape law and the establishment of gender courts, which provide justice for victims of sexual violence and stringent punitive measures for offenders (Adolescent Girls' Advocacy and Leadership Initiative [AGALI] 2012).

In Ghana, Mabel Dove became Ghana's first female member of the Gold Coast Legislative Assembly in 1954, and Her Lordship Justice Anie-Jiaggehe was appointed the first female Supreme Court judge in 1966 (Ghana Statistical Services 2006). Currently women occupy 37 of the 275 seats in parliament (Donkor 2016). While this figure is woefully low, it has created a platform for women to contribute to national government decision-making processes as well as governance issues.

In the traditional and local contexts, women equally contribute to peace, security and justice delivery, although this is seldom recognised and documented. They do so, for example, through everyday community roles, facilitating good relations and conflict management, or by exercising leadership roles. Across Africa, writes Mary Moran (1989), women have been '[q]ueen-mothers, queen-sisters, princesses, chiefs, and holders of other offices in towns and villages; occasional warriors ...' (p. 443).

These roles, however, differ within and among different communities and states. For instance, in Ghana the role and functions of *Obaahemaa* (queen mother) are well known. In Liberia there is the *Sande* group and other forms of female-headed posts such as the *maanaa* (women dance coordinator), *blo nyene* (women's president) and *gyide* (high priest's wife), who contribute to traditional governance and promote the needs of women (Moran 1990; Moran n.d., pp. 9–10). Even within Ghana, the concept of queen mothers is new in the northern part of the country, which is mainly patrilineal, compared with the south, which is predominantly matrilineal and where women are notably strong and occupy some leadership positions. It was only recently that the *Puanaba* and

Pognaa (local names for queen mothers in Northern and Upper East regions as well as Upper West region, respectively) were installed in some parts of Northern Ghana (Ghana News Agency 2011).

Every village and town in most of the southern part of Ghana has a queen mother. The queen mother is 'the embodiment of motherhood and is thus considered to be the mother of her clan in her town and consequently the mother of the chief' (Stoeltje 2003, p. 4). Queen mothers are also positioned as the 'second in command' (Nana Abayie Boaten 1996, p. 35). These women contribute substantially to the promotion of women's and girl's needs and undertake women's empowerment initiatives. They can, however, also select and remove chiefs, and in the past they sometimes provided military leadership where necessary (Adjei and Adebayo 2015; Stoeltje 2003), as illustrated above in the case of Nana Yaa Asantewaa, queen mother of Ejisu. Furthermore, His Royal Majesty Otumfuo Osei Tutu II, the current King of Ashanti, affirmed the important role played by the queen mother in traditional governance: '[T]he Queen mother played a critical role as the custodian of the "royal register" and the person who pronounced on the eligibility of conditions for chiefly office' (His Royal Majesty Otumfuo Osei Tutu II, Asantehene 2004, p. 2). In other words, in the Ashanti political leadership and most traditional settings in southern Ghana, the office of the queen mother has traditionally been vital in ensuring that qualified persons occupy the chiefly position to ensure peace, development and sustainable governance. This role continues today.

Among the Akans of Ghana, the role and contribution of queen mothers includes, but is not limited to: advising chiefs and elders; nominating chiefs for enstoolment; overseeing the welfare of women and other domestic issues in the community; resolving conflicts; leading rituals for community progress and development, as well as puberty rights for teenage girls; organising *durbars* (community gatherings) in their communities; and holding traditional court hearings (Stoeltje 2003). For instance, every Tuesday, the queen mother of Asante sits in her traditional court to mitigate domestic disputes between a man and a woman or between two women (Stoeltje 2003; Boaten 1996).

Another growing trend is the enstoolment of female chiefs in Ghana. This is still a rarity, as chiefs in Ghana have traditionally mostly been men. The female chiefs hold the authority as the supreme custodian of their communities and play the same functions as male chiefs. A case in point is the female Chief Nana Kofi Abuna X of Essipon, a community in the south-western part of Ghana. In addition to undertaking her chiefly duties, she resolves community and chieftaincy disputes, organises outreach and sensitisation campaigns to encourage children to go to school, and has established an education fund for needy but brilliant students in her community. As she indicated in an interview on 21 January 2015, the chief also organises door-to-door visits to ensure that children of school-going age are in school and promotes education in various other ways:

Fifty-five (55) years before I ascended to the throne, there was a lasting litigation, but by God's grace we have been able to put an end to it upon my sixteen (16) years as chief in this community ... I dedicated every Friday [to] visiting the various schools in my community and to encourage pupils and students; sometimes I give money and stationaries [sic] to the pupils ... I also established the Nana Aba Foundation, where I give an award to the best female students based on their senior secondary school results by giving them computers. This motivates and enhances girl child education in my community.

Her efforts have turned Essipon into one of the fastest growing communities in the west. It is interesting to note that even though she is a woman, she bears a male chief name, since the throne is named after men.

It became evident that the chiefs of other Ghanaian communities researched were also focusing on education. This serves as a reminder that those people who most strongly symbolise what are called 'customary' ways of life embedded in many communities can be simultaneously committed to promoting what is associated with the 'modernisation' of communities. Tradition or custom does not have to be fixed in the past, but can also be shaped around practical responses to real problems identified by communities.

In Liberia, the *Sande* secret society dates back to pre-colonial Liberia. This group provides leadership to women in communities, undertakes rituals and initiations of adolescent girls into adulthood, trains girls in the roles that women should play in their communities and empowers them with income-generating skills. KL Little categorises the functions of the secret society in four domains:

a) General education, in the sense of social and vocational training and indoctrination of social attitudes; b) Regulation of sexual conduct; c) Supervision of political and economic affairs; d) Operation of various social services, ranging from medical treatment to forms of entertainment and recreation.

(Little 2009, p. 200)

The contribution of the *Sande* has become even more important in Liberian society as the government has reportedly been taking initiatives to streamline their initiation schools, where girls are taught sanitation and cleanliness, 'as a medium for modern methods in hygiene' (Little 2009, p. 211). At the same time, some locally embedded NGOs are working with the Sande to encourage them to move away from practices that are violent and discriminatory (notably female genital mutilation, FGM).[7] There is also the *gyide* (wife of the high priest) who works with her husband to provide health care to their communities (Moran 1990). The *blo nyene* (women president) provides leadership for the women in the community, representing the women at council meetings and challenging the views of the male-dominated council on issues affecting women and other people in the community (Moran 1990). Furthermore, so-called traditional women (made up of elderly women in the community) help to mediate disputes. One female respondent in Liberia noted:

If you and your friend are walking together and someone insults you, you take the complaint to the traditional women. They will call the two of them and investigate, and a fine will be imposed on the person found guilty to serve as a deterrent. If the husband and his wife are in confusion, they intervene and make peace; they usually call upon one of the women in the community.[8]

Moreover, in traditional settings, community women's groups also organise to promote peace and stability. In Kalsegra, for instance, a community in the Upper West region of Ghana, '[t]he women compose songs to send messages of peace and abate conflict because they know that they will suffer if there is conflict. Also during elections, they sing peace songs'.[9]

Similarly, during the civil war in Liberia, local women's groups that included both Christian and Muslim women mobilised and organised outreach programmes, prayer sessions and peaceful demonstrations for peace (Gbowee 2009; Alaga 2007). Their efforts contributed to the signing of the Comprehensive Peace Agreements in 2003 by Charles Taylor and the other warring factions, restoring relative peace in the country.

The limitations of women's influence in the provision of peace, security and justice

As noted above, the patriarchal nature of most African societies often places limitations on women, in particular with regard to education, technical expertise, decision-making capacity, financial independence, and choice of career. This affects their contribution and roles in traditional and modern state governance. Ghana and Liberia are no exception. The social and cultural constructions of gender help to perpetuate these limitations. The social perceptions, beliefs, practices and norms used to determine who and what women or men ought to be, and how they ought to be treated, places pressure and limitations particularly on women, who are mostly relegated to a subordinate position. For instance, in Kalsegra, Upper West region of Ghana, it is believed that women are like children who ought to be groomed and disciplined when they misbehave.[10]

Most of the women are unable to voice their views or seek help when mistreated by their spouse or family, because the culture of 'not washing your dirty linen outside' prevents women from reporting mistreatment to the relevant institutions or channels.[11] Additionally, the notion that women are supposed to be married with children by a certain age further limits their contribution and respect. In Busua, a community in the Western region of Ghana, young women who decide to gain an education and establish their career before getting married are negatively labelled and disrespected in the community. Their opinions and contributions are disregarded, since they are perceived as 'not woman enough' or 'incomplete women'. One voice in the female youth focus group held in the community expressed that 'the people in this community make mockery of young ladies who are without children (have not given birth) by calling them "PAPAYEWA"' (meaning barren).[12]

Some of these perceptions and practices can be perpetuated by the women themselves. This is linked to their socialisation, which persuades them to uphold these practices and beliefs. Again, a participant in the female youth focus group in Busua said that,

> [m]ost parents, including the mothers in this community, normally influence their daughters to give birth [by comparing them to their mates who have given birth]. In actual fact, our parents prefer children [i.e. their daughters giving birth outside of marriage] to proper marriages.[13]

Such perceptions and ideologies limit the ability and desire of the women to seek 'education or any personal advancement'.[14] This is potentially one reason why women are still less educated in Ghana. The country records about 46 per cent literacy for women as compared with 67 per cent for men, while in Liberia the figure is 61 per cent of women compared with 86 per cent of men in urban areas, and 26 per cent of women as compared with 60 per cent of men in rural communities (Ghana News Agency 2013; Piah 2009). Most of the queen mothers are also less educated compared with their male counterparts, which makes them less competitive and knowledgeable and limits their ability to integrate contemporary governance approaches with cultural leadership demands and practices (Stoeltje 2003). Moreover, while men are culturally perceived to be the income earners and guardians in Ghana and Liberia, women are often seen by the society to be feeble, lacking the ability to lead and make critical decisions. In his study on the role of women in traditional governance, Nana Abayie Boaten I revealed that 'the male stool would not have been in existence in the Akan Traditional area, since it is a matrilineal society, if not for the fact that women have physical inferiority and are seen to be soft' (Abayie Boaten 1991, cited in NCCE 2011, p. 13).

Such a perception and portrayal of women's leadership capabilities serves as an obstacle preventing most women from attempting to attain such leadership positions, and the few who dare to do so are labelled 'iron ladies'. These perceptions are demonstrated both in the traditional and modern state institutions. The men in these societies find it difficult to accept women in leadership positions. When interviewed on 18 August 2013, the female chief of Essipon, Nana Kofi Abuna, shared her experiences when she ascended the throne: 'When I was made the chief, some of the men in the community disobeyed my orders and disrespected me in the beginning because I am a woman'.

Having been socialised not to take orders from women, these men found it difficult to accept the leadership and authority of a woman as their chief. It is important to note, however, that these limitations exist not only in the traditional setting but can be found also within modern state institutions, where women are still struggling to gain recognition in politics and key leadership roles.

Conclusion

> If Africa wants peace, truth and justice; if Africa wants to restore its traditional values of being each other's keeper; if Africa genuinely recognizes deep weaknesses in its developmental agenda, then I can only say that it is not too late to critically look for convergences between the modern state and the traditional state.

The above statement by His Royal Majesty Otumfuo Osei Tutu II, Asantehene (2004) is a clear indication that the traditional institutions not only exist but remain instrumental agents of governance. According to Enyinla and Edo (2013), any state government that disregards the influence and power of traditional authorities in peace formations, national unity and cohesion 'does so at its own peril' (Enyinla and Edo 2013, cited in Sesay 2014, p. 14). It is imperative for the state to recognise the influence of traditional authorities and find avenues for collaboration and interaction. While doing so, it is essential to recognise the role and contribution of women in traditional and local contexts, and to develop gender-sensitive strategies and programmes which will create the platform for them to be equal and effective actors in governance. Thus, in order to establish more gender-sensitive institutions for governance, especially in the traditional context, the first thing to do is to build capacity and empower both men and women with regard to emerging approaches to governance, at the same time finding ways to integrate traditional practices of governance that have proven to be useful for the maintenance of peace, security and justice into state structures.

Another strategy consists of outreach and sensitisation campaigns. Organising community *durbars*, workshops and seminars to discuss gender inequalities and their negative impact on inclusive governance will contribute to behavioural and attitudinal transformations that can enhance women's capacity and roles in governance. Related to this is the need to overcome the current exclusion of men from discourses on gender equality and women's empowerment. Bringing men on board is a necessary approach to changing the mindset of other men in the society on gender issues. Furthermore, state actors must work with the traditional institutions to develop gender-sensitive policies that highlight and acknowledge the contributions of women while dealing with social practices that impede the capacity and role of women in governance and other areas of life. Here, perhaps, there is something to be learned from Nana Kofi Abuna, who challenged the status quo by taking the reins as a female chief, breaking and overcoming the barriers and limitations placed on women in her community. State actors must also ensure that these policies address the needs of men, women and children, so that they can become functional members of their societies. The state and traditional institutions must develop and establish accountability measures to ensure that gender-sensitive policies are pursued in both the state and traditional contexts. Research and documentation of best practices, lived experiences and contributions of women in traditional governance will further sensitise the public to women's capacity in leadership. Developing gender-sensitive strategies and approaches will not only enhance the contributions of women but also create the space for traditional and modern governance structures to further converge.

Notes

1 The research topic was 'Understanding and working with local sources of peace, security and justice in West Africa' with a focus on Ghana and Liberia. It was a two-year AUSAID-funded project conducted in collaboration with the University of Queensland, Brisbane, Australia.
2 Interview with personnel from the Ghana Police Service, Takoradi, 18 August 2013.
3 These secret societies are reportedly still present and command authority in Liberia, although they are hardly talked about due to their clandestine nature.
4 Quoipa women's focus group, Liberia, 10 December 2013.
5 Interview with respondents in Takoradi, Kumasi, Busua and Kalsegra, Liberia, August–October 2013.
6 A matrilineal lineage system means that inheritance is through the mother's bloodline. A patrilineal lineage system means that inheritance is through the father's bloodline.
7 Interview with NGO (anonymity preferred), Monrovia, Liberia, 10 December 2013, 2015.
8 Quoipa women's focus group, Liberia, 10 December 2013.
9 Interview with World Vision, Kalsegra, October 2013.
10 Kalsegra men's focus group, 12 January 2015.
11 Kalsegra women's focus group, 12 January 2015.
12 Busua female youth focus group, 22 January 2015.
13 Ibid. The term 'proper marriage' means being a wedded wife or having a wedding.
14 Ibid.

Bibliography

Adjei, KG 2015a, 'Traditional Akan royal chiefly institution: evolving ceremonial protocol in chieftaincy at Duayaw-Nkwanta in Ghana', *Legon Journal of the Humanities*, vol. 26, pp. 1–18.

Adjei, KJ 2015b, 'The role of the chieftaincy institution in ensuring peace in Ghana from precolonial times to the present', in Adebayo, AG, Lundy, BD, Benjamin, JJ and Adjei, JK (eds), *Indigenous conflict management strategies in West Africa: beyond right and wrong*, Lexington Books, New York, pp. 85–101.

Adjei, KJ, and Adebayo, AG 2015, 'Colonial justice and conflict management: the case of Chief Seniagya and the Ashanti Golden Stool', in Adebayo, AG, Lundy, BD, Benjamin, JJ and Adjei, JK (eds), *Indigenous conflict management strategies in West Africa: beyond right and wrong*, pp. 103–14, Lexington Books, New York.

Adolescent Girls' Advocacy and Leadership Initiative (AGALI) 2012, 'The Rape Law', *Policy in Brief*, www.riseuptogether.org/wp-content/uploads/2016/09/AGALI_Policy_Brief_Rape_Law_-_Liberia-1.pdf (accessed 26 July 2017).

Alaga, E 2007, ' "Pray the Devil back to Hell": women's ingenuity in the peace process in Liberia', *Background brief*, Peacebuild, Ottawa.

Andersen, L 2007, 'Democratic governance in post-conflict Liberia: an interview with Dr. Amos Sawyer', *DIIS Working Paper 2007:20*, Danish Institute for International Studies (DIIS), Copenhagen.

Asogwa, FC 2015, 'Women's involvement in indigenous conflict management: an analysis of the role of Umuada in conflict management in traditional Igbo society in Southeastern Nigeria', in Adebayo, AG, Lundy, BD, Benjamin, JJ and Adjei, JK (eds), *Indigenous conflict management strategies in West Africa: beyond right and wrong*, Lexington Books, New York, pp. 135–44.

Ballah, H and Clemente, A 2003, 'Ethnicity, politics and social conflict: the quest for peace in Liberia', *Penn State McNair Journal*, vol. 10, pp. 52–69.

Boaten, NA 1996, 'Gender relations in traditional administration: the case of discrimination against women', *Research Reviews*, vol. 12, nos. 1,2, pp. 32–41.

Boulton, T 2004, 'Interactions between the local government and the traditional authorities: manifestation of justice, order and development in Ghana', *Paper 63*, African Diaspora ISPs, http://digitalcollections.sit.edu/cgi/viewcontent.cgi?article=1054&context=african_diaspora_isp (accessed 7 July 2017).

Busia, KA 1951, *The position of the Chief in the modern political system of Ashanti*, Routledge and Kegan Paul Ltd, London.

Connell, RW and Messerschmidt, JW 2005, 'Hegemonic masculinity: rethinking the concept', *Gender and Society*, vol. 19, no. 6, pp. 829–59.

de Zwaan, N, and Frerks, G (eds) 2011, *Gender practices and policies in a fragile setting: the case of Eastern Congo*, Peace, Security and Development Network (PSDN), no. 00030, December.

Donkor, S 2016, 'More women for seventh parliament of 4th Republic', *Graphic Online*, www.graphic.com.gh/news/general-news/more-women-for-seventh-parliament-of-4th-republic.html (accessed 24 February 2017).

Elias, J and Beasley, C 2009, 'Hegemonic masculinity and globalization: "transnational business masculinities" and beyond', *Globalizations*, vol. 6, no. 2, pp. 281–96.

Enloe, C 2004, *The curious feminist: searching for women in a new age of empire*, University of California Press, Berkeley.

Forbes, M 2013, *Lessons in courage from Africa's first female president*, www.forbes.com/sites/moiraforbes/2013/11/21/this-is-what-courage-looks-like-lessons-in-strength-from-liberias-ellen-johnson-sirleaf/#66983c3c57d5 (accessed 29 March 2015).

Gbowee, L 2009, 'Effecting change through women's activism in Liberia', *IDS Bulletin*, vol. 40, no. 2, pp. 50–3.

Gerdes, F 2013, 'The evolution of the Liberian state: a study in neo-patrimonial state formation and political change', *Arbeitspapier 2013:1*, University of Hamburg, Hamburg.

Ghana News Agency 2011, *Northern traditional councils – role of queen mothers*, www.modernghana.com/news/343874/northern-traditional-councils-role-of-queen-mothers.html (accessed 29 March 2016).

Ghana News Agency 2013, *Illiteracy rates among women still high in Ghana*, www.ghananewsagency.org/human-interest/illiteracy-rate-among-women-still-high-in-ghana-fao-54631 (accessed 1 April 2016).

Ghana Statistical Services 2006, *Women and men in Ghana: a statistical compendium*, www.statsghana.gov.gh/docfiles/Gender%20Statistics%20%20%28Women%20&%20Men%29.pdf (accessed 1 April 2015).

Girard, AM 2015, 'Gender and public choice in rural India: can female leaders really influence local governance?', *Journal of Gender Studies*, vol. 24, no. 5, pp. 528–48.

His Royal Majesty Otumfuo Osei Tutu II, Asantehene 2004, 'Traditional systems of governance and the modern state', Keynote address presented at the Fourth African Development Forum, Addis Ababa, 12 October, 2004, http://dspace.africaportal.org/jspui/

bitstream/123456789/10101/1/Traditional%20Systems%20of%20Governance%20 and%20the%20Modern%20State.pdf?1 (accessed 28 February 2017).

Kamara, S and Kanubah, J 2013, *Liberia's ten years of peace*, www.dw.com/en/liberias-ten-years-of-peace/a-17030374 (accessed 29 March 2016).

Kessey, KD n.d., *Traditional leadership factor in modern local government system in Ghana: policy implementation, role conflict and marginalization*, Department of Planning, Kwame Nkrumah University of Science and Technology, Kumasi.

Little, KL 2009, 'The role of the secret society in cultural specialization', *American Anthropologist*, vol. 51, no. 2, pp. 199–212.

Luckham, R and Kirk, T 2013, 'The two faces of security in hybrid political orders: a framework for analysis and research', *Stability: International Journal of Security and Development*, vol. 2, no. 2: 44, pp. 1–30.

Mac Ginty, R 2010, 'Hybrid peace: the interaction between top-down and bottom-up peace', *Security Dialogue*, vol. 41, no. 4, pp. 391–412.

Mahama, A-F 2014, *Effects of empowerment of women on role changes in Ghana: the case of Nanumba North District*, Department of Planning, Kwame Nkrumah University of Science and Technology, Kumasi.

McLeod, L 2015, 'A feminist approach to hybridity: understanding local and international interactions in producing post-conflict gender security', *Journal of Intervention and Statebuilding*, vol. 9, no. 1, pp. 48–69.

Moran, MH 1989, 'Collective action and the "Representation" of African women: a Liberian case study', *Feminist Studies*, vol. 15, no. 3, pp. 443–60.

Moran, MH 1990, *Civilized women: gender and prestige in Southeastern Liberia*, Cornell University Press, London.

Moran, MH n.d., *Glebo: civilizing the anthropologist*, http://wps.prenhall.com/wps/ media/objects/12330/12626747/myanthropologylibrary/PDF/NDS_83_Moran_92.pdf (accessed 14 March 2017).

National Commission for Civic Education (NCCE) 2011, *Role of women in traditional governance in Ghana: a case study of the three northern regions*, NCCE Research Department, Accra.

Nmoma, V 1997, 'The civil war and the refugee crisis in Liberia', *Journal of Conflict Studies*, vol. xvii, no. 1, Spring.

Nyei, IA-B 2014, 'Decentralizing the state in Liberia: the issues, progress and challenges', *Stability: International Journal of Security and Development*, vol. 3, no. 1, pp. 1–13.

Owusu, M 2006, *Self-government or good government: traditional rule and the challenge of constitutional democracy and development in Africa*, Department of Anthropology, University of Michigan, Ann Arbor.

Piah, J 2009, *Gender and statistics in Liberia*, Ministry of Gender and Development, Government of Liberia, Monrovia.

Puechguirbal, N 2010, 'Discourses on gender, patriarchy and resolution 1325: a textual analysis of UN documents', *International Peacekeeping*, vol. 17, no. 2, pp. 172–87.

Republic of Ghana 1992, *Constitution of the Republic of Ghana*, Ghana Publishing Corporation, Accra.

Rich, A 1986, *Of women born: motherhood as experience and institution*. Norton, New York, pp. 57–8.

Sawyer, A 2005, 'Social capital, survival strategies, and their potential for post-conflict governance in Liberia', *Research Paper 2005:15*, United Nations University (UNU-WIDER), Helsinki.

Sesay, A 2014, *African governance systems in the pre and post-independence periods: enduring lessons and opportunities for youth in Africa*, Center for Peace and Strategic Studies, University of Ilorin, Ilorin.

Stoeltje, BJ 2003, 'Asante queenmothers: pre-colonial authority in a post-colonial society', *Research Reviews*, vol. 19, no. 2, pp. 1–19.

UN Office for the Coordination of Humanitarian Affairs (OCHA) 2012, 'Gender definitions and mandates 2', *Gender Toolkit*, 19 December.

Walby, S 1990, *Theorizing patriarchy*, Basil Blackwell Ltd, Oxford.

Part II

Case studies in West Africa and Oceania

7 Hybridity and expressions of power, legitimacy, justice and security provision in Ghana

Kwesi Aning, Nancy Annan and Fiifi Edu-Afful

Introduction

There is growing scholarly interest in the study of local sources of peace, security and justice as a framework for strengthening responses to the numerous challenges confronting the contemporary state in the provision of these fundamental public goods. In part driving this interest, and in part emerging from it, is the recognition that whether they influence local governance processes positively or negatively, traditional authorities have a part to play in consolidating peace. While various bodies outside the state security and justice services contribute in different ways to peace and social order in particular localities or particular sectors, in Ghana traditional authorities, and the forms of customary social order of which they are a part, remain the most consistently significant across the country. Contrary to widely-held views, modern governance structures have not displaced traditional institutions; rather these institutions have shown strength and resilience, responding and adapting to different regime interventions designed to undermine their authority and power. Historically, traditional authorities have occupied a significant position in African life. In the case of Ghana, these authorities exemplify the many varied cultures, traditions, customs and values of people across the country and are deeply rooted in the earliest forms of societal organisation and governance. They continue to be substantial local providers of peace, justice and security in the areas under their jurisdictions. As Odeneho Gyapong Ababio II, President of the National House of Chiefs, noted, traditional authorities have proved to be resilient within the governance spectrum of Ghana (Darko 2003). As such, they remain a substantial actor in the conundrum of peace and state formation across Africa.

Colonial rule shaped representations and perceptions of African societies, as well as changing the ways governance operated within them. Pre-colonial African societies, however, could be understood as organised on the basis of a social contract whereby people worked together to collectively realise aspirations for peace and security. Procedurally, and despite marked difference across political systems, there has been a long history of significant shared understandings regarding the ideas, principles and worldviews underlying the political system in play and according to which power and authority were generated and exercised across that system. Additionally, there was a range of accountability mechanisms and systems for dispensing justice. Fieldwork in Ghana underlines that there continue to be relatively high levels of shared understanding within traditional governance systems in Ghana today.

As touched on later in this chapter, the impact of colonisation, as well as the nature of many independence struggles and of the entry into the international state system, gave rise to the complex phenomenon of a polarisation between 'modern' and 'traditional' modes of governance, but also their entanglement in practice (Udy 1970). Their interrelations are characterised by the gamut of cooperation, conflict and adaptation. Yet these dynamic relationships are often presented as more adversarial than driven by a shared desire to serve the governed. A conflictual relationship between the traditional and modern system of governance is now treated as an axiom in governance circles across the country, especially in regard to the provision of critical public goods such as peace, security and justice (Edu-Afful 2014). This approach, however, only exacerbates friction and lack of trust, meaning that tensions and disputes have become inevitable in day-to-day interactions. In reality, traditional authorities and state institutions influence and affect each other, shaping the character and experience of contemporary governance (ibid.). This need not be a weakness.

Despite decades of research on 'dual' governance systems, there are enormous gaps in our practical and conceptual grasp of the contemporary realities of power, legitimacy, justice and security provision in Ghana. These issues, however, are essential to understanding and (for Ghanaians) shaping the dynamics of political community in Ghana. They are also essential to effective responses to the myriad development and security questions across the country. Fieldwork has indicated many instances of cooperation in particular places or across particular networks, yet these remain fragmentary, vulnerable to circumstance and often dependent on individuals. To what extent do the many failed development projects, the persistently inadequate infrastructure, latent and actual security dilemmas, and the inadequacy of the police and court system to absorb all cases and uphold justice, emanate from the failure to recognise local or indigenous practices and to build ways of working constructively with them? In communities, traditional authorities assume leading, if not dominant, roles representing the people, and as such, are vital and strategic partners for development (Odeneho Gyapong Ababio II 2003).

There have been many calls for some form of partnership; many workshops, conferences and policy forums have been held to synchronise and encourage some form of consensus building between the traditional and the modern systems of governance. It is suggested here, however, that in several Ghanaian societies, the types of power struggle between representatives of the modern and traditional systems of governance do not submit to a formalised, overarching consensus as a mechanism for understanding and working with local sources of peace, security and justice. On the contrary, the challenges posed by efforts to formalise the relationship between the traditional and modern modes of governance have driven a re-organisation of the internal dynamics and practices within these modes that have created a barrier to the achievement of the supreme interest of an ideal 'African' state – a contemporary state grounded in, intelligible to, and answerable to its own population and their cultures, and serving their collective well-being (Galizzi and Abotsi 2011). Any compromise mechanism that does not place the interactions and relationships between the traditional authorities and other non-state and state institutions at the centre of the discussions will have limited chance of success.

Using Ghana as an empirical case, the chapter draws on fieldwork findings from two urban areas: Takoradi (Western) and Kumasi (Ashanti) regions; and two rural communities, Busua (Western) and Kalsegra (Upper West) regions. Fieldwork was undertaken over a number of visits to each site over 2014 and 2015, and through bringing a number of participants from different sites together to discuss questions raised during the fieldwork. The chapter examines how the traditional mode of governance has survived, adapted and even grown through reverse acculturation processes, in some cases gaining more influence since the early 1950s when Ghana gained self-rule and eventual independence from Great Britain. The interplay between the traditional and the modern systems of governance is discussed, particularly regarding peace formation. The multiple, changing roles of traditional authorities and the institution of chieftaincy in peace, security and justice are touched upon and questions of legitimacy and accountability discussed. The chapter explores how the interdependent, sometimes cooperative, sometimes conflictual relationships between traditional institutions and state institutions epitomise the changing dynamics of power and legitimacy and of justice and security provision in Ghana.

The traditional/modern governance interface

How do we explain the interface between the traditional and modern systems of governance in Ghana?[1] There have clearly been changes and adaptations of the institution of chieftaincy over time, and it is critical to appreciate the state rules and regulations that have historically governed this institution. In the contemporary context, it is important to see the layered interactions between top-down and bottom-up institutional processes and actors and how such interactions can shape a multitude of different relations. These interactions play out in the daily interfaces and expressions of engagement between the modern state structures and the traditional authority structures. As has been argued elsewhere (Mac Ginty and Sanghera 2012), using a hybridity lens allows us to capture what manifests itself as a complex and constantly changing relationship, in which no single actor, be it state or non-state, is able to maintain a totally independent choice of actions.[2] The substantial role of the chiefs cannot be overemphasised at this point in time when society is seeking to redefine its values, priorities, attitudes, and evaluating traditional and customary practices. Though these roles and functions of the chiefs are generally accepted, locating these functions historically in the legal framework of the colonial and post-colonial states demonstrates the tensions, and in some cases outright conflicts, in the state-traditional authority nexus.

Prior to colonisation, chiefs and traditional authorities personified the social and political community that they served; they were the guardians and custodians of the community's common heritage.[3] Kofi Busia captures the position and role of the chief prior to colonial rule as follows:

> A leader revered as the lineal successor of the founder of the state, its subdivisions, divisions and the village. His subjects felt beholden to him for their well-being. He was the custodian of the lands of the political community of which he was the head. He exercised judicial functions in relation to offences classified as hateful to the ancestral spirits and other spiritual beings, to which he offered prayers for the prosperity of the community.
>
> (Busia 1951, p. 196)

During colonial times, the introduction and enforcement of the *indirect rule* policy by the British in 1927 incorporated the traditional authorities into the colonial system of governance. This subsequently resulted in tensions between the educated elites of the then Gold Coast who were critics of colonial rule and aspired to independent statehood on the one hand, and the traditional authorities on the other (Boulton 2004). Explicitly put, 'the chiefs felt that the educated class, the intelligentsia, was only interested in gaining power, while the intelligentsia felt that the chiefs were pawns of the colonial abusers' (Boulton 2004, p. 11).

Such disagreement continued to escalate, with the chiefs demonstrating a lack of visible support for Nkrumah's 'Positive Action'[4] plan for independence in 1950. To this, Nkrumah reportedly retorted: '[S]hould the chiefs refuse to support the people's "just" struggle for freedom, the time would come when they would run away and leave behind their sandals' (Arhin 2001, quoted in Boulton 2004, p. 11).[5] This potent statement epitomises aspects of the tension that characterises the relationships between the protagonists of the independence movement and the chiefs. In practical terms, it is an abomination for a chief to walk without sandals in the Ghanaian culture (Boulton 2004), and Nkrumah's words meant that he was threatening to disgrace, and by extension de-stool, the chiefs if they continued to obstruct his plans. Subsequently, as a follow-up response to the defiance of the chiefs, the quick adoption of the Local Governance Ordinance in 1951 ended the British *indirect rule* system of governance and introduced regulations to limit the inherited powers of the traditional leaders (ibid.). After independence, the 1957 Constitution and the subsequent Chieftaincy Act of 1961, introduced by the Nkrumah government, further reduced the authorities of the chiefs from 'local administrators to being purely cultural custodians, with no means of enforcing their power' (Boulton 2004, p. 12; Kessey n.d.). These historical tensions dating back to the struggle for independence and the early days of independence have had an impact on the relationship between the state and traditional authorities until today. On the other hand, it has to be acknowledged that all subsequent post-independence constitutions have recognised the functional utility of chiefs. According to Ray, successive governments struggled to:

find the optimum relationship with traditional authority, often by adjusting formally the governmental powers and authority that the post-colonial state believed it was granting to traditional leaders. These adjustments were formally manifested through a variety of legislative and constitutional instruments ranging from ordinances and laws to constitutions. Also, the post-colonial state in Ghana has attempted in part to incorporate traditional leaders by creating the House of Chiefs system which operates from the national or state level to the regions and localities.

(Ray 2003, p. 88)

Following Ray's argument, two concurrent dynamics can be identified. First, that real power and authority is vested in the modern state and its institutions. Second, there is recognition that traditional leaders also hold considerable legitimacy, power and authority. This duality is epitomised by the constitutional provisions of 1957, 1960, 1969 and 1979, and the Fourth Republican Constitution of 1992. For the purposes of this chapter, emphasis will be placed on the 1992 Constitution to examine the manner in which the relations between the modern state and traditional institutions have been spelt out.

Chieftaincy – resurgent, legitimate and effective

It has been argued that in Ghana and elsewhere, there is either 'a renewed interest in chieftaincy' (Ubink 2007, p. 123), and in some cases the concept of a 'resurgent heritage' (Owusu-Sarpong 2003) has been introduced, or there is a recognition of 'a resurgence of traditional authorities, who have had their institutions guaranteed and are encouraged to actively promote and facilitate the objectives of decentralization with grassroots level socio-political and economic development' (Englebert 2002, p. 52; Stacey n.d.). While the arguments about a resurgence of traditional power are worthy of note, the reasons given for this development raise more questions than answers. In the literature, several core explanatory frameworks are provided for this development. First, there is the argument put forward by Kyed and Buur concerning a supposed bottom-up coercion leading to the augmentation of the political standing of chiefs (Kyed and Buur 2006). Furthermore, there is the argument that chiefs have virtually appropriated spatial authority in an unofficial manner to implement state activities. There is also the perspective that a top-down process has occurred in which 'a reincorporation of chiefs into state hierarchies' is taking place (Stacey n.d., p. 2).

Elsewhere, 'renewal' and 'resurgence' have been explained as representing a response to the 1990s demand for structural adjustment programmes (SAPs), which gave prominence to 'a small state' with its attendant stipulations. As a result, such developments 'created an increased space for the involvement of traditional authorities in law enforcement, dispute resolution ... [and that this] enlarged distance between people and the state facilitated the resurgence of tradition as an alternative mode of identification' (Englebert 2002, p. 60). While there is no doubt that the period of structural adjustment programmes (SAPs) in the 1980s resulted in a dwindling of state capacity, to link that process to a resurgence of tradition as a mode of identification in our view demonstrates a disturbing ahistoricity about the role and functionality of chieftaincy. Such an argument will be challenged based on the empirical cases in this chapter.

However, there are other more realistic explanations for this legitimacy that are not linked to the failed, weak or fragile state literature. To give just one example for the authority and legitimacy of traditional authorities in Ghana today: As recently as 2016, the national youth organiser of a major political party in Ghana was fined two sheep, two bottles of schnapps and GHS 200 cash by the Mankranso Traditional Authority in Ashanti region for casting a spell or curse (which was against the decree of the traditional authority) on an official of the Electoral Commission (EC) (Boateng 2016, p. 3). In recognition of the power and authority of the traditional leaders and respect for tradition, the offender appeared before the traditional court (upon summons by the traditional authorities), apologising for the misconduct and paying the fine (ibid.). This demonstrates that even political personalities who are representatives of the modern state respect traditional authorities, recognising their power and control, and accepting their position, significance and role. It is a clear indication of the persistent legitimacy of traditional governance institutions, in particular the chiefs.

Legitimacy is one of the major concerns in the hybridity discourse. What makes traditional authorities legitimate and who determines their legitimacy are some of the issues often highlighted. In Ghana, the legitimacy of traditional authorities is derived from three sources. A first pathway to legitimacy is through the *stool, skin* or throne, which is a symbol of authority of the ruler. All traditional leaders, family heads, and lineages have stools (Adjei 2015). For the Ashanti kingdom in Ghana, the *Golden Stool* (or Sika 'dwa), which was conjured by the High Priest of the Ashanti State, Okomfo Anokye, has been the symbol of political authority for centuries, defining the identity, unity and strength of the Ashanti people (Hagan 1968; Adjei and Adebayo 2015). The Golden Stool legitimises the authority of any Asantehene who is enstooled in accordance with Ashanti customs and traditions. As a result, any disloyalty on the part of sub-chiefs and Ashanti people against the Asantehene is considered an unacceptable act with possible punishment by the custodians of the Stool. During the 80th celebration of the Ashanti Confederacy in February 2015, the Asantehene, His Royal Majesty Otumfuo Osei Tutu II, lamented the disloyalty of some of his chiefs towards his leadership and warned them of the consequences of such action. He reportedly stated that 'some of you are not showing total and loyal service to me, but you should know that you are rather offending the Golden Stool and *it will get you one day*'. He further cautioned: '[D]o not underestimate the powers of the Golden Stool' (ibid.). These utterances of the Asantehene are a demonstration of the implied spiritual power of the Golden Stool to punish its offenders as well as hold people accountable.

Second, the 1992 Constitution of Ghana, the Chieftaincy Act 2008 (Act 759), and the Local Government Act 1993 (Act 462) recognise the role of traditional authorities and legitimise their position as the leaders of their people and custodians of traditions and norms. As enshrined in Chapter 22 of the constitution, the state legitimises the institution of chieftaincy and further prohibits any interference. Article 270 (1) and (2) categorically states:

(1) The institution of chieftaincy, together with its traditional councils as established by customary law and usage, is hereby guaranteed.
(2) Parliament shall have no power to enact any law which –
   (a) confers on any person or authority the right to accord or withdraw recognition to or from a chief for any purpose whatsoever; or
   (b) in any way detracts or derogates from the honour and dignity of the institution of chieftaincy.

(Republic of Ghana 1992)

Third, the legitimacy of traditional authorities is drawn from the trust of the community members in their leadership and position as founders of the community. Because the traditional system has been in existence for centuries, communities understand and accept the governance and services they provide. As Adjei observes, 'A chief's legislative power is derived from his position as the legal embodiment of the community and as either the founding father or representative of the founding father of the community or kingdom' (Adjei 2015, p. 91).

This confidence and trust, coupled with the failure of the modern state to adequately meet the needs of the people, has contributed to the resurgence of chieftaincy in Ghana. The citizens have a closer, more trusting relationship with their chiefs than with state actors, since the chiefs are close to them, relate to their daily struggles and provide everyday security and justice that the state does not provide. For this reason, it is important for scholars, policy-makers and practitioners to find avenues to enhance their contributions to statebuilding processes.

To acknowledge that non-state traditional authorities today play an important role in the provision of peace, security and justice has to be the starting point for such an endeavour. These institutions are not only legitimate, but also effective.

Edu-Afful (2014, p. 101) provides an overview of the critical roles that traditional authorities play in governance. These roles include: settling disputes and managing conflict between individuals, families and communities; mobilising people for developmental projects; promulgating customary laws; maintaining law and order and ensuring adherence to values and norms; protecting and managing community resources, heritage and customs; disseminating information of social, political and environmental importance; providing the linkage between the community and 'outsiders'; and soliciting and initiating developmental projects from national government, local and international donor partners.[6]

Especially in land administration, traditional authorities also perform critical functions of administration, since 80 per cent of all available land in Ghana is vested in traditional authorities. However, the nature of land administration can potentially be a cause of conflict between traditional authorities and the state, as the state owns and controls the resources on or in the land – timber, gold, oil, etc. As a result, conflict can potentially arise over the exploitation and use of the land.[7]

Our interviews in Kumasi, Busua, Kalsegra and Takoradi confirm that the provision of security, dispute resolution and law enforcement is, to a large extent, in the hands of the chiefs. This is corroborated by the works of Kwame Boafo-Arthur, who argues that:

> there are many instances, at the rural level, where societal conflicts are referred, first and foremost, to the traditional ruler for arbitration. In most cases, it is where the parties are not satisfied by the judgment of the traditional arbitration system that the case is taken to court.
>
> (Boafo-Arthur 2003, p. 14)

Boafo-Arthur's argument substantiates the evidence provided by the Chiefs of Busua,[8] Kalsegra[9] and Dixcove.[10] However, in sharp contradistinction to these three chiefs, the decisions made by the Adum Chief, Nana Baffuor Addae Kese IV are final and hardly ever challenged.[11] Furthermore, the notion that customary courts are said to be popular and often resorted to as they are easily accessible, cheap, fast and comprehensible may not necessarily always be correct. On the basis of our extensive fieldwork, we see the need for a much more nuanced, differentiated, and locality- and chieftaincy-specific analysis compared with the expenses paid, the volume of work involved and the accessibility of resorting to these traditional mechanisms.

Issues of tension and collaboration

'Sometimes after resolving a problem that is brought before us, we find that some members of the traditional authority are displeased because they feel that we have done their duty for them'.[12]

This statement, made by representatives of the Assembly and Unit Committees[13] in Kalsegra (an arm of the state's local governance instrument in Ghana), demonstrates the tensions and overlaps which sometimes characterise hybrid political contexts. The multiplicity of actors and their diverse roles, coupled with the power dynamics of 'who is who and controls what', can cause tensions that could undermine the potential for peace, security and justice delivery. This is especially so in West Africa, where many of the states are grappling with post-conflict reconstruction challenges and the woes of infant democracies, as well as institutional frictions, and where misunderstandings and tensions between modern state and traditional institutions can become a burden for the recovery and development process. To give just one example: in Busua there were reported incidences of tension between the paramount chief, Nana Agyemang Badu Bonsu X, and the assembly member[14] over the beating of the *gong-gong*[15] to call for communal gatherings (Boateng and Schleef 2014). Customarily, the beating of the *gong-gong*, one of the symbols of traditional authority and power, is reserved for the sole use of the traditional leader in his role as the chief and a symbol of mobilising authority. However, the assembly member usurped that authority, using the *gong-gong* to summon citizens for different activities perceived as the exclusive preserve of the chief, an act which is acknowledged as unacceptable behaviour. This, among other issues, has created a longstanding rift between the assembly member and the chief, hindering the implementation of several developmental projects and programmes in the community. In response to this apparent challenge by a representative of the modern state to the authority of a traditional ruler, the Chief of Essipon, Nana Kofi Abuna V[16] from the Western Region, expressed her disapproval, saying: '[an] assembly man has no right to beat the gong-gong without seeking the consent of the Chief'.[17]

Such tensions exist not only between the chiefs and representatives of the state, but also between community members, the police, religious leaders, youth groups, women groups, judiciary, community-based organisations and local and international non-governmental organisations (L/INGOs). For instance, in most communities in Ghana, the police are accused of engaging in bribery and corrupt activities, which leads to questions about their competence in adequately providing safety and security for the people.[18] In other communities, they are referred to as 'troublemakers instead of peacemakers' (Annan 2013, p. 4).[19] The police on the other hand perceive some of the cultural practices and values of the community as an obstruction to the effective implementation of their role as law enforcers and state security providers. A case in point is the practice of the culture of *TIZAABOYEN*[20] (which means 'we are one') by communities in the Upper West region, including Kalsegra, to shield local criminal suspects from arrest by the police and subsequently from facing justice. A senior police officer in the region opined that:

> While the culture of 'TIZAABOYEN' is good, it also hinders justice as community members cover native criminals from facing the brunt of the law. They would rather expose outsiders who offend the law to the police rather than their own. These same people then turn to accuse the police of not doing its work.[21]

Although this cultural value potentially enhances communal relations, it also affects intelligence-gathering and police law enforcement, as community members are unwilling to give information on community offenders for fear of reprisals or being labelled a traitor.[22] Thus, community members are torn between fulfilling their cultural and communal protection functions and compliance with the bureaucratic processes, expectations and demands of the modern state institutions.

It also must not be forgotten that chieftaincy disputes are one of the major challenges to Ghana's hybrid political landscape. To this day, there are several chieftaincy positions which are not occupied due to litigations. The Ghana News Agency, a national news outlet, reported that in the Upper West region alone, about 10 paramountcies are vacant due to tensions (Ghana News Agency 2015). Furthermore, in 2014, the Ministry of Chieftaincy and Traditional Affairs recorded that about 106 chieftaincy dispute cases were taken to the court, and an additional 300 cases were resolved through an alternative dispute resolution mechanism (ADR) (Ministry of Chieftaincy and Traditional Affairs 2014). These data, however, by no means negate the relevance of traditional authorities and the important roles they play in building resilient communities and consolidating democratic governance. Rather, the challenge is to strengthen and promote interactions and engagements towards common goals. As Luckham and Kirk highlight, '[t]raditional forms of authority are not necessarily inimical to the development of rules-based political systems.... In fact, the challenge is to understand how traditional and formal systems interact in any particular context' (Luckham and Kirk 2013, p. 32).

Indeed, while institutional tensions may not be completely eradicated, finding ways for the various actors to engage and interact is crucial in advancing the resilience of political order. In Ghana, for example, the cultural values of unity and togetherness help to foster collaboration and cordial relationships among different groups irrespective of their differences. For instance, among the Akans, traditional concepts for peacebuilding and conflict resolution such as *Abusuadua, yentwa* (meaning a family tree which symbolises social cohesion that cannot be cut off); *Nkonsonkonson* (meaning unity and interdependence); and *ese ne teky-erema* (meaning the teeth and the tongue – which calls for peaceful cohabitation regardless of existing differences) encourage collaboration among various actors irrespective of the occasional tensions (Brewoo and Abdallah 2015, pp. 35–52). Similar local philosophies can be found in most sub-Saharan societies (Brewoo and Abdallah 2015).

Based on such cultural ethos, the modern state and traditional authorities and other local actors in Ghana have been exploring ways of adaptation and collaboration. One such effort is the establishment of the Alternative Dispute Resolution (ADR) Programme in 2005 by the Ghana Judicial Service to complement the effort of traditional authorities in the adjudication of justice. In practice, there are ADR expert teams formed in the various regions which include judicial officials, chiefs and religious leaders to settle cases amicably out of court.[23] The ADR programme has reportedly become very successful since its establishment, significantly reducing the burden of cases on the state court system. According to a representative from the judiciary:

> without the support of the chiefs, it would have been difficult to settle the loads of cases that are brought to us. We transfer some of the cases to the chiefs to resolve outside the court. This is very helpful to us.[24]

Between 2007 and 2012, out of the 22,004 cases mediated through ADR, 11,524 were successfully adjudicated. Due to the achievements of the ADR programme so far, it has been expanded to 47 other courts across Ghana, with the aim of extending the programme to the remaining courts by 2017.[25] Additionally, the government adopted its first ADR-specific legislation in 2010, Act 798, which works in tandem with the Arbitration Act 1961 (Act 38) (Adjabeng 2012). The unique and innovative aspect of this mechanism is the creation of spaces and opportunities for judges and magistrates to refer cases to chiefs, and vice versa.

Certainly the introduction of this programme represents an extension of traditional conflict resolution approaches where chiefs and community elders meet to resolve conflicts to ensure peaceful cohabitation.

Another collaborative initiative is the Neighbourhood Watch Committees that have been formed by youth groups and community members with support from the police to provide security for their communities. For example, in Busua, the committee which comprises community youth groups has been providing 'escort services' at night for their relatives and community members, against possible attacks.[26] This is a demonstration of how traditional governance approaches that do not only relate to chiefs also contribute to creating interdependent systems such as kinship and other neighbourhood structures where community members become engaged in the provision of peace and safety. There is also the *Crime Combat and Peacebuilding Committee* in Aboabo, a Muslim neighbourhood in Kumasi, which was formed to encourage nonviolent politics by the youth and reduce crimes.[27] In addition to these initiatives, the police work closely with the chiefs and assembly members to resolve security issues. One police official indicated that 'when a case is reported, we write a letter to them (the chief or assembly man) inviting the person against whom the case is made. They then inform the individuals and they come to us'.[28]

Interviews with various traditional authority actors suggest that chiefs also contributed to bringing about stability in their traditional areas through engagement with law enforcement agencies. Added to the above initiatives are joint trainings, workshops, meetings and networks for and between the police, judiciary, chiefs, youth groups, women groups and community-based organisations.[29] These measures create interdependent opportunities for collaboration that enhance the contributions of the various actors towards the effective provision of peace, security and justice in Ghana.

From the above, it is evident that the relationship between traditional nonstatutory institutions and the modern state is not always contentious, but rather, there are also multiple interfaces where mutual interests converge. Hence, it is important that these positive linkages and the interconnectedness between modern state institutions and traditional and other local sources are acknowledged and documented so as to strengthen their relationships towards an even more constructive governance.

The nature of international support in hybrid political contexts

Against the background of the war on terror, which over the last years has become the pivotal priority of most international donors, little attention is given to other relevant security issues (even if there are links to the war on terror). For example, the marginalisation of youths in communities such as Kumasi and Busua could potentially result in the mobilisation and radicalisation of idle youth to engage in terrorist activities; however, these seemingly non-threatening concerns are often disregarded by international donors. Apart from the excessive focus on terror, another explanatory cause for the shift in international develop-ment disbursements has been the fact that donor economies mostly associate themselves with modern states structures, often overlooking traditional or local sources within the states (Verzat 2014). Perhaps this is because the modern states in Africa tend to follow western democratic ideals (since their introduction through colonial rule), which donors are familiar with and recognise. Donors often do not understand how to engage with, and provide support to, non-state local agencies of peace, security and justice, given that they perceive security as being a function and preserve of the state as the overarching democratic institu-tion. Moreover, international donors are restricted by demands and expectations from their taxpayers at home, who also are accustomed to this state-centric view. As a result, the donors are suspicious of institutions whose values and notions are not compatible with theirs, and this consequently 'influences the choice between the options of directly engaging with, leveraging, politically supporting, or funding these institutions' (EEAS 2012, p. 1).

These factors have contributed to the increasing criticisms of international actors by local peace actors and practitioners for their limited or absent engage-ment with local peace agencies and the communities within which they operate (Moe 2011; Boege, Brown, Clements and Nolan 2009). In Ghana, the research findings highlighted this phenomenon. For example, of the two rural com-munities in which fieldwork was conducted, only Kalsegra had the presence of international actors. These were World Vision, an international NGO, and Azumah Resources Limited, an Australian mining company.[30] World Vision, for instance, is based in Nadowli, the district capital, and not located within the community. In essence, this means that there is very limited interaction between the local community and the donors, and the consequence is that the possibilities for collaboration towards peace, security and justice initiatives are limited.

Local peace actors also harbour some suspicion and mistrust concerning the activities of international donors. Representatives of the youth group in Busua indicated that:

> [t]he international NGOs do not have the right motives; there was one INGO which was here before but left after their project ended. In the beginning when they came, they took pictures of our children to solicit for funding for the children but the children did not see the money. The leadership was stealing the monies and parcels intended for the children by their overseas sponsors. This affected our trust in them.[31]

Such continuous suspicion raises issues of trust and transparency between the international and local providers of peace, security and justice. Addressing this mistrust is essential for future collaboration and support. According to Kumar and De la Haye (2011, p. 13), deficiencies in such support systems can be addressed if 'external partners can help bridge the real or perceived gaps between international norms and practices on the one hand and existing internal mechanisms for conflict management on the other'. It is imperative for the international community and donors to understand that the context within which these local peace providers operate, and the principles that guide their work, may not always conform to their notions of peace, security and justice, and as such, they require specific efforts to be flexible in order to establish trusting partnerships towards lasting peace and security. For instance, international funders must, as a matter of course and necessity, be interested in, and curious about, their new environments by making efforts to learn and understand the values or principles that guide the approaches and operations of local sources of peace and security so as to find compromises in areas of mutual interest. Despite the gaps between the international and local actors, interactions between them are relevant in contributing to peace, security and justice. Hence, there is the need to explore avenues for more engagement and collaboration.

The foregoing underscores that, to be able to contribute substantially towards sustainable stability in Africa, it is important for international actors to understand the multiplicity of actors which characterises African governance structures, as well as to be open to new thinking about the diversity of sources and providers of peace, security and justice.

Accountability: state and non-state mechanisms

The issue of accountability began taking centre stage in the 1990s when new and old democracies notably failed to deliver equitable service and account to their citizens, which contributed to the increase in internal uprisings, especially in Africa (Grant and MacArthur 2008). It thus became imperative for states to establish processes, standards, sanctions and norms that would ensure that political leaders and state institutions could be held accountable by their citizens and non-state actors (Grant and MacArthur 2008). Hence, accountability has become an avenue for legitimising institutions, as it contributes to state formation, stability and lasting relationships, as well as equitable and fair peace, security and justice delivery. Especially in hybrid political contexts, which are characterised by multiple actors and complex interactions, issues of accountability are crucial because they are linked to the distribution and utility of power (ibid.). As modern and traditional systems interface to provide security and justice in hybrid contexts, it is important to ensure that those who govern within both spheres do not abuse their power and that if they do, there are sanctions or disciplinary measures in place. In other words, accountability matters in both spheres.

For the modern state system, which is based on the Weberian notion of statehood, channels of accountability have been established in principle and design. However, the practicability or enforcement of these channels or mechanisms remains a challenge. For example, in the Ghana Police Service (GPS), there are institutions such as the Police Council (Aning 2015), Parliamentary Select Committees dealing with different aspects of security and justice, Regional Police Committees, and the Police Intelligence and Professional Standards Bureau (PIPS), which are meant to provide oversight and management of the service (Aning and Lartey 2008). In addition, there are also frameworks such as the

Police Service Instructions, Criminal Procedure Code and the Police Service Act, 1970 (Act 350), which outline the modus operandi of the GPS. Similarly, the judiciary have mechanisms such as the judicial council, the Ghana Legal Council and the complaint unit of the judicial service which address issues of misconduct by its officials.[32]

As can be seen from the above, the state has in place numerous mechanisms for accountability, but the key questions are: how effective are these mechanisms in ensuring that state actors are answerable to the people they serve? Are the people aware of these mechanisms? And do they benefit the populace, or have they just been established to suit and protect society's elites, with little or no practical utility for the needs of ordinary people? These are critical questions and must be comprehensively examined. One official from the Ghana Police Service indicated that '[a] lot of people are not aware of these mechanisms. It is mostly privy to the elite class'.[33]

The traditional sources of justice and security provision on the other hand, such as chiefs, may not always have structured formal mechanisms for accountability, but they are guided by traditional conventions and unwritten norms and processes that have existed for centuries. There are the elders of the community, for example, who ensure that the chief is performing his public duties according to the values and customs of the community and their ancestors. Additionally, there is the presence of the *Tindanas* and other traditional priests and priestesses, for instance, whose roles are to guide the leadership of the community and ensure that they rule according to the precepts of the gods.[34]

Moreover, the establishment of the national and regional Houses of Chiefs by the 1992 Constitution complement existing traditional mechanisms, addressing chieftaincy disputes and providing oversight over the activities of chiefs and other traditional leaders in the country. As a result, traditional leaders who do not conform to accepted behaviour and regulations can be held accountable by the following bodies, as illustrated in Figure 7.1.

These mechanisms help to build stronger relationships between the chiefs and their communities, strengthen interactions among various chiefs, affirm their legitimacy, and enhance interactions and engagements between the traditional institutions and the modern state.

Figure 7.1 Traditional authorities' chain of accountability.

Conclusion

The foregoing demonstrates that Ghana is characterised by hybrid security and justice provisions, albeit not without challenges. This makes it relevant for scholars to understand and appreciate the dynamics of such specific contexts. To do so, there is a need for the recognition of the multiplicity of actors in providing peace, security and justice, as well as the realisation of the symbiotic relationships between them that create avenues and opportunities for mutual learning. While this multiplicity of actors may lead to competition for space, resources and power, it has to be acknowledged and appreciated that for the provision of security, peace and justice, communities rely on the plurality of service providers. Accordingly, there also is the need for a better understanding of *who* provides *what, when* and *how*, so as to prevent duplication and tensions. More importantly, it is also necessary to get a grasp of the credibility and transparency of the provision of such services. It is essential to understand the different perceptions and definitions of security by people and how they inform their choices of the type of providers. For example, for many people in the communities visited for the field research, security is more related to developmental concerns than the lack of violence. Most of the respondents highlighted poverty, illiteracy, land ownership, family disputes and lack of drinkable water among others as their security challenges.[35] Furthermore, another important lesson is the recognition that non-state, societal providers of security are a fundamental part of how security and justice work for people. Subsequently, recognising the imperfections of traditional authorities, and how their roles and actions could even cause insecurity, is crucial for finding ways for effective collaboration with state institutions and other non-state civil society actors for the provision of security and justice.

Moreover, there is no doubt that customary or traditional security actors do matter and perform critical functions in the daily lives of many people, and that this occurs in a wide range of different contexts. While the utility of such security provision has to be acknowledged, questions remain about its effectiveness, the respect for human rights, sustainability and so on. Therefore, according to Luckham and Kirk, hybridity

> should not be seen as a concept in search of a pleasing theory of the traditional. Rather it is an analytical lens that explicitly challenges reductionist positions by focusing on the interactions that make talking of, let alone reverting to, supposedly traditional governance arrangements impossible.
>
> (Luckham and Kirk 2013, p. 12)

Beyond challenging such positions and ideologies, the notion of hybridity allows us to focus on the layered connections and interactions between locally provided security and justice and that of the state. Thus, creating an effective, legitimate and functional system of provision of security, peace and justice, based on the hybridity of political order, cannot be the work of one group or set of actors;

rather it has to be a collaborative effort of a plethora of different types of actors, be they state or non-state (Nkuuhe 2006).

Notes

1 While there are different forms of traditional authority – see Aning and Aubyn, Chapter 2 in this volume – here we are focussing on the dominant, chiefly systems.

2 Mac Ginty's and Sanghera's work on 'hybridity' provides the lens through which the complex and layered relationships between the modern state actors and non-state actors will be examined. According to Mac Ginty and Sanghera, 'the concept of hybridity encourages us to look beyond the state and institution centric analyses and instead see a fuller cohort of actors including local actors and those not on the national stage' (Mac Ginty and Sanghera 2012, p. 4).

3 For more on the traditional structures of governance in pre-colonial times, see Aning and Aubyn, Chapter 2 in this volume.

4 A nonviolent campaign strategy initiated by Nkrumah involving nonviolent protests, strikes, and non-cooperation with the British colonial authorities.

5 It is an abomination for a chief to walk without sandals in the Ghanaian culture. In other words, Nkrumah was threatening to disgrace the chiefs if they continued to revolt against his plans.

6 Interviews with several chiefs corroborated these points. See, for example transcripts of interviews with Baffuor Agyei Kesse IV, Adumhene, Kumasi, 24–27 August 2014.

7 This can be a potential source of conflict in terms of the distribution of land and the signing of contracts for the development of such resources. Therefore, while a formal and legal contract may be signed by state authorities with respect to the usage of such land, it is critical that there is also a social licence which links an investor and the community within which such a contract is to be executed. See, for example interviews in Kalsegra with Azumah Resources Ltd, Nadowli, 18 November 2013.

8 See transcripts of interviews with Nana Badu Bonsu X, Paramount Chief of the Ahanta Traditional Area, 14 August 2013, p. 3.

9 See transcript of interview report: Focus Group interview with Tindana and Men's Group, Kalsegra, Nadowli, 17 November 2013, p. 6.

10 See transcript of interview with the Paramount Chief of Dixcove, Nana Kwesi Agyeman IX, on 13 August 2013, pp. 8ff.

11 This point was also reiterated by Okatakyie Amanfie VII, the Paramount Chief of Asebu Traditional Area in the Central Region, in an interview in Kumasi, 27 August 2014.

12 Interview with Assembly Member and Unit Committee, Kalsegra, 18 November 2013.

13 In every community in Ghana, according to the local government system of governance, there is a Metropolitan/Municipal/District Assembly, a Town/Zonal/Area Council, and Unit Committees. District Assemblies in Ghana are either metropolitan (population over 250,000); municipal (population over 95,000); or district (population 75,000 and over). Unit Committees are the lowest group on the governance structure, with five members each.

14 A representative of the state under the local governance system who serves as an intermediate between the community/people and the state. He/she is sometimes called 'Assembly Man' or 'Assembly Woman'.

15 The *gong-gong* is a symbol of the authority of traditional leaders in Ghana, which they use to gather their people for communal activities. When it is beaten, all community members must obey, as going against it will be a sign of disrespect to authority of the chief.

16 She is a female chief but has a male stool name as per the tradition.

17 Ibid.
18 Interview with representative of World Vision, Nadowli, Upper West Region, 18 November 2013.
19 See also transcripts of interviews in Kalsegra, 2013.
20 It is the belief that community members should resolve matters among themselves without an outsider. Thus, whenever they have problems, the community members prefer to go to the chief, elders, family heads or other local authorities before approaching the police or court as a last resort when all other attempts fail.
21 See transcripts of interviews with representatives at the Regional Police Headquarters, Wa, Upper West Region, 18 November 2013.
22 Interview with representatives at the Regional Police Headquarters, Wa, Upper West Region, 12 January 2015.
23 Interview with representatives of the Ghana Judicial Service, Western Regional Office, Sekondi, 15 August 2013.
24 Interview with the regional Supervising High Court Judge, Sekondi-Takoradi, Western Region, 2013.
25 Ibid.
26 See transcript of interview with youth group in Busua, 12 August 2013.
27 Ibid. Also see transcript of interview with Asawase District Police, Kumasi, 26 November 2013.
28 Interview with representatives from the District Police Office, Nadowli, Upper West Region, 19 November 2013.
29 See transcripts of interviews in Busua, Takoradi, Kumasi and Kalsegra, 2013.
30 See transcript of interview with Assembly Member and Unit Committee Members, Kalsegra, 18 November 2013.
31 Interview with Busua Youth Group, August 2014.
32 Interview with official from the Ghana Judicial Service, Takoradi, 15 August 2013.
33 Interview with representatives from the district police unit, Kwesimintsim, Takoradi, 13 August 2013.
34 Interview with Community elders in Kalsegra and Busua. 2013. The traditional priests and priestesses are a kind of sorcerer who advise the chief of the demands, expectations and sometimes punishments (when there is an offence or taboo committed) of the gods.
35 See transcripts of interviews in Busua, Takoradi, Kumasi, Kalsegra, 2013.

Bibliography

Adjabeng, SM 2012, *An analysis of dispute resolution mechanisms in the corporate governance architecture of Ghana*, www.mediate.com/articles/adjabengS5.cfm (accessed 2 December 2015).

Adjei, JK 2015, 'The role of the chieftaincy institution in ensuring peace in Ghana from precolonial times to present', in Akanmu, GA, Brandon, DL, Jesse, JB and Adjei, JK (eds), *Indigenous conflict management strategies in West Africa*, Lexington Books, London, pp. 85–102.

Adjei, JK and Adebayo, AG 2015, 'Colonial justice and conflict management: the case of Chief Seniagya and the Ashanti Golden Stool', in Akanmu, GA, Brandon, DL, Jesse, JB and Adjei, JK (eds), *Indigenous conflict management strategies in West Africa*, Lexington Books, London, pp. 103–14.

Aning, K 2015, 'Resurrecting the Police Council in Ghana', in Bryden, A and Chappuis, F (eds), *Learning from West African experiences in security sector governance*, Ubiquity Press, London, pp. 19–35.

Aning, K and Lartey, E 2008, 'Parliamentary oversight of the security sector: lessons from Ghana', www.agora-parl.org/sites/default/files/lessons_from_ghana.pdf (accessed 27 July 2017).

Annan, N 2013, 'Providing peace, security and justice in Ghana: the role of non-state actors', *KAIPTC Policy Brief 7*, Kofi Annan International Peacekeeping Training Centre, Accra, p. 4.

Brewoo, S and Abdallah, M 2015, 'Exploring indigenous mechanisms for peacemaking in West Africa', in Akanmu, GA, Brandon, DL, Jesse, JB and Adjei, JK (eds), *Indigenous conflict management strategies in West Africa*, Lexington Books, London, pp. 35–52.

Boafo-Arthur, K 2003, 'Chieftaincy in Ghana: challenges and prospects in the 21st century', *African and Asian Studies*, vol. 2, no. 2, pp. 125–53.

Boateng, JK 2016, 'Youth organizer fined for casting spell on EC official', *The Mirror*, 30 September–6 October, Graphic Communication Group, Accra.

Boateng, M and Schleef, R 2014, 'Understanding and working with local sources of peace security and justice in West Africa', *KAIPTC Report*, Golden Tulip Kumasi, Ghana, 24–27 August.

Boege, V, Brown, A, Clements, K and Nolan, A 2009, 'Building peace and political community in hybrid political orders', *International Peacekeeping*, vol. 16, no. 5, pp. 599–615.

Boulton, T 2004, 'Interactions between the local government and the traditional authorities: manifestation of justice, order and development in Ghana', *African Diaspora ISPs*, Paper 63.

Busia, KA 1951, *The position of the chief in the modern political system of Ashanti*, Routledge, Abingdon.

Darko, KA 2003, 'The relationship between traditional authorities and the District Assembly', in Assimeng, M (ed.), *Strengthening the chieftaincy institution to enhance its performance*, Konrad Adenauer Foundation, Accra.

Edu-Afful, F 2014, *Traditional authorities and governance: a case study of Komenda Traditional area in Ghana*, LAP Lambert Academic Publishing, Saarbrücken.

EEAS 2012, 'Strengthening national capacities for mediation and dialogue: national dialogue platforms and infrastructures for peace', *Factsheet, EEAS Mediation Support Project – Knowledge Product*, European External Action Service (EEAS), Belgium, p. 1.

Englebert, P 2002, 'Patterns and theories of traditional resurgence in tropical Africa', *Mondesen Developpement*, vol. 30, no. 118, pp. 51–64.

Galizzi, P and Abotsi, EK 2011, 'Traditional institutions and governance in modern African democracies', in Fenrich, G and Higgins, TE (eds), *The Future of African Customary Law*, Cambridge University Press, Cambridge.

Ghana News Agency 2015, 'National house of chiefs elevates 15 divisional chiefs', 2 July 2015, www.ghananewsagency.org/social/national-house-ofchiefs-elevates-15-divisional-chiefs-91377 (accessed 28 December 2015).

Grant, E and MacArthur, T 2008, 'Accountability briefing note', *DFID Practice Paper*, February 2008, Department for International Development (DFID), London.

Hagan, PH 1968, 'The golden stool and the oaths to the king of Ashanti', *Research Review*, vol. 4, no. 3, pp. 1–33.

Kessey, KD n.d., *Traditional leadership factor in modern local government system in Ghana: policy implementation, role conflict and marginalization*, Department of Planning, Kwame Nkrumah University of Science and Technology, Kumasi, Ghana.

Kumar, C and De la Haye, J 2011, 'Hybrid peacemaking: building national "Infrastructures for Peace"', *Global Governance*, vol. 18, no. 1, pp. 13–20.

Kyed, HM and Buur, L 2006, 'Recognition and democratisation: "new roles" for traditional leaders in Sub-Saharan Africa', *DIIS Working Paper/11*, Danish Institute for International Studies, Copenhagen.

Luckham, R and Kirk, T 2013, 'The two faces of security in hybrid political orders: a framework for analysis and research', *Stability: International Journal of Security and Development*, vol. 2, no. 2, pp. 1–30.

Mac Ginty, R and Sanghera, G 2012, 'Hybridity in peacebuilding and development: an introduction', *Journal of Peacebuilding and Development*, vol. 7, no. 2, pp. 3–8.

Ministry of Chieftaincy and Traditional Affairs 2014, *Medium term expenditure framework for 2014–2016*, Ministry of Chieftaincy and Traditional Affairs (MCTA), Ghana.

Moe, LW 2011, 'Hybrid and "e" political ordering: constructing and contesting legitimacy in Somaliland', *Journal of Legal Pluralism*, no. 63, pp. 141–75.

Nkuuhe, J 2006, 'Increasing collaboration in peace building', Paper prepared for a Trust Africa web discussion on 'Building Sustainable Peace', September 2006, Trust Africa, Dakar.

Odeneho Gyapong Ababio II 2003, Welcome Address: 'Strengthening the chieftaincy institution to enhance its performance', *Proceedings of tripartite seminar by the national house of chiefs*, Konrad Adenauer Foundation, Accra.

Owusu-Sarpong, C. 2003, 'Setting the Ghanaian context of rural local government: traditional authority values', in Ray, DI and Reddy, PS (eds), *Grassroots Governance? Chiefs in Africa and the Afro-Caribbean*, University of Calgary Press, Calgary, pp. 31–67.

Ray, DI 2003, 'Chiefs in their millennium sandals: traditional authority in Ghana – relevance, challenges and prospects', in Tettey, W, Puplampu, K and Berman, B (eds), *Critical perspectives in politics and socio-economic development*, Brill Publishers, Leiden.

Republic of Ghana 1992, *Constitution of the Republic of Ghana*, Ghana Publishing Corporation, Accra.

Stacey, P n.d, *Constructs of authority and the state-chief contract in Kpandai, northern Ghana*, UNDP, Accra.

Ubink, J 2007, 'Traditional authority revisited; popular perceptions of chiefs and chieftaincy in peri-urban Kumasi, Ghana', *Journal of Legal Pluralism*, no. 55, pp. 123–61.

Udy, SH 1970, *Work in traditional and modern society*, Prentice-Hall, Englewood Cliffs.

Verzat, V 2014, 'Infrastructures for peace: a grass-roots way to do state-building?' *Berghof Handbook Dialogue Series* no. 10.

8   Understanding and explaining hybridity in Liberia

Thomas Jaye

Introduction

African politics is marked by issues surrounding governance and the nature of the state. In Africa, the post-colonial state has never been a classic Weberian one; there have been hybrid forms of governance characterised variously by tension, conflict, complementarity and peaceful coexistence between modern and traditional institutions. However, for those involved in internationally supported processes of peacemaking and peacebuilding, which have been dominated by the liberal peace project, the focus has been on the formal state institutions. The traditional institutions are hardly recognised. For societies emerging out of violent conflicts, processes of peace formation are complex, involving diverse actors and issues. The actors include internal and external state and non-state actors. Locally grounded, traditional authorities also play a crucial role. Prominent issues include reconciliation, the reintegration of ex-combatants, economic recovery and statebuilding.

Historically, modern state formation in Liberia began in 1822, when the first batch of settlers arrived at Cape Mesurado from North America. Initially governed by agents of the American Colonization Society (ACS), Liberia was declared an independent republic on 26 July 1847. Since then, the country has faced the challenge of dealing with a dual administration comprising both modern and traditional systems of governance. It is important to explore and interrogate the history of the evolution of hybrid political order in Liberia over 169 years, and the governance relationship between different actors: how they have coexisted, complemented each other, and why there has been tension or conflict.

A study of the history of Liberia usually begins with the arrival of the settlers from North America in the 1820s; in the bulk of literature on Liberia, very little is written about pre-Liberia experiences. With the exception of the Condo Confederation in north-west Liberia, the history of state formation in pre-Liberia is given a perfunctory attention; knowledge about it is scanty. This gives the impression that the various ethnic groups or 'tribes' (as they are freely referred to in the literature) lacked governance structures, and the people lived and survived in a state of Hobbesian anarchy. In fact however, traditional authorities did provide their communities with security, peace and justice. In post-war Liberia, these authorities continue to play a critical role in this regard: they remain the first point of reference, before the statutory bodies[1] (ADRA Fieldwork 2014–15).

Thus, the provision of security, justice and peace did not derive from the formation of a Westphalian state in the nineteenth century in Liberia. Understanding the complex and contentious nature of the Liberian state, as argued throughout this chapter, requires a deeper interrogation and recognition of the parallel institutions that provide security, peace and justice to various communities. The notion of hybridity can guide such an interrogation, following Roger Mac Ginty, who writes that hybridity should not be construed or understood 'as the grafting together of two separate entities to make a new, third entity. Instead, hybridisation is understood as a complex process involving multiple actors and issues' (Mac Ginty 2016, p. 89).

In this discussion of hybridity in Liberia, while the terms 'traditional' and 'indigenous' can carry different meanings or definitions, they are interchangeably used throughout this chapter. There is also recognition of the fact that traditional and indigenous approaches to the provision of security, justice and peace are mostly localised, and, as Mac Ginty asserts, this can restrict their national relevance. Nevertheless, traditional and indigenous approaches to the provision of security, justice and peace have to be taken into account in the context of hybrid forms of governance. Mac Ginty, however, also makes the salient point that the socio-cultural environment upon which these approaches depend can be altered by civil wars and by broader global social changes, sometimes to the extent that they may no longer operate. For example, rural–urban migration, decline in respect for traditional sources of counsel and power, and monetisation of exchange may have an adverse impact on them (Mac Ginty 2016, pp. 122–3). Liberia is no exception, and thus an understanding and explanation of hybrid political order must be construed within this dynamic context.

This chapter seeks to contribute to the ongoing debate about peace formation in countries like Liberia, and explores the implications of hybridity for working towards peace and security. It provides an understanding of this concept through the empirical experiences and history of Liberia, the first republic in Africa. It argues that the Liberian state that emerged during the nineteenth century was never an archetypal Weberian state. Rather, the emergence of the state in Liberia was heavily influenced by the interaction with local traditional institutions and the enmeshment of state structures with these institutions. In conventional orthodox thinking about statebuilding and peacebuilding, however, the traditional institutions are not recognised. As a consequence, external interventions very often promote technocratic quick-fixes; they do not address the underlying causes of conflicts and fail to realise that many of these conflicts have not only localised roots but also localised manifestations (Autesserre 2010). Hence, the focus on national elites and formal institutions does not necessarily facilitate peace, security and justice, particularly in rural areas.

One last caveat is that this chapter does not seek to romanticise all things traditional and indigenous. They can be flawed, counterproductive and ineffective, given the changing dynamics and environment within which they operate (Mac Ginty 2016, p. 57). At the same time, however, the point should also be made that just as all things traditional or indigenous are not counter-productive and negative, so are all things modern not productive and positive. It is with this understanding that this chapter seeks to contribute to the ongoing debate about hybridity of the Liberian political order and its significance for the theory and practice of peace formation.

Pre-Liberia political communities

The area referred to as Liberia today was previously part of the Upper Guinea Coast, covering the Mano River basin countries, such as Sierra Leone, Liberia and Guinea and beyond. Prior to the arrival of the settlers in 1822, there were waves of migration from different parts of Africa, particularly the Sudan, to settle in this area. By the time the settlers arrived, some of these ethnic groups had already been settled there for around 250 years. The ethnic tapestry includes 16 groups, namely: Kru, Grebo, Krahn, Sarpo, Bassa, Belleh, Dei, Gola, Kissi, Vai, Kpelle, Lorma, Gio, Mano, Mandingo and Gbandi. These groups are sub-stratified into three language groups called: *Kwa*, *Mel* and *Mande*.

Among these groups, there have been different types of political institutions through which the communities have been governed. There were what have been referred to as 'states' and 'stateless' (acephalous) communities. A classic example of pre-Liberian statehood was the Condo Confederation that incorporated various ethnic groups in the north-western part of today's Liberia, led by King Sao Bosoe. Ascephalous communities may not have had centralised authorities, but they certainly had governance structures, as well as unwritten rules and regulations governing the peoples and their respective communities.

Generally, while the Mel and Mande peoples have had centralised chieftaincy, among the Kwa it is the acephalous system that prevailed (Levitt 2005, p. 21). The Mel and Mande have always lived under a hierarchical patrilineal system where political and judicial authority is vested with the family or the lineage of the founding ancestors; descendants of the original founding ancestors became leaders of the political community (Levitt 2005, p. 22). Among the Mel and Mande, the leaders of the *Poro* 'secret society' played a critical role in selecting the kings and other rulers. They also had the power to remove these rulers from their posts for 'inadequately serving the interests of the village-state' (Levitt 2005, p. 23).

In pre-Liberia, kings ruled the kingdoms. These kings were selected by ruling families of sections and towns, but they could also attain their kingdoms through conquest. The kings were supported by sectional chiefs, elders, outstanding men of towns and tribes and heads of social, religious and cultural institutions (Jones 1962, p. 22). There was also a speaker known as the mouthpiece of the king. In the absence of the king, the speaker presided over cases and conducted meetings; he could also assume the duties of king ad-interim when the king was out of town, and he could act as ambassador to neighbouring kingdoms (Jones 1962, p. 23).

Among the Kwa, the political, social, economic, cultural, security and judicial authority rested in a Council of Elders, the highest decision-making authority in the Kwa body politic. In the Kwa communities, authority, legitimacy, prestige and privilege were based on seniority. The war chief and chief priests were selected based on lineage (Levitt 2005 p. 23). Like the Mande and Mel groups, the Kwa have a Poro-oriented secret society referred to as the *Kwee*, which plays similar roles.[2]

In these traditional political systems there are no absolute leaders, because the councils of elders play a major role in providing leadership; they advise the heads of the political communities, and even though there is no police force or army, the parents and relatives ensure that their children do not violate the rules of the community. Older people also have the right to correct or punish a younger person for disobeying the rules (Guannu 1977, pp. 20–1). The political institutions described have strongly been buttressed by the Poro, or Poro-oriented, secret societies, as well as the Sande secret society. Then there are male and female spiritual leaders referred to as the *Zoes*. With the exception of Kru, Gio, Mandingo and Bassa, all the ethnic groups still have Poro or Poro-oriented secret societies. Membership of the Poro (and Poro-oriented) and Sande societies is limited to men (*Poro*) and women (*Sande*), respectively.

According to Hannah Jones, the Poro was the supreme law enforcement body; its laws were absolute and there were no appeals against them; they used fear as a weapon for law enforcement (Jones 1962, p. 34). In terms of sanctions, the death penalty was the ultimate (Liebenow 1987, p. 44). Other types of sanctions or punishment included cooking food for the entire village, payment of fines determined by the Poro, or banishment from the village, depending on the gravity of the issue (Jaye and Bloh 2015). While the Sande has always been associated with the ritual of clitoridectomy or female circumcision, this body did more than this; it was concerned with fertility, fidelity, care of home and family and other issues (Jones 1962, p. 36).

As Gus Liebenow writes, 'the rituals and sanctions of these secret societies took precedence over those of any other association or institution within the ethnic community' (Liebenow 1987, p. 43). The authority of a chief was based on his rank within the Poro or on the backing of Poro officials. The chief would often defer cases to the council of the Poro, and the council could reverse the decision of a chief who did not himself hold high status within the Poro (ibid.).

Quite contrary to the 'secret' and 'barbaric' images painted of the Poro and Sande, these institutions have played, and continue to play, a critical role in providing justice, security and order. For example, the Poro deals with anti-social behaviour, incest, murder, arson and looting by warriors, as well as making sure that there is positive cooperation in matters such as defence, cultivation, house building, bridge construction and community projects.

Declaration of independence and modern state formation

Modern state formation began with the arrival of the settlers. The arrival of the settlers and formation of settlements along the Atlantic coast was never a smooth process. When Jehudi Ashmun, a white Methodist clergyman, arrived in 1822 to take charge of the settlement of Cape Mesurado, which was originally named Christopolis (meaning 'city of Christ'), he met with resistance from the local chiefs. The chiefs did everything possible to stir up dissatisfaction against Ashmun, because they felt that he was interfering with the slave trade and hence depriving them of guns, ammunition, hard liquor and fancy trade goods that these people so prized (Clifford 1971, p. 16). It was against the backdrop of this experience that Ashmun organised the defense of the settlement by constructing a palisade on the crest of the Cape (ibid.).

From the 1820s to the military coup of 12 April 1980, the energy of the ruling elite in Monrovia was absorbed in the struggle to subdue the recalcitrant peoples of the interior, whom they regarded as 'uncivilized savages' (Clifford 1971, p. 27). One of the challenges facing the ruling elite was that for more than a century they had been separated from their African origins and ancestry. Families were split apart when they were forced out of Africa as slaves, and very few of the 'American Negroes' even knew from which part of Africa their ancestors had been taken (Clifford 1971, p. 53). The key ideas upon which the formation of Liberia was centred were: putting a halt to slavery; civilising the Africans; Christianising the Africans; and finding a 'refuge for the Negro' (McPherson 1891, pp. 45–8). All of this had implications for the future of politics in Liberia, especially in terms of relations not just between the indigenous peoples and settlers, but more importantly, between the so-called 'modern state' and 'traditional authorities'.

Hence, from the beginning the idea of Liberia proved that the mere crossing of the Atlantic to Africa did not ensure the freed Africans had thrown away the very systems that had oppressed them in America. On the contrary, the settlers brought with them borrowed 'civilization' and a political system that was alien to the people they met on those shores (McPherson 1891, p. 31). Rather than seeking a political system that would reflect the cultures of the African peoples and those of America where they had been enslaved, what emerged in Liberia was dual administration, with the coexistence, entanglement and friction of two different governance systems.

In light of the above, it is evident that the settlers arrived in Africa with a sense of 'manifest destiny': to civilise the tribal heathens. In order to achieve this objective, they demanded expansion of the modern state structures into the interior (Liebenow 1987, p. 24). Such a sense of 'manifest destiny' carried with it the efforts on the part of the settlers to subordinate the indigenous peoples, their cultures and governance institutions. While these institutions and cultures have undergone dynamic changes over a period of almost 170 years, some of the African traditional institutions have remained resilient and shape the contours of governance in Liberia in fundamental ways even today. This, however, was not expected or intended by the founding fathers of the Liberian state. They pursued deliberately exclusionary politics, as was clearly reflected in the *Declaration of Independence and Constitution of Liberia* (1847).

The Declaration laid the foundation for exclusion of the indigenous Africans. This was done by the same people who complained that in America they did not have equal rights; that powerful public sentiment frowned upon them; they had been excluded from taking part in government; had been taxed without consent; and had been separated and made a distinct class (Clifford 1971, pp. 22–3). Now these very settlers identified more with North American origins than with anything African (Clifford 1971, pp. 22–3). In the Declaration, it was clearly stated that the Liberian state was formed by and for people who were originally from America. It read as follows: 'We, the people of the Republic of Liberia, were originally inhabitants of the United States of North America' (Clifford 1971, p. 22).

As far as the settlers were concerned, they were forming a state and established Liberia on land acquired by purchase from the indigenous peoples of the soil. In fact, what was referred to as Liberia included about 286 miles of Atlantic coast from Cape Mount to Grand Cess, and stretched inland only about 45 miles. The interior was virtually unknown to the settlers and seemingly of little interest to them at that point.

Similarly, while the Constitution was meant to form a state of free people, it 'failed to recognise the political acumen and the social and material cultures of the African tribes which inhabit these regions' (Azikiwe 1934, p. 63). Such behaviour erected a barrier between the two groups of peoples and their respective political institutions or communities. Indeed, when the state was formed, it was not only a legal entity but a socio-cultural one that expressed the nineteenth century racial, religious, political and psychological outlook of American society (Dunn and Tarr 1988, p. 21). Further, the political formula created by the 1847 constitution was a faithful reflection of the core-periphery reality. It established a repatriate state with tacit understanding of gradual indigenous assimilation into that state (Dunn and Tarr 1988, p. 50). The major administrative divisions of the country were meant to sustain this core-periphery dichotomy (Dunn and Tarr 1988, p. 54). The paradox here is that, on the one hand, the settlers made efforts to inculcate western and Christian values, while on the other, they rejected any real assimilation of the indigenous population (Gershoni 1985, p. 23). In effect, they followed not the participatory ideals, but the racially exclusionary practices of the nineteenth century, applying them in this case against the majority of the population.

As with colonial subjects elsewhere in Africa, the indigenous Africans had to prove that they were 'civilised' before being accepted, before they could vote and be voted for. They had to prove that they owned land and cultivated a plot, that they had relinquished paganism and traditional customs, and that they accepted the Christian religion and a western way of life (Gershoni 1985, pp. 22–3).

Consequently, what emerged in 1847 was a 'dual' system of administration or governance in which the institutions of state government existed alongside the traditional authorities, but which was shaped by the paradoxical relations noted above. Governing Liberia under a dual system of administration has presented numerous challenges. For example, the modern Liberian state could enact laws but has had no control over compliance in the interior (Kraij 2015, p. 34). In the interior, people do follow the judgements of their traditional authorities and secret societies more than anything else. The elders, quarter, town, clan and paramount chiefs continue to be the sources of justice, security and order. The chiefs provide both administrative and judicial services. This has implications for governance throughout the country. As indicated before, the resultant relationships between the modern and traditional governance systems has been characterised by conflict and a dynamic of exclusion, but nevertheless also by complementarity and peaceful coexistence.

State consolidation and incorporation of chiefs

As Liberia sought to find a solution to the challenge of dual administration and political exclusion, its problems were further compounded by exogenous factors. After the Berlin Conference of 1885, the scramble for Africa began. Liberia could not be insulated from this scramble because the country's authorities needed to establish that they had control over the territories they claimed. Therefore, just as Europe scrambled for Africa, so was Liberia scrambling for the hinterland. The European scramble for Africa disrupted the Liberian efforts. For example, by 11 November 1885, Britain established the Mano River as the boundary between Liberia and Sierra Leone, and even annexed the Gallinas territory; and in 1892, France also used the Cavalla River to establish the boundary between Liberia and Cote d'Ivoire (Gershoni 1985, p. 34).

The expansion of the Liberian state into the hinterland was also spurred by internal factors, including the desire to consolidate the Liberian state, generate revenue and subordinate the indigenous peoples. In order to do so, in 1905, President Arthur Barclay put forward a plan to consolidate the Liberian state. The plan aimed to integrate the indigenous population into Liberia by establishing permanent administrative units, headed by African chiefs approved by the government to collect taxes and maintain law and order in keeping with local customs, provided they did not contradict the Liberian constitution. These chiefs would be supervised by travelling commissioners (Gershoni 1985, p. 37). The chiefs were paid 10 per cent as honorarium for the hut taxes they collected from their people, which at that time amounted to 1 US$ per annum (Azikiwe 1934, p. 79). This effectively marked an incorporation of the chiefs into the modern state system, and from then on they were embedded both in the traditional and modern state structures. Chieftaincy was imposed on the acephalous communities in the south-eastern part of the country inhabited mainly by Kwa-speaking people.

The Barclay Plan became law: African areas were divided into districts, and the chiefs and the traditional ways of choosing them were recognised. In ascending order, the three levels of political administrative divisions were: the single settlement (township), which was headed by a town chief; clan (not in the anthropological sense), headed by a clan chief; and units of clans called 'chiefdom', headed by a paramount chief. The Barclay Plan also established a dual legal system: the African customary system, led by the chiefs; and the government statutory system, headed by the Commissioner. By 1923, President Charles

DB King had divided the coastal areas into six counties and the hinterland into five districts (Gershoni 1985, pp. 38–59) as part of the state consolidation process. The plan effectively incorporated the hinterland administration into the Liberian state.

Coercive forces, particularly the Liberia Frontier Force (LFF),[3] which was formed in 1908, were used to expand into the interior through conquest (Liebenow 1987, pp. 25–6). The imposition of Liberian authority through force and conquest between 1905 and 1915 sparked a wave of wars of resistance among the Vai, Grebo, Kru, Kpelle and others. Soldiers and officials of the War and Interior Departments were stationed in the Districts, and up to the middle of 1914 most of the District officials, particularly Commissioners, were also military officers in command of soldiers in these areas (Akpan 1988, pp. 4–6).

But it was not all elements of the ruling elites that were in favour of expansion into the interior as part of the process of state consolidation. Some feared that expansion would undermine their supremacy as a minority group. This is one of the reasons why some opposed integration and unification programmes, as well as the promotion of foreign investment and development (Liebenow 1987, p. 28).

Furthermore, it is important to stress that the dual nature of political order was acknowledged by the Supreme Court, which stated that 'sovereignty does not curtail the authority practically exercised over said Africans by their own kings and other authority leaving the question of right as to such authority entirely open to subsequent judicial exigencies' (Azikiwe 1934, p. 79). In other words: indirect rule did recognise the significance of indigenous authority. For example, District Commissioners were appointed by the state government, but chiefs were selected in keeping with the customs of their local communities (Levitt 2005, p. 138).

> The creation of four new counties in the hinterland in 1964 under President William V. S. Tubman Sr. did not abolish the role of traditional authorities in Liberia. Their creation incorporated the hinterland more deeply into the Liberian body politic, but the traditional institutions remained resilient, even to the extent that almost every male president since Tubman has had to become a member of the Poro or Poro-oriented secret societies. More than half of the country's population are members of these societies even today.
>
> (Kraij 2015, p. 34)

The Constitution of 1984, which repealed the 1847 version, implicitly recognised the hybrid nature of the state. Under Chapter I, which defines the structure of the state, Liberia is declared a 'unitary sovereign state divided into counties for administrative purposes'. In Chapter II, Article 5(b), there is reference to the need to 'preserve, protect and promote positive Liberian culture, ensuring that traditional values which are compatible with public policy and national progress are adopted and developed as an integral part of the growing needs of the Liberian society' (Republic of Liberia 1986, p. 3). Article 56(b) of Chapter VI recognises the Paramount, Clan and Town Chiefs. It reads:

[T]here shall be elections of Paramount, Clan and Town Chiefs by the registered voters in their respective localities, to serve for a term of six years. They may be re-elected and may be removed only by the President for proved misconduct. The Legislature shall enact laws to provide for their qualifications as may be required.

(Article 56(b), p. 24)

Under this Constitution, the dual legal system is maintained. For example, under Article 65 of Chapter VII, which covers the judiciary, it reads that 'the courts shall apply both statutory and customary laws in accordance with the standards enacted by the Legislature' (Republic of Liberia 1986, p. 27). Thus, in the constitution of the republic frequent references to traditional authorities can be found. The paramount, clan and town chiefs serve dual administrative purposes – on the one hand, they fall into the category of traditional authorities; but on the other hand, they are part and parcel of the modern state structure. Chiefs have, therefore, been hybridised through encounters with external actors over a long period of time, especially since the establishment of the modern Liberian state. This illustrates the fact that political order in Liberia has always been hybrid.

Post-war Liberia, statebuilding and consolidation

Liberia was engulfed by civil war from 1989 to 1997. After two years, there was a relapse into conflict from 1999 to 2003. As part of the process of statebuilding and, implicitly, state consolidation in post-war Liberia, the Governance Commission (GC)[4] has been preoccupied with formulating plans for governance reforms. In pursuance thereof, in 2013, the GC crafted the Local Government Act, which was enacted by Legislature in 2016 (Governance Commission 2016). Among other undertakings, it repeals the 'Aborigines Law of 1956' and provides details for the administration of the hinterland, calling for the election of a Superintendent, District Commissioner, Paramount Chief,[5] Clan Chief and General Town Chief (ibid.).[6] The District Commissioner, Paramount Chief, Clan Chief and General Town Chief are to have advisory boards with elders, chiefs, youth, women and prominent citizens as members.

In principle, decentralisation is part of the process of devolving powers to local people and is also meant to limit the over-centralisation of powers in the 'imperial presidency'. It is suggested that the process seeks to devolve government from Monrovia to the counties and districts as part of the *Agenda for Transformation.*[7] The idea is to bring the state closer to the people, improve service delivery (health, education, etc.) and promote reconciliation (World Bank and UNMIL 2013, p. 3). As vital as these objectives are, achieving them remains a tall order. It should be borne in mind that the governance reform process in Liberia should be seen as part and parcel of the overall process of statebuilding and a core element of the liberal peace project. While 'governance' refers to the guiding principles, decision-making processes and operating procedures of organisations and collectives generally, the emphasis of governance intervention in the context of the liberal peace project has been on the modern state structures and institutions and, more specifically, it has been about 'reforming state bureaucracies in the developing world so that they operate in a manner deemed to be transparent and equitable' (Mac Ginty 2016, p. 160). However, a critique of such interventions makes the point that 'good governance' interventions are inherently normative and are political projects that seek to overwrite local and traditional forms of governance with supposedly superior modern forms of governance (Mac Ginty 2016, p. 163).

In this vein, while the language of reducing the over-centralisation of power in Liberia's 'imperial presidency' seems enticing, the governance reform project could also undermine traditional forms of governance. It could replace it with a new form of governance that is not embedded in the culture and traditions of the people. Indeed, such institutional transfer or imposition can create institutions and processes that are 'disconnected from prevalent social practices and values, and divorced from the actual socio-political and economic dynamics shaping people's lives' (Brown and Gusmao 2009, p. 61), whereas the engagement of 'state entities and political leaders with traditional governance values and practices is fundamental to the quality of democracy and to peacebuilding, security, justice, and livelihood' (Brown and Gusmao 2009, p. 62).

In post-war societies like Liberia, the role of traditional authorities must not be underestimated. Chiefs (in their dual roles) and traditional authorities (elders, Poro and Sande) continue to provide for the broader security needs of the people, including peace and justice. Basic social services in the towns and villages are also facilitated by the traditional authorities. This is all the more significant given the limited presence of modern state institutions in every part of the country. When the state is weak, fragile and fails to provide the sort of public services that constitute a contract between it and its citizens, it is, as Sawyer argues, through the informal institutions like these traditional authorities that local people reach understanding among themselves, including resolving conflicts and undertaking a variety of collective actions that are critical foundations for self-governance (Sawyer 2005, p. 1). He further asserts that 'local community sought recourse in traditional institutions in order to cope with the security dilemmas they are facing' (Sawyer 2005, p. 4). There may be differences among the diverse ethnic groups, but generally the traditional authorities and agencies do provide security, justice and peace among the people at the local level (Kofi Annan International Peacekeeping Training Centre 2015). By imposing liberal democratic values such as electoral politics on people whose traditional method for choosing leaders is based on reaching consensus, this project could undermine the role of traditional authorities, cultures and values. It could also generate conflicts at the micro level. In post-conflict situations in particular, the introduction of local elections and, therefore, of electoral campaigning can re-open the wounds of violent conflict, generate humiliation and undermine fragile trust among groups at the local level (Brown and Gusmao 2009, p. 120). Whether or not this leads to violence, it can result in withdrawal of cooperation.

Thus, while the efforts of external actors are primarily focused on rebuilding the modern state institutions in post-war peacebuilding, it is also vital to acknowledge that peacebuilding, as a complex and multifaceted undertaking, has to reach beyond this state-centricity. It requires the efforts of diverse actors from various societal realms to contribute to this process. While it is fully acknowledged that there is diversity among the different ethnic groups and cultures that make up Liberia today, this does not undermine the critical role of traditional authorities in peace-making processes in the communities. Even after more than a decade of UN-sponsored governance and security sector reform, the so-called modern state's territorial reach is still basically confined to the urban areas. The farther one travels into the rural areas, the more it becomes evident that the remit of the modern state is limited (Kofi Annan International Peacekeeping Training Centre 2015). It is the traditional authorities that enjoy more authority in these areas than the modern state. In these areas, chiefs and other traditional authorities such as elders and secret societies coexist in providing justice, security and order. The modern state exercises its jurisdiction through the paramount, clan, general town, town and quarter chiefs (who, as outlined above, are doubly embedded in the state structures and the local communities), their legitimacy depends on their relationship with the elders and 'secret' societies.

The chiefs rely on the modern state for certain forms of authority but are also expected to perform customary roles, which they are powerless to do unless they are a member of the Poro or Sande (Fahey 1971, p. 14). While the chiefs handle everyday matters, fundamental domains of their authority rest more often than not with the Poro. Whatever the Poro tribunal decides is final (Fahey 1971, p. 13). Chiefs in the past were powerful members of the secret societies and chosen by elders and prominent people through consensus. The irony is that even though they were not elected, these chiefs enjoyed a high degree of legitimacy. Importantly, unlike the other officials who are subject to elections under the new GC supported Act, paramount chiefs have already been subjected to elections since 1976 under the Tolbert Administration. One would have thought that the elected paramount chiefs would enjoy legitimacy, as opposed to those chosen through consensus, but on the contrary, the legitimacy of the former has been undermined by lack of experience and charisma, and other characteristics that are required in order to govern in local areas.

Finally, when talking about providers of peace, security and justice in postwar Liberia beyond the state institutions, one has also to take into account religious authorities like the imams, Pentecostal pastors, and grassroots bodies such as trade unions and market people's associations. These actors and institutions also play a role in resolving disputes and maintaining everyday peace and order (Jaye and Alao 2013, pp. 125–61). So do novel institutions which do not easily fit into the state/non-state divide. Tribal governors are an interesting case in point.

Tribal governors

'Tribal governorship', which is considered as a traditional authority, is based in the urban areas. It was established in the early twentieth century as part of the administrative units in the urban areas to cater for 'tribal' people migrating to the cities. Unlike the 'secret societies' that may not easily cross-fertilise with the modern state institutions, the tribal governors can easily undergo such a process. In Liberia, tribal governors work in different parts of the country and handle various types of cases, sometimes beyond their jurisdictions (N'tow 2011, p. 5). According to Saah N'tow, a tribal governor (TG) is a representative of his or her ethnic group living within a given municipal area; he/she is responsible for coordinating administrative activities among his/her people and the government of Liberia. He or she investigates tribal matters and settles disputes among them (N'tow 2011, p. 7).

Tribal governors play three inter-related roles in the Liberian society: social, political and quasi-judiciary. Socially, TGs provide networking for their people, host 'stranded strangers' and promote the cultures of their people. Politically, they serve as a political liaison person for their people with local and national state authorities and mobilise their people when high-ranking officials are guests. And as a quasi-judiciary agency, they mediate, maintain peace and harmony among the people, adjudicate cases and for that purpose convene courts to hear cases.

As part of the customary justice system, the tribal governor's court has three features which distinguish it from the formal courts system (N'tow 2011, p. 8):

- TGs are not required to have knowledge of the law
- TGs are not appointed by the president
- TGs have little or no power to enforce their courts' rulings.

Despite this, tribal governors deal with very serious issues. Cases coming before them include family matters, debt, community level cases, land disputes, marital issues and all other matters threatening the peace and security of the communities. Their judicial duties may include domestic violence, fighting, inheritance, property cases, assault and mysterious deaths (N'tow 2011, pp. 16–17).

The way the TGs' courts operate is very similar to the judicial proceedings of councils of elders in the customary context: in cases or disputes involving two parties, the process of decision-making involves listening to both of them; then witnesses are called to testify; there will be representatives from both parties; and once the hearing is completed, both are asked to leave before a judgement is rendered.

In terms of structure, the governor system includes the governors themselves and a host of volunteers such as messengers, clerk, vice governor, an interpreter and advisory body, comprising elders, youth and women. Very often, they lack training, logistics and transportation (N'tow 2011, pp. 12–23) but are widely used by local people for the purpose of dispute resolution.

Complementarity and conflict

Writing on the relationship between the modern and traditional systems of governance, Deng asserts that:

> acknowledging the importance, richness and competence of traditional laws and systems paves the way for a much-needed process of cross-fertilization between the formal and informal systems, encouraging traditional and modern systems to coexist, learn from each other, and evolve accordingly.
>
> (Deng 2008, p. 116)

Despite the history of tension and conflicts, the relationship between these two different types of institutions can indeed be complementary and peaceful. This has to a certain extent been the experience in Liberia over the course of its history: diverse governance systems performing overlapping or complementary functions in hybrid political order. For example, during the Ebola crisis, both traditional and modern structures collaborated to respond to the threats of the disease.

In this context there are, without doubt, concerns about gender issues – specifically, about the role of women; about youth exclusion and human rights issues. Both youth and women complain about exclusion, whereas the elders complain about the way in which the interpretation of human rights by local and international NGO advocates has undermined traditional authorities, even in cases where village ordinances are supposed to be observed (Kofi Annan International Peacekeeping Training Centre 2015). Accordingly, it is important to stress that, while the ancestral line in most of Liberia is traced through the male members and is thus male-oriented, the role of women should not be underestimated. This point is reinforced by Deng, who writes that the 'influence of the mother is considered so great that she is seen as a potential threat unless she supports the value system' (Deng 2008, p. 78). As he further posits, the children are 'highly prized because they are the pillars on which the ancestral line is maintained' (ibid.). However, the fact remains that women often feel excluded from decision-making processes. In an environment dominated by patriarchy, the dominant role of men will certainly lead to tension (Kofi Annan International Peacekeeping Training Centre 2015).

When it comes to human rights, Deng recognises that they – in their locally embedded forms – constitute a perennial feature of the customary governance system, and he calls for a recognition of the African cultures in the evolution of human rights standards, as well as for recognising the culturally oriented values of Africans towards human dignity, and finding ways in which these values can influence international and national human rights frameworks (Deng 2008, p. 143). One might argue that the 'African system' is one in which the protection of the individual is inherent in the solidarity of the group (Deng 2008, p. 148). In this system, the individual has reciprocal obligations to the group and its interests (ibid.). Hence, the sweeping assumption that Africans who live according to customary values and norms do not observe human rights, should be corrected.

Hence, there are indeed issues of tension and conflict between the modern state and traditional authorities, on understandings of human rights and gender equality in particular. This plays out as tensions with regard to, for example, female genital mutilation or trial by ordeal (known as *sassywood*) (Leeson and Coyne 2012; Pajibo 2008).[8] Finally, different understandings of accountability also figure prominently. One of the common accusations made against traditional authorities is that there is a lack of accountability. However, such an accusation does not acknowledge the way in which traditional institutions work. Importantly, there is no absolute leader in the traditional system. As Mac Ginty would argue, the 'indigenous and traditional practices rest on the moral authority of respected community figures such as village or other sources of counsel', and very 'often these figures demand deference and there is a strong social expectation that their judgement or advice will be adhered to' (Mac Ginty 2016, pp. 54–5). This has been the experience in Liberia. Village elders and authorities are deferred to on many issues because of their wisdom and moral authority. Nevertheless, such moral authority must be upheld and can be withdrawn by the community. Moreover,

> many of the practices have a public element that adds to the transparency or decision-making processes. They are deliberately accessible (perhaps held at a central point in a village or at a location between two disputing villages), with this public dimension providing a visible affirmation of legitimacy.
>
> (Mac Ginty 2016, p. 55)

In Liberia, the Palava Hut process constitutes a classic example of what Mac Ginty describes. Under the Palava Hut system, decision-making processes are transparent; proceedings are held at an accessible place in the village; and decisions are reached based on consensus (Jaye and Bloh 2015).

From fieldwork data gathered in Liberia over a two-year period, the point was also made that the chiefs or elders do not have absolute powers; they govern with the support of a council of elders upon whom they rely to make decisions. Moreover, chiefs and elders can be removed from their positions by their respective councils if they are guilty of unacceptable behaviour such as corruption, abuse of power, insulting elders and women publicly, or violating the laws of the area (Kofi Annan International Peacekeeping Training Centre 2015). Hence, there are accountability mechanisms also in the traditional context – they might be different from those in the modern state context, and less visible to outsiders, but they nevertheless do exist. As with the issues of human rights and gender, there can be conflict and tensions with regard to the topic of accountability. But there is also potential for complementarity. Whether this potential is utilised depends on the will of all actors involved in meaningful dialogue.

Conclusion

Liberia constitutes a hybrid political order, which has not only evolved over a long historical period, but has been influenced by both endogenous and exogenous factors. Its emergence has involved diverse actors, processes and issues. After more than 169 years of independence, the reach of the modern Liberian state remains limited. At the same time, the traditional authorities have provided and continue to provide security, peace and justice in their locales. As elsewhere on the continent, the Liberian state is no classical Weberian one; what exists is a hybrid political order. Africans are still engaging in reflections and negotiations about the political arrangements that could manage the diversity of their cultures, values and institutions as sources of strength and legitimacy (Deng 2008, p. 3). The fact of the matter is that because its power overwhelmingly has not been used to meet the broader security needs of the people, it has been difficult to legitimise the African state which, after all, was arbitrarily and artificially imposed upon the people by external colonial powers.

The Liberian experience illustrates how people emerging out of a protracted conflict situation have no choice but to refer to the existing structures for peace, security and justice. They are caught in the entanglement of modern, traditional, indigenous, local, national and external factors that influence the post-war environment and therefore the peacebuilding process. The long years of civil war have had a negative impact on some of the traditional or indigenous institutions and practices. Nonetheless, the war has not totally undermined their significance; they have remained resilient and therefore are referred to for security, peace and justice at the local level. Understanding these intricacies and the hybrid nature of political order is critical to better understanding the possibilities for peace formation.

While the enactment of the Local Government Act (2016) could help to improve accountability, de-concentrate service delivery from the capital, and reduce the enormous powers of the 'imperial' presidency, there is nothing apolitical about this. The process has the trappings of the liberal peace project that seeks to institutionalise reforms by means of a top-down approach; as such, it could undermine traditional institutions and in some ways produce the opposite of what it seeks. It is part and parcel of the process of consolidating the modern Liberian state – an institution that has failed over the years to serve as guardian angel for the broader security needs of the people. On the contrary, this state has been a threat to the security of the people. Thus, centrally driven decentralisation is not a panacea for Liberia's problems. If not properly designed, it could create local monsters and increase the cost of governance. Further, there are no guarantees that this would achieve the noble objectives it seeks to obtain. Electoral politics at the local level could lead to marginalisation of minority ethnic groups and politically exclude them through discrimination.

On the other hand, the current hybrid political order has the potential to create an enabling environment for a decentralised system that is embedded into the cultures and traditions of the people. Without romanticising traditions and cultures, the coexistence and (potential) complementarity of the modern with the traditional could create the basis for a hybrid order in which both are acknowledged and recognised as part of the country's governance architecture. In order to properly undertake this project, there is need to interrogate the relationship between these institutions. It is evident that there is still poor understanding and explanation of the traditional African institutions, which are too quickly labelled as backward and authoritarian. Such labels are flawed, because the leaders in these communities are subject to the will of the people through their respective village councils; these councils can even be seen as 'an assembly, an embodiment of representative democracy and as nearest to perfect democracy as can be found elsewhere' (Azikiwe 1934, p. 24). Further, Azikiwe writes that while the chief or 'king'[9] in the context of customary communities is sovereign, the exercise of that sovereignty is within the powers of the councillors. The 'king' has never been divine, but abides by tribal sanctions and customary laws (Azikiwe 1934, p. 24). These are positive elements of the traditions that should inform constitution-making and statebuilding in countries like Liberia. But to do so, there is a need to avoid the intellectual pitfalls of the past. It is important to invoke the words of Azikiwe, who correctly observed that:

> the more research one makes in African political institutions, the more amazed one becomes at the unforgiveable errors made by unfinished scholars who have failed to grasp that the rudiments of African political theory and government, the village assemblies in small African communities and in the hinterlands of the Republic as well, exhibit as true a type of pure democracy as could be found in the Greek City-States, or in the earlier New England town meetings, or in the Saxonian Witenagemot.
>
> (Azikiwe 1934, pp. 82–3)

Against this backdrop, further research would be most useful, and African policy-making bodies, including those involved with statebuilding, should recognise the contributions that Africa's past and its traditions could make in peacebuilding and peace-making; peace formation can also borrow and benefit from such experiences without romanticising them.

Notes

1 ADRA Fieldwork Notes (Inc. FGDS and individual interviews) in Palala and Quoipa (Bong County), and Gbojay and Tubmanburg (Bomi County), Republic of Liberia, 2014–15. See Kofi Annan International Peacekeeping Training Centre (2015).
2 Among the Kwa Group it is only the *Kru* people that do not have the Kwee.
3 The LLF constitutes the embryo of the modern day Armed Forces of Liberia (AFL).
4 The Governance Commission was created as a result of the Comprehensive Peace Agreement (CPA) signed by Liberian stakeholders during the Accra peace talks. It was originally called the 'Governance Reform Commission'.
5 The election of paramount chiefs started in 1976 under the Tolbert administration; hence the new act only reinforces what already exists. There is nothing new about this.

6 The difference between the 1984 Constitution and the Local Government Act of 2016 is that in the latter, the posts of Superintendent and Commissioners are subject to elections. Previously, only the paramount chiefs were elected.
7 A Government of Liberia development strategy for lifting Liberians out of poverty to prosperity.
8 Sassywood can be administered as a drink from a poisonous tree. The drink is given to the accused, and if he or she dies or becomes seriously ill (near death), then he or she is found to be guilty, but if the drink is vomited, the accused is found not guilty. Usually, sassywood was applied in cases involving witchcraft, death or theft of property. Sometimes referred to as 'trial by ordeal', sassywood sometimes involves a red hot metal being rubbed on the accused's leg, and depending on his/her reaction (such as removing the foot from the heat), it signifies that the accused is guilty or not guilty. Both methods have been banned by the Government of Liberia under the administration of President Ellen Johnson-Sirleaf.
9 In some parts of the country, these two terms ('chief' and 'king') were used interchangeably.

Bibliography

Akpan, MB 1988, *African resistance in Liberia: The Vai and the Gola-Bandi*, Liberia Working Group Papers, Bremen.

Autesserre, S 2010, *The trouble with the Congo: local violence and the failure of international peacebuilding*, Cambridge Studies in International Relations, Cambridge University Press, Cambridge.

Azikiwe, N 1934, *Liberia in world politics*, Arthur H. Stockwell Ltd., London.

Brown, MA and Gusmao, AF 2009, 'Peacebuilding and political hybridity in East Timor', *Peace Review*, vol. 21, no. 1, pp. 61–9.

Clifford, ML 1971, *The land and people of Liberia*, JB Lippincott, Philadelphia.

Deng, FM 2008, *Identity, diversity and constitutionalism in Africa*, USIP Press, Washington DC.

Dunn, DE and Tarr, SB 1988, *Liberia: a national polity in transition*, The Scarecrow Press Inc., Metuchen.

Fahey, RP 1971, 'The Poro as a system of judicial administration in Northwestern Liberia', *Journal of Legal Pluralism and Unofficial Law*, vol. 3, no. 4, pp. 1–25.

Gershoni, Y 1985, *Black colonialism: the Americo-Liberian scramble for the hinterland*, Westview Press, Boulder.

Governance Commission 2016, *Local Government Act of 2016*, Republic of Liberia.

Guannu, JS 1977, *Liberian history up to 1847*, Exposition Press Inc., New York.

Jaye, T and Alao, CA 2013, 'Islamic radicalisation and violence in Liberia', in Gow, J, Olonisakin, F and Dijxhoorn, E (eds), *Militancy and violence in West Africa*, Routledge, Abingdon, pp. 125–61.

Jaye, T and Bloh, O 2015, *Ethnographic study on national forums to assess/research the traditional Palava Hut systems of Liberia*, INCHR and UNDP.

Jones, HAB 1962, 'The struggle for political and cultural unification in Liberia 1847–1930', PhD thesis, Northwestern University, Evanston, Il.

Kofi Annan International Peacekeeping Training Centre 2015, *Ghanaian and Liberian Fieldwork Notes*; (incl. FGDS and individual interviews in Palala and Quoipa [Bong County], and Gbojay and Tubmanburg [Bomi County], Republic of Liberia, 2014–2015), Australian Development Research Awards Scheme Project, University of Queensland, Brisbane.

Kraij, FV 2015, *Liberia: from the love of liberty to paradise lost*, African Studies Centre, Leiden.

Leeson, PT and Coyne, CJ 2012, 'Sassywood', *Journal of Comparative Economics*, vol. 40, pp. 608–20.

Levitt, J 2005, *The evolution of deadly conflict in Liberia*, Carolina Academic Press, Durham, North Carolina.

Liebenow, JG 1987, *Liberia: the quest for democracy*, Indiana University Press, Bloomington.

Mac Ginty, R 2016, *International peacebuilding and local resistance: hybrid forms of peace*, Palgrave Macmillan, Basingstoke.

McPherson, JHT 1891, *History of Liberia*, University of Michigan, Michigan.

N'tow, SC 2011, *Report of Tribal Governors' Court assessment in Bassa, Bomi, Bong, Lofa, Grand Gedeh, and Montserrado [Counties]*. UNMIL, Monrovia.

Pajibo, E 2008, *Traditional justice mechanisms: the Liberian case*, International IDEA.

Republic of Liberia 1986, *Constitution of the Republic of Liberia*, 6 January, 1986.

Sawyer, A 2005, *Social capital, survival strategies and their potential for post-conflict governance in Liberia*, United Nations University and WIDER Research Paper No. 15.

World Bank and UNMIL 2013, *Liberia: public expenditure review note: meeting the challenges of the UNMIL security transition*. World Bank and UNMIL.

9 How hybridity happens

Unpacking plural security and justice provision in Sierra Leone

Lisa Denney

Sierra Leone is considered one of the first cases of post-conflict security and justice reform (SJR) – in which the institutions responsible for safety, protection and the rule of law in primarily post-colonial states are the subject of 'transformation' by mostly Northern donors and countries. SJR is an effort to improve the capacity of these institutions to deliver security and justice and strengthen the legitimacy of the state itself. It is thus a core feature of internationally-led peacebuilding efforts. Yet, Sierra Leone provides a striking example of the disjuncture between SJR practice as part of wider peacebuilding efforts and the manner in which people obtain peace, security and justice locally. In addition, it also highlights the limitations of our conceptual frameworks for understanding security and justice provision. This chapter draws attention to these limitations by examining both the general neglect of hybridity within particularly early SJR efforts in Sierra Leone, and the simplistic manner in which hybridity tends to be understood when it is acknowledged.

As awareness of the plurality of security and justice providers has grown, analysis often presents this plurality as dichotomous, competitive and in need of harmonisation. However, examining both the users and providers of Sierra Leone's plural security and justice system helps to overcome the tendency to view multiple providers in binary and oppositional terms of 'state' versus 'non-state' or 'formal' versus 'informal', and rather to engage with them on their own merits as an interactive system. This matters for peace formation because it draws attention to the inadequacies of dominant statebuilding approaches that tend to favour formal institutions and deepens efforts to understand the hybrid realities in more fluid ways that better capture how people access security and justice and build peaceful and protective communities.

This chapter proceeds by first examining the history of Sierra Leone's plural or hybrid security and justice system. Second, it considers how international actors have engaged with this system through post-conflict SJR. This highlights the initial neglect of security and justice providers outside of the state, followed by a tentative embrace of some elements of hybridity. Third, the chapter problematises the way in which plural security and justice orders are conceptualised, by considering three often overlooked features of hybridity. Taking an end-user perspective to consider how citizens in reality navigate the multiple avenues available to them reveals a more symbiotic system in which people move between different providers in order to find the most suitable outcomes. This is true in relation to security and justice, just as it is in relation to other services such as health care, in which people utilise a range of providers, from government clinics to traditional healers to drug peddlers. Indeed, security and justice work could usefully learn from the ways in which hybridity manifests and is dealt with in these other sectors. Examining the relationship between security and justice providers themselves demonstrates their interconnections and suggests they are often not purely competitive, but an interactive and interdependent ecosystem that is also cooperative. And, finally, understanding how individual providers themselves can simultaneously occupy both 'state' and 'non-state' roles blurs neat categorisations of 'state' and 'non-state' providers, suggesting that both the security and justice system *and* individual providers can be examples of hybridity. Discussion of these three overlooked features draws on literature on security and justice in Sierra Leone, the author's own observations over multiple visits since 2007, and an in-depth interview with the current Head of the National Council of Paramount Chiefs (NCPC) conducted by the author in Freetown on 10 October 2015.

Ultimately, it is argued that in order to meaningfully connect with the ways in which people obtain and experience (in)justice and (in)security we need a more granular and nuanced understanding of hybridity. Such an understanding should enable us to move beyond general prescriptions about the nature of 'state' or 'non-state' security and justice providers to more empirically grounded conversations that take each provider on their merits. More broadly, this would allow for peace formation efforts to be more relevant and responsive to the lived realities of those whom international interventions are ultimately intended to serve.

Plurality and hybridity

It is now widely acknowledged that security and justice in Sierra Leone – as in most other places – is characterised by a wide spectrum of providers (Baker 2006, 2008; Baker and Scheye 2007; Dale 2008; Albrecht 2010; Denney 2014a). Yet our understanding of the nature of these multiple providers, and how they interact to provide a system of security and justice, remains patchy (Hunt, see Chapter 5 in this volume). Before briefly recapping the nature of Sierra Leone's security and justice system, however, it is important to clarify the language employed to describe this reality.

In examining how people construct order and secure themselves in post-colonial settings, this book strongly brings out the important role of hybridity. The concept of hybridity has been employed to capture the empirical reality of political orders in what are often termed 'fragile states' in international policy discourse (Boege, Brown, Clements and Nolan 2009, p. 6). This builds on the recognition that '[t]he state' is only one actor among others, and 'state order' is only one of a number of orders claiming to provide security, frameworks for conflict regulation and social services (Boege *et al.* 2009, p. 6). That is, in constructing order and security, people in post-colonial settings (and beyond) draw on not merely state actors and institutions but a range of others as well.

Using the term *hybridity* to highlight the diversity of political orders within a given society draws an analogy with the process by which a new plant is created by blending two different plants. That is, the political orders in many parts of the world are not merely the 'fragile' or 'failed' projection of western political orders but are, different orders entirely, influenced by western political orders to some degree but also by a range of other political, legal and normative orders, thus resulting in a hybrid system.

Plurality refers to multiple security and justice orders and derives from the extensive literature on legal pluralism, which has long been used to capture the multiple legal orders that exist in many contexts (Benda-Beckmann 2002; Tamanaha, Sage and Woolcock 2012). While the terms *hybridity* and *pluralism* are not fixed and are used in many different ways, a distinction is drawn here between the two terms for the analytical clarity of the argument. Throughout this chapter, Sierra Leone's security and justice system is characterised as plural, as it draws attention to the multiple providers that constitute a complex system. The term *hybridity* is used to highlight the manner in which some of the providers that constitute the plural system occupy *both* state and non-state roles – drawing legitimacy from both sources – and are themselves thus hybrids (a blend of more than one system). The argument made here, therefore, is that Sierra Leone's security and justice system is plural in nature, made up of multiple, often hybrid, providers. Unpacking 'pluralism' or 'hybridity' in this manner, to go beyond just recognising its existence to interrogating what it means for how security and justice is delivered, is key to a more granular understanding that can inform and improve SJR efforts.

Sierra Leone's plural justice and security system

Sierra Leone has long been characterised by a plural legal system. While little is known about the pre-colonial legal order, records suggest that laws varied from kingdom to kingdom, which were presided over by cultural leaders and assisted by secret societies and spiritual leaders (Kane, Oloka-Onyango and Tejan-Cole 2005, p. 16; Little 1967, p. 255; Fyfe 1962, pp. 3–4, 22–3). Formal English law – as it is known – was introduced during colonialism to apply to the British and consenting Africans, while customary law continued to apply to the rest of the indigenous population (Jearey 1960, pp. 409–10; Denzer 1971). Formal English law was administered by a formal legal system, while customary law was administered by local chiefs and district administrators in the case of appeals.

Formal and customary law have since continued to operate alongside one another. Formal law continues to be administered by the formal courts and the Sierra Leone Police (SLP), while customary law is now administered by the Local Courts, headed by a Local Court Chairman and chiefdom police. Islamic law is also constitutionally recognised in Sierra Leone in relation to marriage, divorce and intestate succession and is understood to be encompassed by customary law (Joko Smart 1980, pp. 87–102). These multiple legal orders have existed simultaneously and continue to the current day.

Since the end of Sierra Leone's civil war in 2002, significant legal change has been underway. Numerous laws have been updated or introduced, including in an effort to make clear the relationship between customary and formal law. According to the 1991 Constitution (currently undergoing review), customary law cannot contradict formal law; however, the Constitution currently provides for exceptions to non-discrimination in relation to customary practices, and in relation to marriage, divorce, death and adoption (providing a loophole for practices such as early marriage and clitoridectomy, and enabling discrimination against women) (Kamara 2005). Some of the most important legal changes, as they relate to the relationship between formal and customary law, include the Local Courts Act and the Chieftaincy Act (2009). The 2011 amendment to the Local Courts Act (1963) clarified the jurisdictional limits of the Local Courts (responsible for administering customary law), limiting them to civil cases and criminal cases in which punishments are less than six months imprisonment or 50,000 Leone (approximately US$10).[1] The Chieftaincy Act makes clear that while chiefs can arbitrate disputes of a non-criminal nature, adjudicating matters and issuing punishments of fines or imprisonment is expressly illegal.

Yet it is questionable to what extent these formal laws apply in practice and affect customary law. In conducting research into the justice system in Sierra Leone in 2009, Clare Castillejo notes that:

> [a] number of local court chairmen and officers interviewed were unaware of the legal limits of their jurisdiction. For example, one local court officer in Koidu town reported that his court could hear cases that carry fines of up to 1 million Leones.
>
> (Castillejo 2009, pp. 7–8)

Ryann Manning (2009, p. 131) notes that 'in a Bombali chiefdom, a previous court chairman was alleged to have consulted the Paramount Chief on all cases before ruling'. In 2012, I witnessed a chief's adjudication in which the plaintiff paid a fee to the chief to adjudicate a dispute, believing the chief could act more quickly and effectively than the police (Denney 2014a). Such examples of practice flouting the law are believed to be widespread, indicating the resilience of customary law and the challenges of regulating one legal order with another.

These processes of legal change should not suggest the decline of customary law. While it is often implicit in much statebuilding discourse and practice that customary law will eventually disappear as the state, its services and formal laws extend deeper into the provinces (because a reliance on custom is rationalised as being due to state weakness), this is by no means a certainty and is at least a very long-term process (Forrest 1998; Rotberg 2003). Indeed, the continuing legitimacy and relevance of customary law to many Sierra Leoneans was highlighted by the importance of chiefdom bye-laws in enforcing government policies during the Ebola epidemic in 2014–15. Chiefs put in place by-laws banning a range of practices that could contribute to the spread of Ebola. This included customary burial practices that involve washing the deceased, secret society initiations that involve initiates being brought together and, in some cases, female circumcision. Some have argued that it was only when customary authorities were brought into the Ebola response that behaviour change among the population really took effect (Oosterhoff and Wilkinson 2015).

In part, the customary justice system remains popular because it is more accessible to the predominantly rural population (13 years after the war ended, there was still not a magistrate resident in every district), and perceived to be more affordable (Thompson 2002; Dale 2008; Castillejo 2009; Suma 2014). However, it has also retained its popularity because it is viewed by many as more relevant to their daily lives and more in keeping with their attitudes towards crime, conflict and dispute resolution (Varvaloucas, Koroma, Turay and Saddiqi 2012). Despite progress in reforming state institutions since the end of the civil war, the Ebola epidemic underscored an ongoing lack of confidence in state institutions that still needs to be overcome and helps to drive a continued reliance on alternative service providers.

The post-conflict period has also given rise to another important change in the justice and security space in Sierra Leone. As more NGOs were established or arrived, and discourses around human rights and justice became more widespread, multiple alternative dispute resolution (ADR) mechanisms have emerged. This is not to suggest that no such mechanisms were in place previously – indeed, a number of forums such as the market women's association and the Bo Peace and Reconciliation Movement had been conducting conflict resolution for some time. However, a range of paralegal and mediation organisations emerged in the post-conflict period that have augmented the justice and security system in Sierra Leone, providing another avenue for dealing with disputes, insecurity and injustice.[2] Post-conflict transitions and statebuilding in Sierra Leone have thus not led to the supremacy of the state as the sole legitimate security and justice provider, but rather has seen the continuation of plural security and justice orders, as well as the emergence of some new non-state security and justice providers.

Dispute resolution in Sierra Leone can thus take place along one of at least four 'chains' (Denney 2014b). These include:

- formal English law through the formal courts
- customary law through the Local Courts
- customary law through chiefs and secret societies (technically illegal)
- alternative dispute resolution.

These are conceived of as chains because there are multiple steps – or links – in the process (these chains, of course, are not discrete but interact, as becomes clear later in this chapter). Within formal English law, for instance, someone might first report to the Sierra Leone Police, who might then investigate the crime and potentially charge the matter to the formal courts, which would then hear the matter and, if the accused was found guilty, decide on a punishment. By

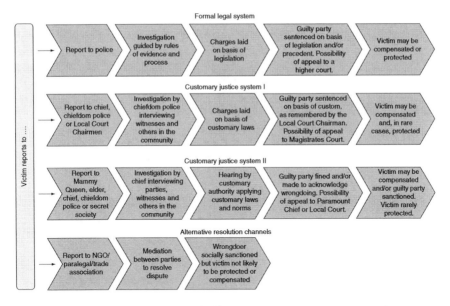

Figure 9.1 Security and justice chains in Sierra Leone.

contrast, if someone were to use the customary law administered by the chief, they might first report to an elder or the chief, who would then call the parties to discuss the matter and provide judgement, which could be appealed before a higher-ranking chief. Yet, these 'chains' should not be understood as purely linear processes, and it is important to note that people move between providers (both of their own accord and through referrals from one chain to another) or pursue matters through multiple chains at once. The plural security and justice chains available, at least in theory, look something like the depiction in Figure 9.1.

This plural security and justice system is historically embedded and yet resilient in the face of significant change in the post-conflict period.

Approaches to security and justice reform (SJR)

Despite this plurality, 18 years of reforms to the security and justice sectors have resulted in only limited engagement with all those a part of Sierra Leone's hybrid system. Security and justice sector reforms in Sierra Leone have been led primarily by the United Kingdom's Department for International Development (DFID), with the former colonial power playing the role of lead donor in the sector. Some more targeted assistance has also been provided by other donors, in particular the United Nations Development Programme, but UK programming is by far the most influential in shaping Sierra Leone's post-conflict security and justice sectors. Despite the widespread recognition that the state is just one provider of security and justice in Sierra Leone, reforms have focused overwhelmingly on the formal state level.

In the early stages of reform, from 1999 to 2005, the focus was primarily on stabilising the country (peace was only declared in 2002) and (re)building the capacity of the SLP to enforce order. As reformers from that time note, while they were aware of the importance of chiefs in the governance of daily life of much of Sierra Leone, embracing a 'non-state' actor in the wake of a civil war waged against a non-state armed group (the Revolutionary United Front) was not politically feasible or desirable. Rather, the emphasis was on enabling the state-sanctioned police force to maintain law and order (Denney 2014a). This is in keeping with the wider statebuilding prerogative of SJR. The overarching goal of post-conflict reforms in Sierra Leone (and internationally) is to rebuild a functioning *state*. In part, this is connected to dominant understandings in international politics going back to Weber that a legal-rational state provides the most effective and desirable mechanism for maintaining order and delivering services to citizens (Weber 1968).

A new security and justice programme – the Justice Sector Development Programme (JSDP) – that ran from 2005–11, funded by DFID, attempted to redress the heavy focus on policing and formal security and justice actors. A stronger justice sector focus was taken and support to the police scaled back. Under this programme, the Local Courts were engaged and codification of customary law (which varies across Sierra Leone's 149 chiefdoms) explored. Development of the Local Courts Act was also supported and paralegal organisations were funded to expand services, providing an alternative dispute resolution service. The JSDP thus engaged more extensively with Sierra Leone's plural security and justice system, in part because this was more possible a few years after the formal end of conflict and also due to the stronger focus on justice than security – where non-state actors tend to be more readily accepted (Denney 2014a). However, while the JSDP was an important step towards engagement with a wider range of security and justice actors, it ultimately continued to focus primarily on state providers, engaged with only some elements of the customary system and tended towards an approach that sought to formalise them (Denney 2014a, pp. 105–6).

Indeed, Albrecht notes that at least until 2010, limited efforts were made to engage with chiefs, despite them being arguably the most central security and justice actor to the lives of most Sierra Leoneans (Albrecht 2010, p. 1). Following the JSDP, DFID launched another security and justice programme, known as the Access to Security and Justice Programme (ASJP). This programme shifted focus away from state security and justice institutions to community level engagement, at least in its early stages. While continuing some support for government ministries, the judiciary and the Family Support Units (police stations set up to deal with crimes involving women and children), the ASJP focused to a larger degree on voice and accountability, supporting local civil society organisations providing paralegal, legal aid and other support at the local level. This programme ended in June 2016 and was also interrupted by the Ebola epidemic in 2014–15. The scope of future programming by the UK is not yet clear but appears to signal a shift towards commercial justice (fitting with UK ideas of the 'golden thread' that links together rule of law with a sound investment environment that – so the thread thinking goes – will lead to economic growth and development (Cameron 2012).

Sierra Leone's SJR programmes have clearly evolved over time to include a greater recognition of the role and importance of plural providers. While this is certainly a welcome development and DFID has, according to Steven Golub, 'played a trailblazing role in studying customary and other non-state justice systems', the approach has not been without its limitations (2007, pp. 48–9). As the final section of this chapter demonstrates, while there is an increasing acknowledgement of the reality of plural security and justice orders, these are often viewed as dichotomous to state provided services, characterised by competition between providers and often criticised for being more prone to human rights concerns than state providers. This view misses the more complicated and overlapping nature of the plural security and justice system in Sierra Leone, which in fact reveals a more integrated and cooperative system of hybrid providers that span – and thus challenge – the state/non-state binaries. Moreover, human rights abuses are hardly limited to one part of Sierra Leone's security and justice providers but cut across all providers.

Unpacking hybridity

While it is of course welcome that there is a greater acknowledgement of plural security and justice orders, the manner in which this is conceptualised often remains a highly stylised account of reality. Even the language used by many researchers (this author included) to explain the phenomenon is often misleading – state versus non-state, formal versus informal, etc. This language reinforces the idea that plural security and justice orders are made up of discrete, oppositional actors that compete. Indeed, Peter Albrecht suggests that the overwhelming neglect of chiefs within Sierra Leone's SJR,

> has been informed by a rigid dichotomy between state and non-state actors that has dominated and continues to dominate the thinking of many academics and policy-makers. It is moreover informed by the fact that, fundamentally, the role of chiefs in Sierra Leone is not well-understood by international actors.
>
> (Albrecht 2010, p. 5)

This chapter attempts to provide a more nuanced understanding of how the plural security and justice system operates in Sierra Leone – not from a top-down perspective of someone external looking in, but rather from the perspective of the users of security and justice services, and the providers of those services. This 'end-user' approach (Luckham and Kirk 2012) recognises the importance of human behaviour in understanding security and justice and shifts the focus from one that seeks to rationalise and neaten reality into systems, to one that opens up the messy and interactive reality of practice. This reveals a much more complicated and interconnected system that cannot easily be separated into dis-crete dichotomous categories – nor as a system of multiple single-entity provid-ers.[3] Rather, it is more usefully understood as a plural order of hybrid providers. Three interrelated points are made. First, the ways in which people access security and justice reveals not discrete opting for 'state' or 'non-state' providers but rather more fluid movement between multiple providers, sometimes using 'state' and 'non-state' simultaneously. Second, different security and justice pro-viders refer disputes between both 'state' and 'non-state' avenues, demonstrating an at times cooperative relationship. Third, looking at the roles and sources of legitimacy of individual security and justice providers shows how they do not all fit neatly into a 'state' or 'non-state' category but rather span both, thus compli-cating the categorisations of the providers that make up Sierra Leone's plural security and justice system.

How people use the system

Perhaps most importantly, people who access security and justice services in Sierra Leone do not survey the options as discrete systems and then decide whether to opt for 'state' or 'non-state' systems. From their perspective, there is just one system that combines multiple (though often wanting) avenues for dispute reso-lution. Different providers are viewed as being more or less accessible and afford-able, depending on one's geographic and financial position. Different providers will also be more or less trusted depending on personal and community norms and experiences of a provider – not all police or all chiefs are viewed homogenously. And finally, different providers will be seen as more or less relevant to specific crimes or conflicts. Often family disputes, for instance, are not seen as being within the remit of the police and are considered more appropriately dealt with by chiefs or elders (although campaigns to prevent domestic violence and treat gender-based violence seriously are attempting to change this). If we are to develop a more nuanced understanding of plural security and justice orders, we must first under-stand why people make the decisions they do in reporting to different providers and how they weigh different factors in making those decisions.

People use the range of justice chains available to them in different ways. People do not necessarily just use one of these chains. They may use multiple chains at once – for instance speaking both to local paralegals as well as the chief. Use of the various chains can also be instrumental – often people report to the police without the intention or belief that the case will proceed through to the formal courts, but the act of going to the police itself can elicit greater readiness to compromise on the part of the accused. Similarly, using ADR mechanisms to deal with cases of domestic or gender-based violence, which have often not been taken seriously by either the formal or customary system is increasingly prompt-ing formal and customary providers to take these matters more seriously so as to remain relevant providers (and access the resources, legitimacy and power that this can confer). This underscores the degree to which people make functional use of the multiple providers in the security and justice system to achieve different outcomes. While it is certainly true that someone seeking justice by way of criminal conviction will find this difficult (given the weak capacity – and will – of the police, lack of forensic capacity in the country, the cost and slow pace of the judicial system, etc.), someone looking to receive financial compensation settled out of court can use the system to their advantage by going to the police to increase the stakes for the accused, and then settling out of court. Similarly, someone looking for justice for gender-based violence is likely to trigger a more serious response from the police or the customary justice system if they can show that paralegals are registering the case as a serious matter. Again, this is about understanding why and how people use different chains within the system as they do. It also helps us to think about the various providers as an interactive system, rather than as discrete chains.

One useful way to think of this is to consider other sectors in which plural providers exist – such as health or education. Sierra Leone's health sector, for instance, is made up of government hospitals, traditional healers and traditional birth attendants, community health workers, drug peddlers, etc. These providers are often not seen as competitors but as multiple components of a wider system, differing in terms of their accessibility, affordability and competitive advantage (see Denney and Mallett, with Jalloh 2014). Some illnesses are more likely to be referred to traditional healers because they are seen to have spiritual causes that modern medicine cannot address. Other illnesses are viewed as having multiple causes and thus require treatment by both traditional healers and government health clinics. Drug peddlers are viewed as filling an important gap, given the frequent failure of drug supply that affects government health clinics. While donors or international aid workers may view some of these actors as more or less desirable, from the perspective of people who use the system, they are an ecosystem of providers that has developed to fill various needs (ibid.). While some may be preferred in certain circumstances to others, they exist because they fulfil a function or a need within communities.

As with other services, understanding security and justice from the perspective of those who use the multiple providers available reveals a more fluid network of providers that people move between to maximise their chances of achieving some form of justice.

Relationships between different actors in the system

Looking at the security and justice system from the perspective of the providers also presents a more complex picture of plurality than the state/non-state dichotomy suggests. The security and justice providers themselves regularly refer cases between different chains within the system, suggesting they are not discrete but rather interactive. Some of the common referral pathways are depicted in Figure 9.2. This is critical to local attempts at peace formation that international interveners must recognise and engage with.

Some of the referrals shown in Figure 9.2 are through the process of judicial review – with appeals from the legal customary justice system possible to the

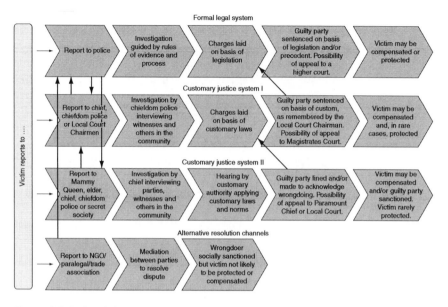

Figure 9.2 Referrals between security and justice chains in Sierra Leone.

formal justice system (although this process is rarely used in practice). Other referrals are more ad hoc and reflect both the continuation of and changes in norms surrounding how certain disputes are resolved. For instance, police continue to refer some cases of neighbourhood disputes, debts, petty theft or domestic violence to customary channels, in the belief that these will provide more appropriate remedies. Particularly in the case of domestic violence, customary channels are often understood as providing justice that allows the marriage to remain intact, in a way that is seen as less possible when the formal justice system is used (Denney and Ibrahim 2012). The Head of Sierra Leone's Council of Paramount Chiefs explains that justice provided by the chiefs is more about getting people back together after a problem or conflict and re-establishing community harmony, as opposed to achieving more 'winner-takes-all' individualised forms of justice.

However, there is a growing trend of chiefs referring complaints of sexual assault and other serious crimes to the SLP. In part, this is due to sensitisation efforts around the 2012 Sexual Offences Act, as well as clearer articulation of the roles of chiefs in the 2009 Chieftaincy Act (although as discussed earlier, this technically makes it illegal for chiefs to adjudicate any matters). In 2012, I witnessed a chief's adjudication in Freetown in which the chief agreed to hold a hearing regarding a matter of verbal abuse of a woman, but declined to adjudicate on a matter of election posters being defaced. As a matter of electoral law, the chief insisted the matter had to be taken to the SLP, despite the plaintiff's pleas that the chief could act more quickly than the police. Cases can thus move between different security and justice chains and must be understood in a fluid rather than fixed manner. This suggests that the security and justice providers who make up the plural system themselves do not view the system as a series of discrete chains, but rather an interactive network. Building our knowledge of how cases move between different providers within the security and justice system, and with what effect, is thus important to understanding the nature of plural security and justice in Sierra Leone.

Hybrid nature of individual actors themselves

A third underexplored feature of the plural security and justice system in Sierra Leone is the hybrid nature of some of the individual providers of security and justice themselves. Thus, while Sierra Leone's security and justice system can be seen to be a 'hybrid' of state/non-state providers, in the same way some of the individual providers of security and justice themselves do not fit neatly into the state or non-state category. Sierra Leone's hybridity, therefore, is not simply made up of a plurality of state and non-state actors, but also some actors who are themselves both state and non-state. This is most apparent in relation to chiefs.

While those writing on chieftaincy in Sierra Leone note their 'betwixt and between' character (Albrecht 2010) and the manner in which they draw on dual sources of legitimacy (Manning 2009), they are frequently talked about as 'customary', 'informal' or 'non-state' security and justice actors. Their more formal or statist role is overlooked. In fact, chiefs occupy a hybrid role and are simultaneously part of the state and part of cultural institutions seen to be outside of the state. Recognising only one part of their character simplifies the complexity of chieftaincy and misses a key feature of the hybridity of Sierra Leone's security and justice system.

Indeed, the head of the NCPC in Sierra Leone describes the role of chiefs as a delicate balancing act. On the one hand, chieftaincy is a constitutionally recognised role. Chiefs have seats in Parliament (although there are some moves to change this from within the chieftaincy itself), have powers embodied in legislation and can – in theory – be dismissed by the Minister for Local Government and Rural Affairs (although it has never happened in practice). Chiefs are crucial in collecting tax at the community level on behalf of the state – perhaps their most important state function. In this sense, they are very much 'of the state'. Indeed, the Head of the NCPC notes that chiefs are 'an agent of government to bring services to the people'. Importantly, they are not political agents, however, and any chief wishing to enter into politics must resign as a chief (Hunt, see Chapter 5 in this volume). They thus fulfil a kind of civil servant role.

However, on the other hand, chiefs see themselves as obtaining their legitimacy from their subjects whose interests they represent – not from the government. When putting the civil servant analogy to the Head of the NCPC, he only partially agreed – pointing to the fact that as chiefs, their work is not guided by state administrative guidelines but by custom and tradition.[4] Theirs is a personalised form of rule, in contrast to Weber's impersonal rule (Weber 1968, p. 958).

While part of their role requires them to participate in state functions (e.g. Parliament or tax collection) they understand their role mostly to exist parallel to the state – in a supportive but separate governance system. This can be seen in their role as custodians of culture, for instance, whereby chiefs are patrons of secret societies (the groups that carry out initiation rites for adolescents, including female circumcision). Chiefs are also custodians of the land in rural areas – holding it 'in trust' for the people.

Chiefs thus serve *both* the people and the government of the day. This is not without its difficulties. The Head of the NCPC spoke of the challenge of serving the people by advocating for their needs to government while being sure not to be seen as opposing the government – which would be viewed as a chief being politicised. Of course, in practice, many chiefs are aligned with one political party or another, but the appearance is meant to be one of political neutrality and support for 'the government of the day'. These challenges are partly at the heart of moves to withdraw chiefs from Parliament to enable them to play more of a representative function without fear of accusations of politicisation.

The hybrid nature of chiefs can even be seen in the roles of the current Head of the NCPC himself – the highest ranking chief in the country. Through his various jobs and roles, he embodies both state and non-state governance functions. Prior to becoming a Paramount Chief, the Head of the NCPC served as a District Officer in the provinces. He was later a civil servant in the Ministry of Health and in the President's Office before being elected as Paramount Chief in 1984, following the death of his father. He is now also a member of the Public Services Commission Board, given his long experience in various forms of governance, a role which he executes according to the national goals of the Public Services Commission and the Constitution, not according to chieftaincy interests or customs.

In the same way that it makes little sense to think of officers within the SLP as existing in some 'modern' world of security and justice outside of the wider social norms that give rise to the prevalence of plural security and justice (see Denney 2014a), it similarly makes little sense to think of chiefs as purely 'traditional' or 'non-state'. Rather, they too possess complex multiple identities and roles that cannot be reduced to 'state' or 'non-state'. As Albrecht notes, chiefs

> belong neither to a pure non-state nor to a pure state category. This condition has made it difficult for international actors to engage robustly with chiefs, who have essentially refrained from clearly defining their functions and role as in-between state and non-state. In short, there does not seem to be a space for the type of actor that falls between categories.
>
> (Albrecht 2010, p. 7)

As research on peace formation – and the central role of hybridity within this – continues, these issues of the multiple hats that individual security and justice providers wear offers a potential avenue for deepening and nuancing our understandings. This is true not only in Sierra Leone or other supposed 'fragile states' but in all places. Rather than neatly categorising actors and the systems to which we ascribe them, their intersectional and contingent identities and affiliations should be opened up in order to understand how hybridity operates in practice for those seeking security and justice (Hunt, see Chapter 5 in this volume).

Unpacking hybridity to explore how users of security and justice services navigate multiple providers, how providers interact and how a single provider can simultaneously embody multiple affiliations provides a richer account of the realities of security and justice in Sierra Leone. This helps to nuance our understanding of hybridity and to move beyond the simplistic binaries that are often the default characterisation of plurality. It can also help processes of statebuilding and peace formation to begin not with templates of how service provision is meant to operate in theory, but with how it in fact operates in practice. This means engaging with providers of security and justice – as well as of other plural services, such as health – that people actually use, even if these take international organisations out of their comfort zones of formal authorities. Not engaging with such realities means that international peace formation efforts work with only one dimension of the ways in which people access services and therefore have a more limited impact and potentially harmful consequences.

Conclusion

Security and justice reform (SJR), as a key component of dominant statebuilding practices, has been roundly criticised for failing to engage with the realities of how security and justice are accessed and how peace is locally formed, as well as for interpreting multiple political, legal and security orders as a failed form of the Weberian state and its monopoly on the legitimate use of force (Schroeder, Chappuis and Kocak 2014; Boege *et al.* 2009). In response, a growing literature recognises that hybridity and plurality are in fact distinct orders in which institutional multiplicity is the norm and not a failing. These constitute the very ways in which communities form their own peace. Yet, how hybridity functions remains underspecified, and both research and (to a larger extent) practice have tended to explain or operationalise hybridity in narrow, binary terms, such as state versus non-state; formal versus informal.

In an effort to move away from such oversimplifications, this chapter has sought to unpack hybridity and what it means for how security and justice are delivered in Sierra Leone. This provides a much more complicated picture of security and justice providers and their overlapping roles, identities and relationships. Understanding hybridity in this more complex – but also more empirically accurate – manner can help to refine SJR, and peace formation efforts more broadly, to engage with hybridity. This, it is hoped, will lead to programming that better connects with the realities of how people access security and justice and takes seriously the unique political orders that characterise the ways in which peace formation takes place.

Notes

1 For a comparison with the situation in Ghana and Liberia, see Boege, Chapter 12 in this volume.
2 For more on how post-conflict interventions contribute to hybridity, see Schroeder *et al.* (2014).
3 See Hunt, Chapter 5 in this volume.
4 Of course, in practice, chieftaincy powers are guided and limited by state laws, and chiefs are meant to uphold the same laws (although not in all cases the same administrative rules and procedures) as civil servants. However, the degree to which the actual exercise of chieftaincy powers is subject to legislative limitations is open to question.

Bibliography

Albrecht, P 2010, 'Betwixt and between: chiefs and reform of Sierra Leone's justice sector', *DIIS Working Paper* 33, www.diis.dk/files/media/publications/import/extra/wp2010-33-albrecht-betwixt-and-between_web.pdf (accessed 26 November 2015).

Baker, B 2006, 'Beyond the state police in urban Uganda and Sierra Leone', *Afrika Spectrum*, vol. 41, no. 1, pp. 55–76.

Baker, B 2008, 'Beyond the tarmac road: local forms of policing in Sierra Leone and Rwanda', *Review of African Political Economy*, vol. 35, no. 118, pp. 555–70.

Baker, B and Scheye, E 2007, 'Multilayered justice and security delivery in post-conflict and fragile states', *Conflict, Security and Development*, vol. 7, no. 4, pp. 503–28.

Benda-Beckmann, F 2002, 'Who's afraid of legal pluralism?', *Journal of Legal Pluralism*, vol. 47, pp. 37–82.

Boege, V, Brown, A, Clements, K and Nolan, A 2009, 'On hybrid political orders and emerging states: what is failing – states in the Global South or research and politics in the West?', *Berghof Handbook Dialogue Series* no. 8, Berghof Research Centre for Constructive Conflict Management, Berlin.

Cameron, D 2012, 'Combating poverty at its roots', *Wall Street Journal*, 1 November 2012, www.wsj.com/articles/SB10001424052970204712904578090571423009066 (accessed 6 November 2016).

Castillejo, C 2009, 'Building accountable justice in Sierra Leone', *Working Paper* 76, FRIDE, Madrid.

Dale, P 2008, *Access to justice in Sierra Leone: a review of the literature*, World Bank Justice for the Poor Programme, http://siteresources.worldbank.org/INTJUSFOR POOR/Resources/Access2JusticeSierraLeoneLitReview.pdf (accessed 26 November 2015).

Denney, L 2014a, *Justice and security reform: donor agencies and informal institutions in Sierra Leone*, Routledge, Abingdon.

Denney, L 2014b, 'Overcoming the state/non-state divide: an end-user approach to security and justice reform', *International Peacekeeping*, Special Issue on Security Sector Reform, vol. 21, no. 2, pp. 251–68.

Denney, L and Ibrahim, AF 2012, *Violence against women in Sierra Leone: how women seek redress*, ODI Country Evidence, www.odi.org.uk/sites/odi.org.uk/files/odi-assets/publications-opinion-files/8175.pdf (accessed 5 December 2015).

Denney, L and Mallett, R with Jalloh, R 2014, *Understanding malnutrition and health choices at the community level in Sierra Leone*, Secure Livelihoods Research Consortium, www.securelivelihoods.org/publications_details.aspx?resourceid=324&Category ID=2265 (accessed 7 January 2016).

Denzer, L 1971, 'Sierra Leone – Bai Bureh', in M Crowder (ed.) *West African resistance*, Hutchinson, London.

Forrest, JB 1998, 'State inversion and non-state politics', in LA Villalon and PA Huxtable (eds), *The African State at a critical juncture: between disintegration and reconfiguration*, Lynne Rienner, Boulder.

Fyfe, C 1962, *A history of Sierra Leone*, Oxford University Press, Oxford.

Golub, S 2007, 'The rule of law and the UN Peacebuilding Commission: a social development approach', *Cambridge Review of International Affairs* vol. 20, no. 1, pp. 47–67.

Jearey, JH 1960, 'The structure, composition and jurisdiction of courts and authorities enforcing the criminal law in British African territories', *International and Comparative Law Quarterly*, vol. 9, pp. 409–10.

Joko Smart, HM 1980, 'The place of Islamic law within the framework of the Sierra Leone legal system', *African Law Studies*, vol. 18, pp. 87–102.

Kamara, J 2005, *Investigating discriminatory laws against women in Sierra Leone*, Centre for Accountability and Rule of Law, 18 December 2005, www.carl-sl.org/pres/investigation-discriminatory-laws-against-women-in-sierra-leone/ (accessed 26 November 2015).

Kane, M, Oloka-Onyango, J and Tejan-Cole, A 2005, 'Reassessing customary law systems as a vehicle for providing equitable access to justice for the poor', paper presented at the New Frontiers of Social Policy Conference, Arusha, 12–15 December.

Little, KL 1967, 'The Mende chiefdoms of Sierra Leone', in Forde, D and Kabbery, PM (eds), *West African kingdoms in the nineteenth century*, Oxford University Press, Oxford.

Luckham, R and Kirk, T 2012, 'Security in hybrid political contexts: an end-user approach', *Justice and Security Research Programme Paper* 2, Justice and Security Research Programme, London.

Manning, R 2009, 'Landscape of local authority in Sierra Leone: how "traditional" and "modern" justice and governance systems interact', in Zhou Y (ed.), *Decentralisation, democracy and development: recent experience in Sierra Leone*, World Bank, Washington DC.

Oosterhoff, P and Wilkinson, A 2015, 'Local engagement in Ebola outbreaks and beyond in Sierra Leone', *Practice Paper in Brief* 24, Institute of Development Studies, Sussex.

Rotberg, R 2003, *State failure and state weakness in a time of terror*, Brookings Institution Press, Washington DC.

Schroeder, U, Chappuis, F and Kocak, D 2014, 'Security sector reform and the emergence of hybrid security governance', *International Peacekeeping*, Special Issue on Security Sector Reform, vol. 21, no. 2, pp. 214–30.

Suma, M 2014, 'Sierra Leone: justice sector and the rule of law', Review by AfriMAP and the Open Society Initiative for West Africa, http://issat.dcaf.ch/esl/layout/set/print/content/download/48039/758786/file/Sierra%20Leone%20Justice.pdf (accessed 7 January 2016).

Tamanaha, BZ, Sage, C and Woolcock, M (eds) 2012, *Legal pluralism and development: scholars and practitioners in dialogue*, Cambridge University Press, Cambridge.

Thompson, N 2002, *In pursuit of justice: a report on the judiciary in Sierra Leone*, Commonwealth Human Rights Initiative, www.humanrightsinitiative.org/publications/ffm/sierra_leone_report.pdf (accessed 7 January 2016).

Varvaloucas, A, Koroma, S, Turay, M and Saddiqi, B 2012, 'Improving the justice sector: law and institution-building in Sierra Leone', in Johnson OEG (ed.), *Challenges and policy issues in early 21st Century Sierra Leone*, International Growth Centre and the Bank of Sierra Leone, London.

Weber, M 1968, *Economy and society: an outline of interpretive sociology*, vol. III, Bedminster Press, New York.

10 The international-local interface in peacebuilding

The case of Bougainville

Volker Boege

Introduction

For more than two decades, international peacebuilding practice has been informed by what has been called the 'liberal peace' approach, and the academic debate has revolved around this approach and its critique.[1] Linked to the discourse on state fragility and the fragility-conflict nexus, liberal peacebuilding was and is conceptualised as closely linked to statebuilding, with a rather narrow understanding of 'the state' as its backdrop: the state as the western Weberian state and the central machinery of government with its variety of institutions in charge of security, welfare and representation. Accordingly, statebuilding was operationalised as building the institutions of the state and their capacity, and the ultimate aim of peacebuilding was the establishment of a 'proper' (that is, Weberian) state as the superior guarantor of peace, with a liberal market economy and a liberal democratic civil society as underpinnings of the liberal state. This paradigm of peacebuilding-as-statebuilding (Richmond 2011), however, has failed to achieve the expected positive outcomes. It turned out that the recipient societies were not just blank pages on which the international liberal agenda could be written, that the weakness or absence of formal state institutions did not equate to the absence or weakness of institutions of social order, and that local populations were not just passive recipients of a peace and state delivered to them from the outside. Local people demonstrated agency of their own, often beyond the political structures familiar to liberal western views. Instead of the mere 'delivery' of liberal templates of peace and state by benevolent outside actors, what is taking place in reality is the collision, interaction and entanglement of profoundly different understandings of socio-political order and of the appropriate conduct of conflict.

This reality has been acknowledged by the more recent 'turn to the local' (which, it has to be said, has so far been a turn more in the academic discourse and at the conceptual level rather than in actual peacebuilding policies and practice). Local actors, most notably 'non-state' societal actors, are now seen as impacting on the internationals' predetermined peacebuilding agenda and its implementation through various forms of agency, including obstruction, resistance, capture, re-appropriation, co-optation, adoption, adaptation, mimicry, redirection, etc., and as capable of appropriating international agendas and resources for their own purposes, according to their own functional logic and political economy (Mac Ginty 2013; Richmond 2011; Richmond and Mitchell 2011; Mac Ginty and Richmond 2013). In this context, the local is acknowledged as the core arena of peacebuilding, the site of ongoing processes of interchange, entanglement, permeation, reassemblage and reconfiguration (Mac Ginty and Richmond 2013; Albrecht and Moe 2014; Mac Ginty 2015), and the locals are found to be worth engaging with.[2]

This local turn nevertheless has its limitations and pitfalls. Its bureaucratic, ideological and epistemological confines, as well as its constraints, grounded in power relations and power politics, should not be glossed over (Chandler 2013b). Furthermore, it can lead to consequences that are highly questionable from a peacebuilding perspective (e.g. the evasion of responsibility and accountability on the part of the internationals, or the modernisation of counterinsurgency strategies) (Moe 2014). Criticism of the local turn as pursued 'mainly for instrumental or rhetorical reasons' (Mac Ginty and Richmond 2013, p. 771) is therefore valid. At the same time, however, the local turn opens avenues for new approaches in the scholarly discourse on peace formation, as well as for innovative peacebuilding practice.

In what follows, the case of Bougainville peacebuilding will be analysed through the lens of the local turn and as an example of it, tracing the international/liberal and indigenous/local interactions and entanglements, and demonstrating how this leads to the emergence of hybrid forms of peace and political community.

Violent conflict on Bougainville

From 1989 to 1998, the island of Bougainville in Papua New Guinea was the theatre of the longest and bloodiest war in the South Pacific since the end of World War II.[3] Its root cause was the negative social and environmental effects of a giant mining project, the Panguna gold and copper mine, which in the 1970s and 1980s was one of the largest open-pit mines in the world. The immense environmental destruction caused by the mine endangered the land-based way of life of the local population. An influx of large numbers of workers from outside Bougainville added to the pressure on local communities. Local people blamed outsiders – workers, expatriate company management and the agents of the central government – for not respecting indigenous culture and their special status and rights as the traditional owners of the land. They demanded meaningful environmental protection measures, compensation for environmental damage and a larger share of the revenues. The mining company and the PNG government rejected these demands, and as a consequence, members of local clans brought the mine to a standstill by acts of sabotage in late 1988 and established the Bougainville Revolutionary Army (BRA). Fighting between the BRA and the security forces of the PNG government soon spread across the whole island. The BRA adopted a secessionist stance and called for independence for Bougainville. BRA fighters managed to overrun and shut down the Panguna mine in

1989, and the mine has remained closed ever since; even today it is in the hands of a faction of the secessionists.

In its war against the BRA, the PNG military was supported by local Bougainvillean auxiliary units, the so-called 'Resistance Forces'. Over time, it became the Resistance that bore the brunt of the fighting on the government side. Moreover, long-standing local conflicts between clans were also fought under the umbrella of the war of secession. Parties entangled in local conflicts either joined the BRA or the Resistance, which were both made up of largely independent units. The war became more and more complex, and the frontiers blurred.

The time of war was to a large extent a time of statelessness. The institutions of the PNG state were forced to withdraw from Bougainville. This opened the space for a resurgence of non-state local customary institutions, which had been sidelined during colonial times and during the formation of the independent state of PNG after 1975 but had not completely disappeared. In many places 'traditional' authorities such as elders and chiefs again became responsible for regulating conflicts and organising community life.[4] They drew upon long-standing customary norms and ways of operating – to the satisfaction of their communities, as most accounts testify (Regan 2000). Elders and chiefs were also responsible for dealing with violent conflicts in the local context. They were often successful in achieving reconciliation at the intra- and inter-community level, utilising customary methods of conflict resolution. Thus, localised 'islands of peace' were established even at the height of the war. Local peacebuilding had already generated positive results well before a formal Bougainville-wide ceasefire was achieved in 1998, paving the way for a high-level political peace process.

The hybridisation of peacebuilding

As noted above, the violent conflict on Bougainville was not just a war of secession. It was a complex mixture of such a war and localised sub-wars between societal entities such as clans, lineages or villages. Therefore, peacebuilding had to address not only political issues at the 'higher' level of Bougainville-PNG relations, but also issues at the 'lower' level of (inter-)communal conflicts. This (inter-)communal peacebuilding largely followed customary approaches. Countless customary peace processes have taken place between opposing villages and clans all over the island since the end of the war, some of which are still continuing, and many more are yet to come.[5]

The aim of customary peacebuilding is the restoration of social harmony in communities and amicable relationships between the conflicting parties. This is achieved by reconciliation processes. Reconciliation is based on the development of a common understanding of the causes and the history of the conflict. It necessitates willingness to accept responsibility for wrongdoings and to apologise, as well as willingness to accept apologies and forgive, and the negotiation of the – material and spiritual – conditions for the restoration of relationships.

Reconciliation culminates in the exchange of gifts (compensation) for damage done and wrongs committed during formal peace ceremonies. Given that the vast majority of Bougainvilleans are devout Christians, Christian understandings of reconciliation and activities such as church services and prayers are integral elements of local customary peacebuilding and of peace ceremonies.

Customary peace processes were 'modernised' in various ways. Local 'peace committees' or 'district reconciliation steering committees' were formed, and local peace treaties were elaborated, put into writing and signed. Local peacebuilders also adopted 'foreign' conflict resolution knowledge and adjusted it to their specific needs. For example, the NGO Peace Foundation Melanesia (PFM) trained locals as mediators, facilitators and negotiators. PFM's courses did not impose fixed western-style concepts of conflict resolution but built on local approaches, in particular by referring to reconciliation and restorative justice, revitalising customary ways and adapting them to contemporary needs, e.g. by introducing more 'modern' training techniques (Howley 2002).

Local peacebuilding was thus a local-liberal hybrid, with local customary ways (of reconciliation and the restoration of relationships) predominating.

High-level political peacebuilding was also hybridised, although the local aspects were less visible here. At first glance it appears that activities at this level followed a typical international liberal template: negotiations facilitated by an external third party (New Zealand), a cease-fire (1998), a peace agreement (2001), a constitution (2004), elections (2005, 2010, 2015), etc. At the same time, however, the high-level activities were also infused with local practices. Chiefs and elders, women and church leaders successfully claimed a role in the realm of 'high-level' politics and at least partially introduced their ways of peacebuilding into that realm, e.g. with regard to inclusiveness and the style of negotiations.

With regard to inclusiveness, customary dispute settlement necessitates the participation and commitment of all members of the parties involved in conflict. Accordingly, a very broad process was organised, in an attempt to include all stakeholders. 'High-level' peace talks were each attended by dozens, if not hundreds, of Bougainvilleans, not only by the political and military leadership. Truce and ceasefire agreements were signed not only by the leadership, but also by local commanders as well as traditional authorities and representatives of civil society, such as church leaders and representatives of women's groups. This made the agreements more binding and easier to implement. Given the matrilineal organisation of most communities on Bougainville, the involvement of women was of particular importance.[6]

Local actors were able to put into practice their understanding of proper representation and participation in political negotiations. Accordingly, the forms of negotiations differed from what would be seen as 'normal' through the international liberal lens. Extended times of prayer and singing together, for example, were integral parts of the negotiations – activities that, from the liberal internationals' point of view, can easily be misjudged as folkloristic and tokenistic accessories to the 'real' business of political negotiation but in the eyes of

Bougainvilleans are peacebuilding tools in their own right, tools that can be more powerful than mere spoken or written words.

High-level peacebuilding on Bougainville was thus a liberal-local hybrid, following a liberal international template, but infused with patterns of locally appropriate behaviour.

To sum up the local-liberal interface of peacebuilding on Bougainville, it can be said that while the process at the top followed more the international-liberal template, the processes at the bottom were dominated by local customary practices. However, the logic of local customary peacebuilding also permeated the top processes, and liberal approaches coloured and re-formed processes at the bottom. It was due to the permeation of liberal forms with local ways that the negotiations at the 'higher' political level led to a comprehensive peace settlement, the sustainability of which was grounded in customary conflict resolution practices at the bottom. The combination of top-down (liberal-local) and bottom-up (local-liberal) processes made Bougainville peacebuilding a success, and while in conventional western academic and political thinking 'the top-down story is the master narrative and the bottom-up reconciliations are subsidiary' it can be argued that in the Bougainville case 'in important ways the bottom-up micro narratives subsume and infuse the top-down peace' (Braithwaite 2011, p. 140).

The international-local interface

While peacebuilding on Bougainville built on the resilience of local actors and institutions, it also needed external support, and the relatively constructive international-local interaction contributed to success.

New Zealand (NZ) played a constructive part in initiating the peace process by offering facilitation services, providing logistical assistance, hosting the initial rounds of peace talks and negotiations, and creating a warm atmosphere for negotiators (Braithwaite, Charlesworth, Reddy, Dunn 2010, pp. 46–9). With the consent of the conflict parties, neighbouring states and the UN conducted a peacebuilding mission on Bougainville. The UN sent a small but highly effective contingent, known successively as the UN Political Office in Bougainville (UNPOB, August 1998–2004) and the UN Observer Mission in Bougainville (UNOMB 2004–05). Its symbolic value, demonstrating the international community's commitment, its contribution to the weapons disposal process and its role as mediator in negotiations between conflict parties were of major importance for the peace process. Not least, the UN provided the external interveners with international legitimacy (Regan 2008, p. 202). Furthermore, a regional Truce Monitoring Group (TMG), which later became the Peace Monitoring Group (PMG), arrived on the island in late 1997 and stayed until June 2003. It was followed by a small, entirely civilian Bougainville Transitional Team (BTT), until December 2003.

The TMG/PMG was an unarmed force comprised of both military and civilian personnel, men and women, from Australia, New Zealand, Fiji and Vanuatu.

NZ led the TMG and Australia led the PMG, with Australia providing the bulk of personnel and resources.[7] The TMG/PMG's mandate was to support the peace process 'through logistics, monitoring, verification, mediation and confidence building' (Australian Government 2012, p. 20).

Most importantly, the presence of the international actors provided a secure space for former enemies to come together. The internationals played an important role in initiating conversations between the conflict parties and keeping conversations going, even in critical stages of the peacebuilding process (Braithwaite 2011).

The Bougainvilleans largely controlled the extent and content of the activities of the external actors. They were successful in their insistence on having an unarmed intervention, despite initial concerns of the interveners, who felt uneasy about going into a volatile post-conflict situation unarmed. This arrangement meant that the interveners were dependent on the locals for their security and protection and were not in a position to enforce anything against the locals' wishes or interests. At the same time the locals developed strong feelings of responsibility for the safety of their international 'guests' (and, in fact, TMG/PMG personnel were never attacked) (Regan 2010, p. 69).[8] In Bougainville, as in many other societies of the Global South, the hosts' responsibility for the security and well-being of their guests is taken very seriously. Hence, this arrangement provided a rather robust security guarantee for the internationals. On the other hand, it impacted on the power relations between the internationals and the locals in the latter's favour (Regan 2010, p. 156).

The intervention initially followed the conventional liberal peacebuilding agenda, but this did not align neatly with local understandings and practices of peacebuilding. This holds true not least regarding the conceptualisation of peace itself. One peace monitor said:

> I began to realize that my understanding of 'peace' was too narrow to encompass its much more complex meaning for many Bougainvilleans. We peace monitors tended to define peace in terms of the formal truce and cease-fire agreements.... We went to villages with copies of the Burnham, Lincoln and Arawa agreements.... We poorly grasped that peace meant dealing with ... less tangible elements ... On a more complex level, which I only glimpsed, Bougainvilleans seemed committed to 'spiritual rehabilitation'. Calls for 'spiritual rehabilitation' were linked to attempts to articulate the kind of society that they wanted to build.
>
> (Ruiz-Avila 2001, pp. 98–9)

The last sentence indicates how misleading liberal peacebuilding notions of 'local culture' as apolitical are, and it hints at the fundamental political significance of culture and spirituality.

The importance of the spiritual dimension also becomes clear in the account of another peace monitor: 'I experienced one healing ceremony, two crusades and a number of discussions with women who had just talked with Jesus' (Parry

2001, p. 106). Engaging with this dimension was not planned for. However, sitting through five-hour-long church services, for example, became common practice over time. The internationals realised how useful this was for building relationships with the devout locals.

For internationals coming from a western secular, presumably enlightened and rational background, it is difficult to earnestly engage with the spiritual, to actually become open to emotional and spiritual sensation and intuition and appreciate the role of myth and ritual for peacebuilding. In peacebuilding on Bougainville, however, God, the spirits of the ancestors and the unborn, the holy bushes and trees and the totem animals of the clans on Bougainville, who are embedded in networks that transcend the culture-nature divide and the human-nonhuman divide, are 'actors' in their own right, with the capacity to make a difference. Accordingly, peace cannot be conceptualised without taking this non-human dimension of the world, both material and spiritual, into account. The ni-Vanuatu, the Fiji iTaukei, as well as the Maori in the NZ contingent, had far fewer problems relating to this spiritual dimension than the white Australians and New Zealanders; they shared a common cultural background with the Bougainvilleans.[9] This proved to be important also during the first rounds of peace negotiations between conflict parties in NZ, when Maori peace rituals were deliberately used to build an atmosphere of trust and commitment (Braithwaite *et al*. 2010, pp. 46–8).

Another area easily discredited as 'soft' and 'non-essential' by international peacebuilders is that of 'gender issues'. A female monitor explains that the peace intervention 'risked missing the boat with a key peace process resource – the women. We had applied our European attitudes to Bougainville and had not realized the role that women had customarily played' (Castell 2001, p. 121). Engaging with the women was of utmost importance for the recalibration of exchanges between interveners and locals. Given that male and female spheres are to a large extent separate in Bougainville society, male peace monitors could not have built relationships as the females did. Hence the participation of women in the intervention was of major importance. Bougainville women had female counterparts among the TMG and PMG. When presenting the success of the PMG to the outside world, the male political and military leadership of the intervention managed to bolster its image by stressing the gender and female component, but this was originally not in the plan. In fact, it was initially met with ignorance and even resistance in the context of the military as a masculine hierarchical organisation and by a male leadership that made a distinction between 'real', that is men's, politics and 'soft' women's issues. Only in the everyday exchange with the locals in the course of the intervention did the gender dimension emerge as a factor of major political significance.

The same can be said about different conceptualisations of time. On Bougainville, as in other international peacebuilding interventions, the external actors tried to impose their (tight) timeframes. But at the end of the day they had to adjust to 'Melanesian time'. The Australian military commander of the PMG, for example, makes the point that 'Canberra' (that is, the Australian Government) underestimated the complexity of the Bougainville situation and therefore presented the PMG with over-ambitious timetables. He says:

> But I learned that Melanesian clocks differ from other timepieces ... I quickly adapted to the Melanesian approach ... [and] although there was significant early pressure from Canberra to speed up the process, I learned that it had to progress at the pace of the locals.
>
> (Osborn 2001, pp. 52–3)

Nevertheless, 'many in the Australian system did not really understand why the peace process moved at what, to them, seemed a frustratingly slow pace' (Regan 2010, p. 79). On the ground, the PMG initially 'concentrated on patrolling to as many villages as possible to hand out printed material. They convened peace awareness meetings, delivered their message and left' (Breen 2001, p. 45). The locals disapproved of this rushed approach. As a result, 'over time patrols spent longer in villages.... Patrols took the time to listen to stories, appreciating the world of villagers and creating empathy and trust' (Breen 2001, p. 47). Similarly, the 'high-level' peace process proceeded at the locals' pace. Dozens of rounds of talks and negotiations and a host of intermediate agreements, memoranda of understandings, protocols, etc., were necessary to make progress – very slowly, as it might seem, from an outsider's perspective. During negotiations, participants took their time, too. The first rounds of talks between the parties in NZ in 1997 and 1998 took weeks. The NZ hosts were prudent enough not to dictate a timetable. Rather they provided for a lot of 'free' time, enough time for the representatives of the parties to adjust and be together without the duress of a tight schedule. Furthermore, no timeframe was given regarding demobilisation and disarmament. At the beginning, there was only general agreement on a three-phased, open-ended weapons disposal process. It only started in December 2001, four years after cessation of armed conflict, and no dates were set as to when the single stages of the process had to be accomplished. Weapons disposal was not finalised officially until the year 2005 (and in reality, it has not yet been completed). Peacebuilding on Bougainville is now in its seventeenth year, and it will continue for some time.

The focus on process and long timeframes is very much in line with local customary principles and methods of peacebuilding. At the same time, it poses a major challenge for the international actors, whose mindset is determined by the notion of achieving 'outcomes' and 'getting things done as quickly as possible'. Overall, the locals largely succeeded in maintaining their pace of doing things and adjusting the international's pre-planned timetables to local needs and customs.

The limits of that adjustment, however, should not be glossed over: the PMG commander in the quote above, for example, speaks about the difference between 'Melanesian clocks' and 'other timepieces'. This way of talking implies a shared universal concept of time and ignores deeper cultural differences. Perhaps Melanesian time is not clock time at all – that is: linear measurable time.

A different cultural understanding of time can have profound impacts on peace-building, e.g. if past events of linear clock time (the time of the internationals) are still 'present'. In Bougainville the dead fighters of the war are still fighting today, because their bodies could not yet be laid to rest according to the appropriate customary burial and reconciliation ceremonies. Time is not a universal given – it is something different for peacekeepers, villagers in the mountains of Bougainville, politicians in Canberra or the UN headquarters in New York.

The examples given above demonstrate that in the local-international interface both a recalibration of relationships between the actors and a renegotiation of the content, aims and strategies of peacebuilding took place. The liberal peace agenda was re-articulated and reshaped.[10]

At the end of the day, 'the way the intervention developed was not so much a matter of careful planning, but rather a product of complex interactions of numerous often distinct interests among both international and local actors' (Regan 2010, pp. 162–3). In the course of everyday interaction with the locals, the internationals' peacebuilding agenda had to change considerably. However, one cannot escape the impression that the internationals' engagement with local understandings of peace(building) remained within their own cultural and epistemological comfort zone and confines, with 'the other', the local ways of being, doing and knowing (conflict, peace, culture) merely seen to challenge and/or enrich liberal ways. On the other hand, the locals' responses to the internationals' agenda instigated self-reflection processes in the internationals' camp and led to a renegotiation of the liberal peacebuilding agenda, resulting in outcomes more conducive to the locals' interests, needs, norms and understanding of peace. The seemingly all-powerful liberal peace approach was re-articulated by its 'recipients' on the ground, who turned out to be not simply grateful and abiding subjects of external agendas and strategies but powerful actors in their own right, maintaining autonomy and agency, neither merely adopting the liberal peace agenda nor resisting it totally.[11] The all-too-often misused phrase of 'local ownership' has real substance in the Bougainville case, with local ownership taken by the locals rather than 'granted' and 'nurtured' by the internationals (Krogstad 2014). The fact that most people and leaders on Bougainville would have liked the PMG and UNOMB to stay longer, is proof of positive changes in the local-international relationship; over time a generally genuine and respectful partnership developed between the internationals and the Bougainvilleans (Braithwaite *et al.* 2010, p. 55).

With regard to the internationals, the encounters in Bougainville (and other places in the Pacific) have contributed to a debate at home (in this case, in Australia and NZ) about the need to rethink and recalibrate one's own understandings of the international-local interface in peacebuilding.[12] Hence, it can be posited that the Bougainville experience contributed to the above-mentioned turn to the local and to the emergence of a discourse on 'relational sensibility' among international peacebuilders.[13]

Looking ahead

After the stabilisation of the security situation on the ground, a considerable number of foreign development agencies, international NGOs and United Nations programmes and institutions became active on Bougainville.[14] Currently, this international engagement is intensifying again as Bougainville is entering another critical phase in its peacebuilding process: according to the 2001 peace agreement, a referendum on its future political status – autonomy or independence – has to be held sometime between 2015 and 2020, and the ABG and the central government of PNG have set 15 June 2019 as the target date for the referendum. Australia is supporting a comprehensive 'Bougainville Peace Building Strategy', which receives considerable funding and which comprises core aspects of sustainable peacebuilding and fostering good governance (law and justice, leadership, civic education, etc.). Furthermore, a variety of community-based organisations and NGOs are working on peace and conflict resolution issues, often applying a combination of indigenous and introduced approaches, e.g. combining western trauma healing programmes and counselling with customary healing rituals.

These initiatives are all the more important as currently people and leaders are faced with the challenge of linking post-conflict peacebuilding with the formation of a political order that can provide for the nonviolent conduct of conflict and sustainable peace in the future. Again, this is a process in which local/ indigenous and international/liberal approaches come together.

Depending on the outcome of the referendum on its future political status, Bougainville will become either a completely independent state (with autonomy as a transitional phase to independence) or will remain a widely autonomous political entity within PNG (Bougainville Peace Agreement 2001). Both options necessitate some kind of statebuilding. At the same time, local customary institutions of governance are in place on the ground that have proven to be legitimate and effective in peacebuilding and that govern everyday life in local communities. They have to be taken into account in the current process of state formation, all the more so as many Bougainvilleans – out of bitter negative experience – nurture a deep mistrust of western-style centralised government structures and processes. The vast majority of people appreciate central elements of liberal democracy (e.g. voter turnout in elections is generally high), but they also want a system of governance that acknowledges their own indigenous norms and values. People wish to 'marry' local customary and introduced liberal institutions and processes. The Bougainville constitution of 2004, although a liberal statebuilding document, reflects this desire (Bougainville Constitutional Commission 2004). It not only provides for western liberal institutions (a president, a parliament, elections, an independent judiciary, an executive controlled by the legislative, etc.), but also makes comprehensive reference to custom and customary institutions. It explicitly institutionalises forms of governance stemming from the local customary sphere, for example, by including direct democratic elements into the formal procedures of liberal democracy (e.g.

voter-initiated legislation and plebiscites or the recall of members of parliament), or by an 'Advisory Body' as a second house of parliament beside the House of Representatives. This Advisory Body (which has not yet been set up) is to be made up of chiefs, elders and other traditional authorities.

Even the liberal institutions are imbued with local characteristics. For example, the ABG President, John Momis, is not only the elected president of the Autonomous Region of Bougainville but also a chief. In public, he is regularly referred to as President Chief John Momis. Thus, although Momis himself sees and presents himself as an elected president bestowed with rational-legal legitimacy, for the people on the ground, there is more to his legitimacy than just that – and Momis is well aware of it. In another example, the current Regional Member for Bougainville in the national parliament of PNG, Joe Lera, was initiated as a paramount chief in his home district after his election to parliament in 2012. Being elected bestowed him with legitimacy in the liberal state context. However, this was obviously not sufficient. He needed further legitimisation by way of becoming a traditional chief. Lera's (as well as Momis') legitimate authority is hybrid: he is a legitimate leader not only because he is an elected parliamentarian but also because he is a chief, and the elements of his legitimacy are inextricably interwoven. He is not only chief for his local people, but his people bestow him with chieftaincy to serve the whole of Bougainville (and PNG), and what he does in this wider 'political' context is legitimised by his chiefly status. He only became chief because he had been elected as a parliamentarian, and what he does in the local context is legitimised not only by his chiefly status but also his status as Member of Parliament (Boege 2014).

In a similar vein, the police and the judiciary – core elements of domestic peace and order in the liberal state – inhabit an ambiguous position. In most places on Bougainville today, police only have a chance to function relatively effectively and with legitimacy when working together with the chiefs. In fact, Bougainville's police service is constitutionally obliged to cooperate closely with traditional leaders in the communities (Autonomous Region of Bougainville 2004, Clause 148). The police in general are not really seen as an important provider of law and order. Large swathes of Bougainville are no-go zones for the police. In some areas, there is competition between chiefs and police; in other areas they cooperate well. Police can only gain access to most villages after invitation by the chiefs (although this is not a legal provision, it is the reality on the ground). The chiefs make use of the police only under exceptional circumstances. They have their own means of 'policing' their communities, at present often together with the community auxiliary police (CAPs).[15] In doing so, they apply customary means of dispute resolution and customary law, which are perceived as providing solutions to most issues related to the maintenance of order in the communities in everyday life. The formal justice system, on the other hand, is weak and seen with considerable suspicion, removed from the people both physically and psychologically: difficult to access, costly, highly formalistic, time-consuming, with confusing procedures and unpredictable outcomes.

There is a lot of debate, however, on where to draw the line between the realm of customary law and state law.[16] Moreover, the distinctions between the two spheres are blurred. For instance, village courts are officially institutions of the formal state system, but often they apply customary law – and when doing so, they often go well beyond the limits of their formal competencies.

This state of governance arrangements and provision of peace and security can be called a 'hybrid political order' (Boege 2010)[17]: the liberal state and the local customary domains not only coexist – with complementarities and synergies, as well as frictions and incompatibilities – but also overlap and become enmeshed. Moreover, on Bougainville, efforts towards deliberate combination and integration of these two domains are pursued for the sake of establishing socio-political order. The ABG is interested in improving the capacity and effectiveness of state institutions, but not as the only means for maintaining peace and order. It is aware that the enforcement of law and justice solely by the respective state agencies is not a viable option and that collaboration with non-state providers of peace and order is needed. The ABG, in other words, deliberately abstains from trying to implement a state monopoly over the legitimate use of force. Instead, it aspires to positive mutual accommodation of introduced liberal state and local customary institutions as an alternative vehicle for maintaining an orderly political community. This means that a core dimension of statehood – maintaining law and order, controlling violence, providing security for citizens and a framework for the nonviolent conduct of conflicts – is organised in a way that decisively differs from the western Weberian model. In other words: the hybridity that characterises peace formation on Bougainville is also a main feature of Bougainville state formation. In processes of mutual accommodation of local customary and introduced liberal institutions and procedures, the templates of liberal peace and state become localised and local institutions liberalised, bringing about a unique Bougainvillean form of political community and post-liberal peace.

Even if Bougainville becomes independent as an outcome of the referendum, consequently having to establish itself as a state so as to fulfil its obligations as a member of the international community of states, in the domestic realm this polity will not be a proper western-style Weberian state, but a home-grown variety imbued with the features of hybrid governance and security arrangements. Such a home-grown form of polity does not necessarily have to be seen as 'second best' in comparison to the ideal type Weberian state, but potentially can serve the needs and interests of the people in effective and legitimate ways, not least in the domain of peace and security.

Notes

1 For this debate, see Paris and Sisk (2009); Newman, Paris and Richmond (2009); Richmond and Franks (2009); Paris (2010); Richmond (2011); Tadjbakhsh (2011); Campbell, Chandler and Sabaratnam (2011); Mac Ginty (2013). More recently, critiques of the liberal peace critique have introduced new aspects into the debate (see, e.g. Chandler 2011, 2013a, 2013b, 2014), pointing to the discursive and practical

limitations of the critique while arguing that it turns a blind eye to issues of power and political economy, and that its epistemological and ontological presumptions tie the critique back into the liberal peace concept it set out to criticise.

2 This engagement with local realities and local actors is a challenge that goes well beyond the conventional international liberal commitment to 'participation' and 'ownership', which usually boils down to expectations of the locals having to buy into the international liberal agenda: 'they' have to own 'our' ideas and concepts (the ideas and concepts of the liberal west), and 'they' have to 'participate' in the implementation of those ideas and concepts. By contrast, Krogstad demonstrates how 'under the radar' local ownership that is simply taken by the locals can be very different from – and more important than – the kind of local ownership international interveners intend to 'nurture' (Krogstad 2014).

3 For an overview of the war on Bougainville, an island of about 9000 sq km and 250,000 inhabitants, and of post-conflict peacebuilding, see Regan (2010); Braithwaite *et al.* (2010); Carl and Garasu (2002). For the historical, societal and political context, see Regan and Griffin (2005).

4 Care needs to be taken not to misinterpret the term 'traditional'. Today's 'traditional' authorities are not the same as those of a distant pre-contact, pre-colonial and pre-statehood past. 'Tradition' is not static; it changes over time, all the time. Today the term 'chiefs' and 'elders' designate 'modern' social categories that emerged in the course of interaction between indigenous societies and external actors, first missions and the colonial administration, and later the institutions of the 'modern' state. While chiefs are usually men, women hold their own forms of traditional authority, based on the matrilineal structure of most communities on Bougainville. In the following, the terms 'traditional' or 'customary' actors or authorities are used in order to differentiate them from other – state or civil society – actors. This follows the terminology used by people and leaders in Bougainville themselves (in official documents, public political speech and everyday conversations). It has to be kept in mind, however, that these terms, and the social institutions to which they refer, are not well-defined and static but contested, fluid and constantly hybridised.

5 For an overview of peacebuilding Bougainville-style, see Boege and Garasu (2011).

6 For an account of the role of women in peacebuilding, see the contributions in Havini and Sirivi (2004).

7 For a comprehensive account of the TMG and PMG, see Wehner and Denoon (2001); Adams (2001); Braithwaite *et al.* (2010); Regan (2010); Breen (2016).

8 In hindsight, the Australian side concedes that:

> the arrangements under which local parties would provide security to unarmed monitors worked well. An unanticipated benefit was that it also encouraged the members of the Truce and Peace Monitoring Groups to place greater importance on building good relationships with local leaders and communities so as to prevent misunderstandings that might result in threats of violence against the operation.
>
> (Australian Government 2012, p. 34)

9 Again, in hindsight 'Australia recognises that its personnel rarely match the cultural skills, understanding of context and appropriateness of approach of our Pacific Island partners in regional settings' (Australian Government 2012, p. 43).

10 It has to be noted that the focus of this account is on the changes on the side of the internationals. Of course, there were also changes on the side of the locals: their attitudes, norms and practices were more or less 'liberalised'; they partially and selectively accepted, adopted and adapted to liberal attitudes, etc., in a mix of intentional deliberate strategy and unintentional emergent adaptation. These processes cannot be retraced here.

11 One aspect of the locals' agency that rarely attracts attention is that they were very smart in utilising the capacities provided by the external actors for purposes that at

first sight were diverting resources from the 'real' peacebuilding tasks. For instance, transport by PMG helicopter was extensively used by chiefs and others to get them to and from meetings; villagers made comprehensive use of the PMG medical facilities or used the paper of all the leaflets, flyers, newsletters etc. distributed by the PMG for rolling their bush tobacco. Hence, it was not only the 'core business' prescribed by the liberal peacebuilding agenda (e.g. supervising the ceasefire, assisting in weapons disposal) that made the intervention useful for the locals, but also the 'collateral goods' that its presence provided – surely a distinct form of 'under the radar' local ownership (Krogstad 2014).

12 See, e.g. Australian Government 2012 as an official document that is touched by the spirit of relational sensibility, cultural sensitivity and acknowledgement of local cultural context. For a scholarly discussion of this emerging trend, see Hughes, Hunt and Curth-Bibb (2013).

13 On relational sensibility, see Chadwick, Debiel and Gadinger (2013). Brigg describes relational sensibility as 'an attitude in which international and local interlocutors are focused, much more centrally than had previously been the case, on partnership, relationship and exchange' (Brigg 2013, p. 13). For a critique of the relational sensibility approach, see Chandler (2013b).

14 Australia was, and is, the biggest of these external players, providing assistance in the areas of law and order, education and health, reconstruction of infrastructure and economic recovery/employment generation and, more recently, direct capacity-building for the ABG and the Bougainville administration. Others involved are the aid agencies of Japan, NZ and the US, the European Union, the World Bank and the Asian Development Bank, as well as several UN agencies: UNDP, UNHCR, UN Women, UNICEF. International NGOs are also present, e.g. Save the Children, World Vision, Oxfam.

15 The CAPs themselves are a hybrid institution. They come under the supervision of the ABG and are designed to build the capacity of the state's security sector; at the same time they are members of their respective communities, obliged to work together closely with the chiefs and community leaders. The whole arrangement of 'community policing', Bougainville-style, transcends the state/non-state divide.

16 For example, opinions differ as to whether the conflict parties, the victim of an offence or the chiefs should decide whether to deal with an issue in the customary or the state law context. Some say that whenever a victim is happy with a customary resolution, the case has to be seen as settled, and the state law does not have to come in, whatever the matter. Others differentiate according to the seriousness of cases, positing that cases of murder or rape should go to the courts. Some strongly believe, however, that even these cases should be dealt with in the customary context.

17 The concept of hybrid political orders challenges the conventional state fragility and statebuilding discourse, which evaluates states against a Weberian ideal type (which, it must be said, is hardly a reality even in the most 'developed' western OECD states) and focuses on deficiencies, on what is lacking (namely statehood in the western sense) instead on what is actually there. By contrast, the hybrid political orders approach draws attention to the situation on the ground. It acknowledges the coexistence, competition, entanglement and blending of different types of legitimate authority, thus clarifying that the realms of liberal state and customary non-state, and their institutions and practices, do not exist in isolation from one another but intersect and permeate each other in everyday encounters (Boege, Brown, Clements and Nolan 2009). 'The emergence of hybridity is the result of the clash and connection of fundamentally different forms of political organisation and community' (Richmond 2011, p. 19).

Bibliography

Adams, R (ed.) 2001, Peace on Bougainville – Truce Monitoring Group. Gudpela Nius Bilong Peace, Victoria University Press, Wellington.

Albrecht, P and Moe, LW 2014, 'The simultaneity of authority in hybrid orders', *Peacebuilding*, vol. 3, no. 1, pp. 1–16.

Australian Government – Australian Civil–Military Centre 2012, *Partnering for Peace. Australia's peacekeeping and peacebuilding experiences in the Autonomous Region of Bougainville in Papua New Guinea, and in Solomon Islands and Timor-Leste*, Australian Government, Canberra.

Autonomous Region of Bougainville 2004, *The Constitution of the Autonomous Region of Bougainville* adopted by the Bougainville Constituent Assembly at Buin on 12 November 2004.

Boege, V 2010, 'How to maintain peace and security in a post-conflict hybrid political order – the case of Bougainville', *Journal of International Peacekeeping*, vol. 14, nos. 3–4, pp. 330–52.

Boege, V 2014, 'Vying for legitimacy in post-conflict situations: the Bougainville case', *Peacebuilding*, vol. 2, no. 3, pp. 237–52.

Boege, V, Brown, A, Clements, K and Nolan, A 2009, 'On hybrid political orders and emerging states: what is failing – states in the Global South or research and politics in the West?', *Berghof Handbook Dialogue Series* no. 8, Berghof Research Center for Constructive Conflict Management, Berlin, pp. 15–35.

Boege, V and Garasu, L 2011, 'Bougainville: a source of inspiration for conflict resolution', in Brigg, M and Bleiker, R (eds), *Mediating across difference: Oceanic and Asian approaches to conflict resolution*, University of Hawai'i Press, Honolulu, pp. 163–82.

Bougainville Constitutional Commission 2004, *Report of the Bougainville Constitutional Commission*, Report on the third and final draft of the Bougainville Constitution, Bougainville Constitutional Commission, Arawa and Buka.

Bougainville Peace Agreement, 30 August 2001, in Carl, A and Garasu, L (eds), 'Weaving consensus: the Papua New Guinea–Bougainville peace process', *Conciliation Resources Accord*, no. 12, 2002, Conciliation Resources, London, pp. 67–85.

Braithwaite, J 2011, 'Partial truth and reconciliation in the *long duree*', *Contemporary Social Science*, vol. 6, no. 1, pp. 129–46.

Braithwaite, J, Charlesworth, H, Reddy, P, Dunn, L 2010, *Reconciliation and architectures of commitment: sequencing peace in Bougainville*, ANU ePress, Canberra.

Breen, B 2001, 'Coordinating monitoring and defence support', in Wehner, M and Denoon, D (eds), *Without a gun: Australians' experiences monitoring peace in Bougainville, 1997–2001*, Pandanus Books, Canberra, pp. 43–9.

Breen, B 2016, *The good neighbour: Australian peace support operations in the Pacific Islands, 1980–2006*, Cambridge University Press, Cambridge.

Brigg, M 2013, 'Relational sensibility in peacebuilding: emancipation, tyranny, or transformation?', *Global Dialogues* no. 2, Centre for Global Cooperation Research, Duisburg, pp. 12–18.

Campbell, S, Chandler, D and Sabaratnam, M (eds) 2011, *A liberal peace? The problems and practices of peacebuilding*, Zed Books, London.

Carl, A and Garasu, L (eds) 2002, 'Weaving consensus: the Papua New Guinea–Bougainville peace process', *Accord*, no. 12, Conciliation Resources, London.

Castell, J 2001, 'Opening doors', in Adams, R (ed.), *Peace on Bougainville: Truce Monitoring Group. Gudpela Nius Bilong Peace*, Victoria University Press, Wellington, pp. 120–4.

Chadwick, W, Debiel, T and Gadinger, F 2013, 'The (liberal) emperor's new clothes? relational sensibility and the future of peacebuilding' *Global Dialogues*, no. 2, Centre for Global Cooperation Research, Duisburg, pp. 7–11.

Chandler, D 2011, The uncritical critique of 'liberal peace', in Campbell, S, Chandler, D and Sabaratnam, M (eds), *A liberal peace? The problems and practices of peacebuilding*, Zed Books, London, pp. 174–89.

Chandler, D 2013a, 'Peacebuilding and the politics of non-linearity: rethinking "hidden" agency and "resistance"' *Peacebuilding*, vol. 1, no. 1, pp. 17–32.

Chandler, D 2013b, 'Relational sensibilities: the end of the road for "liberal peace"', *Global Dialogues*, no. 2, Centre for Global Cooperation Research, Duisburg, pp. 19–26.

Chandler, D 2014, 'Beyond neoliberalism: resilience, the new art of governing complexity', *Resilience: International Policies, Practices and Discourses*, vol. 2, no. 1, pp. 47–63.

Havini, MT and Sirivi, JT (eds) 2004, *... as mothers of the land: the birth of the Bougainville Women for Peace and Freedom*, Pandanus Books, Canberra.

Howley, P 2002, *Breaking spears and mending hearts: peacemakers and restorative justice in Bougainville*, Zed Books/The Federation Press, London.

Hughes, B, Hunt, C and Curth-Bibb, J 2013, *Forging new conventional wisdom beyond international policing: learning from complex political realities*, Martinus Nijhoff, Leiden.

Krogstad, EG 2014, 'Local ownership as dependence management: inviting the coloniser back', *Journal of Intervention and Statebuilding*, vol. 8, nos. 2–3, pp. 105–25.

Mac Ginty, R (ed.) 2013, *Routledge handbook of peacebuilding*, Routledge, Abingdon.

Mac Ginty, R 2015, 'Where is the local? Critical localism and peacebuilding', *Third World Quarterly*, vol. 36, no. 5, pp. 840–56.

Mac Ginty, R and Richmond, O 2013, 'The local turn in peace building: a critical agenda for peace', *Third World Quarterly*, vol. 34, no. 5, pp. 763–83.

Moe, L 2014, 'The strange wars of liberal peace: the "local", hybridity, and the governing rationalities of counterinsurgent warfare in Somalia', paper presented at the ISA conference, Toronto, 26–29 March.

Newman, E, Paris, R and Richmond, O (eds) 2009, *New perspectives on liberal peacebuilding*, United Nations University Press, Tokyo.

Osborn, B 2001, 'Role of the military commander', in Wehner, M and Denoon, D (eds), *Without a gun: Australians' experiences monitoring peace in Bougainville, 1997–2001*, Pandanus Books, Canberra, pp. 51–8.

Paris, R 2010, 'Saving liberal peacebuilding', *Review of International Studies*, vol. 36, no. 2, pp. 337–65.

Paris, R and Sisk, T (eds) 2009, *The dilemmas of statebuilding: confronting the contradictions of postwar peace operations*, Routledge, Abingdon.

Parry, T 2001, 'Peace monitoring in Wakunai, 1998', in Wehner, M and Denoon, D (eds), *Without a gun: Australians' experiences monitoring peace in Bougainville, 1997–2001*, Pandanus Books, Canberra, pp. 103–7.

Regan, AJ 2000, '"Traditional" leaders and conflict resolution in Bougainville: reforming the present by re-writing the past?', in Dinnen, S and Ley, A (eds), *Reflections on violence in Melanesia*, Hawkins Press and Asia Pacific Press, Annandale and Canberra, pp. 290–304.

Regan, AJ 2008, 'The Bougainville intervention: political legitimacy and sustainable peace-building', in Fry, G and Kabutaulaka, TT (eds), *Intervention and state-building in the Pacific: the legitimacy of 'cooperative intervention'*, Manchester University Press, Manchester, pp. 184–208.

Regan, AJ 2010, *Light intervention: lessons from Bougainville*, United States Institute of Peace, Washington DC.

Regan, AJ and Griffin, HM (eds) 2005, *Bougainville before the conflict*, Pandanus Books, Canberra.

Richmond, OP 2011, *A post-liberal peace*, Routledge, Abingdon.

Richmond, OP and Franks, J (eds) 2009, *Liberal peace transitions: between statebuilding and peacebuilding*, Edinburgh University Press, Edinburgh.

Richmond, OP and Mitchell, A (eds) 2011, *Hybrid forms of peace: from everyday agency to post-liberalism*, Palgrave Macmillan, Houndmills.

Ruiz-Avila, K 2001, 'Peace monitoring in Wakunai, 1998', in Wehner, M and Denoon, D (eds), *Without a gun: Australians' experiences monitoring peace in Bougainville, 1997–2001*, Pandanus Books, Canberra, pp. 97–100.

Tadjbakhsh, S 2011, 'Introduction: liberal peace in dispute', in Tadjbakhsh, S (ed.), *Rethinking the liberal peace: external models and local alternatives*, Routledge, Abingdon, pp. 1–15.

Wehner, M and Denoon, D (eds) 2001, *Without a gun: Australians' experiences monitoring peace in Bougainville, 1997–2001*, Pandanus Books, Canberra.

11 Customary conflict resolution in a state environment

Cases from Vanuatu

Volker Boege and Miranda Forsyth

Introduction

The Pacific Island country of Vanuatu is a so-called microstate, consisting of 82 islands, 65 of which are inhabited, with a landmass of around 4700 sq km and a population of approximately 280,000. Apart from a short secessionist conflict during the transition from British–French colonial rule to independence in 1980, Vanuatu has so far been spared large-scale violent conflicts such as have shaken several of its neighbours in the more recent past, in particular Solomon Islands and Papua New Guinea/Bougainville.[1] Nevertheless, Vanuatu has to struggle with similar conflict-prone problems, such as frictions between different regions of the country and associated intercommunal conflicts, uneven economic development and inequities in the distribution of its costs and benefits, tensions over access to state power and state coffers, rapid urbanisation, a youth bulge and youth unemployment. All of this has to be seen against the backdrop of rapid social change, which severely affects societal structures, values and worldviews, coupled with the weakness of the institutions of a rather young nation-state.

Since independence, Vanuatu has experienced occasional outbreaks of violence that have led to disruptions of civic life and borne the potential for violent conflict escalation. So far, however, policies and practices of conflict prevention and the maintenance of order have been relatively successful. This is largely because, as shall be argued in this chapter, local customary forms of dealing with conflict were utilised in combination with state-based forms of maintenance of peace and order. It will be shown that customary conflict resolution (*kastom* conflict resolution) makes an important contribution to internal peace at various societal levels – not only in the everyday life of people in the villages and conflicts in the local context, but also in urban environments and in the sphere of state institutions and national politics. This chapter presents a number of cases in which *kastom* conflict resolution played a major role in the management and transformation of supra-local conflicts that had the potential to have escalated into major violence at the national level. It describes and analyses how conflict resolution worked in these cases (or why it did not work), with a focus on the role of *kastom* and its interplay with state institutions and procedures. Before having a closer look at the cases, however, it is necessary to explain the meaning(s) of *kastom* in the contemporary societal context of Vanuatu and its significance for the maintenance of peace, security and justice.

Kastom and *kastom* conflict resolution

Kastom is strong in contemporary Vanuatu, and conflict resolution is a major dimension of *kastom*.[2] Today's *kastom* is not identical with the customs of the pre-contact and pre-colonial past. Rather, *kastom* has developed since the times of first contact, colonisation and missionisation, incorporating exogenous influences into pre-colonial customs and adapting them to those influences. *Kastom* has evolved in interaction with outside powers, both distancing local ways of doing things from 'modern' introduced ways and absorbing certain elements of the introduced ways, Christian elements in particular. Hence, *kastom* has emerged (and constantly emerges) as a hybrid in the course of intercultural interaction.

Kastom is nowadays self-consciously referred to by 'ni-Vanuatu' (as the local people call themselves) to stress the difference between local ways and foreign, introduced ways, often depicting *kastom* as rooted in ancient pre-colonial traditions, a set of rules developed by the ancestors. *Kastom* governance is thus presented as the 'other' of, or alternative to, introduced state-based institutions and forms of governance, and customary law as the 'other' of, or alternative to, the law of the state (White 1993, p. 475). In other words: *kastom* 'derives both its force and its content oppositionally: by the symbolic contrasts in which it is juxtaposed to its opposites' (Keesing 1993, p. 589). The term *kastom* 'operates primarily by way of dialectical relationships with significant "Others"' (Taylor 2010, p. 281), such as 'skul', 'bisnis' or 'politik' (school, business, politics).

Kastom is thus not so much concerned with the rediscovery and preservation of the way of living of the ancestors; rather, 'selective representations of the past (are) constructed in and for the present' (Keesing 1993, p. 588). Accordingly, 'discourses about custom ... represent the past in and for the present' (Keesing, p. 588), and *kastom* 'evokes not so much the totality of ancestral practices as a particular selection of such practices for the present' (Jolly 1997, p. 139). At the same time, 'modern' issues are 'translated' into and debated in the language of *kastom*.

This becomes apparent in the political sphere, with *kastom* being transformed to an ideology with the purpose of shaping and strengthening a distinct Vanuatu national identity. During 'the struggle for independence in the 1970s *kastom* was selectively rehabilitated in the interests of forging a nation and uneasily enshrined, along with Christianity, in the national constitution and symbols' (Douglas 2002, pp. 18–19). Consequently, *kastom* operates as both a unifying concept and as a marker of diversity (Jolly 1992, p. 347). There is *kastom* as a national ideology, but at the same time different regions, islands, language groups and clans have their own specific *kastom*s. In the first context, *kastom* is a means of nation-building. On the other hand, however, differences in local *kastom*s can be divisive, even posing conflict-prone problems, for example in urban environments where people with different *kastom*s live together and where there is uncertainty about which *kastom* to follow.

Although *kastom* derives its strength from reference to tradition, to the ancestral rules of conduct, it is not unchangeable and static. Rather, it is in constant flux, being exposed to ever new external influences it adapts to new circumstances (Tarisesei 2012). Consequently, there is continuous debate about what *kastom* is; the understanding of *kastom* is constantly negotiated in everyday discourses against the background of rapid social change. On the one hand, this fluidity leads to much contention about the content and practical application of *kastom*, while, on the other, it makes it easier to bring about change – '[I]nnovations in Melanesia often succeed because they can pass as being ancestral and therefore not really new at all' (Lindstrom 1994, p. 81).

In the context of *kastom* it is the chiefs (*jifs*) who bear the prime responsibility for the governance and well-being of their communities.[3] They play an important role in the maintenance of peace, the resolution of conflicts and the development of communities. In tackling these tasks, they refer to *kastom* and apply *kastom* ways. In fact, 'chiefs can only function effectively through *kastom* governance' (Nolan and Tevi 2012, p. 48).

The capacities of *kastom* to deal with conflict is one of its decisive strengths.[4] In fact, 'the vast majority of disputes in every rural and urban community' in Vanuatu are dealt with according to *kastom* (Forsyth 2011, p. 176). *Kastom* conflict resolution addresses conflicts within a given community, among members of the community, or between neighbouring communities. Some of these conflicts (e.g. over stealing garden produce or pigs, pigs destroying gardens, swearing, adultery, etc.) might look quite trivial, but if not appropriately dealt with, they bear the potential for dangerous escalation. For it is never only individuals who are in conflict, but social groups, such as families or clans, because each individual is perceived as a member of a group, and the group is held responsible for the deeds of its members.

Given the relative weakness and limited geographical reach of the state institutions in charge of order and security (the police and the judiciary in particular), respective tasks and responsibilities very much rest with chiefs, who regularly refer to *kastom* in order to prevent and resolve conflict and to maintain peace. 'The central idea of the *kastom* system is that the chief or chiefs of a community are responsible for managing conflicts' (Forsyth 2009, p. 97).

At the same time, chiefs are the intermediaries between *kastom* and the communities on the one hand and the institutions of the state on the other. They 'operate both inside and outside the state' (Lindstrom 1997, p. 228). Post-independence chiefs were incorporated into the state system of governance. The Malvatumauri National Council of Chiefs is a constitutional body;[5] in theory it is the top of a layered chiefly system, with the levels of village councils of chiefs, area councils and island councils, and the Malvatumauri as the national council. In real life, however, this system is not put into practice everywhere; there are local variations and gaps in the system. The Malvatumauri is still working on the establishment of a uniform chiefly system, and it is engaged in furthering the codification and regulation of chieftaincy.

The ambiguity of chiefly status – rooted in *kastom*, but linked to and with obligations towards the state – can lead to tensions, in particular with regard to conflict resolution and the maintenance of peace and order. However, it can also be conducive in this regard, with the chiefs acting as bridging institutions that align *kastom* conflict resolution with state-based approaches.[6]

The rest of this chapter documents and analyses four conflict cases in which the *kastom*-state interface, and the ambiguous position of the chiefs and their intervention, came into play and had a decisive impact on the conflict outcomes. All four cases are of supra-local significance; all had the potential for violent conflict escalation that would have had a major impact well beyond the local context, even at a national level. They demonstrate that *kastom* conflict reso-lution matters not only with regard to remote rural communities (as conventional wisdom has it), but also with regard to the 'modern' sphere of (national) politics and the state. The first case is that of a conflict between two communities in the capital city of Vanuatu, Port Vila. In this case, *kastom* and state approaches were not aligned, and both showed considerable deficiencies. The second case deals with a serious conflict between different state agencies. It demonstrates that state institutions can be the cause of the problem, while *kastom* and chiefs can decisively contribute to the solution. The third case again shows the power of chiefs and *kastom*, with state institutions reluctantly coming on board. The fourth case finally provides proof for the possibility of a combination of *kastom* and state approaches and for deliberate collaboration of chiefs and state institutions.

The March 2007 state of emergency in Port Vila

A serious conflict between two communities in Port Vila occurred in March 2007 over a case of sorcery, leading to violent clashes between the communities from the islands of Ambrym and Tanna living in Port Vila. The belief in sorcery is widespread throughout Vanuatu, and accidents, misfortune, sickness and death are often blamed on individuals identified as being sorcerers or witches (Forsyth and Eves 2015). In this case, four people were killed, houses burned to the ground and property destroyed; dozens more were wounded and hundreds forced to flee their homes following accusations of sorcery (Public Report 2007; Jowitt 2008, p. 476). A state of emergency had to be declared for Port Vila and the sur-rounding regions.

This conflict between two communities from different islands living side-by-side in the urban environment of the country's capital city exemplifies the importance of 'islandism' in a 'modern' context.[7] This is a common phenom-enon found throughout Melanesia; it encompasses a kinship-derived system of obligation and support (Brigg 2009). It means there are extremely strong bonds between kinship and language groups, and the self-identification of people according to their particular ancestral 'ples' (place of origin) – which can be a whole island or a particular part of an island.

The report of a commission of inquiry into the events found that the police had totally failed (Public Report 2007, p. 10). They had done nothing to prevent or stop the fighting. Police reacted heavy-handedly only after the day of violence, with more than 140 people arrested and detained. However, neither had the chiefs been prepared to step in and dissolve the tension: fighting 'occurred because there was no proper mediation between the parties by their chiefs' (Public Report 2007, p. 3). Later the chiefs of the Tanna and Ambrym communities tried hard to achieve reconciliation, but this proved to be difficult because of the differences in *kastom* between the two communities. The Tanna community was prepared to bestow a young woman in marriage to the Ambyrm community for the loss of life, but the Ambrym people refused because this was not congruent with their *kastom*.

The Tanna chief, Tom Numake (a former President of the Malvatumauri and leader of the Tanna community in Port Vila), explains:

After the events of 3 March 2007, the chiefs from Tanna prepared a *kastom* reconciliation. Everything was ready from their side: pigs and mats and a girl. In Tanna *kastom* you have to give a girl (of 21 years or older) when somebody from the other side has been killed in a conflict. The girl is to marry a man from the other side and have children so as to compensate for the loss of life on that side. From the Tanna side a girl was ready to go. If a person is killed, it is not enough to give pigs and mats, you have to give a girl too. However, the Ambrym chiefs were not ready for this kind of reconciliation.[8]

Furthermore, the Ambrym community argued that the government also had a responsibility for the clashes and had to be involved in any reconciliation (and ensuing compensation arrangements). Hence, they asked the Tanna chiefs to wait until the government had come clear on the issue. As a consequence, the Tanna-Ambrym reconciliation had to be put on hold. This case clearly demonstrates how the *kastom* sphere and the state sphere are linked. Lack of progress in the one sphere (in this case: the state) can hinder progress in the other sphere (*kastom* reconciliation). In more general terms, this case raises the problem of how to include state institutions in *kastom* conflict resolution.

An important lesson of the March 2007 events was that as the national chiefly institution the Malvatumauri has a special role to play in intercommunal disputes. The report of the commission of inquiry recommended that 'any meeting between two islands over a nakaimas [black magic] issue should be handled by the Malfatumauri Council of Chiefs or any of its agencies' (Public Report 2007, p. 4). It even went as far as to recommend 'that meetings of sensitive nature must be held at the Malfatumauri National Council of Chiefs *nakamal* [traditional meeting place] and that adequate security is provided at all times by VPF [Vanuatu Police Force]' (Public Report 2007, p. 12).[9] These recommendations are based on the commission's assessment that the

alternative agency to provide peace and security of the people in Vanuatu especially in our local communities are the Chiefs. There are Chiefs throughout Vanuatu and the Government must be ready to use them to work alongside [*sic*] the police.

(Public Report 2007, p. 12)

The report thus acknowledges that the state institutions are not expected to be the sole (or even primary) providers of peace, security and justice. Responsibility is given to the chiefs, with state institutions in a supporting role. *Kastom* and chiefs are expected to operate also in a 'modern' urban environment; it is assumed that they have the capacity to deal with new challenges resulting from social change – in this case urbanisation and the ensuing coexistence of different island groups (that is, different *kastom* groups). On the other hand, it is accepted that state institutions and the government cannot properly deal with important conflict-prone issues (in this case: black magic) and that they have to rely on *kastom* and the chiefs. Unfortunately, in this case, the chiefs initially were not up to their task, but nor were the state institutions. Serious violence was the result. A further escalation of violence, however, was avoided due to the repressive reaction of the police and the reconciliation efforts of the chiefs. Nevertheless, these were uncoordinated activities that led to sub-optimal results and, as a consequence, to the harsh criticism by the commission of inquiry.

The August 2002 VPF-VMF stand-off

In 2002, a conflict between the Vanuatu Police Force (VPF) and the Vanuatu Mobile Force (VMF) pushed Vanuatu to the brink of civil war. A dispute over leadership positions in the VPF led to a stand-off between VPF and VMF in Port Vila, with both sides ready to use force. While government representatives were not present in this critical situation (rumours spread that the Prime Minister had gone into hiding), several chiefs were, and they talked to the two sides and managed to dissolve the stand-off.

In the follow-up, the chiefs held separate talks with the different conflict parties as well as the government, and then brought them together in the Malvatumauri's *nakamal* for negotiations facilitated by the chiefs. Negotiations resulted in a reconciliation ceremony held at the *nakamal* between the chiefs, the government, the police and the VMF.

The police and the VMF apologised for the disturbance of the peace and the trouble they had caused. The then prime minister, himself a high chief from Futuna Island, apologised to the chiefs and acknowledged 'the effort put in place by the chiefs through the Vanuatu National Council of Chiefs, the Malvatumauri, to enable the parties to resolve the dispute through a customary way and in a peaceful manner' (*Trading Post*, 3 September 2002, pp. 1–2). Pigs were killed and traditional mats and kava exchanged. Tears were shed and hands shaken as a sign of reconciliation. Hymns were sung and a church service held. Hundreds of people witnessed the reconciliation ceremony. According to all accounts, the ceremony was a very moving experience. The *Trading Post* commented on its success:

Custom and religion saved the day for the Government, Police and VMF as they hugged and said sorry to each other in a highly emotional reconciliation ceremony at the Chiefs Nakamal last Saturday evening, followed by prayers at the Police Station and VMF Barracks on Sunday.... Observers from across the board of the community have praised the settlement giving all the credits to the lively custom values and the religious principles that Vanuatu has been leaning on through the years.

The meaning of the reconciliation ceremony, however, was defined in differing ways.

While some argued that once customary reconciliation had been accomplished, there should be no involvement of the state legal system, others posited that *kastom* reconciliation should not prevent state justice from taking its course. The newly appointed commander of the police expressed his support for the reconciliation, but at the same time made it clear that in his opinion it could not be used as a 'blanket' to throw over any allegations which were before the courts. 'The law, he stressed, has to be allowed to take its course' (*Trading Post*, 31 August 2002, p. 2). In his view, the customary reconciliation could not replace the legal process: 'To agree to a traditional reconciliation ceremony and withdraw any allegations against a suspect pending before the courts would be like saying that there is no need for law and order to be seen to prevail' (ibid.).

This position was reiterated by the prime minister when he stated 'that any custom ceremony should not put a break to any matter that is before the court, proceedings that have been initiated must be completed' (*Trading Post*, 5 September 2002). The chiefs shared this view. Chief Paul Tahi, then president of the Malvatumauri, reiterated that there was consensus that after reconciliation, the chiefs would give the issue back to the state and the laws of the state.[10] In fact, the state legal system took over, and the matter was dealt with in several court cases in the following months.

The whole saga, however, only came to a close years later, and again, *kastom* provided for the closure. On 19 January 2010, a final reconciliation ceremony between the VMF and the VPF took place. This event was termed 'historic' as it was seen as 'the first national reconciliation' (*Vanuatu Daily Post*, 20 January 2010). All the main protagonists of the 2002 conflict were present at the ceremony, which 'drew to a close with a special ritual that saw all taking part in the Lord's Supper, shaking hands over water under the bridge and a sumptuous lunch' (ibid.).

The story of the 2002 stand-off between the VPF and the VMF provides an example of the complex relationship and interplay of *kastom* and state institutions in national politics. On the one hand, there was complementary cooperation. The intervention of the chiefs and the customary reconciliation ceremony diffused the immediate tension, prevented the conflict from escalating and secured a basis for its peaceful resolution. Once this had been achieved, the institutions of the state legal system – the courts – took over and brought the conflict to an end in legal terms by the application of the laws of the state. The final settlement then was again in the context of *kastom* (the reconciliation in 2010). In hindsight, the course of events can thus be interpreted as an indication of complementarity of *kastom* and state approaches. On the other hand, however, it is important to note that this had not been deliberately planned; there was no organised collaboration. State institutions had either been the cause of the problem or had proven weak and incapable of a planned response to the conflict, and it was only the intervention of the chiefs that saved the day for the government. It was they who were instrumental in the immediate dissolution of the tension, and it was they who brought the government back in.

It had been the state security forces that were responsible for the violence-prone escalation of the conflict in the first place. They had become a threat to order and peace instead of being providers of peace and order. Confronted with this situation, the government proved to be helpless. It appears that under these circumstances, the chiefs and the recourse to *kastom* were the only possible means of prevention of further conflict escalation and of conflict resolution.

The chiefs were able to offer a way out of the stalemate, namely *kastom* reconciliation. They succeeded in transferring the instruments of *kastom* conflict resolution to the context of the state and politics. Finally, this case also shows that state institutions can be subject to, and agents of, *kastom* conflict resolution.

The May 2006 prison escape

The resolution of the August 2002 crisis can be seen as evidence for the possibility of the complementarity of *kastom* and state. On other occasions, however, the differences between *kastom* and state approaches, and the potential for conflict between the two, become more apparent. The case of a prison escape in Port Vila provides a telling example.

In May 2006, 20 prisoners escaped from prison and turned to the president of the Malvatumauri, Chief Paul Tahi, for help, complaining about maltreatment by the police within the prison quarters and the poor state of the prison building.

The Malvatumauri president decided that the chiefs would take ownership of the issue. He explained his stance by saying: 'Whether you are a prisoner, Prime Minister or a woman, or a child, you belong to a *nasara* and you are still under the care and direction of your chief' (*Vanuatu Daily Post*, 8 May 2006, p. 1). (*Nasara* means 'meeting place' and in this context, membership of a particular community/kinship group). He met the prisoners who had gone into hiding and told them that they would have to go back to prison, but that the chiefs would organise a reconciliation first. The prisoners moved into the Malvatumauri's *nakamal* and thus were under the protection of the chiefs. When the police insisted on coming in and arresting the prisoners, this was rejected by Chief Paul, pointing to the sanctuary that the *nakamal* provided.

The leadership of the police did not dare to enforce arrest orders, but warned the chiefs: 'In accordance with law you cannot harbour a criminal.... They escaped from lawful custody. Any person who tries to entertain or harbour the prisoner then they are just as guilty' (*Vanuatu Daily Post*, 10 May, 2006, p. 2).

From this strictly legalistic point of view, the chiefs had committed a crime by guaranteeing the prisoners refuge in the *nakamal* and protecting them from the police.

There was a clash of positions: on the one hand the legal position of state institutions (to help escaped prisoners is a crime), on the other hand the *kastom* position (prisoners are also members of the community and deserve the protection that the *nakamal* provides). The strict legal perspective did not prevail. Instead, the issue was dealt with as a political one. The government was prudent enough to agree to the chiefs' proposal for a resolution of the problem, and finally the police had to join the process as well.

On 10 May 2006, a reconciliation ceremony was held at the *nakamal*, with the exchange of gifts between prisoners, chiefs and state representatives. Afterwards, the chiefs and the prisoners staged a march through town from the *nakamal* to the prison, where the chiefs handed the prisoners over to the police, and a government representative promised 'that the concerns of the prisoners will be taken up at the highest level of government' (*Vanuatu Daily Post*, 10 May 2006, p. 2). The chiefs demanded a pledge from the police not to punish or maltreat the prisoners after they had been returned to the prison – and the police complied.

Several months later, there was another reconciliation ceremony, involving the chiefs, the government and the prisoners, with the prisoners apologising to the chiefs for breaking *kastom* law and to the Prime Minister, the Speaker of Parliament and the Justice Minister for breaking the laws of Vanuatu.

By means of the prison escape and the reconciliation, the chiefs and the prisoners managed to draw political and public attention to the grievances of the prisoners. In June 2006, a new Correctional Services Act was enacted by Parliament. It established a correctional service apart from the police. The new system 'builds on the traditional communal system and ... integrates traditional values and processes within a new Correctional' (*Vanuatu Daily Post*, 14 March 2007, p. 4). It incorporates the *kastom* system of reconciliation between (the families of) the offender and the victim, and it tries to overcome the 'prison centric criminal justice system' (ibid.) by focusing on rehabilitation and reintegration.

Whereas the outcome of the prison escape crisis was a success for the prisoners and the chiefs, the police were left with 'mixed feelings' (*Vanuatu Daily Post*, 16 May 2006, p. 4). On the one hand they had to be happy that a serious crisis had been averted. On the other hand, their authority had been undermined. It was the chiefs who solved the problem, which – according to statutory law – had been clearly a police issue. The police had to comply with the terms set by the chiefs, not the laws and regulations of the state. The chiefs, however, were sensible enough (as in the case of the August 2002 stand-off) not to stress their success but rather the common aims – order and peace – and to pursue a cooperative approach that took the police and other state institutions on board. In order to make this clear, the prisoners were formally handed over to the police – as the state institution in charge – by the chiefs, and reconciliation ceremonies were held that included the institutions of the state.

In this case, *kastom* conflict resolution clearly prevailed, but it did not trump or supersede state institutions. Rather, there was positive mutual accommodation, made possible by the conciliatory approach of the chiefs and prudent government politics. Furthermore, the case demonstrates to what extent *kastom* and chiefs can impact on national state politics, in this case even leading to new national legislation and the establishment of new state institutions.

The August 2006 Ulas incident

This incident, involving a threat of civil unrest rather than actual violence, arose during the time of the annual independence celebrations in the last week of July 2006 in Luganville, the second biggest city in Vanuatu, situated on the island of Santo. It provides an illustration of the possibility of chiefs, police and politicians working together to resolve potential civil unrest before violence erupts.

At the centre of the incident were members of the Ulas family, the Luganville Town Council of Chiefs (LTCC), and the Sanma Island Council of Chiefs (SICC). The SICC is comprised of representatives from different chiefly area councils in Sanma Province,[11] whereas the LTCC is comprised of representatives of different island groups living in Luganville. The Ulas family, numbering over 500 in Luganville, are originally from the island of Paama in a different province. However, they have been living in Luganville since long before independence and owned a string of properties in Luganville and outside of town. The family had a history of being involved in disputes with indigenous 'man Santo'.

The unrest was initiated by some members of the Ulas family when they assaulted a man from Sara (a village in rural Santo) during the independence celebrations, apparently in retaliation for a previous incident involving a man from Paama (*Vanuatu Daily Post*, 4 August 2006, p. 1). Members of the Sara community then started to come into town to seek reparations for this injury. The SICC (which represents the interests of the people from rural Santo) issued a demand that the Ulas family was to leave Santo within a number of days. More and more people from rural Santo started to come into Luganville, and the situation became extremely tense. Some schools were shut down, civilians mounted road-blocks, and people kept to their houses in fear (*Vanuatu Daily Post*, 3 August 2006, p. 6). It was reported that there were men with bows and arrows and knives on the outskirts of Luganville ready to attack members of the Ulas family. There was a real risk of considerable bloodshed.

The context of the incident was the underlying tension between people from Santo and people from other islands who live in Santo as a result of urban drift or in-migration from other islands to the major towns of Port Vila and Luganville. Urban drift is an increasing phenomenon in Vanuatu and has the potential to create significant discord between the different communities living in urban areas, who all compete for scarce work in the formal sector of the economy and for scarce land. Relationships between the people from Santo and the Ulas family at the time of the incident had been brought to breaking point because of the perception of continuing criminal assaults committed by members of that family in Santo.

The police were involved in the incident right from the start. Luganville is the headquarters of the Northern Command,[12] and there is a large police station based there. As in many other parts of Vanuatu, there is a perception that, due to limited resources, the police in Luganville are reluctant or unable to engage in regular patrols in town, and in particular to go out to the rural areas of Santo. The commander of the Northern Command approached the incident by keeping the use of force as a last resort and trying to facilitate a chiefly *kastom* resolution. Police officers were, however, deployed to provide security for the LTCC in their efforts to open dialogue with the SICC. Other prominent leaders, including the Minister for Internal Affairs[13] and his First Political Adviser, as well as some church leaders, were also called in to liaise between the various groups and to urge them to reach a settlement. A number of meetings between the two chiefly councils were held. However, negotiations broke down over the issue of the demand by the SICC that the entire Ulas family leave Santo, and the response by the provincial authorities and the police that this would be unconstitutional (due to the guarantee of freedom of movement in the constitution).

This impasse was eventually overcome in two ways. First, the police arrested and charged five of the men who had been involved in the assault on the man from Sara with crimes of threatening and intentional assault, and had them evacuated to Port Vila. Second, when the SICC was still reluctant to back down on their demands, the commander warned them that if any violence resulted in Luganville as a result of their stance, he would consider them to be responsible for it and would arrest and charge them. As a consequence, the SICC eventually agreed to compromise on their claims that the Ulas family must leave Luganville and to accept reconciliation by the LTCC. The chiefs of the SICC then went and spoke with all the people who had gathered in Luganville from the rural communities and told them that the dispute was finished and they must go back to their communities. A few were apparently angry, but they obeyed.

The LTCC were then in a position to go and make a customary presentation to the SICC. They organised two tusked pigs (paid for by the Minister of Internal Affairs as the state representative for that constituency), food, kava, mats and other items and walked in procession to the SICC. The president of the LTCC gave a *namele* leaf and a *nangarria* leaf[14] to the president and secretary of the SICC, who accepted them. The road was then clear for negotiations to begin, the tension was dispelled, and life returned to normal. Further customary reconciliations took place over the following years with the purpose of re-establishing good relations between the LTCC and the urban communities they represented on one side, and the SICC, and all the people of Sanma who were affected by the incident, on the other.

A number of factors contributed to the successful resolution of a tense situation that could have escalated into violence on a large scale. The first was the involvement of many different types of community leaders in managing the unrest – town chiefs and rural chiefs, church leaders and provincial and national politicians originating from the locality of the conflict. This meant that a relatively united front was presented to the people of Luganville and rural Santo, and that the agreement reached had a high degree of legitimacy. Second, the chiefs were involved by the police right from the start in order to find a peaceful resolution, rather than being brought in to contain violence after it had broken out. Third, there was a continuing and open dialogue between the chiefs, politicians and the police and a great deal of mutual respect. This allowed difficult issues, such as the conflict between the chiefs' desire to regulate who is allowed to live in their communities, and the constitutional protection of freedom of movement, to be dealt with in a sensitive way, rather than by denying the chiefs the right to make decisions. The open nature of the dialogue also allowed compromises to be made such as the arrest and deportation of the five men, which were crucial in reaching the final peaceful settlement.

This is a case of positive mutual accommodation and constructive interaction of *kastom* and state approaches to the provision of peace, security and justice. It demonstrates that deliberate planned collaboration of state and *kastom* actors and institutions has the potential to resolve conflicts and maintain order in the context of 'modern' problems and in an urban environment.

Conclusion

These case studies demonstrate that in critical violence-prone situations, the maintenance of law and order and internal peace depend on the intervention of both state and non-state institutions – chiefs and police, *kastom*/customary law and state law. *Kastom* conflict resolution plays a major part in maintaining peace and order in different societal contexts; it is not only applied to and applicable in minor localised cases in remote rural communities (as conventional wisdom has it), but also in cases from 'modern' life – in urban environments, and with regard to conflicts of a supra-local, even national, relevance, involving not only local actors, but also state institutions, and addressing outright political issues of wider public interest. As conflicts in the latter cases have the potential to severely disrupt public order and to put internal peace at risk at a national state level, *kastom* conflict resolution is of major political significance. It usually comes into play in combination with state institutions such as the state laws and law enforcing agencies; at times the *kastom* approach is dominant, at times it only plays a supporting role, but even then it is an indispensable element of the conflict resolution configuration.

In the cases presented here, it was the complementarity of efforts or direct cooperation of state agencies and chiefs and the combined utilisation of state-based and customary instruments of conflict resolution (such as court cases and customary reconciliation) that prevented violent conflict escalation or contained violence. The cases illustrate complementarity at work, with *kastom* approaches supplementing state-based approaches and vice versa. At the same time they also disclose frictions, competition and incompatibilities, thus demonstrating that the linkages and relationships are profoundly problematic. This means that we are confronted with a complex and fluid mix of approaches, institutions and actors that coexist, interact, compete, collaborate, become enmeshed, intertwine, overlap, entangle and disentangle all the time. In other words: what takes place is the ongoing hybridisation of conflict resolution, emerging from people's engagement with both *kastom* and introduced approaches, according to their own needs; and this hybridisation transcends the binaries of *kastom* and non-*kastom*, state and non-state. What really matters are the relations, the interspaces and interstices, the liminality and performativity that let hybridity emerge.

For peacebuilding practice, the challenge is to work with this hybridity and to make use of (the potential for) complementarity it entails, so as to enable deliberate planned collaboration of the plurality of providers of peace, security and justice. For attempts to introduce uniform, exclusively state-based systems are almost destined to fail. In a societal environment like Vanuatu, the state institutions have only limited capacity and/or are not perceived as legitimate by substantial sections of the populace, and this will not change quickly. On the other hand, customary institutions have proven their capabilities and legitimacy, and the cases presented here have contributed to strengthening their position – beyond the local realm of the village – in the sphere of state politics. It seems that it is not so much what their actual impact on the course of events in these cases really was that matters most, but how their role was perceived and assessed by the people; this perception enhances the appreciation and hence the (belief in the) power of *kastom* and the chiefs and their legitimacy.

These findings have implications for the wider debate about and the praxis of statebuilding. They indicate that it is prudent to pursue positive mutual accommodation of state and non-state systems, rather than a narrow course of statebuilding that merely focuses on the central machinery of government and the state apparatus. A central question therefore is how to articulate state-based institutions, customary institutions and civil society institutions so that new forms of governance and statehood that are more capable, effective and legitimate than western models of the state, emerge. How this can be done is for the people and the leaders of Vanuatu to decide; it will be, of course, an issue of contention and protracted political negotiations.[15] In fact, the people in Vanuatu today in their everyday lives are engaged in constantly exploring ways of positive mutual accommodation of *kastom* and state, of indigenous and introduced forms of governance and conflict resolution. 'Bridging' institutions committed to *kastom*, but at the same time able to speak with government, are necessary to and capable of organising such future-oriented debates and of providing a forum for what are often topics of intense conversation in villages, towns and settlements. They are urgently needed in order to find ways of stabilising peace and order by means of constructive engagement of state and indigenous customary institutions. What is really needed is 'link-building as opposed to state-building' (Baker 2010, p. 613). This implies working with *kastom* as a living system instead of rejecting it as an anachronistic 'traditional' residue of pre-modern times. Such an approach opens space for the emergence of hybrid forms of peace (Richmond and Mitchell 2012; Mac Ginty 2010, 2011) and of political community that provides the framework for the nonviolent conduct of conflicts and sustainable conflict resolution.

Notes

1 Regarding these cases, see Boege, Chapters 10 and 12 in this volume, for further references.

2 The term '*kastom*' is a Bislama derivative of 'custom'. Bislama is the *lingua franca* used by ni-Vanuatu (the people of Vanuatu). There are 113 different local languages spoken in Vanuatu. Bislama is an important means of communication between ni-Vanuatu from different language groups. It is the official language of Vanuatu, besides English and French. A lot has been written about *kastom* in anthropology, sociology, law and other academic disciplines, in an effort to reach a categorical hold of it. Out of the vast literature on *kastom*, see Forsyth (2009); Rousseau (2004, 2008); Jolly (1992, 1994, 1997); Lindstrom (1990) and the articles in Lindstrom and White (1993).

3 Again, there is a considerable body of scholarly literature on chiefs in Vanuatu, see for instance Lindstrom (1997); White and Lindstrom (1997); Rousseau (2004); Forsyth (2009). Although it has become commonplace to refer to chiefs as 'traditional' authorities, chiefs emerged in the course of interaction between local indigenous societies and external actors, namely missions and the colonial administration. As a consequence, different types of chiefs evolved (e.g. chiefs that drew their legitimacy from pre-contact customs, chiefs installed by the missionaries, chiefs appointed by the colonial administration), and all these types overlapped and mixed over time (Lindstrom 1997). Today's '*kastom jifs*, although undoubtedly *kastom*, are not simply customary. The emergence and construction of the popular identity *jif*, from a plethora of local leadership positions, were shaped by the events and interests of postcontact, colonial society' (Lindstrom 1997, p. 212).

4 On the other hand, *kastom* can also be a cause of a broad range of conflicts, not least conflicts over chiefly status.

5 Chapter 5 of the *Constitution of the Republic of Vanuatu* provides for the establishment of the National Council of Chiefs. It stipulates that the Council 'shall be composed of custom chiefs elected by their peers' (Republic of Vanuatu 1988, Article 29 [1]) and that the Council 'has a general competence to discuss all matters relating to custom and tradition and may make recommendations for the preservation and promotion of ni-Vanuatu culture and languages' (Republic of Vanuatu 1988, Article 30 [1]). The National Council of Chiefs Act (2006) clarifies the structure of chiefly councils at various levels, without giving them additional powers, as originally marked out in the bill for the Act. This is why Selwyn Garu, the then CEO of the Malvatumauri, commented 'that the act that had finally been passed through Parliament was like a dog that had had all its teeth removed and yet the dog was still expected to hunt pigs' (Forsyth 2009, p. 164); see also the interview with Selwyn Garu on Radio Australia (Radio Australia 2006).

6 On this bridging role, see *Kastom Governance* (2012).

7 *Wantok* is 'one talk': kin, member(s) of the same language group.

8 Interview with Chief Tom Numake, Port Vila, 4 July 2007. He said that he was involved in two cases of *kastom* conflict resolution in Tanna, in which the bestowal of girls in marriage worked well to solve the conflict.

9 The *nakamal* are meeting houses in the villages where chiefly business, rituals and ceremonies are conducted and where *kastom* conflict resolution meetings take place. They also signify the 'whole interconnected web of relationships between people past (ancestors), present and future and other realities of life – flora, fauna, weather, spirits and so forth – and enshrine harmony as the primary goal' (Brown and Westoby 2007, p. 79). Hence, they are places of peace. The idea of the *nakamal* is 'that it offers the opportunity for different knowledge bases to come together and share information in a common space in which all can participate' (Huffer and Molisa 1999, p. 10). Accordingly, the '*nakamal* way' is 'a way of sharing customary and contemporary experiences in an inclusive and educational manner' (ibid.).

10 Interviews with Paul Tahi, 2 March and 27 June 2007, Port Vila.
11 Vanuatu is divided into six provinces. Sanma Province contains the islands of Santo, Malo and Malekula.
12 There are two commands in Vanuatu, the Southern Command with headquarters in Port Vila; the Northern Command with headquarters in Luganville.
13 Luganville was the Minister's constituency.
14 These leaves have a special significance in *kastom* and are used to show peace.
15 A discussion of various options that could be pursued, at least in relation to conflict management, can be found in Chapters 7 and 8 of Forsyth 2009.

Bibliography

Baker, B 2010, 'Linking state and non-state security and justice', *Development Policy Review*, vol. 28, no. 5, pp. 597–616.

Brigg, M 2009, 'Wantokism and state building in the Solomon Islands: a response to Fukuyama', *Pacific Economic Bulletin*, vol. 24, no. 3, pp. 148–61.

Brown, MA and Westoby, P 2007, 'Peaceful community development in Vanuatu: a reflection on the Vanuatu *Kastom* Governance Partnership', *Journal of Peacebuilding and Development*, vol. 3, no. 3, pp. 77–81.

Douglas, B 2002, 'Christian citizens: women and negotiations of modernity in Vanuatu', *The Contemporary Pacific*, vol. 12, no. 1, pp. 1–38.

Forsyth, M 2011, 'The *kastom* system of dispute resolution in Vanuatu', in Taylor, J and Thieberger, N (eds), *Working together in Vanuatu. Research histories, collaborations, projects and reflections*, ANU E-Press, Canberra, pp. 175–82.

Forsyth, M 2009, *A bird that flies with two wings: kastom and state justice systems in Vanuatu*, ANU E-Press, Canberra.

Forsyth, M and Eves, R (eds) 2015, *Talking it through: sorcery and witchcraft practices and beliefs in Melanesia*, ANU Press, Canberra.

Huffer, E and Molisa, G 1999, 'Governance in Vanuatu: in search of the Nakamal way', *SSGM Discussion Paper* 1999, no. 4, Australian National University, Canberra.

Jolly, M 1992, 'Custom and the way of the land: past and present in Vanuatu and Fiji', *Oceania*, vol. 62, pp. 330–54.

Jolly, M 1994, *Women of the place: kastom, colonialism and gender in Vanuatu*, Harwood Academic Publishers, Chur.

Jolly, M 1997, 'Women-nation-state in Vanuatu: women as signs and subjects in the discourses of *kastom*, modernity and Christianity', in Otto, T and Thomas, N (eds), *Narratives of nation in the South Pacific*, Harwood Academic Publishers, Amsterdam, pp. 133–62.

Jowitt, A 2008, 'Melanesia in review, issues and events 2007: Vanuatu', *The Contemporary Pacific*, vol. 20, no. 2, pp. 475–80.

Kastom Governance 2012, *Kastom governance is for everyone: activities and impacts of the Vanuatu Kastom Governance Partnership 2005–2012*, The University of Queensland and Malvatumauri National Council of Chiefs, Brisbane and Port Vila.

Keesing, RM 1993, '*Kastom* re-examined', *Anthropological Forum*, vol. 6, no. 4, pp. 587–96.

Lindstrom, L 1990, *Knowledge and power in a South Pacific society*, Smithsonian Institution Press, Washington.

Lindstrom, L 1994, 'Traditional cultural policy in Melanesia', in Lindstrom, L and White, GM (eds), *Culture, kastom, tradition: developing cultural policy in Melanesia*, University of the South Pacific, Suva, pp. 67–81.

Lindstrom, L 1997, 'Chiefs in Vanuatu today', in White, G and Lindstrom, L (eds), *Chiefs today: traditional Pacific leadership and the postcolonial state*, Stanford University Press, Stanford, pp. 211–28.

Lindstrom, L and White, GM (eds) 1993, 'Custom today', *Anthropological Forum*, Special Issue, vol. 6, no. 4.

Mac Ginty, R 2011, *International peacebuilding and local resistance: hybrid forms of peace*, Palgrave Macmillan, Basingstoke.

Mac Ginty, R 2010, 'Hybrid peace: the interaction between top-down and bottom-up peace', *Security Dialogue*, vol. 41, no. 4, pp. 391–412.

Nolan, A and Tevi, D 2012, 'Reflections', *Kastom governance is for everyone: activities and impacts of the Vanuatu Kastom Governance Partnership 2005–2012*, The University of Queensland and Malvatumauri National Council of Chiefs, Brisbane and Port Vila, p. 48.

Public Report 2007, 'Commission of Inquiry: the summary of the findings and recommendations into the actions of the Vanuatu Police Force before, during and after the events of March 3, 2007', Ministry of Justice and Community Services, Port Vila.

Radio Australia 2006, 'Vanuatu: chiefs want rethink on new Bill', *Pacific Beat*, 29 June.

Republic of Vanuatu 1988, *Constitution of the Republic of Vanuatu*, Laws of the Republic of Vanuatu, Revised edn., Port Vila.

Richmond, OP and Mitchell, A (eds) 2012, *Hybrid forms of peace: from everyday agency to post-liberalism*, Palgrave Macmillan, Basingstoke.

Rousseau, B 2004, 'The achievement of simultaneity: kastom in contemporary Vanuatu', PhD thesis, University of Cambridge, Cambridge.

Rousseau, B 2008, ' "This is a court of law, not a court of morality": *kastom* and custom in Vanuatu state courts', *Journal of South Pacific Law*, vol. 12, no. 2, pp. 15–27.

Tarisesei, J 2012, *Today is not the same as yesterday, and tomorrow it will be different again: kastom on Ambae, Vanuatu*, Vanuatu Cultural Centre, Port Vila.

Taylor, JP 2010, 'Janus and the siren's call: kava and the articulation of gender and modernity in Vanuatu', *Journal of the Royal Anthropological Institute*, vol. 16, pp. 279–96.

Trading Post, 'Acting Police Chief supports reconciliation legal process', 31 August 2002, p. 2.

Trading Post, 'Tension resolved the custom way', 3 September 2002, pp. 1–2.

Trading Post, 'PM says reconciliation will not stop legal proceeding', 5 September 2002.

Vanuatu Daily Post, 'Escapees seek Chiefs' help', 8 May 2006, p. 1.

Vanuatu Daily Post, 'A clash of power. Chiefs help prisoners return to jail', 10 May 2006, p. 2.

Vanuatu Daily Post, 'Letter to the editor', 16 May 2006, p. 4.

Vanuatu Daily Post, 'Family Ulas prepared to leave Luganville', 3 August 2006, p. 6.

Vanuatu Daily Post, 'Police arrest five in tense Luganville', 4 August 2006, p. 1.

Vanuatu Daily Post, 'Correctional Services ensure rehabilitation and reintegration', 14 March 2007.

Vanuatu Daily Post, 20 January 2010, 'Vanuatu Security Forces heal rift through reconciliation', p. 1.

White, GM 1993, 'Three discourses of custom', *Anthropological Forum*, vol. 6, no. 4, pp. 475–94.

White, GM and Lindstrom, L 1997, *Chiefs today: traditional Pacific leadership and the postcolonial state*, Stanford University Press, Stanford.

12 The hybridisation of peace, security and justice

Cases from West Africa and Oceania

Volker Boege

Introduction

From 1989 to 2003, Liberia in West Africa was the theatre of devastating large-scale civil wars. After a political settlement in August 2003, it became the theatre of a huge UN peacebuilding operation, in fact, the largest UN intervention of its kind so far. The Pacific Island Country (PIC) of Solomon Islands was the theatre of large-scale internal violent conflicts from 1998 to 2003. From June 2003 onwards, it was the theatre of a far-reaching regional peacebuilding operation, the largest intervention of its kind in Oceania to date.

Ghana in West Africa is hailed as a haven of (relative) stability and good (enough) governance in a region of fragile, conflict-affected and post-conflict states. Nevertheless, it is not free from violent conflicts in certain parts of the country and at certain times. The small PIC of Vanuatu has so far been spared conflict on a scale experienced by its neighbour, Solomon Islands. Yet in its short history as an independent nation-state it has had its share of internal violent conflict, albeit of a locally and temporarily confined nature.

Thus, although on the basis of their geographical proximity and similarities with regard to environment, culture and societal structures, Ghana and Liberia (both West Africa) seem to belong together, as do Solomon Islands and Vanuatu (both Melanesian countries), Liberia and Solomon Islands can both be categorised as fragile post-conflict countries, while Ghana and Vanuatu could be seen as stable and orderly states. This is not to deny that within these categorisations, there are differences: Liberia's civil wars were much more protracted and deadly than the 'tensions' in Solomon Islands, and the international post-conflict peacebuilding intervention in Liberia was on a much larger scale than in the Solomons. Ghana has a relatively long history as an independent state (gaining independence in 1959 as the first decolonised African state), and is a major player on the international stage in Africa and beyond, with a population of 26 million people and a territory of 240,000 sq km, while Vanuatu was the most recent country to gain independence in Oceania (in 1980); its population is less than 300,000, and its land mass is just 12,000 sq km.

Exploring the provision of peace, security and justice in these four countries can cover a broad variety of situations. While the far-reaching international intervention in Liberia was carried out by *the* quintessential international organisation, the United Nations, the comparatively small regional intervention in Solomon Islands was conducted by neighbouring countries in the context of a regional organisation, the Pacific Islands Forum. As described above, Vanuatu is a small PIC and a latecomer as a nation-state, while Ghana is a large country with a relatively long history as a post-colonial state.

In this chapter, it will be argued that the concepts of the hybridisation of security, and hybrid forms of peace and political order, can explain the configuration of peace, security and justice in such a broad variety of situations as is represented by these four countries.

The concept of hybridisation allows us to overcome a state-centric perspective on issues of peace, security and justice, a perspective informed by the dominant discourse of failing and failed states that over the last two decades has guided the politics and strategies of major western donor countries and international organisations. The so-called fragile, or conflict-affected, post-colonial states of the Global South have become the subject of externally driven peacebuilding and statebuilding, or rather: peacebuilding-as-statebuilding (Richmond 2011). All four countries in question here are subject to such an approach to a greater or lesser degree. This is clearly visible in the post-conflict cases of Liberia and Solomon Islands, with their far-reaching and long-term international interventions, but it can be also found in Ghana and Vanuatu, where external support is also geared towards, inter alia, good (enough) governance, conflict prevention, security sector reform, state capacity building. By contrast, it will be argued in this chapter that one has to look beyond the formal state institutions to understand the provision of peace, security and justice in the four countries, taking into account the broad variety of societal actors in this field, and their relations and interactions with state institutions.

As Ghana, Liberia and Vanuatu also figure in other chapters of this volume,[1] it is not necessary to give a general account of the situation in these countries. Rather, this chapter shall focus on selected aspects that are particularly indicative of the hybridisation of peace, security and justice. The interface of a variety of peace and security actors – 'state' and 'non-state', 'international' and 'local', 'formal' and 'informal', will be explored, examining in particular how this interface plays out in an everyday local context. It will become clear that the fragile–stable divide, as well as the above binaries, have to be called into question. In this chapter, an argument for a complex and relational understanding of peace and state formation is made and finally, some policy-oriented conclusions are drawn.

Community policing in Liberia: neither state nor non-state

Liberia endured extremely bloody violent conflicts from the end of the 1980s until 2003.[2] In August of that year, a Comprehensive Peace Agreement (CPA) was signed, providing for the establishment of a National Transitional Government and the deployment of a UN peace mission – the United Nations Mission in Liberia (UNMIL). Since 2007, the UNMIL presence has been gradually reduced, and on 1 July 2016, the Liberian government reassumed full responsibility for the security of the country, with all of UNMIL's remaining residual security responsibilities handed over to the security institutions of the Liberian state. There is, however, still a reduced UNMIL presence on the ground.

After 2003, international peacebuilders focused on (re-)building the central machinery of government and the main state institutions, such as the army, police, judiciary and finance. Enormous efforts were put into Security Sector Reform (SSR): the army and the police, as well as other security services, were rebuilt almost from scratch.

Empirical data, however, show that most people are sceptical regarding the effectiveness and legitimacy of these institutions.[3] Police capacities remain limited, severely constrained by logistical shortcomings (in large rural areas there is no police presence at all), and people complain about police corruption, mismanagement, brutality, human rights violations, low morale and discipline (Zanker 2015). The judiciary, the court system and corrections have similar problems. The court system is seen as 'inaccessible and unaffordable' for ordinary people (Tubmanburg women focus group, 24 September 2013; see Kofi Annan International Peacekeeping Training Centre 2015). Consequently, there is widespread lack of trust in the judiciary. It is seen as 'usually for the rich. Many felt that justice in the formal system has a price tag: it was generally held that without affluence and influence your chances of getting justice are between slim and none' (Quoipa men's focus group, 11 December 2013; see Kofi Annan International Peacekeeping Training Centre 2015).

Although the legitimacy of the police seems to be improving, and people in principle want the police to function better (Robinson and Valters 2015), people put more trust in societal providers of security who are embedded in community life. A recent conflict analysis of Liberia comes to the conclusion that 'social networks and community dispute settlement have been key sources for peace' (Herbert 2014, p. 2).

In this context, chiefs have to be mentioned first. Chiefs had been incorporated into the de facto colonial rule by the Americo-Liberian elite through the establishment of a state-sanctioned system of 'traditional' – de facto indirect – rule, bestowing the chiefs with the right to govern their communities, while making them into quasi-state institutions under presidential control (Jaye, see Chapter 8 in this volume). Today's system of chiefs, with its quarter chiefs, town chiefs, sectional chiefs, clan chiefs and paramount chiefs is a hybrid, with legitimate authority stemming from the state as well as the communities. Although chiefs are seen – and present themselves – as traditional authorities, at the same time, they 'quite clearly think of themselves as the local extension of the authority of the Liberian state' (Isser, Lubkemann and N'Tow 2009, p. 33).

Religious actors and institutions also figure prominently. Besides Christian and Muslim religious leaders, so-called witch doctors and other representatives of indigenous spirituality, the secret societies (in particular, the *Poro* [male] and the *Sande* [female]) are of major importance.[4] Their realm of responsibility and the influence of their priests/leaders goes well beyond the 'religious' sphere in a narrow sense. They are in charge of the socio-cultural, mental and spiritual well-being of communities, and they exert some 'political' influence, albeit indirectly. They draw their legitimacy from the invisible world of the spirits (of the ancestors, the forest, the animals) (Ellis 2007, pp. 201–4). They are involved in the maintenance of order in the communities (Vinck, Pham and Kreutzer 2011, p. 45). Against the backdrop of the collapse of other governance institutions, secret societies took over governance functions during the civil wars, and 'Poro authorities were attributed with a deeper order of legitimacy than any group of secular rulers and commanders' (Neumann 2013, p. 205). Today, secret societies are officially recognised by the state; they come under the Assistant Minister for Cultural Affairs within the Ministry of Internal Affairs.[5]

In securing peace and order, community leaders including chiefs and priests, make use of self-help organisations like Neighbourhood Watch or Community Watch Forums or other forms of self-organised security groups. They play a much more important role in everyday community life than the state police. Even where there is some police presence (in urban areas), people tend to turn to these groups first. Finally, there is the grey area of vigilante groups, which oscillate between the spheres of criminal activity, community protection and commercial enterprise, providing services to private businesses and individuals.

Attempts to institutionalise community policing are entangled in these complex webs of local everyday security governance. As part of internationally sponsored SSR, there have been considerable efforts to implement community policing. Yet, understandings of the meaning of community policing, and of its legitimate activities and purpose, differ markedly (Zanker 2014). The boundaries between community policing groups and vigilante groups, or even mob justice, are blurred. The relationship between the state police and community policing groups is ambiguous, with support and collaboration in some places but not in others. There are no clear lines of distinction between state-sanctioned community policing and informal/illicit vigilantism (ibid.).

Community policing is generally seen as positive by locals, contributing to their everyday safety, be it in its more formal state-controlled or in its informal autonomous form. By contrast, internationals differentiate between 'good' community policing (formalised, under state control, organised top-down) and problematic community policing (informal, community-controlled, bottom-up), which they see as questionable with regard to accountability, compliance with human rights and state law, and other aspects. In other words, there is a gap between the internationals' and the locals' perceptions and assessments of appropriate, legitimate and effective provision of peace, security and justice, with the internationals focused on the strengthening of the respective state institutions (Robinson and Valters 2015).[6] This approach misses the fuzzy realities on the ground, which are characterised by a mix of the formal state system, a formalised 'traditional' system sanctioned by the state, and informal local systems, The latter combine various customary and civil society elements in different and flexible ways, depending on local circumstances, and they are pretty much in flux (Jaye 2009).

Chiefs and state in Solomon Islands – complementarity in weakness

Between 1998 and 2003, Solomon Islands was plagued by violent conflicts (locally referred to as 'the tensions'), mainly caused by disputes over land between the local Guale people of the main island of Guadalcanal and immigrants from neighbouring Malaita.[7] Over time, Malaitan and Guale militias, as well as the (paramilitary) police forces, became entangled in increasingly blurred violent encounters. The majority of the state security forces sided with the militias and the rest fell into disarray. State institutions became less and less capable of providing basic services to the population; central government institutions and the state finances were hijacked by militant factions. This led to Solomon Islands being labelled a 'failing state' (Australian Strategic Policy Institute 2003).

In July 2003, RAMSI, the biggest peacebuilding intervention in the Pacific region to date, was enacted through the Pacific Islands Forum upon the invitation of the Solomon Islands government, sanctioned by the United Nations. Formally it was a multilateral regional endeavour, although in reality, it was dominated and led by Australia, which provided the bulk of resources, finances and personnel (Hayward-Jones 2014). It was driven by an Australian agenda – a liberal peace agenda, with the restoration of law and order, economic recovery and building the machinery of government at its core (Kabutaulaka 2005; Hameiri 2007). From 2011 onwards, RAMSI started to withdraw gradually; in 2013, its military component came to an end, and its development programmes were transitioned to bilateral aid programmes. RAMSI thus became a policing-only mission, with its Participating Police Force (PPF) assisting and training the Royal Solomon Islands Police Force (RSIPF).

During the tensions, many communities beyond the capital city and the hotspots of violent conflict managed to maintain everyday life relatively undisturbed, based on the subsistence economy and local customary governance, with chiefs and church leaders in charge of the maintenance of day-to-day social order and communal peace.[8] These leaders are present on the ground everywhere. Conversely, state agencies have only limited presence. As community leaders, chiefs refer to *kastom* or customary law when dealing with conflicts, anti-social behaviour and other disturbances of the peace in the local context. They do not have any formal governing powers and are very dependent on the willingness of community members to abide by *kastom*.

At the local level, *kastom* ways of conflict resolution have been used to deal with the effects of the tensions. Locals pursue their own customary processes of peacebuilding, detached from, and parallel to, RAMSI, albeit in its shadow. They are engaged in reconciliation processes that are often locally instigated by church leaders and chiefs, independent of government or other external support. Nevertheless, there is some overlap and interaction with more centralised peacebuilding efforts, initiated from the political 'top' of the state, such as the National Peace Council or the Ministry of National Unity, Reconciliation and Peace or the national Truth and Reconciliation Commission.

The police and other formal justice agencies (courts, correctional services) face significant resourcing challenges. As in Liberia, this hinders their presence on the ground and their effectiveness. One attempt to bring the police closer to the people is a community policing project, the Community Officer Project, which was launched with the support of RAMSI/PPF in 2009 in order to bridge the gap between state and international providers of peace and security on the one hand and chiefs and communities on the other. Community Officers, appointed by the communities, are supposed to closely collaborate with local leaders in maintaining peace and order and at the same time, serve as a link to the state police (Dinnen and Peake 2015, p. 30).

Apart from this project, state institutions, internationals and community leaders usually act in isolation of each other. Chiefs feel that their capacity to maintain order is undermined by lack of support from state institutions. Communities want better links and synchronicity between the work of chiefs and church leaders on the one hand and that of state agencies on the other. Chiefs are aware that they cannot deal with all the challenges to peace and order on their own, and that they need the support from state actors who can deal with problems beyond their reach. On the other hand, state actors such as the police are aware that chiefs and church leaders are important for the maintenance of order. However, in comparison to the other cases – Liberia, Vanuatu and Ghana – collaboration between police and chiefs is less well established and routine. Whereas in the other three countries there are links between them, chiefs in Solomon Islands remain formally outside the state system. While their contribution to the provision of peace, security and justice is de facto acknowledged by state institutions, this does not lead to formal recognition and cooperation. As a consequence, the situation in Solomon Islands is characterised by complementarity in weakness instead of a mutually reinforcing collaboration.

'Turtle-chiefs' in Vanuatu – at home in water and on land

Vanuatu borders on Solomon Islands. As in the Solomons, it is customary that conflict resolution first and foremost contributes to the maintenance of order and peace in Vanuatu, with the chiefs playing crucial roles.[9] As in other colonial contexts, the leadership category of 'chief' emerged in the course of interaction between local societies and external actors, such as missions and the colonial administration. Different types of chiefs evolved, and these overlapped and mixed over time (Lindstrom 1997). Today's '*kastom jifs*, although undoubtedly *kastom*, are not simply customary. The emergence and construction of the popular identity *jif*, from a plethora of local leadership positions, were shaped by the events and interests of postcontact, colonial society' (Lindstrom 1997, p. 212).

Chiefs are the intermediaries between the communities on the one hand and the institutions of the state and (inter-)national economic and political processes on the other.[10] The former CEO of the Malvatumauri (the National Council of Chiefs), Selwyn Garu, compares chiefs to turtles, because turtles, too, have to live in two worlds, in the water and on land. They have to swim in the water and to crawl on land. They cannot swim on land or crawl in water. They have to adapt to the environment. While chiefs in their locality can act according to *kastom*, in the National Council of Chiefs, which is a formal constitutional body, they have to act according to the law of the state, in particular the Chiefs' Act.[11] The turtle-chiefs cross the water/land, i.e. the state/non-state divide, all the time. It would thus be misleading to separate the 'informal [non-state] sector' from the 'formal [state] sector', since the two are intertwined.

Chiefs are in charge of the prevention and resolution of conflicts in the community context. In fact, 'the vast majority of disputes in every rural and urban community' are dealt with by the chiefs according to *kastom* (Forsyth 2011, p. 176). *Kastom* conflict resolution is supported by all sectors of the population, including women and youth, although they are in some places discriminated against in the *kastom* context. Women and youth complain about biased or incompetent chiefs and demand more of a voice, but they are not against the chiefly system and *kastom* as such. It is also their system, whereas the state system is seen as alien, for example, courts are often called 'kot blong waetman' (the white man's court) (Forsyth 2011, p. 181).

While *kastom* conflict resolution generally functions within and between communities in rural areas, difficulties arise in urban environments, where people from different islands live together and interact in everyday life. People have brought their varying forms of *kastom* from their villages to the cities, and they still have their chiefs with them (now often called 'town chiefs'); they still make use of *kastom* conflict resolution. But the *kastom* of different island groups varies, and often disputes emerge as to which *kastom* applies. Moreover, non-*kastom* means of conflict resolution are more accessible: the police and the courts, or influential individuals (politicians or public servants, businessmen or leaders of civil society organisations) who might get involved in the resolution of a conflict affecting people from their own home islands. People can take disputes to these individuals or to the state system if they are not happy with *kastom* decisions – and vice versa ('forum shopping'). This can undermine both systems – those of *kastom* and the state. On the other hand, however, often *kastom* and non-*kastom* ways are combined constructively, with (mostly tacit, informal) collaboration between the police, the courts and the chiefs. In a strictly legal sense, the formal state law trumps *kastom*, and *kastom* has to operate within the boundaries of state legislation, confining itself to dealing with minor disputes and leaving serious cases to the state system. In reality, however, the relationship between state law and institutions on the one hand, and *kastom* and chiefs on the other, is much more complex (Forsyth 2009, 2011; Rousseau 2004).

State institutions espouse a rather instrumentalist attitude, expecting the chiefs 'to maintain law and order where the state resources cannot reach, or are not accepted', while they 'deny any requests from the chiefs for state power to assist them in carrying out their duties' (Forsyth 2011, p. 180). This leads to frustration and feelings of neglect and disempowerment on the side of the chiefs (very similar to the Solomon Islands situation), all the more so, as it is obvious that the state institutions are incapable of maintaining peace, order and justice in the everyday context of rural communities; they are dependent on the functioning of the *kastom* system. As in Solomon Islands and Liberia, the police, the courts and other state institutions cannot cover the entirety of the country and are far away from the majority of the population. They lack capacity, effectiveness and legitimacy.

Conventional wisdom has it that *kastom* conflict resolution is applied and applicable only in localised cases in remote rural communities. Yet it is also of significance for contemporary cases in urban environments, and for conflicts at a supra-local, even national, level involving state institutions and addressing political issues – conflicts that have the potential to severely disrupt public order and put national peace at risk (Boege and Forsyth, see Chapter 11 in this volume). Hence, *kastom* conflict resolution is of major political importance.

Chieftaincy in Ghana: source of conflict escalation and resolution

Compared with its neighbourhood in West Africa, Ghana is a haven of stability, peace and democracy. It has been spared large-scale violent conflict at a national level, and there is no imminent threat of such a conflict. Nevertheless, the country is not free from sporadic outbreaks of violence, although they are confined in space and time. Furthermore, there are a variety of lingering conflicts that are violence-prone. On several occasions these have escalated, costing thousands of lives, causing widespread damage to property and infrastructure and displacing tens of thousands of people.[12] In absolute terms, these conflicts are far more costly than similar conflicts in the Pacific cases, not only in stable Vanuatu, but even in conflict-affected Solomon Islands. They had and have detrimental effects on Ghana's governance and development at the national level. In most cases, they are disputes over land and other natural resources, over chieftaincy and (ethnic/religious) identity, and most occur in border regions or other remote parts of the country, the Northern Region in particular (Tsikata and Seini 2004).

In comparison to Liberia, Solomon Islands and Vanuatu, state structures are sophisticated and dense, and state providers of peace, security and justice such as the police, the army, courts and corrections are stronger, more effective and more visible. In other words, state structures have permeated society to a greater degree in Ghana than in Vanuatu, Solomon Islands and Liberia. Nevertheless, the degree of permeation varies: in urban areas and in southern parts of the country, the state is more present than in rural areas and in the north, or in border regions.

Notwithstanding the greater role of state institutions, a broad variety of non-state providers of peace, security and justice can be found, just as in Liberia, the Solomons and Vanuatu.[13] As other chapters in this volume address the relationships between these non-state providers and the state, and their relationships to each other (Aning, see Chapter 7 and Annan, see Chapter 6, both in this volume), this chapter will focus on the role of chiefs, making the argument that for the provision of peace, security and justice, chieftaincy can be both a solution and a problem.

The 'chiefly system' is more formalised in Ghana than in Liberia, Solomon Islands or Vanuatu. The institutionalised system of customary rule/chieftaincy is acknowledged by the state. The 1992 Constitution of Ghana and the 2008 Chieftaincy Act (Act 759) clarify the relationship and connection between the chiefly system and the state system.[14] The chiefly system is multi-layered, from the village chiefs or head chiefs at the local level up to paramount chiefs or kings of larger ethnically and territorially defined social entities (most notably the king of the Ashanti kingdom, the Asantehene).[15] This system is reflected in the state context by the formal institutionalisation of the National Register of Chiefs, the National House of Chiefs and Regional Houses of Chiefs. There is a special Ministry of Chieftaincy and Traditional Affairs.

The relationship between state authority and chiefly authority is uneasy. The state tries to subordinate the chiefly system, and it has been successful to a considerable extent. Nevertheless, even today, the

> chief is a political and social power centre (if even in a circumscribed sense) in the area he rules and ipso facto a microcosm of authority who at times rivals the central government in legitimacy, recognition, and loyalty by subjects.
>
> (Boafo-Arthur 2003, p. 134)

Chiefs still enjoy traditional legitimacy in the eyes of the people, particularly in the rural areas, where according to Asamoah (2012) they function very effectively as a form of local government. Chiefs are not only community leaders who play important roles in the governance and development of their communities, but the skin or the stool are also imbued with spiritual meaning, making the institution a sacred office.[16] Chiefs are the embodiment of the culture, history and identity of their communities. Dispute resolution is one of their main tasks (Dzivenu 2008). Given the prominent role of chiefs in society, it is 'little wonder that a lot of people continue to turn to traditional authorities for the resolution of their security and justice issues' (Badong 2009, p. 46). Chiefs deal with family, land and chieftaincy disputes and other non-criminal issues. They have their own customary courts, where they settle cases together with their council and according to customary law, which is acknowledged as a source of justice in its own right by the state, albeit with the elimination of those customs 'that are outmoded and socially harmful' (Republic of Ghana 1992, Article 272c).[17]

> The primary concern of the chief's court is not to be vindictive or punitive unless circumstances necessarily mandate such a solution. The primary purpose of justice in the chief's tribunal is to promote harmony and reconciliation between parties. The ultimate aim is the restoration of social equilibrium.... The adjudicators work to ensure that parties thereafter continue to live and relate to each other as good neighbours, friends and relatives even after the dispute.
>
> (Dzivenu 2008, p. 26)

People often prefer chiefs' courts to the state legal system because procedures are simple, cheap and culturally embedded. Decisions are mostly respected, but people have the option to carry cases through the hierarchy of customary courts or to the state justice system (similar to Vanuatu). In some parts of the country, chiefs have their own 'traditional' security organisations, which fulfil similar functions as neigbourhood watch committees in urban centres (night patrols, arrest of suspects, mediation in minor disputes within communities, etc.), e.g. the Nachimba (youth) organisation in Tamale in the Northern Region (Badong 2009, pp. 34–8), or chiefs make use of private land-guards (Badong 2009, p. 39).

The institution of chieftaincy itself is a source of – occasionally violent – conflict, much more so than in Liberia, Vanuatu and the Solomons. It even has been posited that chieftaincy is at the centre of communal conflicts in Ghana, with conflicts mostly about chieftaincy succession (Tsikata and Seini 2004). Conflicts surrounding the question of who the 'right' chief is also occur in Liberia, Vanuatu and the Solomons, but on a much smaller scale and with much less devastating effects. In fact, some of the most violent conflicts in Ghana to date have been chieftaincy disputes. Competing parties in such disputes often align with political parties, and thus the conflicts take on a national political dimension. Such chiefly entanglement with political party politics and associated groups of 'macho-men' (Badong 2009, p. 43) is also detrimental to the dispute resolution role of chiefs. This seems to happen more and more often, and it undermines the legal obligation which forbids chiefs' active involvement in politics.[18] Chieftaincy contenders try to utilise the political parties' resources and influence for their purposes, and political parties expect the support of chieftaincy contenders in elections. Hence, national and party politics on the one hand and chieftaincy politics on the other become enmeshed; this leads to conflict escalation and makes conflict resolution more complicated. The Dagbon and Bawku conflicts, as well as the succession dispute in the Wenchi Traditional Area, amply demonstrate this point (Ahorsu and Gebe 2011; Bukari and Guuroh 2013; Boafo-Arthur 2003).

These connections show that the chiefly sphere of governance is not isolated from the state sphere, and that chiefs are far from being just 'local' institutions. Chiefs are linked to supra-local networks, and it is often those chiefs who are not purely local who can contribute to local peace particularly effectively, because they can tap into supra-local, even national, resources and connections for support (Simons and Zanker 2014). On the other hand, this connectedness can also be used for non-peaceful purposes, such as in chieftaincy disputes or power struggles in the local context (Joensson 2007). With regard to the provision of peace, security and justice, chiefs thus are not only part of the solution, but also part of the problem. This is particularly obvious in Ghana, but the argument could also be made regarding chiefs in Liberia, Solomon Islands and Vanuatu. 'Traditional authorities' are not per se benign keepers of peace and order.

Hybridisation

A comparative look at the provision of peace, security and justice in the four countries proves the concept of hybridisation of governance and security to be a useful explanatory tool.

Although the four countries are all formally constitutional liberal democratic states, based on the rule of law and democratic procedures and institutions, there is a wide gap in all of them between the 'paper form' of such a political system and the realities of governance on the ground. State institutions and procedures have not permeated the territory, the society and the communities in these four countries in a way that makes the state the dominant framework for the maintenance of peace and order. Rather, political order is hybrid: diverse legitimate authority structures, sets of rules, logics of order and claims to power coexist, compete, overlap, interact, intertwine and blend, emerging from genuinely different societal spheres – spheres that do not exist in isolation but permeate each other (Boege, Brown, Clements and Nolan 2009). As the four countries are post-colonial states (Liberia having a special history with its home-grown variety of colonialism based on Americo-Liberian domination), statehood is imbued with the legacies of colonial and pre-colonial forms of governance. Customary institutions, which have their roots in the pre-colonial past, continue to matter in the everyday life of communities. They change in the course of the interaction with 'outside' forces. In particular, they are subjected to re-formation as they engage with, respond to, are influenced by and partially incorporated into, state structures and processes. In recognition of the relative weakness of state institutions and the relative strength of traditional authorities, some governments deliberately incorporate traditional authorities into state structures and hand over state functions to them, as is the case with chiefs in Liberia, Ghana and Vanuatu. 'Traditional' authorities take an ambiguous position with regard to the state, appropriating state functions and 'state talk', but at the same time, pursuing their own agenda under the guise of state authority (Kyed and Buur 2006).

In this context, 'hybrid security governance' (Schroeder, Chappuis and Kocak 2014) brings together, as the four countries show, a plethora of actors and institutions from the state sphere and the societal sphere of civil society, private business and traditional-customary networks. The actors and institutions from these spheres are usually referred to as 'state' on the one hand, and 'non-state' on the other. Indeed, it is often argued, both by stakeholders on the ground and external scholarly observers, that in cases like Liberia, Solomon Islands, Vanuatu and Ghana one is confronted with 'two parallel security systems' (Badong 2009, p. 6, with reference to Ghana), namely the state system and the informal sector. In fact, in the four countries discussed here, everyday peace is maintained not so much by state institutions, but by societal actors such as chiefs or neighbourhood watch groups whose strength is rooted in the life of closely-knit communities, with kinship-based networks underpinning social order and well-being and regulating everyday life. By contrast, police, courts and other state institutions lack the capacities to make their presence felt in the communities; they hardly penetrate the rural areas of the four countries. Police posts and courts are far away from the people on the ground; they do not function effectively, and they lack legitimacy with the locals. More often than not these state institutions do not even assume that peace and order is primarily their responsibility; they leave this responsibility to local customary authorities such as chiefs or religious leaders, or to societal groups such as neighbourhood watch committees.

Thus the state/non-state distinction is helpful for grasping the realities of the provision of peace, security and justice in the four countries, but one cannot stop there. For it also has been shown that the state/non-state boundaries are blurred, and actors and institutions are often embedded both in the state and the non-state context at the same time.

While there are some entities which can, at first sight, be seen as 'state' (the police, the army, the courts) and some as 'non-state' (elders, vigilantes, landguards, chiefs), a closer look reveals intersections and transgressions. There are chiefs, for instance, who are both state and non-state ('turtles' living in the water and on land) or community police who are more 'state' in some contexts and on some occasions, and more 'non-state' in others. A closer look also reveals intense interactions and relationships which, again, blur the boundaries between entities – between police and community/neigbourhood watch groups, or between the formal state justice system and informal customary law. Accordingly, the provision of peace, security and justice is hybridised.[19]

The concept of the hybridisation of order and security governance draws attention to the state/non-state distinction, overcoming the state centricity of liberal peacebuilding scholarship and practice, introducing to it the non-state dimension and at the same time transcending it, focusing on the transgressions of the state/non-state boundary, on interactions and enmeshment, on the informal within the formal and the formal within the informal. It is not the mere 'coexistence' of two 'parallel systems' that characterises the provision of peace, security and justice in the four countries, but ongoing processes of mutual permeation and emergence. The state/non-state dichotomy 'that informs the statebuilding framework rarely reflects reality. Linkages and overlaps exist between institutions that represent and draw authority from the central state and institutions that generate authority at the local level' (Albrecht and Kyed 2010, p. 2). Such hybridity is not per se benign – it is imbued with power disparities and structures of dominance; it can be oppressive and marginalise certain societal groups along the lines of age, gender, class, religion or ethnicity. But it is the case on the ground and, hence, it is necessary to engage and work with hybridity wherever the aim is to improve peace, security and justice.[20]

This conceptualisation of political order, peace and security governance as hybrid renders the idea of the state as the central overarching entity, holding the monopoly over the legitimate use of physical force, obsolete. In the four countries no such state monopoly can be found – the government might claim (and its international supporters might wish) that it does exist but in reality, there is no central dominance over, and control of, the vast variety of providers of peace, security and justice and their fluid and constantly changing relationships and interactions (Baker, see Chapter 4 in this volume). Hybridisation, as an ongoing process of becoming through mixing, reconverting, leaching and blending, is the main feature of the provision of peace, security and justice, not the centrally orchestrated and controlled 'building' of a uniform system of maintenance of peace and order. Hence, respective projects of governments and their international supporters – security sector reform, state capacity building, justice sector reform, etc. – are only elements in a much broader mix of state and peace formation.

The international protagonists of the liberal peacebuilding and statebuilding agenda are powerful actors in this mix. This is obvious in post-conflict situations such as in Liberia and Solomon Islands. UNMIL and RAMSI decisively contributed to peace and order after violent conflicts, and the diverse local actors and processes in the provision of peace, security and justice flourished against the backdrop of their presence. But this is also the case, albeit less visible, in largely stable situations, as in Ghana and Vanuatu. Governance and politics here are also shaped by the mainstream liberal peacebuilding and statebuilding paradigm, with a variety of donor-funded projects and programmes geared towards building and/or reforming the capacities of state institutions, supplemented by support for civil society organisations (human rights organisations, women's and youth groups, peace institutes, etc.).

The internationals' interventions, however, do not necessarily have the pre-programmed effects. Solomon Islands and Liberia provide ample evidence that societies which in the view of international interveners are to be the recipients of international liberal peacebuilding and statebuilding are not just blank pages on which the internationals' agenda can be written. Instead of the mere 'delivery' of liberal templates of peace and state by benevolent outsiders to passive and grateful local recipients, these 'recipients' have agency of their own, and in the process of interaction, the distinction between local and liberal is at the same time called into question and reinforced (Simons and Zanker 2014, p. 12), resulting in hybrid forms of peace, order and security.[21]

Conclusion

The four countries discussed here demonstrate that there are ways of securing peace and order beyond the state (which does not mean in opposition to or against), with actors and institutions constantly operating at and transgressing the state/non-state boundary. Relationships between actors are characterised by a mix of tension, suspicion and competition on the one hand and complementarity and partial collaboration on the other (Hunt, see Chapter 5 in this volume).

In the interests of improving the provision of peace, security and justice, collaboration has to become more conscious and planned. This necessity is voiced in all four countries. For example, with regard to Ghana, Nancy Annan identifies a 'need for better collaboration and partnership' (Annan 2013, p. 5), recommending an exchange of knowledge and expertise between the various actors and institutions, and the development of common understandings of problems and their solutions; one example could be to better educate customary authorities on the state judicial system and statutory law, and to better educate state actors on customary law.[22]

Obstacles to collaboration can be overcome by deliberate attempts to bridge the divides, to engage in dialogue and to pursue policies of positive mutual accommodation. Instead of trying to impose uniform, exclusively state-based peace and order, such positive mutual accommodation has to be based on the complementarity of efforts of the vast variety of providers of peace, security and justice and make it the basis for improved collaboration.[23] This means working with the hybridity of political order, not against it, acknowledging that hybridity of order and security governance is not just a transitional phenomenon (with 'non-state' actors merely filling 'gaps' until the time when state actors will be ready to take over full control), but here to stay.[24] Consequently, what is needed is 'link-building as opposed to state-building' (Baker 2010, p. 613).

Such a relational and dialogic approach necessitates profound changes in attitudes and approaches from international actors. They will have to liberate themselves from the state-centric mindsets that informed RAMSI and UNMIL, and other similar international interventions, as well as governance capacity-building programmes in more stable environments such as Ghana or Vanuatu. They will have to acknowledge and engage with the hybridity of political and security order and also work with 'unconventional' local providers of peace and security.[25] For this to happen, much more modesty and willingness to learn on the side of the internationals is a prerequisite. In this regard, we have found promising examples in all four countries, but they are still the exception, not the rule.

Locals generally acknowledge international actors as capable and effective, and they enjoy legitimacy due to their performance. In Liberia and Solomon Islands, the internationals succeeded in implementing peace and order at the national level, and people are thankful for that. Concerns emerge when it comes to the internationals' capacities and willingness to engage with local societal actors. People find the internationals' understanding of local culture and social conditions wanting, which limits their effectiveness and negatively impacts on their legitimacy.[26]

In stark contrast to the relative inflexibility of international actors, the flexibility of the people on the ground is visible everywhere, all the time: people in Liberia, Ghana, Solomon Islands and Vanuatu show formidable pragmatism and adaptability when it comes to combining the indigenous and the exogenous, exploring what works for their circumstances and incorporating it into their culture and customs – which are far from static 'traditional', but fluid and inter-culturally adaptive, constantly hybridising. People are engaged in negotiating the emergence of forms of peace, political order and belonging that best suit their needs, history, culture, aims and aspirations, and that can provide the framework for the peaceful conduct of conflicts – beyond the ideal-type western state with its monopoly over the legitimate use of physical force.

Notes

1 See the contributions of Annan (Chapter 6); Aning/Annan/Edu-Afful (Chapter 7); Jaye (Chapter 8); and Boege/Forsyth (Chapter 11) all in this volume.
2 For an in-depth analysis, see Jaye (Chapter 8) in this volume.
3 The following is based on field research conducted in Liberia between 2013 and 2015 by the Liberian team members of a joint KAIPTC-UQ research project (see Kofi Annan International Peacekeeping Training Centre 2015). Unless otherwise indicated, quotes in this chapter are from fieldwork reports.
4 For an overview over secret societies, see Ellis (2007).
5 The inclusion of secret societies in the formal state system goes back to the time of Americo-Liberian domination. After attempts to crush the secret societies failed, they were incorporated into the system of domination. A National Traditional Council was established as an umbrella body for all secret societies. Several presidents became members of secret societies and, even today, high-ranking state representatives are members and as such, are bound to their norms, rules and decisions.
6 There is a gap between the internationals' and the locals' perceptions and assessments of appropriate, legitimate and effective provision of peace, security and justice.

> The UN and other donors have invested considerable effort and funds into the formal system, but widely neglected the customary system.... Customary institutions and secret societies are seen as a root cause of the war that would best be abolished, and democracy continues to be touted as the solution to Liberia's problems by the international community. The rural population has a different view. They remember the abusive practices committed in the name of the state.... Many complain that the international community is applying double standards, devaluating customary approaches and overestimating formal democracy.
>
> (Neumann 2013, p. 261)

7 For an overview of causes and the course of the violent conflict, see Moore (2004); Dinnen and Firth (2008); Allen (2013).
8 The exposition that follows this point in the chapter is based on field research conducted in Solomon Islands in 2010 and 2011.
9 For an exploration of the concept of *kastom*, see Boege and Forsyth, Chapter 11 in this volume.
10 The exposition following this point in the chapter is based on research conducted in the context of a seven-year project (2005–12). This Vanuatu Kastom Governance Partnership (VKGP) was a collaborative endeavour of the Vanuatu Malvatumauri National Council of Chiefs, a group of researchers at the University of Queensland in Australia and AusAID, the former Australian government international development agency.
11 Interview with Selwyn Garu, Port Vila, 10 April 2011. For the role of chiefs and chiefly institutions in the state system, see Chapter 5 of the Constitution of the Republic of Vanuatu (Republic of Vanuatu 1988) and the National Council of Chiefs Act (2006). The Malvatumauri's CEO has to have one leg in *kastom* and the other in the state system. He has a position with the Public Service Commission but at the same time has to do *kastom* work. The Malvatumauri itself is linked to the Ministry of Justice.
12 A particularly gruesome example is the conflict between the Konkomba and Nanumba/Dagomba in Ghana's Northern Region in 1994/95, which led to the loss of 2000 lives, the displacement of almost 80,000 people and the destruction of almost 150 villages (Joensson 2007). Other examples are the conflict between the Gonja and the Nawari, also in the Northern Region; the Dagbon chieftaincy dispute (Ahorsu and Gebe 2011); and the conflict between the Kusasis and Mamprusis in the region's Bawku Traditional Area. These are mainly chieftaincy conflicts (as outlined further

on in this chapter), which often go back to colonial and even pre-colonial times (Bukari and Guuroh 2013).

13 These include private security companies, neighbourhood watch committees, land-guards, traditional authorities, NGOs and civil society organisations; and so-called 'macho-men'. For an overview, see Badong (2009).

14 For the history of chiefs and chieftaincy in the colonial and post-colonial era and the multiple challenges to the institution in the course of that history, see Kludzie (2000); Boafo-Arthur (2003); Joensson (2007); Dzivenu (2008). Here it suffices to note that the 'chiefly system' has survived many onslaughts in the course of (in particular post-colonial) history.

15 In northern Ghana, chieftaincy is historically less elaborated, with several originally acephalous (chiefless) ethnic groups. This makes the situation of customary govern-ance in the north more complicated and contributes to the frequency of (violent) chieftaincy disputes.

16 The skin of an animal is the symbol of authority of chiefs in northern Ghana, and the stool is the symbol of authority in the southern regions. Chieftaincy is therefore often talked about as 'skin' or 'stool'.

17 The National House of Chiefs was given the task of undertaking an evaluation of rel-evant customs and compiling a list of those customs that have to be done away with. This has not been done to date.

18 By law, chiefs are prohibited from actively participating in politics; for example, they are not allowed to become members of political parties or members of parliament. If they wish to do so, they have to resign from their chiefly position. However, they may be appointed to public offices, and chiefs do serve on constitutional or statutory com-missions, as boards of public agencies and corporations or as advisors to government officials.

19 Such hybridisation also includes boundary-making as the complement of boundary transgression. Although institutions and actors such as police and chiefs interact and intertwine, they also insist on their distinctiveness and autonomy, reinforcing it by acts that have the purpose of strengthening the boundaries between them.

20 This use of the hybridity concept as a descriptive-analytical tool is fundamentally different from other, prescriptive-normative, understandings of hybridity. I share Mac Ginty's and Richmond's view that the 'most important contribution the concept of hybridity can make … is an analytical device. It is primarily a way of seeing the world and capturing change and lack of fixity between categories' (Mac Ginty and Richmond 2016). In my understanding, hybridity cannot be designed, pre-programmed and implemented (certainly not as an 'alternative' to 'the state'); it emerges due to relations and processes.

21 For more details, see Schroeder, Chappuis and Kocak 2014.

> Security governance models are thus not 'downloaded' in their entirety from the international level, and reform processes instead result in outcomes that combine external and domestic forms of security governance in different, and unantici-pated, ways. These mixed or 'hybrid' security orders combine elements of domestic and external security governance.
>
> (p. 216)

22 These recommendations come against the backdrop of a 'growing feeling among non-state groups and the public that the state security forces and the judiciary are corrupt and unresponsive to citizens', and this is 'a probable factor accounting for the strain in relationship' (Annan 2013, p. 4). The police in particular have to struggle with 'the negative legacy of being seen as a corrupt, "buyable", non-performing service'; there is 'public disaffection with the conduct, integrity and effectiveness of the Ghana Police Service', resulting in police-community relations 'based on mistrust and hostil-ity' (Aning 2006, p. 29).

23 For Liberia, for example, Robinson and Valters found 'significant scope for the formal and informal security sectors in Liberia to be better linked and coordinated' (Robinson and Valters 2015, p. 41).

24 'Hybrid contexts are not necessarily part of a transition from one condition (possibly traditionalism) to another (possibly modernity). Instead, they deserve to be accessed in their own right' (Mac Ginty and Richmond 2016).

25 Regarding Solomon Islands, for example, Allen and colleagues posit that,

> [t]he substantial level of donor assistance to Solomon Islands in recent years has not reached most parts of the country, however, and there have been few attempts to engage, directly or indirectly, with those nonstate rule systems that remain critical to the management of everyday disputation in most rural localities.
>
> (Allen, Dinnen, Evans and Monson 2013, p. 57)

26 For Liberia, for example, Schia and de Carvalho found that the UN 'has little understanding of the traditional customary system' (Schia and de Carvalho 2010, p. 11). Accordingly, they posit that '[f]irst and foremost, the challenge is for the international community to understand how these traditional systems work' (Schia and de Carvalho 2010, p. 14). This also holds true for other situations and countries.

Bibliography

Ahorsu, K and Gebe, BY 2011, *The Dagbon Chieftaincy Crisis: governance and security in Ghana*, SIPRI/OSI African Security and Governance Project, WACSI, Accra.

Albrecht, P and Kyed, HM 2010, *Justice and security: when the state isn't the main provider*, DIIS Policy Brief, DIIS, Copenhagen.

Allen, MG 2013, *Greed and grievance: ex-militants' perspectives on the conflict in Solomon Islands, 1998–2003*, University of Hawai'i Press, Honolulu.

Allen, M, Dinnen, S, Evans, D and Monson, R 2013, *Justice delivered locally: systems, challenges, and innovations in Solomon Islands*, The World Bank, Washington DC.

Aning, EK 2006, An overview of the Ghana Police Service, *Journal of Security Sector Management*, vol. 4, no. 2, pp. 1–37.

Annan, N 2013, 'Providing peace, security and justice in Ghana: the role of non-state actors', *Kofi Annan International Peacekeeping Training Centre Policy Brief*, no. 7, Accra.

Asamoah, K 2012, A qualitative study of chieftaincy and local government in Ghana, *Journal of African Studies and Development*, vol. 4, no. 3, pp. 90–5.

Australian Strategic Policy Institute (ASPI) 2003, *Our failing neighbour: Australia and the future of Solomon Islands*, ASPI, Canberra.

Badong, PA 2009, *Security provision in Ghana: what is the role and impact of non-state actors?*, ALC Research Report no. 5, King's College, London.

Baker, B 2010, Linking state and non-state security and justice, *Development Policy Review*, vol. 28, no. 5, pp. 597–616.

Boafo-Arthur, K 2003, Chieftaincy in Ghana: challenges and prospects in the 21st century, *African and Asian Studies*, vol. 2, no. 2, pp. 125–53.

Boege, V, Brown, A, Clements, K and Nolan, A 2009, 'On hybrid political orders and emerging states: what is failing – states in the Global South or research and politics in the West? Building peace in the absence of state: challenging the discourse on state failure', *Berghof Handbook Dialogue Series* no. 8, Berghof Research Center for Constructive Conflict Management, Berlin, pp. 15–35.

Bukari, KN and Guuroh, RT 2013, Civil society organizations (CSOs) and peacebuilding in the Bawku Traditional Area of Ghana: failure or success?, *Research on Humanities and Social Sciences*, vol. 3, no. 6, pp. 31–41.

Dinnen, S and Firth, S (eds) 2008, *Politics and state building in Solomon Islands*, ANU E-Press and Asia Pacific Press, Canberra.

Dinnen, S and Peake, G 2015, Experimentation and innovation in police reform: Timor Leste, Solomon Islands and Bougainville, *Political Science*, vol. 67, no. 1, pp. 21–37.

Dzivenu, S 2008, The politics of inclusion and exclusion of traditional authorities in Africa: chiefs and justice administration in Botswana and Ghana, *Political Perspectives*, vol. 2, no. 1, pp. 1–30.

Ellis, S 2007, *The mask of anarchy: the destruction of Liberia and the religious dimension of an African civil war*, New York University Press, New York.

Forsyth, M 2009, *A bird that flies with two wings: kastom and state justice systems in Vanuatu*, ANU E-Press, Canberra.

Forsyth, M 2011, The *Kastom* system of dispute resolution in Vanuatu, in Taylor, J and Thieberger, N (eds), *Working together in Vanuatu: research histories, collaborations, projects and reflections*, ANU E-Press, Canberra, pp. 175–82.

Hameiri, S 2007, The trouble with RAMSI: re-examining the roots of conflict in Solomon Islands, *The Contemporary Pacific*, vol. 19, no. 2, pp. 409–41.

Hayward-Jones, J 2014, *Australia's costly investment in Solomon Islands: the lessons of RAMSI*, Lowy Institute for International Policy, Canberra.

Herbert, S 2014, *Conflict analysis of Liberia*, GSDRC, University of Birmingham, Birmingham.

Isser, DH, Lubkemann, SC and N'Tow, S 2009, *Looking for justice: Liberian experiences with and perceptions of local justice options*, Peaceworks no. 63, United States Institute of Peace, Washington DC.

Jaye, T 2009, *Liberia: parliamentary oversight and lessons learned from international security sector reform*, Center on International Cooperation, New York.

Joensson, J 2007, 'The overwhelming minority: traditional leadership and ethnic conflict in Ghana's Northern Region', *CRISE Working Paper* no. 30, CRISE, Oxford.

Kabutaulaka, TT 2005, Australian foreign policy and the RAMSI intervention in Solomon Islands, *The Contemporary Pacific*, vol. 17, no. 2, pp. 283–308.

Kludzie, APK 2000, *Chieftaincy in Ghana*, Austin and Winfield, Maryland.

Kofi Annan International Peacekeeping Training Centre (KAIPTC) 2015, 'Ghanaian and Liberian Fieldwork Notes', Australian Development Research Awards Scheme Project, University of Queensland, Brisbane.

Kyed, HM and Buur, L 2006, 'Recognition and democratisation: "New Roles" for traditional leaders in Sub-Saharan Africa', *DIIS Working Paper* 2006/11, Danish Institute for International Studies, Copenhagen.

Lindstrom, L 1997, 'Chiefs in Vanuatu today', in White, G and Lindstrom, L (eds), *Chiefs today: traditional Pacific leadership and the postcolonial state*, Stanford University Press, Stanford, pp. 211–28.

Mac Ginty, R and Richmond, O 2016, The fallacy of constructing hybrid political orders: a reappraisal of the hybrid turn in peacebuilding, *International Peacekeeping*, vol. 23, no. 2, pp. 219–39.

Moore, C 2004, *Happy Isles in crisis*, Asia Pacific Press, Canberra.

Neumann, H 2013, 'Through the eyes of the locals: two post-war communities and their struggles from war to peace', PhD thesis, Freie Universität Berlin, Berlin.

Republic of Ghana 1992, *Constitution of the Republic of Ghana*, www.ghanaweb.com/GhanaHomePage/republic/constitution.php (accessed 6 July 2017).

Republic of Vanuatu 1988, *Constitution of the Republic of Vanuatu*, www.paclii.org/vu/legis/consol_act/cotrov406/ (accessed 6 July 2017).

Richmond, OP 2011, *A post-liberal peace*, Routledge, London.

Robinson, KB and Valters, C 2015, *Progress in small steps: security against the odds in Liberia*, ODI Development Progress Case Study Report Security, ODI, London.

Rousseau, B 2004, 'The achievement of simultaneity: kastom in contemporary Vanuatu', PhD Thesis, University of Cambridge, Cambridge.

Schia, NN and de Carvalho, B 2010, 'Peacebuilding in Liberia and the case for a perspective from below', *NUPI Working Paper* 778 Security in Practice, no. 8, NUPI, Oslo.

Schroeder, U, Chappuis, F and Kocak, D 2014, Security sector reform and the emergence of hybrid security governance, *International Peacekeeping*, vol. 21, no. 2, pp. 214–30.

Simons, C and Zanker, F 2014, 'Questioning the local in peacebuilding', *DFG Working Paper* Series, no. 10, DFG, Leipzig and Halle.

Tsikata, D and Seini, W 2004, 'Identities, inequalities and conflicts in Ghana', *CRISE Working Paper*, no. 5, CRISE, Oxford.

Vinck, P, Pham, P and Kreutzer, T 2011, *Talking peace: a population-based survey on attitudes about security, dispute resolution, and post-conflict reconstruction in Liberia*, Human Rights Center University of California, Berkeley.

Zanker, F 2014, 'Mixed messages: efforts at community policing in post-war Liberia', Paper presented at ISA Annual Convention 2014, Toronto, 29 March.

Zanker, F 2015, *A decade of police reform in Liberia: perceptions, challenges and ways ahead*, SSR 2.0 Brief, no. 4, Centre for Security Governance, Kitchener.

13 Peace formation in heterogeneous states

Concluding thoughts

M Anne Brown and Kwesi Aning

This book has considered questions of security, justice and peace in a number of socially and politically heterogeneous post-colonial states in two distinct regions. The United Nations (UN) and other international agencies have repeatedly identified strong or resilient states as an essential basis for peaceful, stable and just societies. This raises two sets of fundamental questions. First, what do we mean by 'the state', and how is strengthening the state, or supporting its resilience, to be pursued, particularly in those states that have historically been significantly shaped by struggles with colonialism? Second, if inter-state bodies such as the UN emphasise the critical significance of states for peace, where and how do the communities or populations making up many post-colonial states actually seek security, peace and justice? When communities to a significant extent seek basic security and justice from sources other than state institutions, what does this mean for the state? Directly and indirectly, the chapters of this collection have reflected on both these sets of questions.

Some chapters have called for the emergence of an 'African' state (or a Pacific Island state) or, perhaps more accurately, have pointed to the potential for, and the already existing elements of, such political communities. This call should not be understood as either the expression of assertive nationalism or a yearning to return to an imagined past. Nor should it entail any weakening of systems of accountability. On the contrary, it recognises the need for 'a contemporary state grounded in, intelligible to, and answerable to its own population and their cultures, and serving their collective well-being' (Aning *et al.* see Chapter 7 in this volume, p. 123). This is not, then, an argument about 'good enough' states, but about 'defining what the state and its government is' in terms that are meaningful to its citizens as well as to other states (Baker, see Chapter 4 in this volume, p. 74). This is a call for deeper processes of state formation, more inclusive of the country's often diverse population; it is not a new aspiration. As Julius Nyerere, the first president of Tanzania, noted:

> [T]he machinery through which a government stays close to the people and the people close to their government will differ according to the history, the demographic distribution, the traditional culture (or cultures), and the prevailing international and economic environment in which it has to operate.
>
> (Lumumba-Kasongo 2005, pp. 11–12, in Roberts 2008)

Several contributions in this volume address the complex network of security and social order upon which communities draw and depend. State institutions are often important players in this mix but are far from having a monopoly over the provision of security and justice; they may not even play the principal role. A range of cases underscore the argument that national or international efforts to support stable peace, or to strengthen the political community of the state, need to recognise and work with the complex patterns of social order, justice and peace-making, that is, the processes of peace formation already in play across communities. In other words, efforts to build peace or to strengthen the state need to be in conversation with a heterogeneous array of bodies and groupings beyond government institutions. As Jaye notes, 'the focus on national elites and formal institutions does not necessarily facilitate peace, security and justice' (Jaye, see Chapter 8 in this volume, p. 141).

Such heterogeneous or hybrid political contexts do not, these chapters suggest, render an effective, accountable and peaceful state impossible or unlikely. Nor do these contributions support an argument that socio-political heterogeneity should be a reason for governments to try to impose greater centralised control across the board. Indeed, it might be the complex network of relations between government institutions and societal bodies, particularly traditional governance systems, that enable the resilience of the state, as the contributions of Aning and Aubyn, and Boege and Forsyth, suggest. Heterogeneous political contexts require more nuanced, flexible notions of the state and state-making practices than those proposed in prevailing models of statebuilding. Inappropriate templates of the state have arguably themselves become obstacles to the emergence of more effective, accountable and cohesive political communities and state institutional architectures. They have produced states and governments 'caught between image and reality' (Baker, see Chapter 4 in this volume, p. 65; see also Eriksen 2016). Rather than focussing on implementing such templates, those concerned with strengthening the state could explore the question posed by Bruce Baker's chapter: how do a state's governing institutions and personnel understand their relationship with society, and vice versa? Exploring, clarifying and recrafting the relationship between the state's governing bodies and society is a fundamental way of addressing the ongoing need for state formation and is critical to peace formation in post-colonial and conflict-affected contexts.

The proposition that the state, or the formal structures or arena of the state, are 'not African' but derive 'from arbitrary colonial administrative units designed as instruments of domination, oppression and exploitation' is reasonably well established in academic circles (Englebert 1997, p. 767; see, e.g. Dia 1996; Mamdani 1996). It is not, however, given much practical weight in international policy circles, perhaps because it is not clear what policies or practices to draw from it. A similar argument could be made regarding the Pacific Islands and some other post-colonial regions. A critical part of the history of the state in West Africa and the Pacific Islands is thus that the state's legal-bureaucratic models of leadership, decision-making and accountability have not emerged from those forms of order, authority and collective meaning which to a significant extent shape life for the majority of the country's people. This has led to significant disjuncture and incoherence between forms of accountability. Thus, 'in the affairs of the nation there was no owner, the laws of the village became powerless' (Chinua Achebe 1966 in Englebert 1997, p. 768).

This difficult historical legacy poses critical challenges for the formation of political community, and these play out differently in different contexts. Because the institutional form of the state has weak roots in broader patterns of social order and many widely shared values, the emergence of democratic accountability is more difficult and complex. While the political life of the state is marked by fractures and friction between different logics of socio-political order, however, it is also shaped by their entanglement. These conditions can erode accountability and legitimacy for all forms of authority, generating widespread social alienation, corruption and political dysfunction. The power of statutory institutions and elites is indigenised and customary power reshaped, but this can happen in ways that serve the interests of entrenched and competing elites at the expense of communities and populations (Reno 1999). In Africa in particular, chieftancy institutions were often compromised and weakened in this process, as Aning *et al.* note (see Chapter 7 in this volume; see also Reno 1995).

The arguments put forward over many of the preceding chapters draw on these insights concerning what can be the deeply destructive discontinuities of political life, but they take these insights as a point of departure for a broader set of perspectives. Over decades or generations, state institutions, as well as a wide range of social arrangements and aspirations that have emerged with the life of the modern liberal state, have become relatively well established across West Africa and the Pacific Islands. At the same time, the diverse forms of social order with roots in customary life show no sign of being displaced but have continued to flourish (and to change). For far longer than the modern state, traditional world religions have also become strongly embedded in life across the regions considered here: Islam and Christianity in West Africa, and overwhelmingly Christianity, with the recent introduction of Islam in some places, in the Pacific Islands. These powerful collective patterns of life and meaning have challenged, accommodated, resisted and recreated each other across time, space and circumstance. This interaction has generated transformations of thought and practice and continues to do so, but it has not erased what can be profound difference and tension among them. The destructive patterns noted above are important for understanding the forces driving socio-political life in many post-colonial states, but they are not the only, and not always the dominant, dynamic in play. There are countervailing forces working to establish peace and social order. Depending on the array of historical and contextual conditions in any given set of circumstances, these may or may not be sufficient to undo or restrain the negative potentials of post-colonial discontinuity.

In the face of both spectacular and everyday ingrained misuse of power, it can be easy to overlook the ongoing effort to make things 'hang together' and the creativity and adaptability that enables this to happen. While accounts of corruption and dysfunction are numerous, people in villages, districts, churches, government offices, courts and police stations across countries, and in elite political circles, are working to craft ways of dealing with difficult problems and to support community well-being. Inevitably, such efforts entail competing and counteracting values, practices, priorities and ambitions, but this is the ordinary, if nevertheless profoundly challenging, complexity of political exchange in heterogeneous states. These efforts, in state offices, gatherings of elders, women's collectives, council chambers and so forth, need to be part of a wider view and more inclusive understanding of the working life and governance of the state.

Weberian models of the state maintain a categorical distinction between state and society. This distinction has its purpose, but in its current form at least, it does not serve those states that are working with institutional forms, norms and processes that did not emerge from their own population's systems of value and life (Eriksen 2016). Under these conditions, while the ability to distinguish between, for example, the requirements and processes of a state institution and those of a kin network remain critically important, it is the habit, channels and character of connection and relations interweaving the practices and agents labelled 'state' and those labelled 'society' that become critically important (Brigg 2016; Hunt, see Chapter 5 in this volume). As Volker Boege's chapters suggest, the hybridity of order and security governance is not just a transitional phenomenon (with 'non-state' actors filling 'gaps' until the time when 'state' actors will be ready to take over full control); it is here to stay. Consequently, what is needed is 'link-building as opposed to state-building' (Baker 2010, p. 613). Disjunctions and discontinuities between different logics of social order are constantly being negotiated and relations emerging, but this happens in different ways (Charles Hunt's contribution explores some of these differences). The predominant forms that these relations take will shape the dominant character of socio-political life in a particular domain or region. Relations can operate out of view, in the shadows beyond the reach of any form of accountability, oversight or participation, manipulated by self-interested and perhaps violent elites. They can work as part of a pragmatic, de facto interdependence that is nevertheless not openly acknowledged and remains a context of suspicion and dysfunction. Or they can be more openly or genuinely recognised and worked with by those involved and those affected, open to challenge (even if discrete) and change, and engaging with relevant, even if conflicting, forms of accountability. More open and inclusive processes of discussion and exchange seem more likely to support the emergence of shared forms of accountability. This is not a matter of the collaboration of elites alone, but of the forms of governance that circulate throughout the communities making up the life of the state.

Implications for practice and policy

What do the far-reaching issues raised by the above discussions mean for policy and practice? This question is relevant not only to national governments and large international agencies, although these bodies are of critical importance and their actions carry significant consequences. Working against violence, or with the challenges of difference in heterogeneous communities directly, concerns people in many roles and contexts who undertake very different kinds of activities, from policing, courts and councils of various kinds to ritual and story-telling, research and teaching (Nordstrom 1997; Lederach 2005). Peace formation draws attention to the importance of the everyday and the local as a foundation of political community; it addresses not only formal government or the lives and social order of others, but the agency of our own communities and every arena of governance (Richmond 2013).

The first set of implications are for understanding and analysis. Some guidelines to support analysis could be drawn from the preceding discussions. Understanding the dynamics of social order in post-colonial states requires stepping aside from assumptions and judgements which take a certain model of the state as the only acceptable vehicle for political community or political order, and the only acceptable framework in which to pursue values such as accountability, justice, peace, participation and respect for the person. We need to be able to recognise the profound heterogeneity of many contemporary states and to work positively with this reality. Different logics of governance, alternative sources of law and justice, and competing claims to authority make for challenging state and peace formation; at the same time, this heterogeneity is the field and provides many of the resources from which the political community of the state must be crafted. The structures and institutions of government are a fundamental element of this field. Society, however, in its diverse forms of agency and governance, is at least equally fundamental to, and equally responsible for shaping, the political community of the state. At the most general level, the tasks of policy and practice that follow from this understanding involve openness to observing and engaging with 'politics as it is' in ways that work against violence (Frödin 2012, p. 271) and supporting constructive linkages and habits of accessible dialogue – link-building – across different forms of socio-political order, or between government and societal institutions and actors.

Analysis needs to pay attention to the sources of social order and justice that people actually draw upon and the ways of making peace they engage in – what Lisa Denney frames as an end-user approach to understanding security. Historical and cultural factors often affect how people understand threat, build trust and seek security (Escobar 2008; Lederach 2005). These factors are not always obvious, predictable or even easily observable by outside commentators – the 'secret' societies throughout the Mano River basin countries of West Africa are just one example, albeit a particularly renowned one. Often enough, the people working to build peace or establish stability are women. Women's contribution to peace and to governance can be critical and ongoing but is frequently overlooked or not recognised by external observers and political elites of all kinds (Annan, see Chapter 6 in this volume; Bolton 2003; Lederach 2005). Yet, as Nancy Annan (see Chapter 6, p. 101) points out, 'highlighting gender issues is critical for creating the space for a more nuanced understanding of women's contributions in hybrid political orders'. Without this, interventions are in danger of further marginalising women's roles and authority.

While there are significant general patterns to the occurrence and management of conflict, and the provision of security across countries and regions, social order is often locally underpinned by networks of actors who have established face-to-face patterns of interaction and whose legitimacy is largely local. Disputes and violent conflict may also be deeply embedded in local relations – for example, chieftancy and succession disputes – and play into and shape broader patterns of conflict (Darkwa, Attuquayefio and Yakohene 2012). Engaging with questions of policy and practice around peace thus often requires working with the nuance and grain of local relations.

In understanding the web of relations contributing to order and disorder, it is helpful to loosen the grip of the strong dichotomies that dominate much analysis of governance and security, such as state/non-state and formal/informal. Like these dichotomies, automatic assumptions about whether a particular category of actors, such as chiefs, police, neighbourhood watch groups and vigilantes, are either good or bad (e.g. more or less violent, or patriarchal, or unaccountable) also impede understanding, including understanding from an ethical perspective. As Charles Hunt (Chapter 5, p. 80) argues, it is 'the nature of the *relationships between entities* [and with communities] rather than the *characteristics of entities* that matters most for understanding how hybridisation occurs and how hybrid (dis)orders emerge' (emphasis in the original). Paying attention to how institutions and people collectively and relationally generate social order enables resilience and strength to come into view, as well as disintegration, dysfunction and violence (Hunt, see Chapter 5 in this volume; Brown 2007; Moore 2007). Just as sensitivity to local history and culture, and awareness of the burdens of trauma people may be carrying, are important in contexts of violent conflict, so awareness of local efforts supporting social order not only provides a fuller, richer, more accurate picture: it can also open a path to work with what is there, rather than to assume that peace, order or justice can only be delivered by others (Lederach 2005). This has significant implications for national and international bodies as well as for local actors themselves.

The second set of implications concerns the kinds of actions that might flow from these understandings. Bruce Baker, addressing state bodies considering how to respond to populations drawing on alternate sources of security, notes that '[i]n constructing an answer, the state, and in particular its government, has to begin first by having a clear view of itself ... and how it sees its relationship with society' (Baker, see Chapter 4, p. 61). Constructing answers to questions about the relationship between government and society, or to the challenges of heterogeneous political order, is not simply an analytical process. It is a slow, difficult social and political process of exchange among many players making up the life of the state. Crafting just, peaceful and inclusive answers is likely to require bringing questions of the interdependence of statutory institutions and customary authorities from being a nagging problem embedded deep in the fabric of socio-political life into becoming matters of more open, reflective discussion. Socio-cultural factors will significantly shape how 'open' discussion, or discussion that enables accountability, participation and genuine exchange, is achieved in concrete terms. Processes that enable a functional level of trust, however, take time.

Given the often complex and fractured interplay of different governance, security and justice actors in post-colonial states, there can be different, often contradictory mechanisms at work, operating from different understandings of justice and accountability. Despite various forms of enmeshment, levels of mutual acknowledgement and even understanding between customary and statutory authorities can be weak. As noted in a study of societal justice systems undertaken by UNDP, UNICEF and UN Women, 'formal justice actors often know little about the informal systems that most people use and law school curricula, for example, pay little attention to customary law' (UNDP, UNICEF and UN Women 2016, p. 20). Even though there may be viable local relationships and collaboration, field research has made clear that more broadly these interdependent relationships are also often marked by tension, suspicion and competition. Moreover, while individuals may move between different worlds and institutions may often incorporate a mixture of practices and processes, this does not in itself create a bridge between logics of governance or articulate differences in ways that enable accountable or effective governance. There is nevertheless considerable variation in the dominant character of relations among different actors between districts and countries, and across regions, in part reflecting variations in colonial and independence histories, but also the emergence of different habits of exchange and collaboration. In Vanuatu and the Bougainville region of Papua New Guinea, for example (both discussed in this volume), formal and informal linkages are significant and dense, and concrete relations are more likely to be constructive (see Boege, Chapters 10 and 12, in this volume; Boege and Forsyth, Chapter 11 in this volume; Peake and Dinnen 2013).

Previous chapters have noted some approaches to bringing different logics of governance, or state structures and customary institutions in particular, into closer and more constructive relations. It is instructive to briefly consider two overarching approaches, both commonly pursued by national governments and supported by international agencies. These are, first, decentralisation through the introduction of provincial or district governments and, second, consultation processes between government and (usually) customary authorities aimed at the 'harmonisation' of approaches to governance. For both approaches, we suggest that the way they are undertaken and maintained is at least as important as, if not more important than, the approach itself.

Thomas Jaye's discussion of decentralisation in Liberia indicates that, while this structure of government has potential merit, the process of introducing it has been centrally driven and has largely failed to engage with actual current forms of local governance. Thus, although the new structures are intended to devolve power to localities, they are in danger of remaining predominantly top down. Rather than enabling government to become more genuinely responsive to communities, this new structure could in effect undermine and marginalise local processes of governance in the effort to consolidate a state structure that has a long history of predatory behaviour (Jaye, see Chapter 8 in this volume). Decentralisation in itself does not automatically constitute or enable processes of exchange across a hybrid polity. The character and quality of the engagement, not with abstract liberal citizens imagined from the capital, but with actual communities and their ways of life, is of central importance.

In both West Africa and the Pacific Islands, consultation processes between statutory and customary authorities are commonly part of efforts to 'harmonise' state institutional and customary systems. While such efforts make sense, harmonisation initiatives frequently operate as attempts by state institutions to exercise control, announce limits and protocols, and claim the 'monopoly' that signifies statehood in Weberian models (Baker, see Chapter 4 in this volume). (Efforts to 'formalise the relationship between the traditional and modern modes of governance' have often followed a similar pattern [Aning *et al.*, see Chapter 7, p. 122; see also UNDP *et al.* 2016, p. 21]). This approach does not generate open communication or build trust. Leadership by government institutions may often be appropriate in various arenas of governance, but this is not always or automatically the case, particularly in circumstances where customary authorities carry greater local legitimacy, authority and knowledge. In many circumstances, customary authorities may not even contest leadership by state institutions, or may not seek the same kind or domain of leadership. Communities may see customary authorities as a partner in governance with government, for example, and a channel of communication, rather than a competitor (K. Higgins PhD thesis, forthcoming). Nevertheless, the practical form that government leadership might take in particular matters, may change significantly as a result of more open engagement with customary or traditional leaders rather than attempts to dominate or manipulate them.

While engagement across heterogeneous forms of social order and authority inherently involves questions of power, these are not inevitably contests for domination or to achieve mutually exclusive goals. Rather than efforts to impose control or assert supremacy, the forms of engagement needed are those that enable the different parties to acknowledge and listen to each other, that lay groundwork for a functional level of trust and build habits of dialogue or communication. Efforts to establish control by those who do not enjoy legitimacy or trust may be more likely to lead to resentment and resistance rather than produce the desired outcome. While questions of power and of authority are contentious, difficult and imperative, as Kwesi Aning, Nancy Annan and Fiifi Edu-Afful argue, processes of engagement cannot simply be orchestrated by governments but need to involve genuine exchange and mutual recognition (Aning *et al.*, see Chapter 7 in this volume; see also Tully 1995).

Across the regions, various bodies – from state institutions, customary, community or civil society networks to international agencies – have built creative linkages, often through long-term, low-key grassroots commitments. These connections will remain 'thin', however, if there is little contextual support. Avenues for exchange around concrete issues (e.g. locally identified security threats) can be useful in this context. External or international actors can play roles facilitating processes of exchange. They may at times be active participants – not as rule setters or power brokers, but as part of broader networks of governance and contributors to conversations about forms of state-making. Gradually building patterns of constructive exchange can enable 'collective efforts to manoeuvre relationships towards more productive and less violent forms that generate more legitimate, equitable, efficient and resilient processes of peace formation' (Hunt, see Chapter 5 in this volume, p. 94). Even when marked by friction, local relations and exchanges across networks of security and justice could become sources of innovative response to the challenges of volatility and insecurity facing communities and states.

Working with customary or societal actors does not mean abandoning concerns around human rights or accepting violence or marginalisation, as Anne Brown's chapter points out (see Chapter 3 in this volume). Rather it means entering into mutual exchanges and respectful conversation as part of a long-term commitment to undoing patterns of violence and abuse (Brown 2009). This also applies to state actors, who are equally likely to be associated with violence, systemic discrimination and abuse. Bruce Baker has noted that 'a willingness to reform' should be 'the entry point of partnership with non-state actors' (Baker, see Chapter 4, p. 74; see also UNDP *et al.* 2016). Baker's point is that high international standards should not automatically rule out potential engagement. In the effort to create more inclusive forms and networks of governance, however, not only customary authorities but all parties, whether state, societal, local, national or (where relevant) international, need to be prepared to change.

Hybrid states face the challenge of undertaking state-making in ways that do not marginalise large sections of the population but build links across difference by emphasising processes and habits of dialogue, mutual recognition and meaningful forms of accountability. For governments and broader policy-making circles, change may lie as much with how engagements with communities and community leaders are undertaken as with the structure of those engagements themselves. That is, change in certain processes may have greater value than change in the structure of institutions. Building links means that communication and exchange need to go beyond consultation into deeper processes of listening and dialogue. This need not be exchange for the purposes of agreement but to develop more nuanced mutual understanding. As well as engaging with pressing local issues, discussion could explore, for example, what security, justice and accountability mean in practice for the various parties, how these understandings support or contradict each other, and what current circumstances faced by national and local conditions might demand. The enmeshment of different sources and models of governance could be more openly acknowledged and become a matter of more general discussion.

Many people in towns, villages and districts are already engaged in experimental and practical forms of collaboration, enabling things to 'hang together' under often very challenging conditions (e.g. Yoder 2007; Peake and Dinnen 2013; Menkhaus 2016). Governments, scholars and international agencies could learn from some of these experiments. Government agencies, community and non-government organisations, customary bodies, religious bodies and active citizens could reflect more openly on the character of their local networks of relations, their forms of accountability, levels of trust and friction and how well these networks serve local communities.

For the international community, supporting peace formation and strengthening the state could give priority to relations linking government, societal forms of governance and communities. The models guiding statebuilding and state-strengthening could be more free from the drive for standardisation and open to accommodating more complex ways of understanding and approaching what makes for a working state. More flexible perspectives on the state could enable observers to see what is already working in communities and states; supporting resilience could thus begin from looking at what already generates and supports resilience. The challenge for international agencies is not to abandon principles of accountability, justice, respect for the person and participation, but to seek ways of giving life to these principles that are meaningful to communities, and to do so, where possible, through conversation with them. Ways of being a state that are grounded not only in the accumulated experience of other states but in their own diverse communities may be slowly and quietly taking shape in some areas. International agencies could help facilitate linkages among different peace and governance actors within districts and states and across regions and support processes of exchange. Partnership could become a more genuine process of listening. For all parties, at the most fundamental level, peace formation involves paying attention to others as participants in exchange and co-creators of networks of political community within the state and, where relevant, beyond.

Bibliography

Baker, B 2010, 'Linking state and non-state security and justice', *Development Policy Review*, vol. 28, no. 5, pp. 597–616.

Bolton, L 2003, *Unfolding the moon: enacting women's kastom in Vanuatu*, University of Hawai'i Press, Honolulu.

Brigg, M 2016, 'Relational peacebuilding: promise beyond crisis', in Debiel, T, Held, T and Schneckener, U (eds), *Peacebuilding in crisis: rethinking paradigms and practices of transnational cooperation*, Routledge, Abingdon.

Brown, MA 2007, 'Conclusion', in Brown, MA (ed.), *Security and development in the Pacific Islands: social resilience in emerging states*, Lynne Rienner, Boulder.

Brown, MA 2009, *Human rights and the borders of suffering: the promotion of human rights in international politics*, Manchester University Press, Manchester.

Darkwa, L, Attuquayefio, P and Yakohene, A 2012, *Peacemaking in Ghana: lessons learnt, options for the future*, Legon Centre for International Affairs and Diplomacy, University of Ghana, Accra.

Dia, M 1996, *Africa's management in the 1990s and beyond: reconciling indigenous and transplanted institutions*, World Bank, Washington DC.

Englebert, P 1997, 'The contemporary African state: neither African nor state', *Third World Quarterly*, vol. 18 no. 4, pp. 767–76.

Eriksen, SS 2016, 'State effects and the effects of state building: institution building and the formation of state-centred societies', *Third World Quarterly*, vol. 10, pp. 1–16.

Escobar, A 2008, *Territories of difference: place, movements, life, redes*, Duke University Press, Durham.

Frödin, OJ 2012, 'Dissecting the state: towards a relational conceptualization of states and state failure', *Journal of International Development*, vol. 24, no. 3, pp. 271–86.

Higgins, K forthcoming, *A nation of villages: exploring governance in Melanesia*, unpublished PhD thesis, University of Queensland, Brisbane.

Lederach, JP 2005, *The moral imagination: the art and soul of building peace*, Oxford University Press, Oxford.

Mamdani, M 1996, *Citizen and subject: contemporary Africa and the legacy of late colonialism*, Princeton University Press, Princeton.

Menkhaus, K 2016, 'Managing risk in ungoverned space: local and international actors in Somalia', *The SAIS Review of International Affairs*, vol. 36, no. 1, pp. 109–20.

Moore, C 2007, 'External intervention: the Solomon Islands beyond RAMSI', in Brown, MA (ed.), *Security and development in the Pacific Islands: social resilience in emerging states*, Lynne Rienner, Boulder.

Nordstrom, C 1997, *A different kind of war story*, University of Pennsylvania Press, Philadelphia.

Peake, G and Dinnen, S 2013, 'More than just policing: police reform in post-conflict Bougainville', *International Peacekeeping*, vol. 20, no. 5, pp. 570–84.

Reno, W 1995, *Corruption and state politics in Sierra Leone*, Cambridge University Press, Cambridge.

Reno, W 1999, *Warlord politics and African states*, Lynne Rienner, Boulder.

Richmond, OP 2013, 'Failed statebuilding versus peace formation', in Chandler, D and Siskm TD (eds), *Routledge Handbook of International Statebuilding*, pp. 130–40, Routledge, Abingdon.

Roberts, D 2008, 'Hybrid polities and indigenous pluralities: advanced lessons in statebuilding from Cambodia', *Journal of Intervention and Statebuilding*, vol. 2, no. 1, pp. 63–86.

Tully, J 1995, *Strange multiplicity: constitutionalism in an age of diversity*, Cambridge University Press, Cambridge.

United Nations Development Programme (UNDP), UNICEF and UN Women 2016, *Informal justice systems: charting a course for human rights-based engagement*, www.undp.org/content/dam/undp/library/Democratic%20Governance/Access%20to%20Justice%20and%20Rule%20of%20Law/Informal-Justice-Systems-Charting-a-Course-for-Human-Rights-Based-Engagement.pdf (accessed 6 July 2017).

Yoder, LM 2007, 'Hybridising justice: state-customary interactions over forest crime and punishment in Oecusse, East Timor', *The Asia Pacific Journal of Anthropology*, vol. 8, no. 1, pp. 43–57.

Index

Made in the USA
Las Vegas, NV
28 March 2023

69823836R00142